Of GREATER DIGNITY THAN RICHES

Culture, Politics, and the Built Environment
Dianne Harris, editor

ALSO IN THE SERIES

Improvised Cities: Architecture, Urbanization, and Innovation in Peru
Helen Gyger

Ideals of the Body: Architecture, Urbanism, and Hygiene in Postrevolutionary Paris
Sun-Young Park

Colonialism and Modern Architecture in Germany
Itohan Osayimwese

Modern Architecture in Mexico City: History, Representation, and the Shaping of a Capital
Kathryn E. O'Rourke

Building Modern Turkey: State, Space, and Ideology in the Early Republic
Zeynep Kezer

Re-Collecting Black Hawk: Landscape, Memory, and Power in the American Midwest
Nicholas A. Brown and Sarah E. Kanouse

Designing Tito's Capital: Urban Planning, Modernism, and Socialism in Belgrade
Brigitte Le Normand

Architecture, Politics, and Identity in Divided Berlin
Emily Pugh

Governing by Design: Architecture, Economy, and Politics in the Twentieth Century
Edited by Daniel M. Abramson, Arindam Dutta, Timothy Hyde, and Jonathan Massey for Aggregate

Second Suburb: Levittown, Pennsylvania
Edited by Dianne Harris

Of GREATER DIGNITY THAN RICHES

Austerity & Housing Design in India

FARHAN KARIM

UNIVERSITY OF PITTSBURGH PRESS

Advancing Art&Design

SOCIETY OF ARCHITECTURAL HISTORIANS

Publication of this book has been aided by a grant from the Millard Meiss Publication Fund of CAA. Illustrations in this book were funded in part by a grant from the SAH/Mellon Author Awards of the Society of Architectural Historians.

Published by the University of Pittsburgh Press, Pittsburgh, Pa., 15260

Manufactured in the United States of America
Printed on acid-free paper
10 9 8 7 6 5 4 3 2 1

Cataloging-in-Publication Data is available from the Library of Congress

ISBN 13: 978-0-8229-6569-5
ISBN 10: 0-8229-6569-0

Cover art: Drawing of the courtyard and veranda of the low-cost house designed by Joseph Allen Stein and Bengal Engineering College, Calcutta, 1954

Cover design: Alex Wolfe

To my family

CONTENTS

ACKNOWLEDGMENTS

During the long and winding trajectory of this book, from its origin to a confined written work, I received a lot of help from many people. I hope they all see their contributions to this book, but any failings that remain are entirely mine. I could not have asked for more encouraging mentors than Duanfang Lu and Greg Castillo—their constant support, tough recommendations, wise direction, and helpful arguments helped shape my perspective. Many of the ideas that developed out of this research are owed to Greg Castillo. Long consulting sessions with Duanfang, the topics of which ranged from techniques of research to crafts of teaching, molded my career as an architectural historian.

Peter Scriver has been a great resource, responding to every tiny detail of my queries; his insightful criticisms kept my argument on track. I am also grateful to Chris L. Smith's input at the early stage of this research, especially his assistance in giving my thinking a broad theoretical underpinning. Peter Armstrong's almost daily rounds at my office at the University of Sydney and his kind and enthusiastic words kept me charged even in the darkest hours of this project. It was a happy accident to have Gevork Hartoonian as my office mate in my first year at the University of Sydney. Sitting back-to-back with me in my tiny office, he helped to shape my understanding about critical history. The many formal and informal conversations I had with Glen Hill and Anna Rubbo added nuances and richness to my thinking. I would also like to express my gratitude to Anoma Pieris for her detailed criticism and advice when I was writing an article for a special issue of a journal that she was editing.

Outside Australia, my research benefited from many scholars. Among them, perhaps my greatest fortune was finding Abigail S. McGowan at the library of Indian Institute of Architects in Mumbai. Without her compassionate friendship and formidable wisdom, this work would have taken a lesser shape. Saloni Mathur's many critical comments and kind reviews added value to my thinking in myriad ways. My meetings with Rahul

Mehrotra, Shanay Jhaveri, William J. Glover, Mrinalini Rajagopalan, Arvind Rajagopal, and Amit Srivastava opened new avenues of thinking.

The intellectual environment at the University of Sydney and University of Kansas taught me a lot, especially the encouragement and criticism I received from my peers; their commitment and dedication in their own work has been an example of excellence for me. Jun Yi, Michael Zanardo, and Farzane Haghighi shared many enthusiastic and intellectually whirling moments with me over delicious foods. My book would have taken a very different shape if I hadn't met Gargi Gangopadhaya at the India Office Library of the British Library. Our eventful evening in the summer of London, the endless conversation, and the long stroll I had with her not only enlightened me as a scholar but rearranged and remolded my understandings as an individual.

I am indebted to the infinitely passionate staff members at the interlibrary departments of Sci-Tech and the Fischer Library at the University of Sydney, as well as at the University of Kansas interlibrary loan service. The books and articles they regularly brought to my desk from all over the world were fascinating. I would also like to take this opportunity to express my gratitude to the staff of many archives, record rooms, and libraries I visited and conducted research in through the years.

My work on this book took me to the farthest corners of the world, as every place seems too far from Down Under. My research trip would not have been possible without the assistance from the University of Sydney Postgraduate Research Support Scheme. I also express gratitude to my friends who opened their doors, showed great hospitality, and supported my research. Dipak Roychowdhury and Arundhati Roychowdhury in Kolkata, Naushad Hassan in New York, Sajid Masud and his family in Washington, DC, Abul Abdullah and Suraiya Akther, Anisur Rahman and Kaniz Sultana in Chicago, Sifat Sikandar and Sadequr Rahman in Bristol, Shariful Shikder and Sabrina Afrin in Cardiff, Jamshed Rahman and Mukti Rahman in Berkeley, and Moin J. Mohammad in Adelaide. I would also like to thank my beloved friends in Sydney, Golam Kibria, Galim Saddam, Shakil Mahmud, Imran Hossain, Jannatul Ferdous, Tanvir Ahmed, Hasina Aktar, and Kamrul Islam, as it was their joyful presence that helped me find my way through the gloomy, long, and lonely days of research.

The major portion of this book has been written at various cafés around Sydney: Cafe Azzuri, Leichhardt Café, and Tobby's Estate Coffee in my neighborhood of Dulwich Hill. I thank the staff of these shops for their happy smiles, free coffees, and unbeatable patience as I occupied their tables for hours over cups of cappuccino.

I am grateful to the steering committee of the Australian Leadership Award program for seeing potential in my research and funding it. The book would not have been possible without generous funding from the University of Kansas: the General Research Fund, New Faculty Grant, Friends of the Hall Center Book Award, and Vice Chancellor Research Book Publication Award. The publication of this book has also been aided by grants from the Millard Meiss Publication Fund of the College Art Association and the SAH/Mellon Author Awards of the Society of Architectural Historians.

Getting copyright permission of the images was a challenging task, and I could not have achieved that without the kind help of Ishita Shah and Namrata Sehgal. A special thanks to them. I am also grateful to the staff of the Associated Cement Companies for allowing me to use their images in this book. My thanks to Suraiya Mymuna and Bushra Nayeem for producing drawings from archival documents.

My sincere thanks to Abby Collier; without her patience, careful reading, editing, and profound suggestions, this book would not have been possible. I also want to thank the wonderful production team of the University of Pittsburgh Press.

I am most grateful to my parents, Sk. Azizul Karim and Fatema S. Nahar, for their emotional involvement in my project. Their constant encouragement and irrational faith in my capacity has been a guiding beacon. Nothing can be compared with the love and affection of my sister, Shaila Ahmed; my periodical refuge at her place in Melbourne refreshed my thoughts in many ways. My brothers, Fayad Sultan and Faisal Karim; my brother-in-law, Javed Ahmed; and my nephew, Isfar Ahmed, were constant sources of joy and encouragement. In the past four years this book witnessed births of my two boys, whose confused but determined struggle to claim their positions on the earth blissfully disrupted my work cycle. My final thanks goes to my intimate spiritual and intellectual partner, the only person who commutes with me in light and in silence, Farhana Ferdous; words cannot express the lasting influence her sincerity and compassion has had on me.

ABBREVIATIONS

ACC	Associated Cement Companies (India)
BDD	Bombay Development Directorate
BIT	Bombay Improvement Trust
CBRI	Central Building Research Institute (India)
CIAM	Congrès International d'Architecture Moderne
HCB	Hyderabad City Improvement Board
HfG	Hochschule für Gestaltung (Germany)
LN	League of Nations
MoMA	Museum of Modern Art (US)
NID	National Institute of Design (India)
PWD	Public Works Department (India)
UN	United Nations
USAID	US Agency for International Development

Of GREATER DIGNITY THAN RICHES

INTRODUCTION

> You should not accept or tolerate ugliness anywhere, in your life, in your activities, in your buildings. The worst type of ugliness of course is ugly behavior of individuals and groups. But to some extent, the environment reflects itself in the behavior of the individual, as a beautiful environment helps in developing a sense of beauty in the people who live there. It is desirable, therefore, that what we build, however simple and humble it may be, should have some artistic value. And mind you, do not connect artistic value with money.
>
> **Jawaharlal Nehru, "Building a New India"**

In winter 2010, chasing a rare document on German architect Otto Koenigsberger, I arrived at Hindustani Housing's abandoned factory in Delhi. The olive green skin of the imported German machines was flaking off, exposing the rusted surface of their stout corpses. Jawaharlal Nehru, the first prime minister of India, envisioned the Hindustani Housing factory, which would create prefabricated low-cost houses, as a quick and effective solution to the country's housing problem, and he invited Koenigsberger to help materialize his dream. The factory's machines, which once processed tons of cement each day to produce prefabricated housing components—the first of their kind in the decolonizing worlds—were now settled among the rubble and gravel. Inside the silence of the factory, I saw a muster of wild, bright Indian peafowls from the nearby woods along the Yamuna River. The peafowls were squatting on the cement-casting machines under the piercing light that poured in through the iron walls of the factory shed.

Once hailed as the promise of affordable modernism for everyone, the postcolonial hope of Nehru and Koenigsberger has since transformed into a nuanced surrealism. While this abandoned housing factory reflects the postcolonial state's push for centralization and industrialization, *Of Greater Dignity than Riches* looks beyond the narrative of how the postcolonial state exerted its centralized control to modernize its cities and villages. In this book, I explore an ambiguous territory in which the Indian state gradually relinquished control of its subjects to a body of extra-state agents—village elites, foreign consultants, local designers, aid workers, volunteers, politicians—all of whom contested state power and had a vested interest in India's postcolonial future.

As a relatively stable domestic market emerged between the 1920s and 1950s, the Indian government, in collaboration with local and foreign architects and planners, embarked on various reformation projects to modernize and develop the domestic environment of the country's lower-income population. These projects extensively used the Gandhian political rhetoric of asceticism, which exalted voluntary poverty as the core strength of Indian civilization. Government reform and development projects portrayed economic scarcity, rhetorically called *poverty,* not as an impediment but as a new possibility—the essential ingredient of postcolonial development. Hope and optimism for an alternative future of development mobilized by the village and urban poor was the key to this austerity discourse. The "modernism of austerity," as I call this endeavor, was a compendium of utopian ideal city and village designs in conjunction with pragmatic, low-cost housing prototypes for the urban and rural poor.

The Discourse of Austerity

In 1958 Le Corbusier was overwhelmed with designing the monumental architecture of Chandigarh, capital of the northern Indian states of Punjab and Haryana, now revered as the emblem of a bygone heroic modernism. At the same time, his lesser-known cousin Pierre Jeanneret was commissioned by the Indian Ministry of Food and Agriculture for a different purpose: to design and furnish model interiors of a working-class house for a government publication that would promote the newly crafted state slogan, "Poverty can sometimes give an impression of greater dignity than riches."[1] The state's exaltation of poverty was not meant to offer the riot and famine-torn postcolonial India a makeshift modernism. Instead, the government set out to embrace poverty and resource scarcity as essential ingredients of postcolonial subjecthood.[2] When the Ministry of Food and Agriculture approached him, Jeanneret was designing housing for second- and third-class government employees, which, according to Le Corbusier, was incompatible with modern design principles.[3] But Jeanneret eventually agreed to the government's plea for a different modernity, an inverted model of haute modernity. For a newly decolonized country like India, it was neither a peculiar nor a sporadic effort. In this book, I argue that the scarcity of resources, and sometimes poverty in its crudest sense, were important factors in defining postcolonial Indian modernism as it is known today. The Indian state, along with many other stakeholders such as designers, trade organizations, and cultural activists, aimed to define the limits of poverty and its relationship with an impending industrial development.

Through a discourse of austerity, the state negotiated between "modernizing the poor" and surrendering their fate to the domestic market. It promoted resource scarcity not as a detriment but as a given condition in the path toward development. With this book, I am not proposing another revision of postcolonial modernism, nor do I intend to disagree with the established classification or divisions of design culture that emerged because of the unique regional and political conditions of the decolonizing worlds. Austerity is not about style in the conventional sense. By *austerity discourse*, I mean a unique tendency and sentiment among Indian architects, policymakers, public administrators, and foreign consultants to face the challenge of producing "development" with scarce economic resources. The discourse of austerity does not imply tightening the belt in austere times. Rather, austerity was viewed by most of the decolonizing world as an inevitable precondition to development. More often than not, the actual scarcity of resources was less important than the narratives of scarcity and development.

The narratives of scarcity was constructed through surveys, reports, diagrams, charts, conferences, exhibitions, newspapers, magazines, newsletters, and anecdotal observations of designers and policymakers. This book shows the physical manifestation of the narratives of scarcity, which took the form of "ideal houses" and "model villages" that were either showcased in exhibitions or in the pages of magazines. But these ideal houses or model villages were not real spaces to be occupied and lived in. At best, they were a heuristic narrative petrified in physical form, built as didactic instruments to show members of society how embracing a culture of austerity would lead to prosperity. As a result, the recipe for postcolonial development was envisioned within the confines of an austerity discourse in which a network of metaphors, allegories, and icons of model homes idealized the present and the future. *Of Greater Dignity than Riches* studies the historical context within which this narrative and its physical manifestations took shape. In order to understand this historical context, it is essential to understand how the process of creating icons and metaphors of an idealized future resulted in new modes for the production and delivery of space. The austerity discourse set the tone for India's postcolonial design and architectural modernism, even though the participating low-income population gained little if any power over the actual production of its architecture. The project of austerity eventually idealized the life of the poor, and perhaps even reduced poverty into a stylized architectural representation.

The term *austerity* is loaded with contested meanings. It could refer to Britain's wartime economic state, which even today, as Rebecca Bramall explains, supplies an ideological framework for confronting the contemporary political situation in the United Kingdom.[4] It could also refer to the stringent economic time in interwar Germany, which, according to Paul Betts, inspired designers of East Germany to produce "ascetic objects" with absolute, minimal articulation.[5] *Austerity* could also mean the American New Deal sensibility of assuring unfettered growth with little resources and engaging with the less-affluent social class.[6] Or it could refer to Mao's revolutionary China.[7] In all four cases, design became more than simply a reaction to economic scarcity; it was a cultural expression, the embodiment of a specific way of life. Austerity culture was prescriptive—not an accurate representation of how the poor built houses for themselves or how they actually lived but how others imagined an ideal way of living for them. Resource scarcity, the lack of financial and technological ability to supply housing at an affordable price, is the driving force behind a lingua franca of development. However, a fine line exists between a pragmatic response to resource scarcity and the austerity discourse itself, which engulfed almost every aspect of spatial and material culture in India—from the smallest detail, the scientific design of a broom, to the largest, the rationalized planning of an entire village.

The Indian government embraced the concept of economic growth based on large-scale industrialization and accumulation, while at the same time arguing for a conceptual limit of growth by promoting the idealized, ascetic, and anticonsumerist values of Gandhi. By blending these two apparent opposites—growth and control, abundance and austerity—the government eloquently weaved an ambivalent postcolonial modernity. This apparent Janus-faced design culture, to empower both the consumer fueling the market and the apparent nonconsumers outside the market, was not compatible with the prophecy of pure, industrially oriented modernism.

A Modernism for the Poor

Architectural modernization in India has often been explained as an induced process, prompted by the model of American modernization theory and the Euro-American architectural movement. From this perspective,

India is at the juncture of global flows mediated by occasional interventions by Western modernists such as Le Corbusier and Louis I. Kahn and through large-scale projects. The popular view of India's aspiration toward an industrialized modernity also fodders the import-based model of architectural modernism. Social theory has depicted postcolonial India as obsessively addicted to large-scale development projects. It would be incomplete and inaccurate, however, to interpret Nehru's remark that "Dams are India's new temple" as a general representation of India's development goals. This generalization has turned into an academic myth that often only considers postcolonial history in reference to the capital city of Chandigarh, bolstered by stories that continually reiterate the collaboration between Western architects and Third-World states.

Nehru's India only partially shared a culture of centralized modernization. The continuous reproduction and circulation of that fragmented reality, or the simulation of reality, eventually made it intangible, unimaginable, and unreal—to use Jean Baudrillard's term, it became a *simulacra*. The postcolonial Indian government and its allies, both local and Western, made a great effort to define modernism for the poor, even suggesting that the poor themselves act as agents of development. This version of modernism did not entirely follow the model of centralized, state-controlled modernization, as in Mao's China.[8] Instead, it aimed to engage with local agencies and power structures and focus on the local community and its social condition.

Of Greater Dignity than Riches argues that the discourse of austerity was significantly shaped by the presence and involvement of Western consultant architects and planners in India. A significant number were either invited by the newly formed government or funded by the United States or the United Nations. Their vision of modernity, rooted in the growth-based economic model of industrialization, was challenged in the postcolonial Indian context, where they were constantly juggling growth and limit, abundance and scarcity. Together with local bureaucrats, consultants from the West tried to reconcile these opposing forces and suggested a new austere modernity that was neither heroic nor universal but, as they believed, would flourish at the grassroots level. Architects and planners often expressed hope that what could not be achieved in the industrialized and developed West might possibly be achieved in the new decolonized India. India was considered the last resort, the place where Western modernity would fulfill its prophecy of equality and freedom without falling to the market force. But there is no coherent single story of the modernity of austerity or a grand theory to represent it. It was a multilayered mix of many efforts from local designers, public administrators, and policymakers in tandem with grant agencies, international diplomacy, and hired Western designers interested in India's postcolonial future. In cinematic terms, this book is a long-distance panoramic ripping off of this other modernism—a modernism that was imagined and prescribed for nonaffluent subjects in postcolonial India.

The Myth of an Ideal Home

The modernism of austerity played out most interestingly in the postcolonial state's vision of a new ideal home for the poor—both as an actual artifact and as an analogy of the postcolonial state. Over the course of the anticolonial movement, the notion of home attained a nuanced meaning commensurable to independence, autonomy, public democracy, and private culture.[9] Gandhi's hermit-like ashram was of course the most dominant political icon. The Indian anticolonial struggle nourished the notion of home as an ideological idiom entwining personal memories and national histories.[10] On the one hand, British women in India were held responsible for reproducing imperial power-relations on a household scale by codifying the establishment of the British home.[11] On the other, the incipient notion of the Indian home was in symbiosis with a growing nationalism, where home was a trope that "gave voice and form not to memory, but to [a] personal and collective future."[12] Partha Chatterjee argues that during colonial rule, the development of nationalism was primarily formed by claiming sovereignty in the "inner domain"—the realm of private space of culture practiced in a metaphorical home. By fostering otherness when compared to an array of "outer domains" such as state, trade, and religion, Chatterjee explains, home forged the identity discourse of a colonized community.[13] Chatterjee's dichotomy, however, does not fully explain the complexity of the home icon as an immediate pre-Independence inner domain.[14] The postcolonial Indian state, along with many private business enterprises and cultural institutions, created a nuanced meaning of the ideal home that allowed free interplay between the inner and outer domains. Various house reformation efforts and exhibitions disseminated a concept of the ideal home that suggested permeable boundaries would lead to an interchange of ideas.

Because the notion of an ideal home was already an established metaphor in Indian society, the postcolonial state used it as a symbolic space to define Indian nationalism and citizenship. To fulfill this objective, the Indian government invested in new organizations and ministries and initiated an array of projects to develop a prototype ideal home for the village poor and urban industrial workers. A home of this kind, built in the most economical way, with minimal square footage, symbolized an austere culture and embodied the state's constructed vision of scarcity. Austerity was not a totalitarian imposition; it was reserved only for those who could not afford an affluent lifestyle. A tenet of this selective modernity was to complement growth-based modernity by including the poor and in turn granting them the same respect and dignity as the rich. Set against this context, the ideation process of an ideal home for the poor represents the politics of location-based postcolonial subjectivity and exemplifies the government's conceptions of an idealized life for the less affluent.

Exhibitions

Public outreach was at the heart of the discursive formation of austerity. The concept of the ideal home was disseminated through various exhibitions, seminars, and public demonstrations. Through public displays, the state aimed to gain the public's confidence and generate public opinion about an idealized life of the poor. The displays glorified everyday, mundane life experiences. These exhibits set out to build an array of make-believe worlds, worlds that the audience would accept as factual and real but with an awareness that they might also be unattainable. The friction that resulted is dramatized in figure I.1, in which Prime Minister Nehru observes a prototype house for the less affluent at the first international exhibition of low-cost housing in 1954. The exhibition, co-organized by the Indian government and the United Nations, canonized various techniques of housing production to inspire local builders to construct ideal housing for the disadvantaged. In this photograph, the beholder, representing the state bureaucracy, and the beholden, the anonymous poor, belong to two irreconcilable spheres of reality. It was a matter of debate how the life of the typical and typified Indian could be aligned with the life that was suggested by the housing design at this exhibition. The objects on display, while appearing desirable, were equally unattainable. The ideal home exhibitions constructed an elusive parallel reality, and their effect was framed by the class-consciousness of their audience. They became the catalyst for creating an alternative society, one with a seemingly endless potential to combat the triviality of everyday life.

The austerity discourse was also an integral component even in the discussion of ideal homes for the upper middle class. In the winter of 1937, a group of young Indian architects headed by P. P. Kapadia, the president of Indian Institute of Architects (IIA), organized a display in the town hall

FIGURE. I.1. The South East Asia Regional Conference of the International Federation for Housing and Town Planning was inaugurated by the prime minister, Jawaharlal Nehru, at the International Low-Cost Housing Exhibition Grounds, in New Delhi on February 1, 1954. Source: Photo Studio/February, 1954, A22a(v)/A22a(I) Photo Number: 36915. © Photo division, Government of India.

of Bombay. The institute publicized what it considered to be the ideal Indian home, a site for performing democracy and harnessing a "perfect way of living."[15] Its ideal home was not meant for the poor or industrial workers; rather, the IIA intended to set an example of how middle-class urban families could furnish their houses with economic, modern furniture. The architects who organized the event believed their solution would offset poor building practices and help all economic classes in Bombay. The IIA's exhibition appeared at a time when anticolonial politics wielded underdevelopment as a political weapon and venerated poverty in a metaphoric way, mainly through Gandhi's theatrical display of voluntary poverty. By contrast, this show evinced a picture of an affluent future that was the true objective of India, a future that was available "even for those who [could] afford drastic reforms in the home."[16] According to Kapadia, the show represented an image of a desired future, not of the present that was characterized by "'jerry buildings,' chawls, tenement houses, [and] cheap and shoddy structures."[17] By extrapolating a mode of stern modern living in India, the IIA sought to invoke a "pointer to the future, a substantial step forward towards greater well-being, and let us hope greater happiness."[18] By setting a future-oriented platonic discourse of the "ideal," this show portrayed home as a fictitious destination for Indian society—a place that would stimulate the desire for consumption. However, the irreconcilable lifestyles of the real and imaginary middle class made this an illusionary journey, an illegitimate peek into the lives of strangers.

This ideal home exhibition was criticized for exclusively addressing the urban middle class and excluding the common masses from the discourse of the "ideal." The prime minister, in his inaugural speech, reflected on the palpable problems at hand, stating, "In our search for the Ideal[,] however, we cannot afford to lose sight of the practical realities of life."[19] The prime minister and other stakeholders suggested that the IIA arrange another exhibition demonstrating the unexplored dimension of the Indian "ideal home"—the home that would serve the needs of the poorer segments of society. The press, lambasting the show, protested, "It is all very beautiful, convenient and comfortable, but it is not of the slightest use to the average man with a limited purse, and still less to the poor man."[20] This invocation of mass consumption was fueled by the campaigns of various design organizations, which showed how this standard of modernity could be achieved in a "cheap dwelling" by minimum means.[21] A few days after the IIA's ideal home exhibition closed, in response, the Gujrati Stree Shakhari Mandal (Club for Gujrati Women) displayed drawings and models of ideal one- and two-room tenements at its club fair.[22] Architect Yahya C. Merchant, secretary of the IIA, assisted club members with organizing the display. The institute agreed to arrange a follow-up exhibition on low-cost houses and domestic spaces, but that plan was never realized.[23]

Although the IIA's show lasted only eighteen days, it attracted more than one hundred thousand people who bore witness to the possible, if sometimes drastic changes designed for the Indian home. It might appear that the narrative created by the IIA exhibition was a binary opposite of austerity discourse. And yet the show proposed a model for how Indians could modernize their homes with limited resources and restrained growth. Austerity was not limited to the reformation of housing for the poor and industrial workers. The austerity discourse offered a new mode of thinking that affected almost every aspect of Indian society. A decade before Indian independence, coinciding with the end of the Great Depression, IIA's exhibition brought together an image of a nonfeudal society and stark functional living at a time when India was spawning a class comprised of native urban elite and a boom in the building industry, along with a new wave of domestic consumers.[24] This show was the first of its kind in India to identify the real-estate industry and household goods as two of the prime driving forces for capitalist development and to propose the home as central to consumer discourse.[25] With its selection of Bauhaus furniture and cutting-edge transatlantic household objects, this exhibition heralded a forthcoming postwar, postindependence domestic market that would be based upon industrially produced consumer goods and household objects.[26] By proposing a new material culture—a new way of life based on new household objects—this show was instrumental in bringing about a historical breach with the preceding colonial era and a promise to reestablish the Indian home in a new and democratic modern world.

Modern Design for a New Generation

The Indian architects' longing for contentment through affluence is an integral part of the austerity discourse. The IIA subscribed to the interwar Bauhaus interpretation of modernity based on economy and the liberal socialist view of architectural production, possibly closer to Hannes Meyer's socialist view. However, economy and collectivism were not the only factors deemed important by the IIA. The institute shared a close affinity with the European tradition that relied on domestic space to provide an intimate area for practicing individualism.[27] The home, which promised a personal comfort zone that operated within an exclusive private space of isolated human action, eventually harnessed the "pampered individual."[28] The IIA was well aware that its conceptual ideal home needed a new generation of potential citizen occupants. As reflected in the lantern lecture delivered by architect H. J. Billimoria in the Art and Architecture series under the auspices of the Bombay Presidency Adult Education Association in 1941, only a new Indian generation would be able to realize and appreciate modern "interior decoration" or the modern way of life.[29] An invisible presence of a new kind of citizenship was implicit in the choreographed interior of the IIA's show. This new citizen would be simple, minimum, and austere but at the same time contextual and traditional.

India's exhibitions and the associated discourse of austerity canonized material culture, design, and architecture as manifestations of progress and development. Newly established institutes such as the National Institute of Design (NID) in Ahmedabad or the Building Research Institute at Roorkee helped to foster a new direction in design suitable for the growing and malleable sociocultural and market condition. This institutionalization effort was also a venture to remove the stigma attached to India—the exotic other that was exploited by colonial power to satisfy its own culture of imperial taste. Through new design and research institutes, India affirmed its position in the dominant growth-oriented modernity while simultaneously imagining an idealized material culture and domestic environment that calibrated with its Third-World allies.[30] An emerging India was moving up the scale of development, indicating that it was no longer merely a consumer of the material spectacle produced by the West. It began to disseminate its own version of contemporary spectacle. Absent from the historiography of architecture and modernity in India is an in-depth study of the nature of its resurgence; India explicitly challenged the indulgence of domesticity and the exuberance of material fetish, which is a point of focus for this book.

Austerity in a Global Context

On a global scale, the ideal or model home for the poor attained different political meaning. Developed countries, especially the United States, interpreted a scarcity of resources and resulting reduction of home ownership as the root cause of the global spread of communism.[31] International agencies, including the United Nations, and American NGOs such as the Ford Foundation took considerable interest in creating the myth of the affordable ideal home in the global south. For the US government, India was strategically an important place and a source of political anxiety both because of its geographical location and because of Prime Minister Nehru's inclination toward socialist ideas. This anxiety manifested in a number of collaborative projects between the Indian government, local trade and cultural forces, the United Nations, and the Ford Foundation. Through exhibitions they coordinated together, local and foreign stakeholders made strong statements on a number of new initiatives: municipal bylaws, national policies for industrial housing, rationalized minimum housing, scientific ways to achieve material economy, mortgage and credit systems for new housing, the production of building materials, and the training of unskilled laborers for the building industry. Despite an ephemeral existence, these exhibitions reveal subtle attributes of the modernism of austerity.

My book considers the multidimensional parameters of a broader Cold War *mission civilisatrice* mobilized by the United Nations, the Point Four Program, and the Ford Foundation. The formation of austerity discourse in India was the result of the end of British colonialism, the emergence of conceptual allies of the Third World, and the spread of the global Cold War. It was a time when development-centric and growth-oriented modernization was reified as a discursive device in the name of modernization theory—spilling across finance, culture, and the built environment from the First to the Third World.[32] Poverty, exclusion, and sociopolitical marginalization were no less important topics for cultural studies than issues to be discussed exclusively in relation to political and economic failure. Western and Eastern social scientists came to the consensus that they could not overcome underdevelopment if they only considered development within the realm of economics and politics. Development, theorists of modernization argued, is fundamentally a cultural issue related to the mindset, behavior, and cultural belief system of poor societies, which had little or no motivation to alter their station in life. Major development studies during the 1950s and 1960s concluded that, instead of attempts to change the indigent mindset, it should be viewed as an inevitable ingredient in the constituency of development.[33]

India's modernism of austerity held a similar vision, which maintained that the colonial definition of poverty must be revisited. And if the poor and the affluent altered their thinking process and started to see poverty as a new form of dignity, alluding to Gandhi, they would reimagine the concept of development. In this altered world vision, India would no longer aspire to Western material abundance. Instead, austerity would leave a permanent mark of progress. In this regard, development projects in India assisted by the United Nations and Ford Foundation consultants were not exclusively exported by the West to fulfill its so-called neo-imperialist mission. The case studies in this book explore indigenous agency and problematize the export-biased models of Third World modernization that emphasize unidirectional linear transmission from West to East. Postcolonial India deployed architecture and design as a *performative modernity*, translating ideas about development into images symbolizing postwar, postcolonial national identity.[34]

The exhibitions explored in this book portrayed the modern subject, whether Indian or Western, as willingly submitting to a situation that ultimately challenged her own role in society. This society was a well-organized force to be confronted, a space in which the masochistic pleasure of self-submission to the comfort and security of home was to be unlearned and deconstructed. The exhibitions discussed here did not promote a particular architectural style or material culture; they were recognized by the name of the organizing institutions involved, such as the United Nations; and none canonized a single designer or a single design ideology. In fact, the organizers of these exhibitions conceived the exhibitionary place as an amalgamation of possibilities. The common theme combining each approach was a conviction to form different discourses of modernity. Thus, they were not exclusively devices to import and impose Western ideals, nor were they exclusively places to promote indigenous and vernacular design.

The Scope of the Book

Chapters in this book are organized not in strict chronological order but thematically, focusing on selected aspects of the austerity discourse. Since the themes discussed here emerged concurrently and were entangled at their inception, I could not always maintain a strict chronology, even within a chapter. Most of these case studies recount joint efforts of foreign institutes or architects and designers and Indian government organizations, which means they present at least two different perspectives: from the Western consultants and from the Indian government. Because of a paucity of Indian sources, a substantial number of archival documents used in this book came from Western repositories. As a result, the stories in this book mainly capture the position of Western agencies.[35] While the colonial bureaucracy invested substantial time and effort in documenting its activities, in the postcolonial period, the archiving of design-related documents was marred for a number of reasons, the most important being the feeble mechanisms that were available for archiving institutional documents in individual design and research. Archiving documents, when it comes to so-called events of secondary importance such as design, is in many instances subjective and selection of documents depends on the circumstances. In the case of India, this selection process, and the politics of inclusion and exclusion of archival documents, is crucial. India's past, at least with regard to the case studies that I selected for this book, is mainly approachable through foreign sources.

Of Greater Dignity than Riches explores how an ideal prototype housing unit was formed for industrial workers in India's emerging industrial centers; how the agency of poor citizens tempered threats to state authority; how various government agencies conceptualized and idealized rural poor and village communities; how ideal villages were created as a means to develop what the state viewed as impoverished and disintegrated communities; and how pure austerity values gradually waned from the design discourse. As a result, India's newly established design cells and institutes created multiple transnational connections that were aligned toward global design norms.

Taken together, the chapters in this book posit the Indian subjects within an imagined landscape of ideal homes, model villages, and the country's associated material culture. Showing the conceptual limits of these models and indicating the everyday experience squared by these limitations, I propose that these house reformation efforts, exhibitions, and ideal homes offer the nuances of a new Indian subjectivity.

1

Imagining an Ideal Prototype House for Industrial Workers

In 1918, with much reluctance, Arthur E. Mirams—the "understaffed and over worked" consulting surveyor of the colonial government of Bombay—took up the task of arranging a nationwide design competition to seek the most "suitable house type" for the mill workers of India.[1] The Expert Board of Colonial Bombay, led by Mirams, imagined that the appropriate space for mill workers would be small cottages. The board's imagination resonates with the typical colonial fantasy of an ideal hut for an ahistorical nation in the utopian arcadia.[2] The competition, however, called for formulating a new and "modern" prototype that would support a healthy way of living at low cost. Based on the unsettled construction market at the end of the First World War, the competition set 750 rupees as the maximum cost for one unit, which also determined the required minimum square footage; ergonomic and cultural considerations were hardly taken into account. The minimum square footage designated by the competition eventually became the design factor that controlled the production and supply of working-class housing even in the postindependence period. The idea behind this design competition never materialized in broader scale, but Mirams's attempt helped to reify the emerging discourse of housing for mill workers.

The competition's call for entries explicitly outlined the ideal "types of cottages" the colonial authority desired to be dotted around the rapidly industrialized part of Bombay.[3] This outline mandated what the government of Bombay imagined was most suitable for the emerging urban working class, and it was among the earliest recorded schemes that quantified and made an effort to standardized industrial workers' housing in India. According to the competition instructions, the design should be prepared for two types of "cottages": single or double story, containing not more than a maximum of six-units on each floor. Each unit was to be suitable for a working-class family. Preference was for a double-room tenement with a small veranda in front that would cover a gross area of 275 to 300 square feet, excluding staircases or steps, and the net floor area of any room was not to be fewer than 100 square feet. The instructions also made the participants of the competition aware that the objective was to invent a prototype for the cheapest possible structure, durable and functional, that the city could lease to the urban working class for the lowest possible rent.

The aim of Mirams's competition, to set a new standard for workers' housing, was rooted in a burgeoning discourse surrounding mill workers' housing in Bombay. The global demand for Indian cotton increased rapidly following the American Civil War, and the Indian textile industry expanded quickly, causing a massive influx of workers into Bombay from surrounding rural areas who found jobs in this new industry.[4] The emergence of this urban working class contributed to a phenomenal growth of major Indian cities, such as Ahmedabad, Hyderabad, and Calcutta. Bombay grew substantially because of an abundant supply of local capitals, and it secured a continuous supply of labor from the surrounding villages.[5] In 1875 the executive health officer of Bombay reported that a good portion of the laborers were temporary migrants from the villages and lived in cramped dwellings that had no direct connection to a sewage system.[6] And yet in Bombay, the mill owners or the city authorities were not concerned with accommodating this new working-class population until the bubonic plague broke out in 1896. In addition to disrupting the steady supply of labor, the plague threatened the physical well-being of the elite natives and the white population of the city. Between 1896 and 1897, laborers left the mills of Bombay en masse, disrupting daily operations and drawing attention to their need for suitable housing.[7] The impetus to provide the mill workers with low-density, sanitary housing was ultimately twofold: to create a clean, healthy, and gentrified city in which urban space was divided according to class and race and to secure a continuous and dependable labor supply.

The Bombay City Improvement Trust

Immediately after the bubonic plague outbreak, elite residents in central Bombay blamed the crammed and filthy slums that were clumped together near their neighborhood.[8] A lack of local medical knowledge along with the laissez-faire public health policy of the colonial authority led native elites to believe that slum clearance and gentrification of urban space would solve the problem.[9] In response, the government of Bombay established the Bombay City Improvement Trust (BIT) in 1898, modeled after the Glasgow Improvement Trust. The fundamental idea of any improvement trust in that time was to form a strong alliance between local elite groups and politicians.[10] Over the course of the next half century, the BIT configured a domestic and urban space in which individuals and communities were dispersed and placed according to their respective class identities.[11]

The outbreak naturally initiated discussions of ideal living, cleanliness, and the home and body beautiful in various disciplines. The experience of the epidemic, the main cause of death in Bombay between 1897 and 1907, radically stirred the linear relationship between colonized and colonizers as the subordinated-subordinator couple.[12] As the people of India encountered the disease, their hope for absolute emancipation from colonial rule, both bodily and ideologically, was assessed on two grounds: the corporeal, the question of control over one's own body, and the spatial, the question of one's physical location in one's own home and in urban space. The health measures taken up by the colonial administration to control the epidemic raised important questions about who should control the collective corporeal experience within the city.[13] The epidemic acquired a spatial dimension that resulted in the territorial reconfiguration of Bombay, which significantly framed the lifestyle of mill workers and an emerging middle class.

In order to ensure proper ventilation and adequate light, the municipality enacted the Epidemic Disease Act in 1897, which demolished portions of large tenement houses to widen the *chowk* (narrow alleyway between chawls).[14] The cumulative result of such evictions substantially increased the housing demand of the low- and middle-income population. It also caused a sharp rise in housing rent, as the evicted population sought new accommodations around the neighborhood from which they had been dislodged. Such operations reduced housing space within working-class neighborhoods and dramatically raised real-estate value;[15] together with the unstable market that followed the First World War, these operations quickly caused an unprecedented shortage of working-class tenements, which, to use a colloquial term, resulted in the *house famine*.[16]

In order to "cleanse" the city, the BIT oversaw a substantial dehousing of the working class without giving due consideration to rehousing the evicted communities. The trust rationalized its operation by arguing that the working-class population was not sensible enough to realize the demands of urban cleanliness. According to the municipal commissioner of Bombay, P. C. H. Snow, in 1897: "The people would not believe that the hopeless condition of their own dark, damp, filthy, overcrowded houses was their real danger, they raved about the sewers and became phrenzied if a scavenger was remiss. . . . [E]very form of obstruction was resorted to when the Municipality attempted to deal with their dwellings."[17]

In operation, the trust's main objective was to eradicate the insanitary shanties from the city. Providing public housing was never the main aim of the BIT; to them, constructing a few model houses as examples for private builders would suffice. To implement its objective, the BIT implemented a three-pronged urban intervention: first, on a domestic scale, by making houses "modern" through proper sanitary design; second, by controlling traffic and opening up new space with wide boulevards and roads; and third, by creating a new suburban space at the city's outskirts. By 1909 the trust offered new "sanitary chawls" (long, single- or multistory buildings in which multiple small, single-room units are sheltered under one roof) consisting of 2,844 rooms.[18] As of 1920 the trust had constructed 21,387 tenements and had demolished 24,428.[19] By emphasizing low density in urban spaces, the BIT's policy guidelines eventually subsumed efforts to design and construct feasible housing for the dislodged population. The common theme that underpinned these objectives was a desire to decrease the density of the city's heart.

J. P. Orr, chairman of the trust from 1910, blamed the overdensity of Bombay's buildings—which he called "the sweating of building sites"—for the progressive growth of disease.[20] The BIT had almost no idea how to provide better housing for workers.[21] Various city authorities could not arrive at a common consensus about design, mill owners lacked clear direction, and all stakeholders were very reluctant to actively contribute.

The 1918 Exhibition

With his open competition, Arthur Mirams sought to establish a rational prototype or standard design for workers' housing. But because his solution rested on the economic interest of various stakeholders, their rationality sidelined workers' social and cultural context.

To organize the design competition, Mirams teamed up with J. W. Mackinson, chief engineer of the Bombay Municipality, and R. H. A. Delves, deputy land manager of the BIT. The team carefully selected designs that featured semidetached single- or double-story houses. Their selections were markedly at odds with Bombay's scarce land and heavy demand for housing.[22] The top three prescribed a minimum livable space of 110 square feet, which Mirams later expanded to ten feet by twelve feet, or 120 square feet (figs. 1.1, 1.2). With their proposals for more elementary units, designers suggested a rational inversion of the existing "wretch-

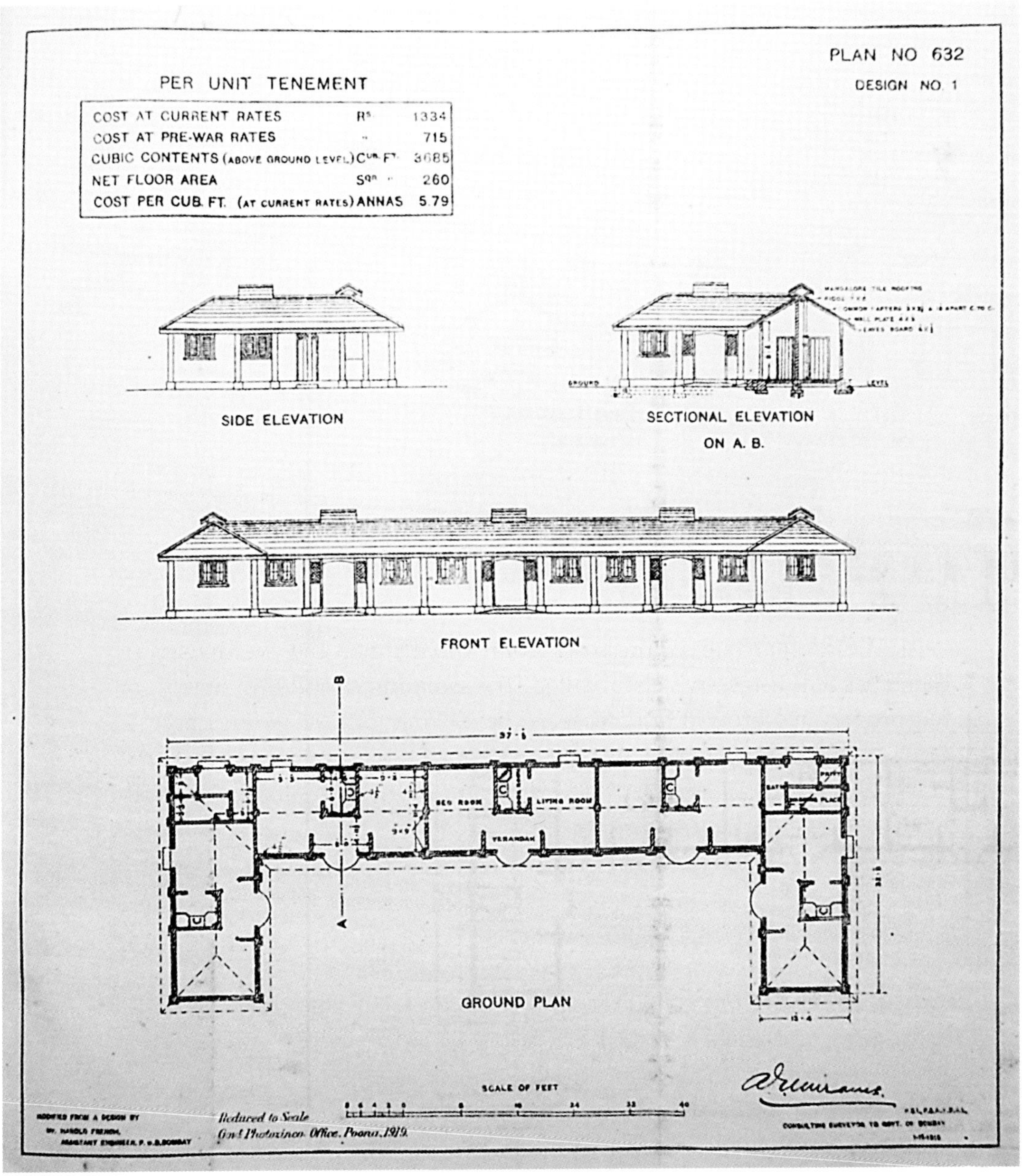

FIGURE 1.1. The plans and elevations of the first prize winner of the 1918 workers-class housing competition. Source: A. E. Mirams, *Plans and Specifications of Houses Suitable for Occupation by the Working Class* (Bombay: Government Central Press, 1919), n.p.

FIGURE 1.2. A model of the first prize winner of the 1918 exhibition. Source: A. E. Mirams, *Plans and Specifications of Houses Suitable for Occupation by the Working Class* (Bombay: Government Central Press, 1919).

edness of the dark and dingy four story chawls [the existing informal multistory dwellings that were popular as cheap accommodations for mill workers] with one roomed tenements, in each of which 6 or 8 persons are huddled," as described by the Industrial Commission in 1927.[23] Mirams and his colleagues believed that the new prototypes would provide more "privacy and comfort" than the multistoried chawls, and thus came the idea of the semidetached, low-density housing complex.[24] According to the colonial government, high-density chawls were politically dangerous spaces that could potentially harbor insurgents against city authority and industrialists.[25] To reduce the possibility of mass upheaval in high-density chawls, the state adopted policies that incorporated privacy and seclusion in low-density dwellings and considered splitting up large community blocks into clusters of small cottages.

Mirams featured the winning entries of the competition in an exhibition at the Special Collectors Courtroom in the Bombay Improvement Trust Office on June 21 and 22, 1918.[26] It was a small-scale exhibit intended to draw the attention only of local entrepreneurs and builders. The first of the exhibition's two sections included drawings of entries to the com-

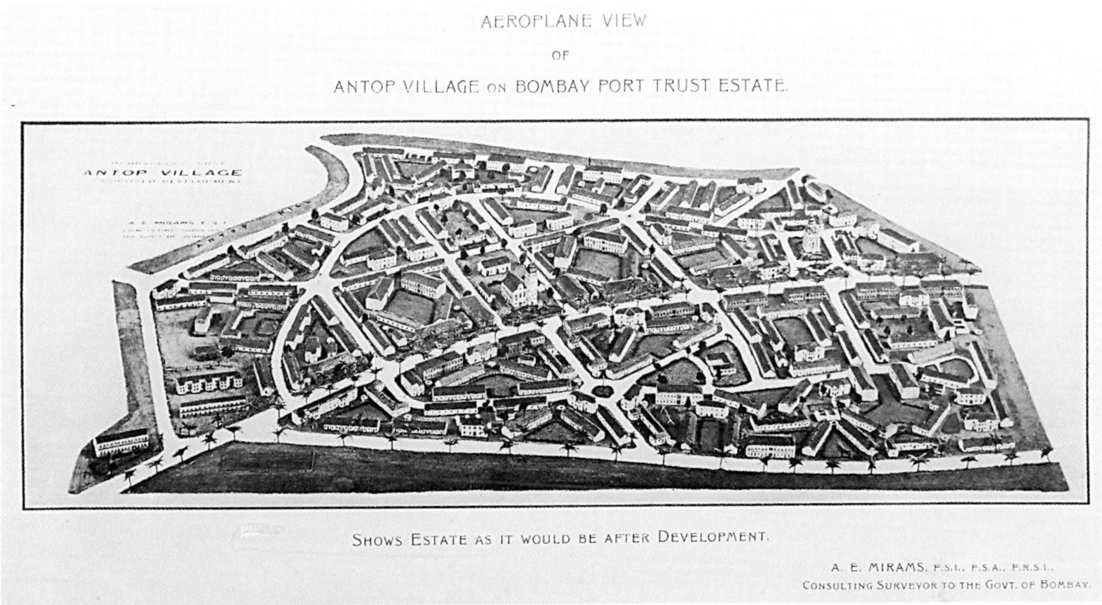

FIGURE 1.3. Antop village on Bombay Port Trust Estate, showing how the different entries of the competition could form an industrial housing estate. Source: A. E. Mirams, *Plans and Specifications of Houses Suitable for Occupation by the Working Class* (Bombay: Government Central Press, 1919), 8.

petition along with estimations of construction costs, elaborate notes, and explanations for contractors and industrialists. The second section displayed recent examples of town planning and city improvement schemes in Bombay and its vicinity, which showcased the British garden town concept. The new Salsette Town Planning Scheme shown by the consulting surveyor to the government, Antop Village on Bombay Port Trust Estate and the Ahmedabad Mill Employees garden suburb attracted popular attention, as they presented the "real and practical" context in which the prescribed workers' houses would be placed (fig. 1.3). Such an idealistic vision reflected the popular elite conception of Bombay, free from the chaos or unruliness of traditional workers' houses. Mirams intended the show to be a didactic display for a more technical audience, as a number of engineering staff from the railway companies, municipalities, BIT, and port trust were present.[27] After the exhibition closed, presidents of municipalities, the chairman of the port trust, the chairman of the improvement trust, factory owners, officials from railway companies, the inspector general of police, and military authorities all asked for a simplified and workable version of the designs—requests that compelled the exhibition committee to publish a catalog.

Improving Labor through Housing

Mirams was a well-regarded land surveyor and urban planning consultant to various colonial governments.[28] During his fifteen-year tenure in India, he was adamant about applying British land reform policy in the colony as a way to control the racially segregated urban space and systematic order of working-class housing. This conviction was reflected in his seminal "social survey" conducted in 1917 on behalf of the Indian Industrial Commission.[29] In addition to a written report, Mirams presented oral evidence before the commission in which he reported that the "improvement of industry" was intertwined with the "improvement of labor."[30] Mirams's recommendations about improving the life of Indian laborers were based on two fundamental premises: that Indian laborers were physically inferior to workers in countries with a temperate climate and that they were politically disorganized, demotivated, and unambitious—so much so that they were not at all interested in improving their current condition by advancing their technical skills and wage-earning capacities. Because of these fundamental characteristics, Mirams contended, and despite low wages and a good labor supply, Indian industries were not efficient or productive. He further suggested that since Indian workers were not ambitious, reduced work hours and increased wages would not develop the life of the working class. Extra money and free time, he argued, would only compel laborers to indulge in sinful activities, such as alcohol and narcotic use. In addition, from his perspective, since Indian laborers were content with a low standard of comfort and were accustomed to an unsanitary rural environment, they were less likely to maintain a sanitary urban environment. Finally, Mirams concluded that mill owners and governments must not expect first-generation Indian workers who still maintained connections with villages to possess the civic senses essential to maintain a well-ordered, sanitary urban environment.

Mirams recommended that, instead of focusing on the workers themselves, the government and the mill owners should train the children of its labor force to be sensible and productive. Since most of these children already worked in the mills and factories, Mirams reasoned, they already fell under the control of their employer. And if they could be trained "under tolerable conditions of life," they would transform into an efficient second generation of workers rooted in new industrial towns.[31] This new generation of workers would be more ambitious and more interested in life. They would consider their work at the mill their only occupation and as a result would be less capricious and more docile and ordered. According to Mirams, training of the factory workers' children should start in their formal education during breaks from work and at home. And, given the influence workers' housing would have over this ideal future labor force, the government should take its design and construction very seriously. Improving workers' housing was about much more than urban sanitation or moral obligation; from Mirams's perspective, it was an economic issue intimately tied to the future of Indian industry.

The 1918 exhibition allowed industrialists to express their commitment to providing a humane living for their workers, which, they argued, would increase the efficiency of human labor and industrial production. Besides outlining the plan, section, and elevation of various housing prototypes, designers presented detailed estimates of the costs involved, as well as new construction techniques. The cost analysis caught the attention of the press and the builders. But what enthused the entrepreneurs caused mixed reactions in press reviews, which highlighted two main concerns: the dearth of any consideration for the aesthetics of the design of elevations and the relevance and implications of a good "environment" in propelling industrial production. While some news reports embraced Mirams's suggestions for confronting the acute housing shortage and endorsed it as a formal, tangible, and rational solution, others demanded a more picturesque setting with a front garden and improved, "'beautiful' elevations."[32] Increasing the aesthetic value, they argued, would provide a more relaxed and leisurely environment to energize and ready workers for their next day in the factory. With the initiation of assembly-line production, the role of human workers was critical; reducing threats to their productivity was paramount. Housing was ultimately interpreted as an extension of the factory production line. Production and efficiency took precedence over considerations of the cultural and social use of space.

Mirams conceived his prototype of the ideal house in support of a new system of centralized production, supply, and housing management that the state and local authority would mediate.[33] This new policy, drawing from the experience of Great Britain, did not envision a complete abolition of the competitive private housing market but raised the necessity to intervene when private enterprise failed to act. The primary concern of the local authority–based housing supply was to develop an effective rent and credit system in which the local authority would either build housing or help private mill owners build housing to rent to the workers. Despite institutional-level propaganda, the local authority never realized its project to build detached working-class housing in garden suburbs. Growing dissatisfaction among industrial workers, food riots, the threat of bubonic plague, and an unmanageable population density shattered its romantic dream of garden-suburbia living.

Defining the New Working Class

Mirams's competition was not an independent initiative but represents a larger tendency by the colonial governments of Indian cities to impose disciplinary and legislative conditions that would accommodate a new emerging working-class population. For instance, in 1913 the Calcutta Improvement Trust published a report, City and Suburban Main Road Projects, in which authors James Maden, a senior trust engineer, and Albert de Bois Shrosbree, the chief valuer to the improvement trust, presented a prototype plan of dwellings for the "poorer class."[34] Maden and Shrosbree proposed a three-storied block divided into two wings. Each story had twelve units, six on each wing, served by a double-loaded corridor in the center. Each unit was divided into a twelve-by-twelve-foot living room and a four-foot-wide veranda, but there was no cooking space. Male and female toilets and bathrooms were located at both ends of the block. Maden and Shrosbree's model was similar to most of the exhibition entries organized by Mirams. Trust engineers had similar working methods and also shared ideas about what constituted an ideal sanitary space for laborers. Their approach to design likely stemmed from colonial officers, who had a parochial understanding about the emerging urban industrial workers of India.

Across official documentation produced by various improvement trusts and industrial commissions, workers were little more than an abstract, an acultural, apolitical labor force akin to factory machinery. Reducing them to an inert component of the production process homogenized the official perception of the industrial worker's life. But the trust engineers and surveyors who prepared these documents all expressed a personal moral obligation to help the poor, not just to solve the problems of the city. In a letter to the Indian Industrial Commission, Mirams wrote, "Although I have observed a good deal of poverty in my walk through life and in many countries, and although I had read a great deal about poverty, I confess I did not realize its poignancy and its utter wretchedness until I came to inspect the so-called homes of the poorer working classes of the town of Bombay."[35] This heightened sense of morality among the trust engineers and officials gave missionary values to their jobs, eventually prepared the basis for their action, and idealized their collective perception of Indian workers' lives.

When considering how to house its industrial workers, colonial governments and mill owners had two fundamental limitations: they did not know how to define or map the sociocultural complexity of the working class and its housing, and they could not arrive at a clear consensus about who constituted the new urban working class. Whether it should be limited to workers in the mill, the dockyard, and the warehouse or expanded to include anyone poor and less affluent—such as third-class government workers and even members of the police forces—remained to be seen. An entirely new discussion emerged from attempts to define industrial workers as an economic class and a cultural construct, to understand their problems, and to determine who was legally responsible for solving this perceived problem. The question of authority and responsibility sparked lengthy, winding debates between various city authorities, nonprofit organizations, and mill owners. No single organization would accept total responsibility. Without coordination or an integrated vision for the future, this impasse jeopardized any undertaking related to the delivery of new housing or the improvement of existing housing.[36] Public discussion of workers' housing centered on murky vicissitude and ambiguous definitions of the working class and its houses in a hasty attempt to deliver something tangible with the limited financial capacity of the city.

As this discourse developed, mill workers and the urban poor gradually became analogous, if not synonymous. And for the first time, both concepts—urban poverty and the working class—found their way into the spatial discourse of India. Debates abounded on the housing crisis of the emerging working class—mainly involving those in the mill, the dockyard, and the mine—and after independence, on refugee housing. To better understand the problem, colonial city authorities looked to create a comprehensible social and physical mapping of the working class informed by census data, which was no easy task. The majority of first-generation industrial workers came from an agrarian background and preferred circular movements between village and city to one-way migration to industry. Despite this, they maintained a complex identity that conflated caste and region with their newly anointed class as industrial workers.[37] However, neither the mill owners nor the municipalities saw industrial workers as permanent residents of the city, let alone active participants in civic life; they were merely understood as numbers of an industrial force, one that was highly unpredictable and contingent.

Many mills in Bombay periodically shut off or reduced their production when it was not profitable, making it impossible to promise a stable, continuous, and permanent supply of labor. For Indian elites, merchants, mill owners, designers, and colonial urban governance of the late nineteenth and early twentieth centuries, the question of industrial workers' housing—its design, construction, management, and delivery—shattered norms of urban areas and established notions about neighborhood, community, and collective housing. It also challenged the stereotypical colonial mindset that conventions and traditions of the Indian city prevented reform according to new modern class divisions and culture associated with the industrial economy. The indefinite, mobile, and unnamable urban working class was a resource for mills and factories, but, paradoxically, that class was at once a constant source of fear and anxiety for the white population and local elites alike.

Government Chawls, Responsibility, and Profit

The indeterminacy of the new working class was followed by another problem—the indeterminacy of the existing dwellings of the working class. Trust engineers, municipal officers, and sanitary inspectors developed their suggestions for a new and improved housing type on chawls. The word *chawl* entered into official documents in 1881. But the 1881 census, having inadequately defined the dwelling, documented 4,139 chawls out of 28,315 different types of tenements in Bombay.[38] The 1901 survey changed the definition of *chawl* to mean one large block of multiple housing units, even though each unit on that block was still understood as one chawl.[39] In the 1901 census document, a rudimentary diagram of a chawl showed an oblong structure with a single gable on top and seven oversized doors on each side, indicating that one chawl housed seven families. This diagram served as the basic architectural scheme of trust, and mill owners built chawls just like this in the coming decades. These new dwellings tackled aesthetic, engineering, and ergonomic issues in a myriad of ways. Gradually they emerged as an architectural type, broadly referred to in official documents and newspapers as a "worker's house." They also formed a discourse in the professional, bureaucratic, and mill owners' imagination to rationalize and systematize working-class living in minimal space.

As the discourse of workers' housing continued to develop, the physical demolition of informal tenements carried on. After a decade of ineffective slum clearance, new measures were taken by the BIT to house the displaced population. Between 1909 and 1918, the trust demolished 7,823 dwellings and constructed 9,311 one-room tenements on its estate.[40] The construction of these new houses aimed not to resolve the housing problem of the working class but to set examples of ideal single-room working-class dwellings and to encourage "private enterprise."[41] According to a 1927 report, Bombay required at least fifty thousand single-roomed tenements for its workers, although there was fierce debate among members of the Special Advisory Committee that the figure did not represent actual demand.[42] The First World War, and the consequent shortage of building materials, raised the rent of the trust's chawls to an unaffordable level for the working class. It was reported that this housing was mostly occupied by the middle-income population or that it was sometimes forced upon the rural migrants.[43] The Bombay Municipal Corporation rebuked the trust's repeated failure to address working-class housing and formed the Bombay Development Directorate in 1919 to solve the housing famine, which eventually merged with the Bombay Municipal Corporation in 1933. The new directorate was empowered in the same manner as the trust, having the authority to enforce compulsory land acquisition without public consultation. It was responsible for building at least fifty thousand single-room tenements. The BDD decided to improve the existing multistoried and high-density chawl model with the help of novel material of the time, reinforced cement concrete. Despite its efforts, however, the new directorate met with the same tragic fate as the BIT, but with much larger financial damage: it constructed fewer than seventeen thousand rooms, of which only one-fifth were ever occupied.

The emerging discourse of the worker's house was mainly based on the anecdotal observation and personal impression of the municipality officers and improvement trust engineers; the social use of space was less important. Despite repeated warnings from the popular press to incorporate opinions of occupants into the design of new model houses, the Bombay Development Directorate (BDD) never engaged the actual dweller in the design process. BDD's model house design proved to be a fiasco, as it operated as an erroneous speculative hypothesis of the working-class lifestyle that excluded essential functions like *nahanis* (washing places), adequate *chulha* (cooking space), and customary verandas for breathing space. As the archbishop of Bombay told architect Claude Batley, "There was no evidence of the milk of human kindness in their design."[44] Another leading architect of Bombay, Perin Jamshedji Mistri, who at that time was serving on the local committee of Back Bay development, complained that the existing chawl layouts were "without sufficient considerations or knowledge of the human needs of labor."[45] H. Stanley Jevons, a professor of economics, was the most outspoken critic of government chawls. In a letter to the *Times of India*, he wrote:

> I cannot sufficiently condemn the practice of going on building block after block of these chawls of exactly similar design, without paying any attention to ascertain need of the people living in those first constructed. An engineer who is quite ignorant of the needs of the working-classes and of principles approved by all housing reformers, may be forgiven for making mistakes for the first one or

> two blocks erected. He cannot possibly be forgiven for going on repeating those mistakes, without any apparent attempt to meet the needs and wishes of the unwilling inhabitants.[46]

By purging the essentials of life, the BDD conjured up an illusion of clean, high-density houses that were more a mirage than functioning working-class dwellings. Despite much propaganda, BDD's model houses were hardly occupied.

As early as the 1890s, several mill-owning groups in Bombay, such as the Petits, Wadias, and Jamsedji Tata, worked on designing and constructing housing for their workers.[47] However, this type of private initiative was extremely limited. Vithaldas Thackersey, chairman of the Bombay Mill Owners Association, strongly contended that the BIT should be solely responsible for ensuring housing for mill workers.[48] Thackersey substantiated his argument by stating that mill owners would face significant financial loss if they were to provide housing.[49] His colleagues also supported his view, adding that the BIT was morally obligated because it profited from the textile industry.[50] In 1913 Jahangir Cowasjee, a prominent nationalist leader and financer of several mills in Bombay and Jamshedpur, condemned the BIT's intention to pass its responsibility to mill owners, since most of the mills in the post-plague decade were already in massive capital debt.[51]

The few mill owners who actually constructed housing for their workers also strongly opposed the BIT's stance that they were legally obligated to provide it.[52] Not only were they reluctant to embrace the idea, but they were also highly critical of the design guidelines provided to them by the BIT, mainly in the form of codes and written instructions, for housing that was expensive and impractical.[53] Although both parties were preoccupied with financial gain, their bigotry was imbedded in the broader political and intellectual debate about who bore responsibility for the working class. The moral dimension of providing housing to industrial workers was apparent in Lord Sandhurst's remarks on the establishment of the BIT, when he stated, "The rehousing of the poorer classes is one of the most important and attractive provisions of the Bill. These people deserve our sympathy and assistance as we desire to place them in better houses."[54] It was common knowledge among the trust engineers and mill owners that the workers, with their limited wage-earning capacity, would never be able to build and own a home in the city. This presented a paradox. On the one hand, mill workers were financially incapable of providing housing for themselves, and mill owners would not increase their wages for the sake of keeping the market competitive and profitable. On the other hand, sanitary dwellings were essential for efficient industrial productivity, but no one would assume full responsibility for building them.

The discussion of the worker's house gradually shifted focus from the morality of ruling elites and civic duty to the potential for profit. Under the leadership of J. P. Orr, the BIT was increasingly a profit-oriented organization. In a 1913 proceeding of the Bombay Development Committee, Orr contended that to make the chawls affordable to factory workers, rent ought to be low, which means a slow return on the BIT's investment in construction and maintenance.[55] Considering the potential financial loss, Orr argued, the BIT should rethink its involvement in the whole process. He also believed that municipal building bylaws were doing more harm than good. In 1912 at the second All India Sanitary Conference in Madras, Orr blamed the limitations and irrelevance of the bylaws for high-density urban development and the proliferation of unsanitary chawls.[56] When Orr, J. F. Watson, and engineers in the BIT presented possible amendments to the building bylaws in 1913, they were viewed by some members of the trust as a means to reduce municipal authority.[57]

On the legislative side of de-densification, these new rules critically reviewed the apparent inefficacy of existing municipal bylaws that had been controlling urban morphology and the configuration of individual buildings.[58] With hindsight, Orr argued that the existing laws had been repressing the urban poor and pressing them into an ever more crowded and chaotic urban pattern. In order to fix this and create order, he outlined his famous "63½-degree rule." According to this rule, two adjacent vertical planes or the exterior façade of chawls must not create an angle of more than 63 ½ degrees when the pick of any vertical plane was connected to the base point of any other. Orr suggested that 63 ½ should serve as the basis of all regulations: for plot size, for the location of a building in a plot, and for the height-to-width ratio of a building to the proportion of a window to its floor area (fig. 1.4). It was assumed to be effective in both urban and suburban areas. This rule played a major role in reforming the regulations of other city improvement trusts, such as those in Hyderabad and Delhi.

Mirams was highly critical of the profit-oriented tendency within the BIT, and in 1916 he spoke out against Orr's view: "The Trust are confronted with the question as to how far it would be right for them to incur loss on schemes which provide for better housing of the poor classes . . . in spite of the objections raised by economists that this would practically amount to subsidizing employers out of public funds. [But] if this argument was carried to its logical conclusions, then no public authority is justified in spending money which benefits the individual at the expense

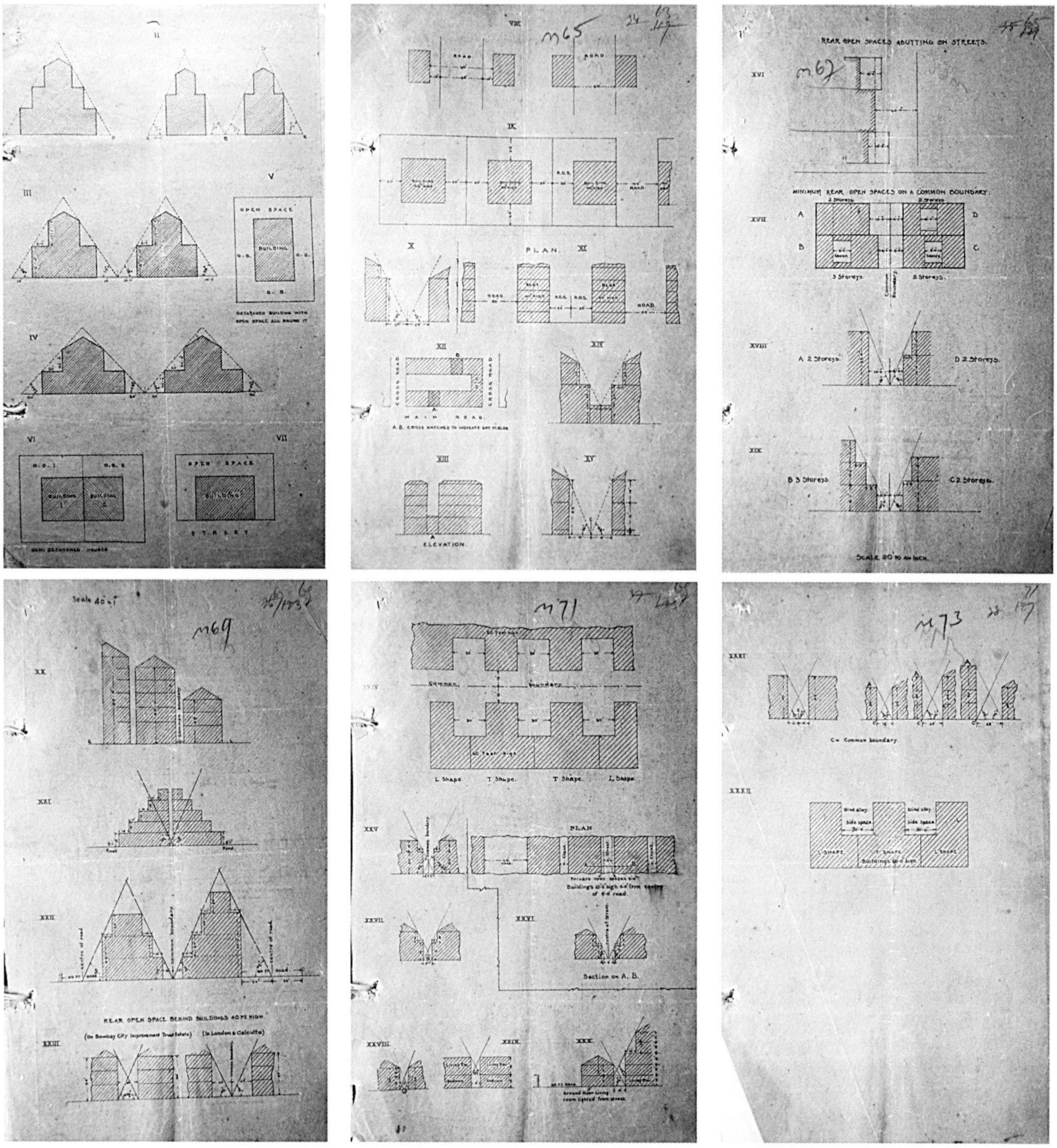

FIGURE 1.4. Drawings showing the implication of the 63½-degree rule in determining the building footprint, distance between two blocks and the limit of height. Source: J. P Orr, "Light and Air in Dwellings in Bombay," 38–39, 40.

of the public."[59] In 1918, while preparing the call for entries for his competition, Mirams estimated that an average Bombay mill worker could only afford to pay two rupees per month for rent, but the contemporary construction market could not possibly build a sanitary building in the city for a monthly rent of less than three rupees.[60] Mirams set up the competition to showcase how even an economic building that could afford to collect less than two rupees could have an aesthetically pleasing design. If, for the government, workers' housing was solely a technical or at best an architectural problem in the narrowest sense, the unaffordability of the renters could be solved architecturally by creating ingenious ways to construct cheap but aesthetically pleasing buildings. The complex economic and social problem of housing was thus flattened and constrained to the premises of techniques and cost. In reality, the housing problem was intricately related to the various structural conditions of the real-estate market, such as land ownership.[61] However, the interest of Mirams and his colleagues in a new workers' housing initiative lay in the techniques of construction and aesthetic. Neither the BIT nor the BDD had any control over the structural condition of the market. No well-coordinated rent policy existed. And on top of that, the definition of a house tenement and the nature of its occupants were always in flux. Mirams observed that the entrepreneurial landlords who operated within this structurally limited market worsened the condition of the working class.[62]

The Worker's House and Its Urban Context

The issue of "working hands housing" in Bombay, as Mirams observed in his report to the Indian Industrial Commission, was very different than in the rest of the country. In Bombay the problem of housing was intrinsically related to the problem of urban development. Mirams argued that the challenge is not solely an architectural problem but rather a problem of the city, and thus he disagreed with the ongoing argument within the BIT that mill owners should assume sole responsibility for housing their workers. Mirams believed that only the BIT was equipped to understand and encounter the complex urban problem. Referring to the success of the small coal-mining towns of Bihar—where employers supplied housing to all their workers—Mirams argued that the same scheme would not be appropriate for Bombay because its urban condition was very unique. Employers in Bihar weren't more inclined to oblige the law, Mirams contended, but they were bound to provide housing to their employees. For them, no other options existed; coal mining was the only economic activity in a town devoid of housing provisions. Unlike Bihar, the income-earning power and economic prosperity in Bombay was not dependent on mills and factories. The city had many moving parts attached to its core industrial strength, and Bombay municipality evolved as a distinct political and administrative entity that had the legal power to impose taxation on every social and economic class.[63] Given this multilayered economic situation, Mirams urged the policymakers of Bombay not to think in a linear fashion, as they might do in Bihar.

According to Mirams, workers' housing in Bombay and elsewhere should be considered against a larger social and urban context. His call to understand the worker's house in this context was different from his peers, such as J. P. Orr, who approached the design and delivery of the worker's house mainly in terms of its plot size, geometric shape, maximum height, and setback space. For Orr the problem could be solved effectively if the municipality identified a standard and ideal geometric and morphological pattern for the city; finding the right shape and numbers for an ideal prototype was key. Mirams, on the other hand, wanted to understand urban form in terms of sociology and anthropology. His sociological approach aimed at substantiating any effort of quantification: the number and shape of that so-called ideal prototype by the collective social behavior of the working class. Mirams believed the recent development of the sociological method in Britain would help the colonial government understand the behavior pattern of Indian workers. Although Mirams argued for an objective, sociological approach, his study was biased because he used sociology as a rational instrument to validate his personal take on Indian workers—that they were naturally immoral and unambitious.

Geddes and the Sociology of the City

Mirams borrowed the sociological dimension of the urban context from Sir Patrick Geddes's recent theory of the city. The Scottish biologist, sociologist, and geographer evinced the city as a living organism constituted of natural terrain, economic resources, and the collective social behavior of its residents. In 1914 Geddes was invited by sociologist Harold Hart Mann, former principal of the agricultural unit in Poona (now Pune), Bombay, and fellow of the University of Bombay,[64] to feature his famous traveling exhibition on Cities and Town Planning. The exhibit portrayed Geddes's argument through various European case studies.[65] The reformation and design of India's urban centers was a pressing issue for the colonial government, which had neither the financial support nor any mechanism to understand the urban dynamics of Indian cities. While traveling in India,

Geddes wrote an open letter to Jamsedji Nusserwanji Tata, pioneer industrialist and founder of the Tata Group, urging Tata to establish a research institute in India. In his letter, Geddes explained that the problem of the worker's house and the design of industrial towns in India was intertwined in diverse sociological aspects and that India needed a sociological approach to understand the issue as a coherent whole.[66]

While Tata was not convinced by Geddes's idea, this sociological approach was welcomed by the colonial government. The state was in need of the right tool to gain knowledge about the emerging urban working class, on which they barely had any data. The Indian census, initiated in 1871, only collected numerical data about the ethnic background or economic production of its subjects. It was not equipped to gain knowledge about the social behaviors of an economic class, one comprised of a complex mix of ethnic groups that shared common time and space both in city and village. Geddes's idea seemed attractive to the colonial government, and he was invited to establish a department of sociology within the University of Bombay, where he served as a professor of sociology between 1919 and 1924.[67]

During Geddes's tenure at the University of Bombay, he initiated a number of academic and student projects to analyze the structure of the city from an interdisciplinary perspective. Geddes's main objective was to create a new epistemological framework to define the problem of the city from a sociological perspective, which would be created through the accumulation of sociological data about housing, its occupants, and its urban context.[68] This new mode of data collection was fundamentally different from the previous census. Reports on social issues related to mill workers' housing were placed within a distinct and integrated social space. A new form of reporting emerged that stressed the condition of life of the working class.[69] Through surveys and reports, the worker's house and its neighborhood were transformed into a self-referential sociological phenomenon. The conversion of the workers' neighborhood into charts of sociological data was intended to make the existing worker's house and neighborhood epistemologically penetrable for the mill owners and the colonial government. Any effort to scientifically and sociologically reform the worker's house was part of an attempt to make sense of the unknown—the life of the industrial worker. Geddes believed the new framework would be crucial in order to manage and deploy urban governance. In his proposal, the worker's house occupied an important location. It was seen as a conceptual space that would be necessary to keep a productive balance between industrial development and the social stability of urban life. For Geddes the technical, mathematical, and financial construct of the worker's house was not more important than how the authority planned to build these ideal prototypes in the context of the city.

Ironically, the intricate urban context of the worker's house also made it equally vulnerable and a constant source of dissent. The year 1918, when Mirams organized his exhibition, was specifically important to the labor history of Bombay. Mirams's team started to plan for the exhibition in 1917, and it was around 1917 and 1918 when the well-coordinated general strikes began to crystallize, resulting in eight large-scale strikes between 1919 and 1940.[70] These strikes were organized both in the factories and in the chawls. On several occasions, city authorities created legislation banning residents from holding any community meetings in chawls, as they were seen as potential danger spots that fueled agitation.[71] These strikes in Bombay were caused by economic hardship, but they were also symptomatic of the formation of a political consciousness among workers and peasants in India and across the industrializing world at that time.[72] This awakening was also propelled by the start of the all-India noncooperation movement under the leadership of Gandhi and Shaukat and Muhammad Ali in 1919.

Some colonial intellectuals realized the broader implications of the strikes—that they were not merely disconnected movements fighting for higher wages but were part of an emerging demand to establish the social and political rights of the working class. Patrick Geddes's essay "University of Bolshevism (established 1920) in Worli Bombay" pointed to this fact in a satirical way.[73] He contended that the unsanitary and dilapidated workers' houses constantly manifested the inequality and urban poverty that would fuel social agitation and fodder revolutionary tendency in the industrial workers. Geddes argued, ironically, that poor housing conditions in Bombay paved the way for bolshevism. He also argued that the government of Bombay, through its own policies, promoted bolshevism in India as effectively as any agitator or conspiracy, as it allowed the deterioration of housing conditions to continue. In his essay, Geddes explained the new and improved worker's house as the enclave or shell to effectively hide out the urban poverty and thus to eschew the potential for revolution. According to Geddes, figuring out the best spatial configuration of the worker's house was not simply a technical question, and determining the appropriate design must be the central concern of labor management.

It was generally believed that if workers had a nice home to live in with their families, it would be easier for the government to tackle rising labor agitation and strikes. Aesthetically pleasing homes and peaceful family life, as conceived by the colonial authority and the mill owner, was the solution to the labor strikes. Without this, as several mill owners of

Bombay reported to the Industrial Commission, mill workers just huddled and strayed into urban areas after long days of mundane factory work, disseminating their frustration about life—routines that might eventually lay the foundation for a revolution.[74] Mill owners, administrators, and scholars alike demanded a state intervention to social management.

Suburbia and Gentrification

With his 1918 exhibition, Mirams wished to overcome this disconnect between the ideal prototype and its urban setting. Although the houses were originally conceived of as independent units, Mirams presented the newly designed Salsette neighborhood as the ideal urban context for the workers' houses. The BIT's initial program meant to open up new areas at the northern end of Bombay and create housing that would negotiate between chawls and picturesque suburban residences. However, the BIT could never figure out exactly how to achieve that goal. Its demolition and relocation scheme for the low-income population eventually caused anxiety among the local elite, who worried that the proximity of working-class housing to the city core would impair hygiene and "import disease into one of our last healthy localities."[75]

In July 1903 the chairman of the trust proposed to erect huts in the Kennedy Sea Face area for the evicted population of the Dhobi Talao and Lohar Chawl area. The members of the BIT, supported by the *Bombay Gazette,* strongly opposed it. As an alternative, they proposed two radical ways to gentrify the city. Their first suggestion was "to divide the island into natural areas for the accommodation of the upper, the middle and the lower classes with special reference to occupation."[76] The second was to place the working class as far as possible from their workplace.[77] These suggestions captured the imagination of the elite for a spatially excluding conurbation of homes, physically separating inhabitants and delimiting the city according to economic class. Although derived primarily from the anxiety associated with the spread of bodily infection and disease, this plan eventually expressed a simplistic mental image of a divided modern society on the basis of economic class.

The development of suburbia for the emerging middle- and working-class population in northern Bombay—a major agenda of the BIT—came into full operation during the late 1910s.[78] The trust conceived of suburbia as the beautiful antithesis to the old inner city. As Sandip Hazareesingh has pointed out, the initial endeavors of the trust lacked coherent planning, which led to unplanned and unexpected outcomes—not what the trust initially thought of as the essential character of the new suburb.[79]

The new northern suburban area at Dadar, Matunga, and Sion was envisaged as a mixed-income, mixed-class neighborhood, bordered by leafy surroundings, with a handful of single-unit residences on large plots connected by straight and spacious roads.[80] In revealing the picture of the future suburbia of Bombay, the BIT was influenced by the English garden city, but a strong internal argument to provide a suburban home to the working class was the most compelling factor. J. A. Macdonald, engineer of the port trust who referred to chawls as "Arch-Hectic-Tecture," wrote in the *Bombay Chronicle*: "This [the chawl method] is in my opinion the wrong way to house the Indian labourer who has been accustomed to open air village life and shady trees. Being an absolute necessity we call upon him to help us develop our large city and in return herd him in huge ugly reinforced concrete erections and then pretend to ourselves that he is happy."[81] It was quite likely that the BIT would seek precedence from examples in Great Britain and set those ideas in an Indian context. However, the initial layouts of housing and new urban blocks of the BIT projects, in many ways, were informed by the colonial authority's knowledge of the reformation effort in the metropole. For example, periodically senior officers were sent to learn from both the English and the European experience.[82] They focused their investigations on land legislation, acquisition, and management and prevention of land speculation. Yet scant attention was paid to the reshaping of workers' lives through the built environment. Neither Great Britain nor its colonies succeeded in creating the "new community" utopia by claiming the countryside and decanting the urban poor into new and healthy surroundings. In Bombay's case, the BIT projects ended up in a small and detached community deprived of adequate facilities and social groundings.[83] The BIT never could attain the garden suburbia of its imagination.

Reinforced Cement Concrete and Quarters for the Poor

Four years before Mirams's team sought unfettered suburban living for the working class, the Hyderabad City Improvement Board (HCB) embarked on providing the low-income population of Nampally with scientific "rat proof" modern housing.[84] As in Bombay, the bubonic plague compelled the city to modernize the worker's quarter. The HCB associated the disease with a lack of modernization, that is, the "unmodern," vulnerable, filthy, and disorderly living conditions of the urban poor. The simple colonial solution of a public or government body replacing informal housing with orderly and standardized housing units was the only available mod-

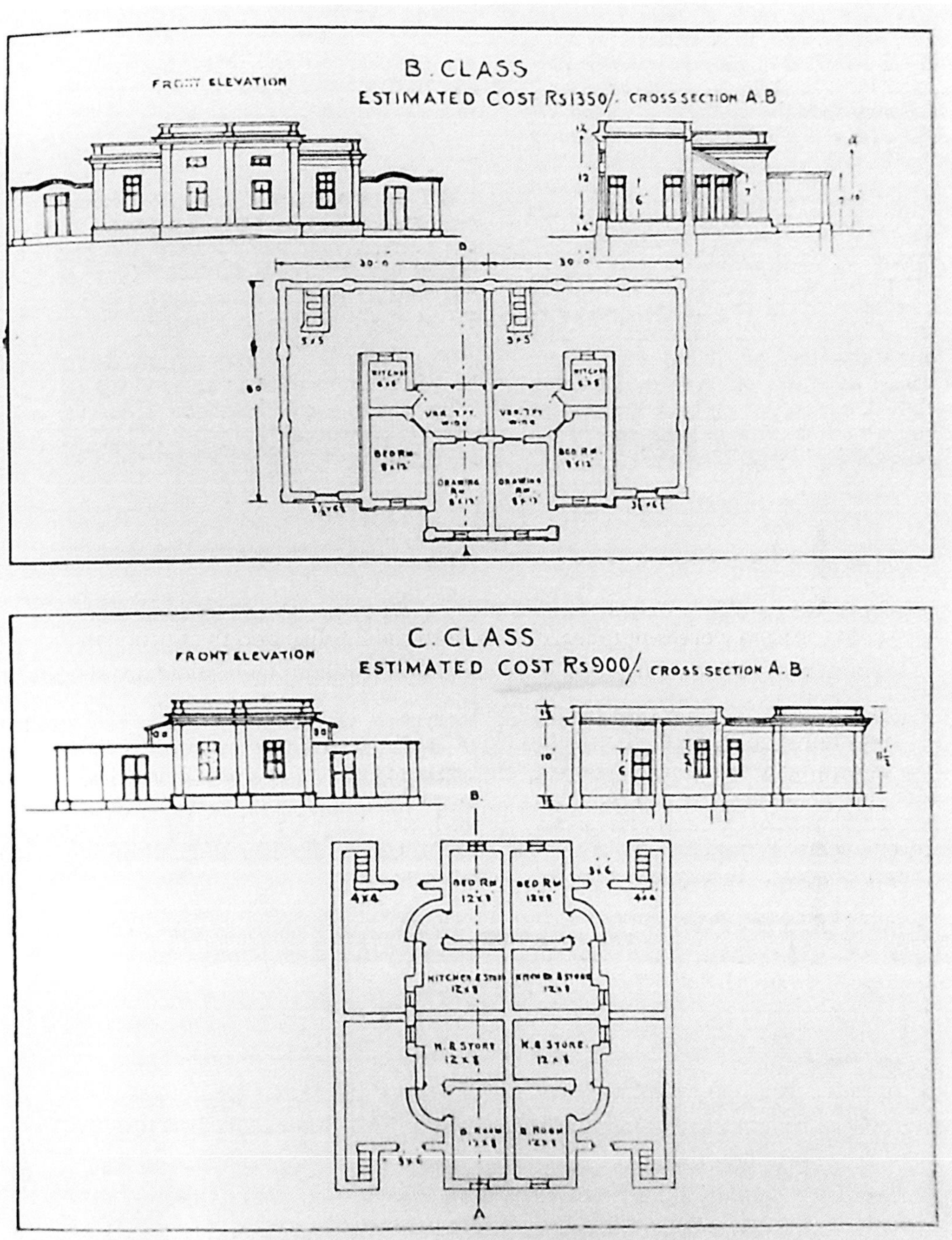

FIGURE 1.5. Plan and elevation of the ideal two-room houses, built by the Hyderabad City Improvement Board in 1914. Source: (1930) "Poorman's Quarters in Hyderabad (Deccan): H. E.H. The Nizam Government's Huge Scheme," *Indian Concrete Journal* 4, no. 6: 169. © Associated Cement Companies.

FIGURE 1.6. The high walls of the Hyderabad City Improvement Board's ideal house to ensure hygiene through seclusion and privacy. Source: (1930) "Poorman's Quarters in Hyderabad (Deccan): H. E.H. The Nizam Government's Huge Scheme," *Indian Concrete Journal* 4, no. 6: 170. © Associated Cement Companies.

el before the HCB. Its efforts started in 1914 with one rat-proof house, and by 1928 this single house was developed into an entire housing complex called Nampally Housing State (figs. 1.5 and 1.6).

The houses were built of reinforced cement concrete, a relatively novel structural system in India. The HCB claimed that this housing complex was the "only disease free portion of the city." According to the Associated Cement Companies Limited (ACC)—the largest association of cement-producing companies established in 1912—it was possible only because of reinforced cement concrete (RCC).[85] The ACC promoted concrete as the most affordable and durable material of the time and established it as a symbol of modernism in contrast to rising *swadeshi* vernacularism. The Nampally model offered two variations: One was a 30-by-30-foot block with two 8-by-12-foot rooms and one small kitchen. The other smaller variation (fig. 1.7) was situated in a 20 by 20 foot block with two 8-by-12-foot rooms—one bedroom and one kitchen and storage area adjoining a small backyard with a separate private toilet. The models were more spacious than Mirams's prototype, as they provided a backyard with one

FIGURE 1.7. The workers quarter, built by HCB, circa 1914. Source: (1930) "Poorman's Quarters in Hyderabad (Deccan): H. E.H. The Nizam Government's Huge Scheme," *Indian Concrete Journal* 4, no. 6: 169. © Associated Cement Companies.

toilet and were deliverable almost at the same cost. The housing's construction, which was entirely of concrete with seven-foot-high boundary walls separating each block, gave its units a strong appearance, an image of security away from urban disease. These units conveyed the message of private refuges from the external world that would enhance personalization, hygiene, and privacy. The small blocks, which could be rented from the government at a rate between two and five rupees per month, are one of the earliest examples of modern housing for industrial workers in India.

In 1932, almost three decades after the HCB's experimentation, the Secunderabad Town Improvement Trust developed its own concrete housing prototype for the plague-torn poor community (fig. 1.8).[86] Under the supervision of W. McLachlan, executive engineer of the Secunderabad Town Improvement Trust, the scheme adopted a set of three prototypes that had evolved through dimensional adjustment, alteration, and expansion of a basic prototype, very similar to that provided by the HCB. The trust eventually built 400 units. Each prototype consisted of a two-room unit placed on a 35-by-32-foot plot. The two rooms were of equal dimen-

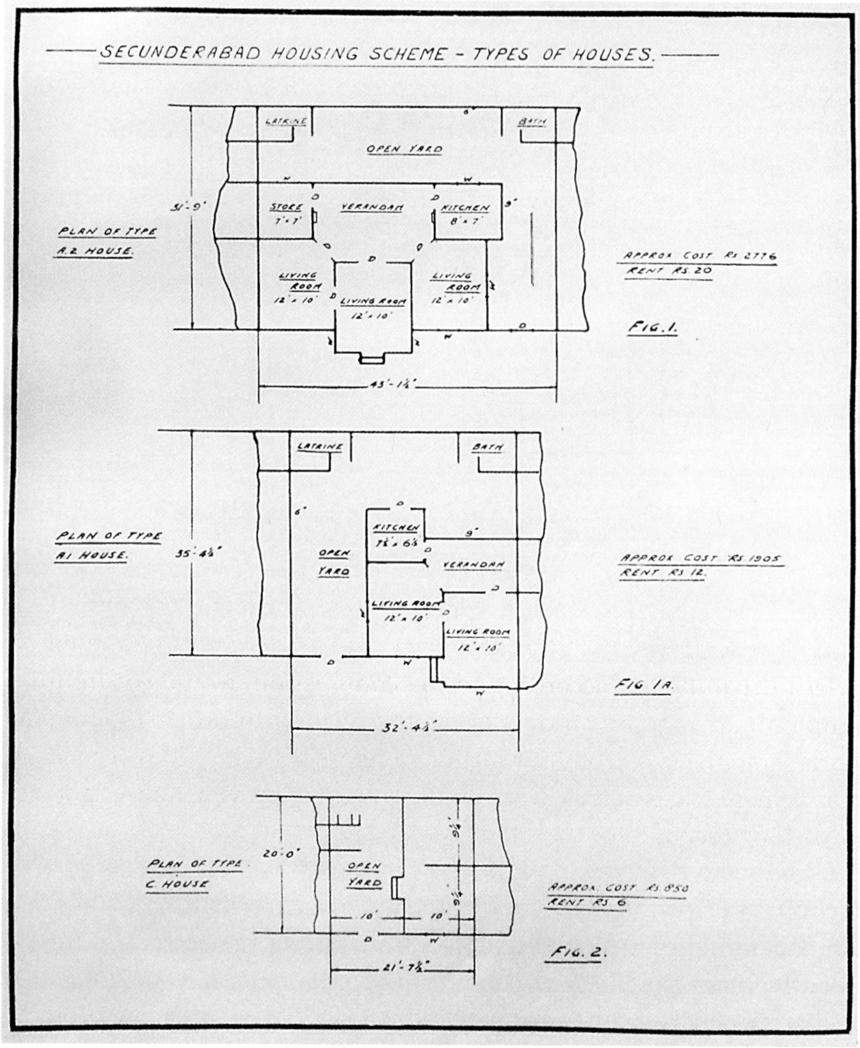

FIGURE 1.8. House floorplans, Secunderabad, 1932. Source: P. D. Padukone, "Slum Clearance in Secunderabad," *Indian Concrete Journal* 6, no. 12 (1932): 419–22, 419. © Associated Cement Companies

sion—12 by 10 feet—one served as a living room and the other as a bedroom adjoining a kitchen, while the sides contained a small yard with a bath and latrine. The one room house included two 10-by-9-1/2-foot rooms adjoined by a 10-foot-wide yard with an outdoor latrine. Although these units were similar in spatial distribution and block size to those provided by the HCB, there were notable differences in their construction. The 400 houses in Secunderabad were built by RCC columns and a triangular system of concrete hollow blocks imported from a factory in East Molesey (Surrey, England), which served as infill material for walls. The Secunderabad Town Improvement Trust assumed that using prefabricated hollow blocks would make the monthly rent (6 rupees) affordable, and it developed two different prototypes of a "durable modern house" at a relatively cheap construction cost (850 and 1,905 rupees). At a slow but constant pace, the discourse of workers' housing moved from the discussion of an ideal spatial layout to the innovative use of modern materials and construction techniques.

Most male laborers in a household spent a few months in the city and did not bring their families with them. The British Labour Commission advised the Indian trusts that if they would provide adequate housing for their employees, workers might consider bringing their families along with them as they traveled from the villages to the city. The intention of course was to create a true urban working class that would be compelled to keep its homes and neighborhoods beautiful and sanitary. The state viewed industrial workers' housing as a means to domesticate the large influx of industrial labor stranded from the surrounding countryside. A modern urban house, according to the commission, would secure uninterrupted and regular production in the factory. In order to assimilate laborers into the urban environment and retain them on a long-term basis, improvement trusts across British India sought to provide houses not only for working men but for their families as well.

One of the first attempts to design houses for the worker's family was done by James A. Jardine, a British engineer. The first batch of four hundred units was constructed at Waverley Jute Mill near Calcutta (now Kolkata). Guided by the Board of Health's rules that shaped municipal bylaws, designers were mainly concerned with durability, hygiene, cost, and reproducibility. The planning scheme was quite rudimentary: a two-story building with two or four two-room apartments on each floor. Each floor had a central corridor to serve the rooms on each side and also provided easy access for health inspectors. The structure was built entirely with RCC, and even the smallest details of door- and window frames were built with prefabricated elements of cement. Gradually the worker's house became more than a bachelor's quarters or mere elements in a factory production line; it was a space to accommodate a heterogonous mix of people of different age groups, genders, and social and cultural backgrounds. The one-room tenements of the "coolie lines" built for the coal miners around 1931–1932 are an early example of this attitudinal shift (fig. 1.9). However, authorities across British India continued to believe that occupants were

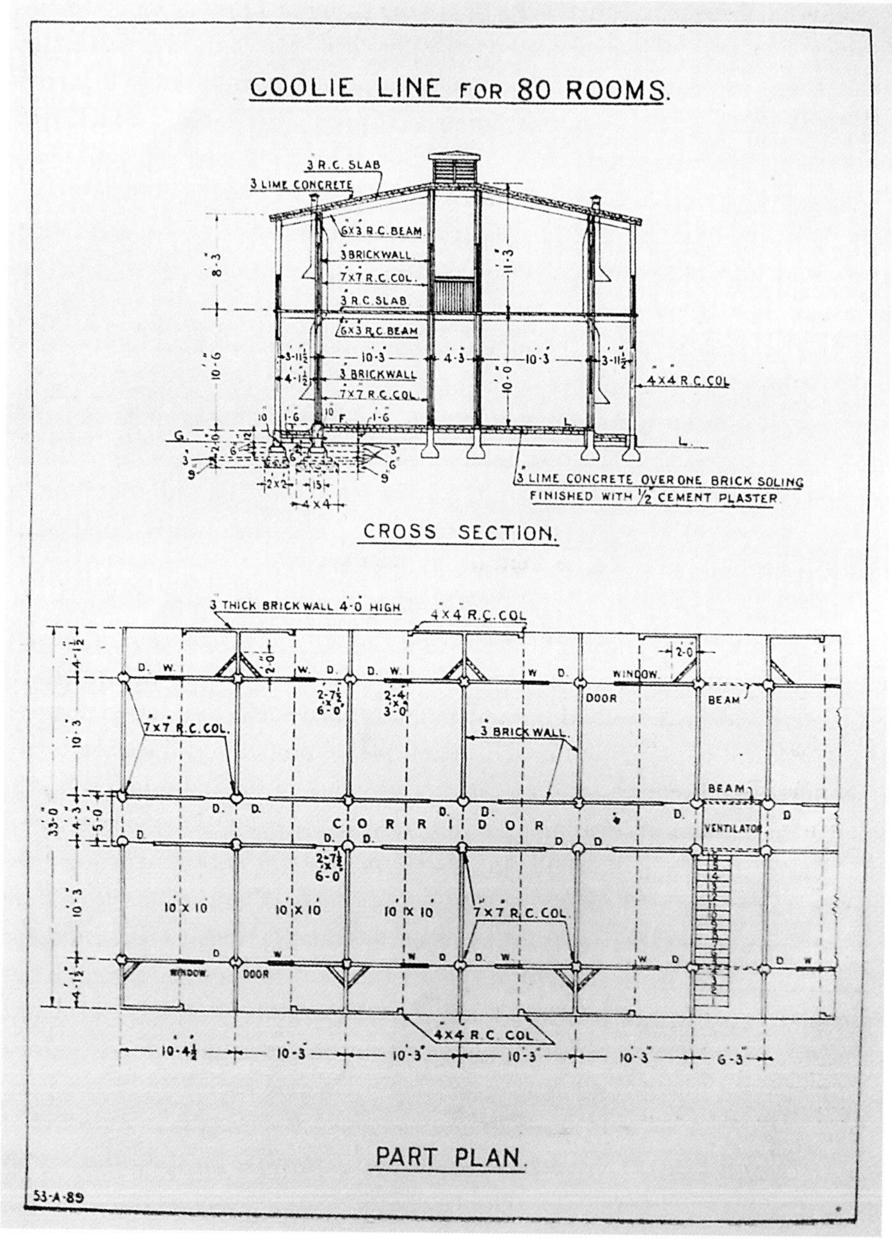

FIGURE 1.9. Plan and section of housing for the 'Coolie lines,' 1931–32. Source: J. M. Jardine, "The Modern Coolie House," *Indian Concrete Journal* 5, no. 2 (1931): 43–45. © Associated Cement Companies.

neither ready to accept the modern way of living nor able to cope with the "developed environment" prescribed for them.[87]

The Associated Cement Companies' Industrialized New India

The engineers of the improvement trusts initially questioned the suitability of RCC structures and hollow cement blocks in India's climatic context. In certain regions, extreme monsoons severely dampened concrete walls, and trust authorities—the major client of the ACC for the construction of low-cost housing—decided to discontinue using this building method. It became necessary for the ACC to win back the confidence of local builders. Through its journal and various publications, the ACC promoted the benefits of RCC structures. By the end of the 1930s, RCC enjoyed a moderate acceptance among builders, especially those who worked for city improvement trusts and their allied departments. By the end of the 1940s, the ACC had established itself as the most efficient modern mode of construction. At the Engineering and Industrial Exhibition arranged by the Institution of Engineers at the South India Centre in Madras from April 20 to May 25, 1947, the ACC erected a full-scale concrete house for the working-class population. This example demonstrated the superiority of concrete and equated the metaphorical value of the material with that of swadeshi and anticolonial spirit.[88] The ACC's worker's house prescribed an alternative modernism for the poor that contrasted the modernism of affluence framed by Bombay's Art Deco buildings along its Marine Drive.

In 1945 the Housing Committee of the Indian National Congress introduced its first housing scheme to synchronize the various efforts made by different local authorities.[89]The scheme was also a strategy to pacify labor unrest and enhance accord between owners and labor unions.[90] Because of a paucity of archival materials, it is difficult to trace how the Housing Committee decided to plan schemes or minimum dimensions for floor space that were greater than Mirams's or the BIT's and BDD's minimum requirement. Given its limited research resources, the committee likely referred to previous efforts of the improvement trusts and the British Housing Standards and Statistics of 1935.[91] However, practicing engineers thought the prototype and minimum dimensional requirements set by the committee were superfluous, a view shared by the dominant trade organization of the ACC. The minimum standard set by the committee, they argued, did not reflect the living habits of residents who mostly came from the country and were used to living in "small spaces" in rural areas.[92] The ACC rather preferred Mirams's 1918 prototype because the optimized

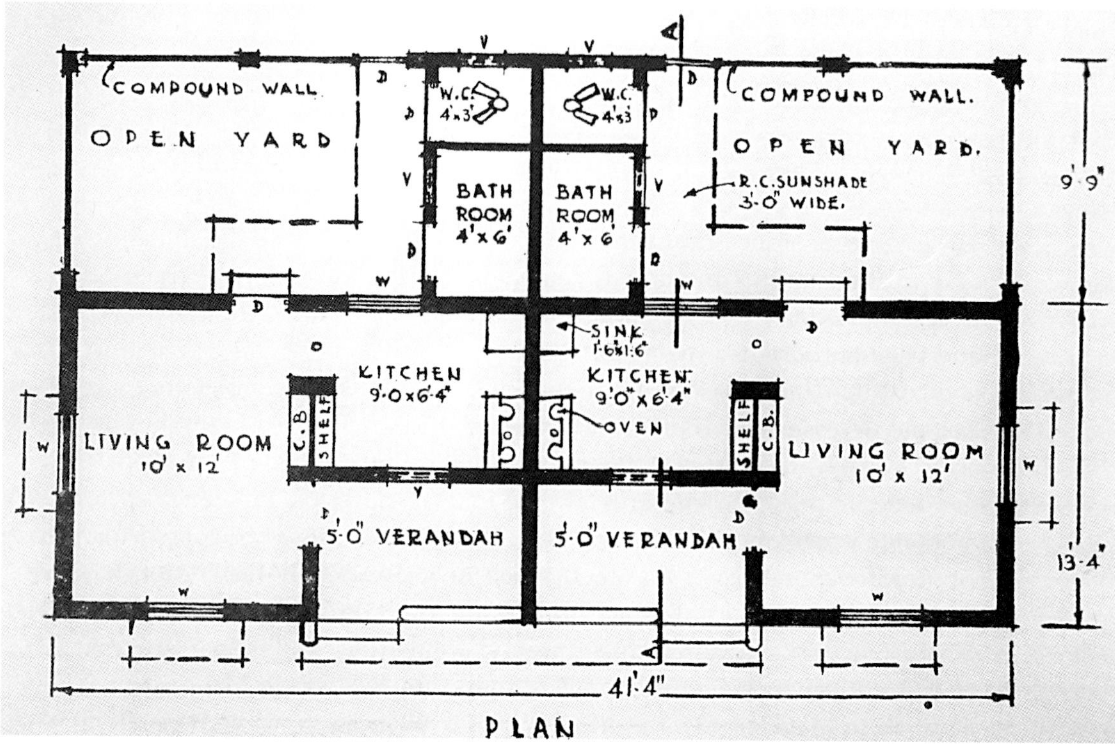

FIGURE 1.10. Type A of the ACC prototype, a two-room semidetached house, 1947. Source: Anonymous, "Labour Housing," *Indian Concrete Journal* 21, no. 2 (1947), missing page numbers. © Associated Cement Companies.

construction cost, which was Mirams's key consideration, was naturally agreeable with the cultural practice of Indian workers. The ACC's argument suggested that the poor working-class population was used to living in tight spaces that might appear inhumanely small according to Western standards but were quite acceptable and normal for Indian laborers. Any provision for workers to possess or own space larger than the culturally acceptable minimum standard, the ACC reasoned, would provoke low-income renters to sublet their apartments to earn extra money.

The Housing Committee's "best suitable figure" was guided by market inflation and a worker's wage. It included a minimum of 120 square feet, or 1,100 rupees per housing unit. To the ACC, the congress model was an "impractical proposal," so it presented a "practical solution" of three different units based on Mirams's 10-by-12-foot prototype. Its one-room version was almost a perfect square, with 671 square feet of plinth area that divided the house into two distinct strips: a service area that contained a kitchen, a toilet, and a bathroom, and a served area with a 10-by-12-foot living room and

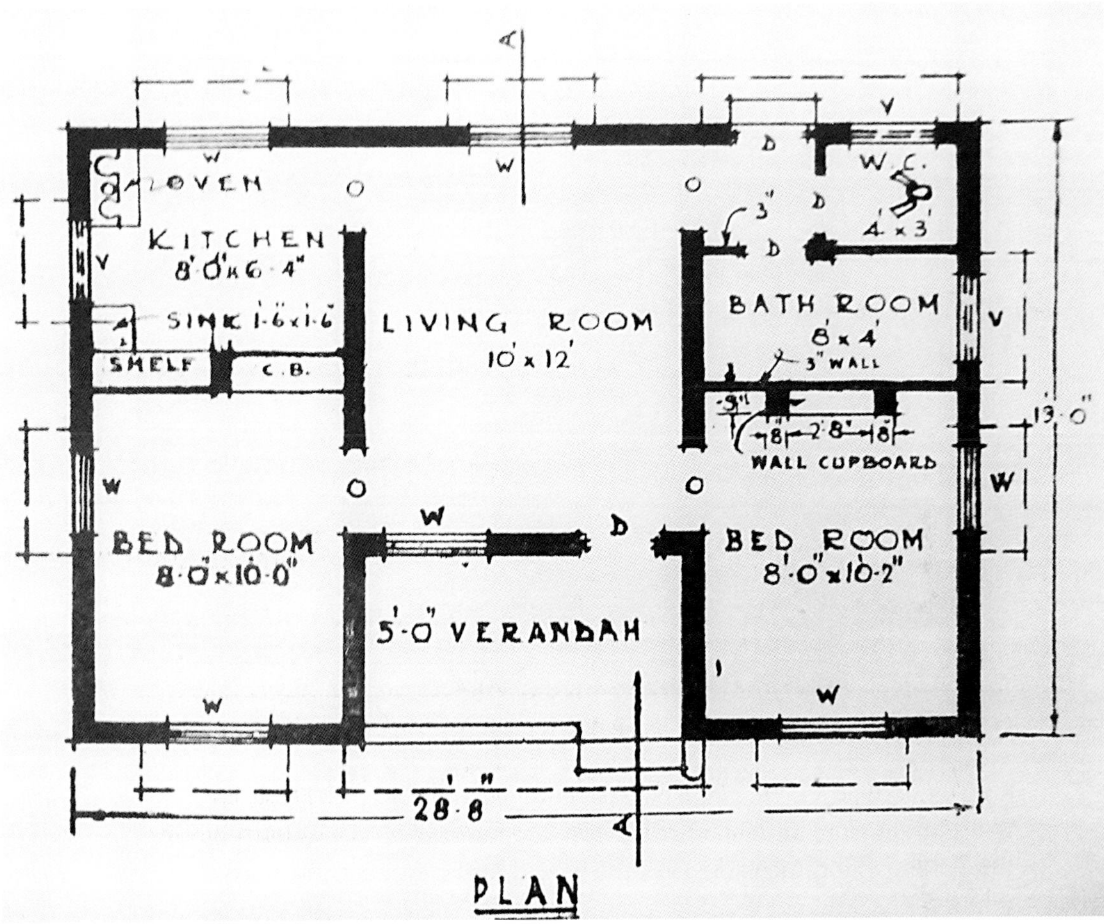

FIGURE 1.11. Type B of the ACC prototype, three-room detached house, 1947. Source: Anonymous, "Labour Housing," *Indian Concrete Journal* 21, no. 2 (1947), missing page numbers. © Associated Cement Companies.

five-foot-wide front veranda (figs. 1.10, 1.11). In all their variations, the units were either presented as a group, or one unit was coupled with another mirroring unit. This layout would produce a disciplined repetition in which the service strips could be clustered together for functional efficiency. In its second variation, the two-room unit had 901 square feet of plinth area and retained the 10-by-12-foot room, but the service strip was pushed back to make room for another small bedroom in the front beside the veranda. This arrangement tampered with the purity of served versus service strips, but retaining such purity was perhaps not the primary concern. In the final version of the three-room unit, the 10-by-12-foot room occupied the focal position of the scheme, while two separate service strips each contained one

FIGURE 1.12. Bedroom of the working-class house of the ACC prototype, exhibited in the Industrial and Engineering Exhibition at Madras, 1947. Source: *Indian Concrete Journal* 21, no. 2 (1947). © Associated Cement Companies.

bedroom in front and a bathroom and kitchen at rear. The consistent repetition of spatial dimensions and the variations between units made it clear that the ACC did not consider providing more spacious rooms for families as they climbed the economic ladder. Instead, this planning scheme included more rooms with the same area and dimensions of its lesser version.

The ACC published two interiors photographs of its prototype house.[93] The first is of an austere bedroom washed by daylight from an adjacent window that occupied the majority of the sidewall (fig. 1.12). The precast concrete grill of the window replaced the traditional pattern of wood and metal grills and thus any visual traces of artisanal practice by industrially produced machine crafts. The window avoided any provision for drapery, challenging the conventional function of a "window," to provide privacy and shut down the interior from the outside world. Even the most private interior spaces of working-class families, such as the bedroom, was imagined as public and made available to the outside world. The discrete spheres of private and public erased territorial boundaries. A bare *khatia* (traditional bed) sprang up to the sill level; a pillow was delicately placed parallel to the window, as if someone was reading or enjoying the view through the window. The bed, slightly depressed in its middle, looks slept in. A collection

FIGURE 1.13. Kitchen of the working-class house of the ACC prototype, exhibited in the Industrial and Engineering Exhibition at Madras, 1947. Source: *Indian Concrete Journal* 21, no. 2 (1947). © Associated Cement Companies.

of paraphernalia is sparsely stacked on the open concrete cabinet; a bag, clothes, and a few other essentials recounted the minimum effort people would need to perform domestic chores. The second photograph, of the kitchen, shows a row of bare concrete shelves with a few kitchen utensils and a cooktop with a newly designed smokeless wood-fired *chula* (stove) (fig. 1.13). With these photos, the ACC imagined an ascetic life for a new industrial worker. The interior of the house was uncannily empty, suggesting its occupants might have gone to the factory. People were not expected to be pampered by domestic comfort, but to live an industrious life on the factory production line.

The ACC had long been struggling to establish concrete houses as the symbol of a new industrialized India. This new symbolism might look like the antithesis of Gandhi's vernacularism, but the ACC reconciled these two polar ideas, swadeshi vernacularism and Western industrialization, and eventually established itself as a progressive force in postcolonial India. An accident at the 1939 Congress exhibition went far in marking the difference between Gandhism and the ACC. A fire reduced the entire exhibition site to rubble, since most of the stalls, inspired by the Congress's swadeshi spirit, had been constructed by "swadeshi material" of bamboo and thatch.[94] Only the ACC's concrete stall remained standing. The ACC used this to its advantage, stressing the functionality, durability, and effectiveness of concrete over the fragility of old-fashioned swadeshi materials.

The Indian nationalist and anticolonial struggle was mainly steered by urban politicians and shaped by the educated middle class in urban centers. Nevertheless, the multitude of the rural and urban poor was also very important in the anticolonial movement, though high culture and high politics rarely sought to monumentalize a visible presence of that multitude. Rather, Congress's politics sought to systematize the multitude of the poor by turning them into an organized work force framed by a disciplined production process. In Gandhian rhetoric, this socioeconomic order was to be achieved through home-based rural industry, while, in Nehru's view, large-scale industrialization and urbanization would restore order.[95] The ACC argued that being technically and industrially advanced does not contradict nationalism and patriotism, of which rural development was a significant component. The ACC's viewpoint, which clearly wanted to negotiate between Gandhian and Nehruvian values, was well substantiated by its prototype house, a concrete structure designed to be produced and distributed through a network of centrally organized industrial efforts. The ACC also assumed that local people were not sufficiently equipped to secure and produce their own homes. Achieving home ownership was not desirable in most cases—if workers spent time building their own homes, the ACC argued, it might impact their contribution to industry. The central concern of the ACC was the condition under which one achieved economic affluence at the family and community level, not the achievements themselves. The ACC also argued that concrete structures would rejuvenate rural India. Through numerous trade publications, it refuted Gandhi's vernacular material culture and thus envisaged an image of developed Indian villages rooted in industrial culture. With the publication of guidelines to construct a modern village, the ACC upended the image of the Gandhian Arcadian village and replaced it with something more compatible with the zeitgeist of industrialization and urbanization, which is discussed in more detail in chapter 4.

By 1947 two things were well established: First, development did not necessarily mean straying away from Western knowledge and functionalism but assimilating industrially oriented modernity with local needs. Second, working-class dwellers had limited roles in which they could contribute to the building of their homes, a process controlled by state and industrial endeavors. The ACC's ideal house incarnated in its motif of a rising sun in a concrete window grill, which debuted at the first free India Exhibition in 1948. Alongside a group of models and photographs of cutting-edge examples from the United States and England, the full-scale ACC house proudly declared, "Precast Concrete House at the Free India."[96] Its prototype design of a two-room house displayed a specific living pattern and worldview for growing nuclear families of industrial workers. The cumulative effect of the ACC units was expected to form an ideological destination in which liberated and modern workers created a perfect harmony with the new Indian bourgeoisie.

Scarcity in the Postindependence Era

In the aftermath of independence, the paucity of financial resources, technical expertise, and institutions left little room for the government to engage in a sophisticated discussion on architecture and design. The government's strategy was to employ the simplest available technology to achieve an affordable construction method—one that was low in cost, simple to perform with unskilled labor, and easily proliferated across the distant corners of rural India. Following this strategy, the newly formed Madras Improvement Trust (circa 1947) erected three "model houses" at three corners of the city of Madras (now Chennai) to demonstrate their efficiency and "modern look." The Madras Improvement Trust preferred basic planning, as suggested by the ACC, but adopted subtle variations to suit local demands. It also started to produce its own hollow concrete blocks. K. K. Nambiar, chairman of the Madras Improvement Trust, was inspired by Louisiana State University's experiment with low-cost housing and its enthusiastic acceptance in the United States and England. For him, the new technology of hollow concrete blocks presented the key to "tackl[ing] the housing shortage" in India. According to Nambiar, an increase in workers' purchasing power was "neither practical nor desirable as it will necessitate an upgrading of wage structure, setting in motion the vicious circle of increased cost of articles produced and consequent increase in costs of dwelling and their rentals."[97] The solution, he argued, lay in the development of effective low-cost construction techniques and government subsidies. Running Nambiar's proposed effective cycle of housing supply and consumption would require a synchronized subsidization of the state, central government, and employers; his proposal was later adopted in the national housing scheme.

The extensive drive for growth in the immediate postindependence era was marked by technical optimism. Among the new techniques, prefabrication and factory-produced housing were major sources of enthusiasm. Prefabrication on a mass scale was first introduced and popularized in India through wartime construction of army barracks and domestic shelters for air-raid bombings. In 1948 Sri A. R. Venkatachari, chief engineer in the Public Works Department (PWD) of Madras at the Irrigation Research Station, Poondi, created one of the most noteworthy designs. Large-scale irrigation across South India required prefabricated and "knock-downable" houses to accommodate the large number of workers moving from one site to another (fig. 1.14).[98] As these houses were not meant to remain permanently in one place, they were smaller than the conventionally acceptable standard of ten by twelve feet. The structures were built in the manner of balloon framing, with seventeen peripherals and three internal thin columns filled in with cement concrete slabs. In a short time, this kind of prefabricated housing became popular. India's first prime minister, Jawaharlal Nehru, was convinced it would solve the postindependence shortage of buildings—so much so that at his behest the first housing factory, Hindustan Prefab Limited, was established in 1948.[99] Nehru invited Otto Koenigsberger, the former chief architect of princely Mysore, to take on Hindustan Prefab's production of housing units to accommodate the incoming migrant population from the fledgling state of West Pakistan. Since then, Hindustan Prefab has been supplying various prefab building parts to government projects.

Besides prefabrication, M. R. Venkataram, chief engineer of Bombay, Baroda, and Central India Railway, promoted the gunite concrete technique for constructing government-built housing. He was convinced by the process's fast pace, economy, and convenience (fig. 1.15). Venkataram called for a total rejection of the brick masonry buildings altogether and contended, "An Aladdin to homes by the millions overnight is required if a roof is to be provided over each head. . . . Still in spite of shortage of men

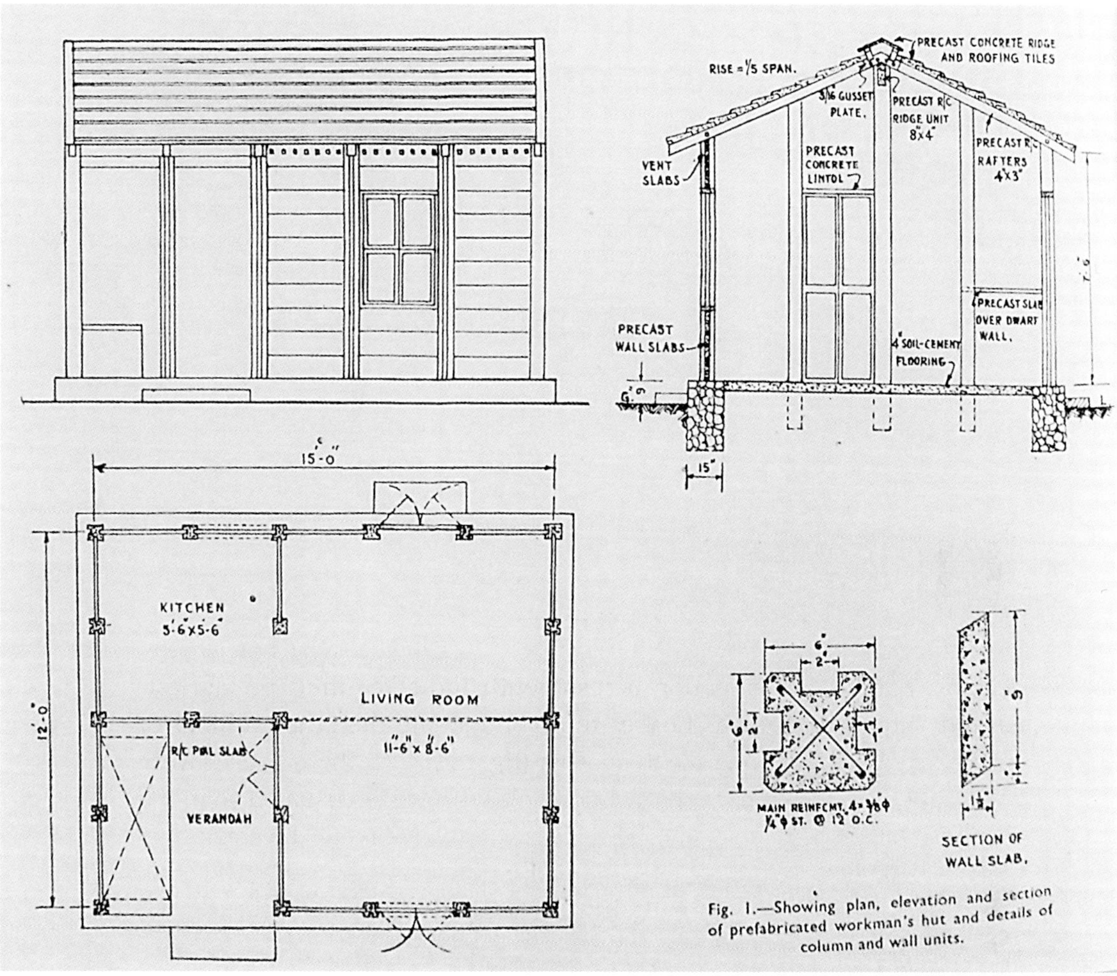

FIGURE 1.14. Drawings of the prefabricated and knock-downable RCC house for the irrigation workers of Madras, 1948. Source: *Indian Concrete Journal* 22, no. 6 (1948): 146. © Associated Cement Companies.

and materials, houses can be put up by the thousand if not by the million in this land, if only the old and snail-like process of the conventional brick or masonry type or foreign types, totally unsuitable to our conditions and which deplete our already thin foreign currency by way of expensive machinery and building materials[,] is discarded."[100] Following his first project, the railway workers' colony at Sen Nagar Santacruz, Bombay, in 1949, Venkataram built railway colonies at Delhi (circa 1950) and for the depots at Godhra and Bolsar (circa 1952). These later projects followed the same planning scheme, but the area of individual rooms varied according to available funding. Like Venkatachari's balloon-frame structures, Ven-

FIGURE 1.15. Prefabricated Gunite workers' housing, Delhi, 1950. Source: M. R. Venkataram, "Prefabricated 'Gunite': A Low-Cost Method of Building Concrete Houses," *Indian Concrete Journal* 24, no. 3 (1950): 66–73. © Associated Cement Companies.

kataram's houses were built on peripheral thin columns with prefabricated concrete wall panels and roof slabs and either double or single walls, depending on the climate. They took the fundamental shape of a basic square, with two separate but attached strips—service and served—that slightly shifted longitudinally to give way for a veranda in the front and a kitchen and toilet unit in the back. Since steel was too expensive for building a low-cost worker's house, bamboo was sometimes used as a tensile material. This type of construction can be dated back to the pre-independence era when Ferguson, a PWD engineer, built lime gunite houses on bamboo framing in Jodhpur. Around 1948 several working-class quarters were built on balloon framing with a mesh of three-eighth-inch-thick bamboo splits.[101]

In addition to dwellings for industrial workers, government engineers turned their attention to housing colonies of refugees of the 1947 partition, one of the major sources of cheap labor in Punjab and Delhi. Punjab PWD engineers adopted planning schemes that echoed local workers' housing, assuming a similar social and economic condition for the refugees. In most cases, prefabrication was deemed the most effective method for refugee colonies, given time and cost considerations. But when it came to erecting refugee housing in places relatively distant from the city, designers wanted to experiment with alternative economical material and construction methods. For example, a four-thousand-unit housing scheme for refugees turned industrial workers in east Punjab circa 1950 adopted a cement-soil (or stabilized) mixture for a rammed earth construction, which took longer to build. But P. L. Varma and S. R. Mehra, superintendent engineers of Punjab PWD, proclaimed that such a technique could reduce 80 percent of the coal costs required for brick burning, a savings of up to 150,000 rupees.[102] The spatial dimensions of the refugee house were quite similar to the ACC prototype. The layout, however, was conceived in such a way that only two houses could be joined to form a cluster, unlike other schemes that allowed a lateral addition to form larger clusters. Residents appreciated the finely rendered external walls and clean massing with a two-arch opening. But because of its slow rate of delivery, at a time when the government was impatient to fix the housing problem, engineers never replicated this particular design.

Industrial Workers as a Socioeconomic Category

The sporadic colonial efforts of local housing reformation coalesced in 1931, when the Royal Commission on Labour in India urged the adoption of legislative and administrative measures for the provision of modern housing.[103] Between the late 1930s and 1940s, the interwar reconstruction program of the League of Nations (the first intergovernmental organization established on January 10, 1920, and replaced by the United Nations on April 20, 1946) likely informed the reformation efforts of India's city improvement trusts.[104] During the 1940s, the LN's central concern was securing an adequate number of "healthy" dwellings for the global urban population and determining universal guidelines for housing. The American Public Health Association Committee on the Hygiene of Housing was established in 1937 as the corresponding organ of the LN Housing Commission.[105] In 1938 it published its first report, *Basic Principles of Healthful Housing*.[106] In 1941 the committee published another volume, *Housing for Health*, which documented the issues raised in a special conference called by the Milbank Memorial Fund.[107] These articles and books prescribed a universally applicable minimum dimensions for human dwellings irrespective of country, culture, climate, or geography. To ensure a healthy home, in addition to the minimum spatial requirements, the LN chartered fifteen fundamental human physiological needs to incorporate within the minimum spatial dimensions. The LN's housing prescription aimed to conjure a new humanism in which human demands were equal and indifferent. Referring to LN's suggestions, the American Public Health Association commented, "Based on fundamental biological requirements of human organism . . . [housing is] believed to be fundamental and minimum required for the promotion of physical, mental, and social health, essential in low-rent as well as high cost housing, on the farm as well as city dwelling."[108]

For the first time, the Labour ministers' conference of January 1940 sought an integrated pull from state governments in India. Five years later, at the seventh standing conference of the Labour Committee of the Tripartite in 1945, attendees appointed a subcommittee to consider and report on various aspects of the problem, and it submitted a report the following year.[109] On the basis of that report, the Ministry of Works, Housing, and Supply formulated an integrated plan that referred to the LN charter but adapted it to the local context. In the ensuing years, state governments introduced the Truce Resolution (December 1947) and the Scheme for Industrial Housing (April 1948), plans that local industrialists rejected strongly on the grounds that they did not clearly indicate financial subsidence or ownership.[110]

After independence, the Planning Commission revisited the issue of finance and ownership in 1950 in consultation with the Ministry of Labor. In 1952, after many transformations, the Ministry of Works, Housing, and Supply published *Subsidised Housing Scheme for Industrial Workers, 1952–53*, which detailed the spatial, financial, and managerial relationship between states, industrial employers, and employees—the major determining factors of industrial housing reform.[111] For the purpose of this scheme, the term *industrial worker* was reinterpreted in legal terms; *a worker* was defined according to the Factories Act of 1948. The plan thoroughly discussed the financial and spatial issues related to the building of housing for industrial workers by state governments or statutory housing boards, as well as employers and registered cooperative societies of those workers. The central government also proposed to assist the program by means of subsidies and loans on relatively favorable terms.

The proposed accommodations were of two types in cities of moderate size where land values were not exorbitant. The first type consisted of single-story tenements containing one living room, kitchen, veranda or lobby, and bathing space with a water tap; later provisions called for one electric bulb. These were significant additions, as demands for running water and electricity had long been a point of dispute between workers and municipalities.[112] The scheme also outlined an expanded role for municipalities. The second type was designed for larger cities with higher land values: multistory buildings composed of one living room, one bedroom, and a kitchen; a group of flats would have community latrines and bathrooms. In both cases, the living room would be 120 square feet at minimum—a standard set by colonial trusts that was still deemed a feasible option in democratic India.[113]

Hygiene and Aesthetics

Soon after the subsidized housing scheme found its legal footing, engineers constructed a large number of workers' houses, which assumed a variety of names: colonies, industrial housing, quarters, houses, tenements, blocks, and flats.[114] Between 1953 and 1954, the government approved the construction of 31,980 tenements, and by the end of 1954, 17,120 were completely occupied.[115] The notion of hygiene underpinned the new industrial workers of independent India and their modern dwellings. However, unlike its colonial predecessor, which employed hygiene as part of its governance and biopolitics, independent India used it to reorder human existence from a preindustrial state to a modern democratic state. For instance, the Public Health Engineering Department of the All India Institute of Hygiene and Public Health developed a series of "type plans" or prototypes and spatial schemes for low-cost houses in both rural and urban contexts (fig. 1.16).[116] Their objective was to provide an interface that could connect qualitative aspects such as hygiene and sanitation with quantitative aspects such as construction costs and spatial dimensions.

Around 1958, a decade after the Indian government initiated its workers' housing scheme, Works, Housing and Supply published a catalog titled *Industrial Housing in India*, which included drawings and photographs of approved and built examples across India.[117] It also supplied a range of type plans as examples for workers or small industries unable to hire professional architects and engineers.[118] The catalog therefore worked as a compilation of homegrown knowledge produced in regional centers, as well as a blueprint of a modernism for the poor.[119]

The experience of working-class modernism in India was consciously devoid of any aesthetic ideology. As in the preface of *Industrial Housing in India*, Swaran Singh—the minister for Works, Housing and Supply—stated the government was committed to ensuring healthy accommodation for

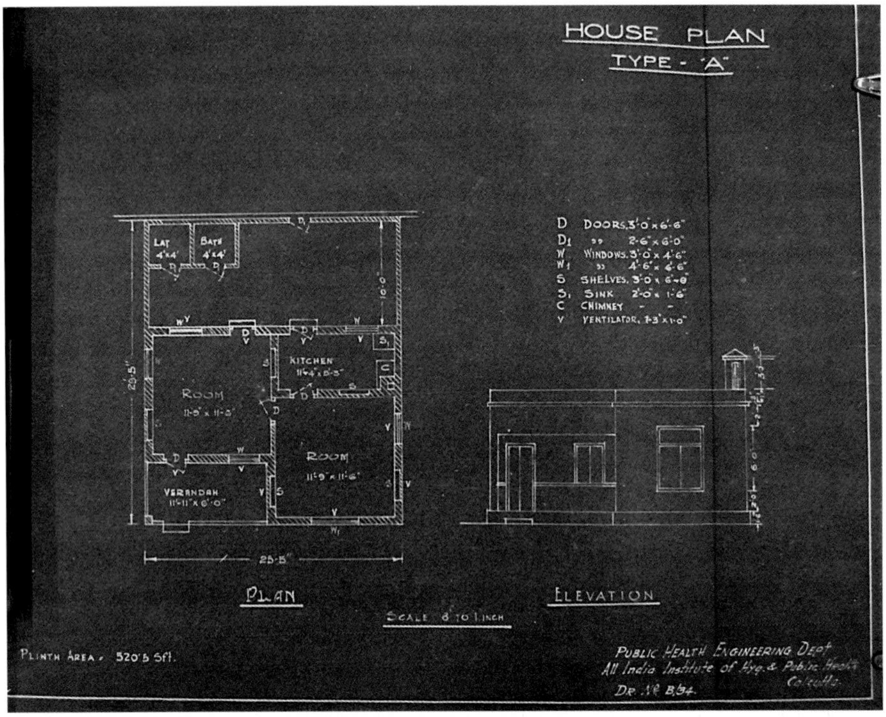

FIGURE 1.16. Prototype plan of detached two-room "hygienic house" designed by All India Institute of Hygiene and Public Health, circa 1948. Source: Public Health Engineering Department, Type Designs for Small Houses (Calcutta: All India Institute of Hygiene and Public Health, 1948).

workers, and aesthetic and architectural expression was only a secondary concern. And yet, by presenting twenty-three examples of housing from sixteen major cities in India, including twelve type plans, the catalog documented the diverse ways architects designed minimal living and managed scarce resources. Although the minister claimed not to prioritize aesthetics, most of the designs shared a strong visual resemblance with interwar European modernism: pure forms, white-rendered façades, and ribbon windows. Singh, optimistic about the new scheme, affirmed in the catalog that "the Challenge is Met."[120] With this catalog, India declared its departure from the utopian sphere of Gandhian villages. Its central argument was predicated on the scientific optimism that if one industrial housing project was successful, the same result could be reproduced anywhere. While colonial schemes were rarely transposed from planning to reality, the postindependence scheme valued praxis over theorization, and state politics capitalized on its material achievement. The departure from the immanence of paper aesthetics was further accentuated by the

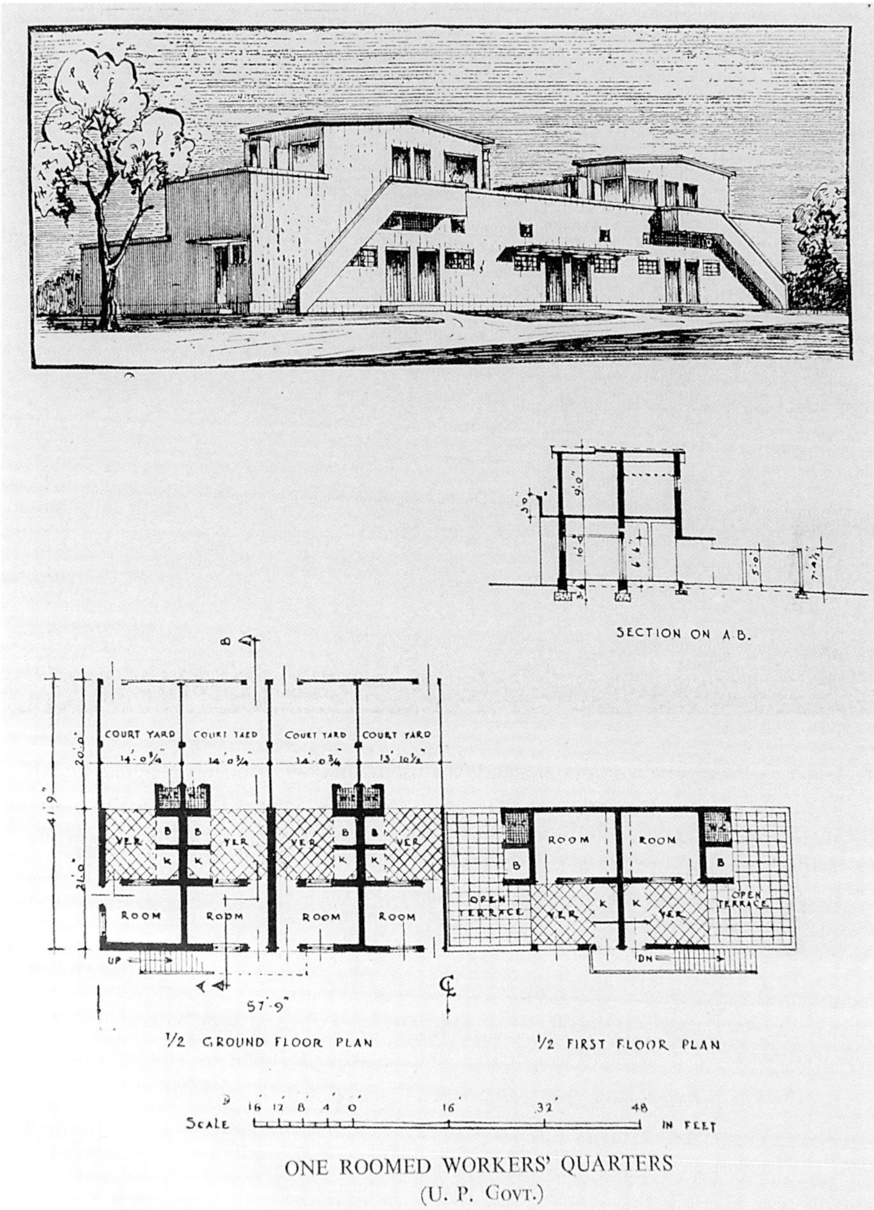

FIGURE 1.17. One-room, two-story prototype of workers' quarters from the Ministry of Works, Housing, and Supply catalogue. Source: Shugan C. Aggarwal, *Industrial Housing in India* (New Delhi: Ministry of Works, Housing, and Supply, 1952): 9.

last section of the catalog, "type designs." This made the brochure not just a closed documentation of the past, but a resilient, open blueprint for what could be regenerated and reproduced in the future.

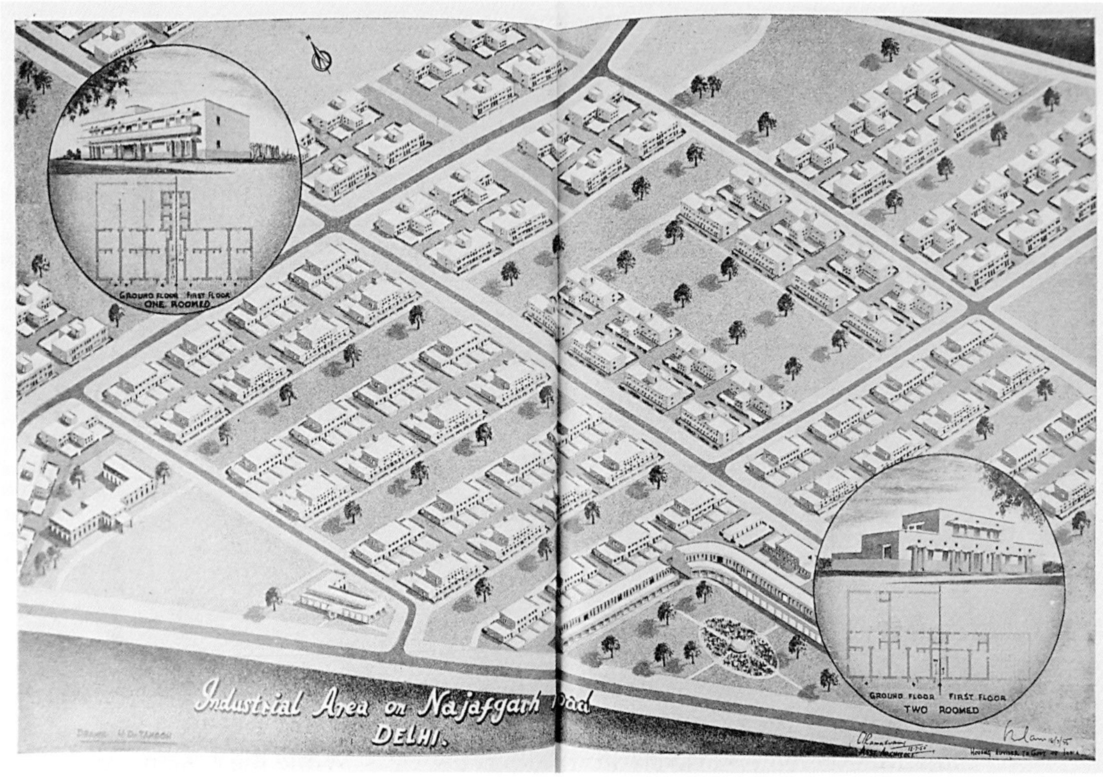

FIGURE 1.18. An ordered community of workers neighborhood made of prototype houses, Delhi, from the Ministry of Works, Housing, and Supply catalogue. Source: Shugan C. Aggarwal, *Industrial Housing in India* (New Delhi: Ministry of Housing, Works and Supply, 1952): 56.

The newly constructed housing in the catalog was developed and constructed by a variety of designers, private practitioners, municipalities, and industrial engineers and was more sophisticated in its formal expression. The catalog classified these houses according to administrative jurisdiction rather than building types or geographical locations. While the plans were not much different from conventional layouts, the significantly improved and sophisticated construction and rendering techniques that utilized modern material, RCC structures, and prefabricated doors and windows gave the houses more of a slick look (fig. 1.17). Their crisp, rectilinear profiles, punctuated by the occasional projection of sunshades or projected verandas, created deep recesses in the south elevation more aligned with the interwar Bauhaus credo. A recurring theme for these two-story units involved the top floor, which often used the flat RCC roof of the lower story as an open terrace. Designers of the houses in this catalog did not conceive of them as independent artifacts but as urban elements contextualized in a neighborhood setting. The community in which they were located assumed a clear hierarchy—small clusters of units formed different small communities that belonged to larger garden suburb communities (fig. 1.18). But designers still strived to retain a lower density, evident in their incorporation of open spaces at both the micro and macro scale.

The ACC's Low-Cost House

To mark the Silver Jubilee of the Associated Cement Companies in 1952, the ACC arranged an architectural competition of low-cost house designs. The sixty-nine entries were exhibited the following year at the Jehangir Art Gallery in Bombay. The competition drew so much public interest that the ACC published the exhibition as a booklet titled *40 Designs for Low Cost Housing*, which was so well received that the ACC produced and sold several editions within just a few years.[121] A copy of the first edition is now kept in a locked cabinet in the ACC library as the most convincing evidence of its achievements during the 1950s. The exhibition produced the idea of modern minimal living for the middle class, a concept that was hitherto reserved exclusively for the working class. While the designs of this 1952 exhibition mirrored the spatial configurations, dimensions, and planning of typical working-class housing, they adopted a new term—the "low-cost house."

By eliminating the working-class identity from the rhetoric, the houses of the ACC competition could be subscribed to or owned by people of any social or economic class. They succeeded in attracting members of the middle-class urban population who did not identify as working class yet wanted to own an affordable house. The competition ruptured the symbolic attachments of building typology to economic class, envisioning a society that hides its class-consciousness. This subversion of class-consciousness was further accentuated by the representation of houses as individual artifacts, without knowing how they could be grouped together to form a community. In an Arcadian landscape, these houses symbolized a happy sanctuary for an urban nuclear family in the postindependence middle class.

Designing for the Tropics

The concept of working class was gradually replaced by a concern for environmental appropriateness. The ACC's *40 Designs for Low Cost Hous-*

ing booklet divided housing into two broad climatic zones (dry and wet) where administrative divisions were insignificant. The publication avoided the idea of a bureaucratically sectarian India at a time when the country was working to define the administrative borders of the state territories. The book evoked the concept of a borderless, classless utopia in which dwellers were categorized mainly according to their climatic setting. The idea of a geoclimate-bound society was reified in another remarkable publication published by the ACC in 1958, *Industrial Housing for the Tropics,* a compilation of articles from the *India Concrete Journal* by architect D. N. Dhar. The book conceptualized the Indian housing problem as part of the architecture of the broader geoclimatic region of the tropics.

In his book, Dhar criticized the passive acceptance of Western standards and the disregard for climatic considerations. According to Dhar, the built environment needed to be viewed as a result of geoclimatic dynamics, with nature as the scientific backdrop for spatial production. He eventually compiled a table of differences between England and India in which the two appeared as binary opposites, mainly in terms of climate. The table charted two imaginary regions of homogenous cultural geography, west and east, destined to collide head-on. These climatic divisions eventually overshadowed the concept of a postcolonial nation-state divided into diverse cultural practices and varied administrative zones.

Significantly, as Dhar observed, people in the tropics tended to spend a significant amount of time outside. Indian designers, he argued, were not aware of how climate influenced the collective social behavior of a population. According to Dhar, this lack of awareness prohibited Indian designers from creating a clean environment. Because Indian workers preferred to huddle outside their climatically insensitive living units, he explained, their houses became nothing more than chaotic repositories of paraphernalia. As a result, designers not only produced scientifically ineffective buildings but gave them the look of slums. He condemned the *charpoy* (traditional bed) as the "greatest offender" and despised the pervasive intermingling of communities between buildings (figs. 1.19, 1.20, 1.21). In response, Dhar suggested a plan that would shut the individual blocks off from each other and create more privacy for families. He presented a detailed criticism of the housing designed and constructed by the Indian government and proposed a range of technical options to increase the scientific efficiency of the buildings (fig. 1.22). His recommendations involved the position and dimension of openings, the role of corridors as ventilation apparatuses, and the selection of tropical vegetation such as *Inga-Delcious* (*sic*) and *Jaitu*. Overemphasizing the site specificity of buildings

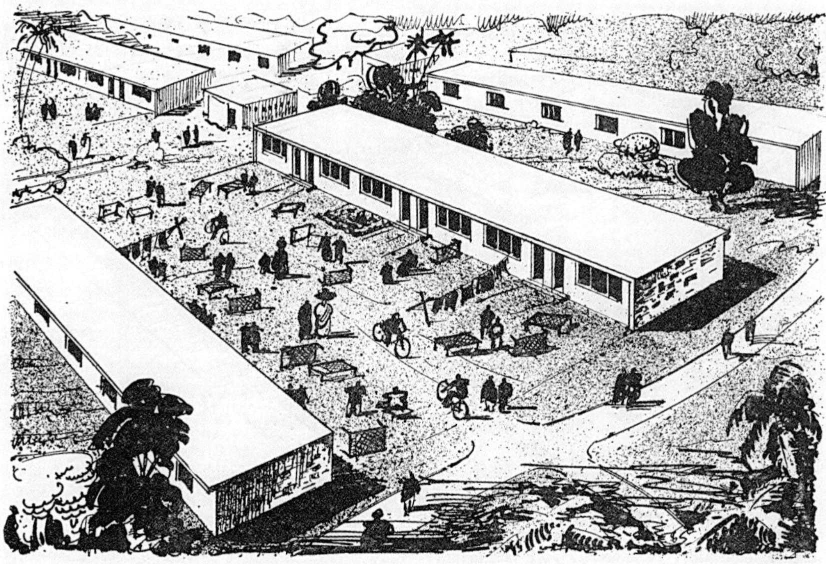

Fig 13 Showing what confusion one-room quarters facing each other can create. Note the use to which the open space between the houses is put. In actual practice the space is not as wide as is shown here (See Fig 14)

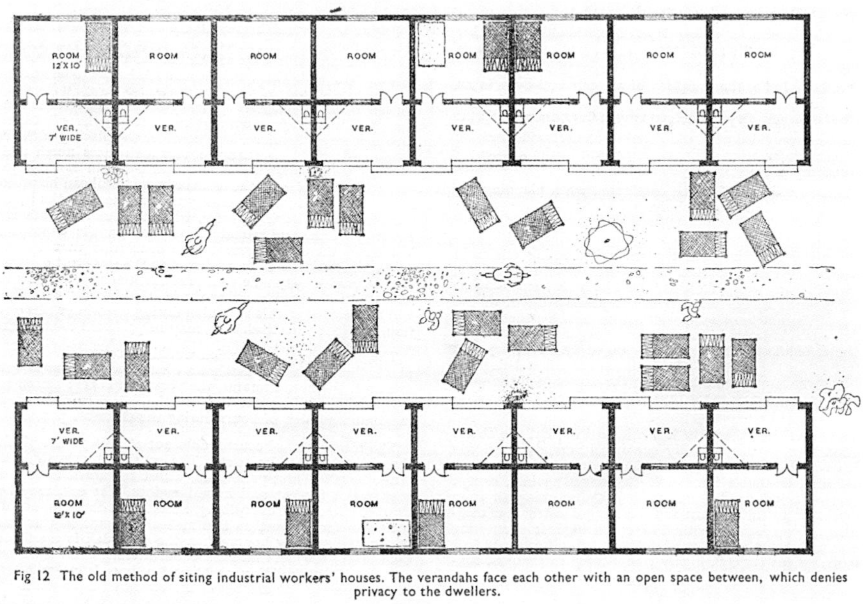

Fig 12 The old method of siting industrial workers' houses. The verandahs face each other with an open space between, which denies privacy to the dwellers.

18

FIGURE 1.19. Dhar's presentation of the chaotic life of the industrial workers. Source: D. N. Dhar, *Industrial Housing for the Tropics* (Bombay: Concrete Association of India, 1958), 18, 19.

FIGURE 1.20. A man seating on a charpoy in a village of Punjab, Chandigarh, India. Pierre Jeanneret, photographer, 1951–1955. Source: ARCH279614, Pierre Jeanneret fonds Canadian Centre for Architecture, Gift of Jacqueline Jeanneret.

strengthened the concept of industrial workers as site-specified beings. This emphasis, as Dhar noted, eventually connected the past of workers with the life of tropical food-producing communities: "An industrial work-

FIGURE 1.21 (*above*). Charpoys have been a constant reference in the design of low-cost housing in India. Sweepers' houses in sector 19, Chandigarh, India. Jeet Malhotra, photographer, 1950–1970s. Source: ARCH279617, Pierre Jeanneret fonds, Canadian Centre for Architecture Gift of Jacqueline Jeanneret.

er once at home should forget the regularity and the monotony imposed on him by his work. . . . [A] small piece of land adjoining his dwelling may be given to him for the expression of his agricultural instincts, for it must be remembered that he is essentially an agriculturalist from a village; a small piece will usually do, for he has not much energy left over after he returns from his work."[122]

The argument to provide open spaces for households went beyond their pragmatic solutions—as leisurely spaces for rejuvenating the worker's mind or as temperature-controlling mechanisms that instilled a notion of comfort. Open space symbolized and nourished its owner's inner primitive tropical being, embedded in the lineage of ecological existence. Workers were seen not as a construct of sociopolitical institutions but as a biological species that had evolved primarily in response to their environment. This biological existence was unimpaired by colonial rule or

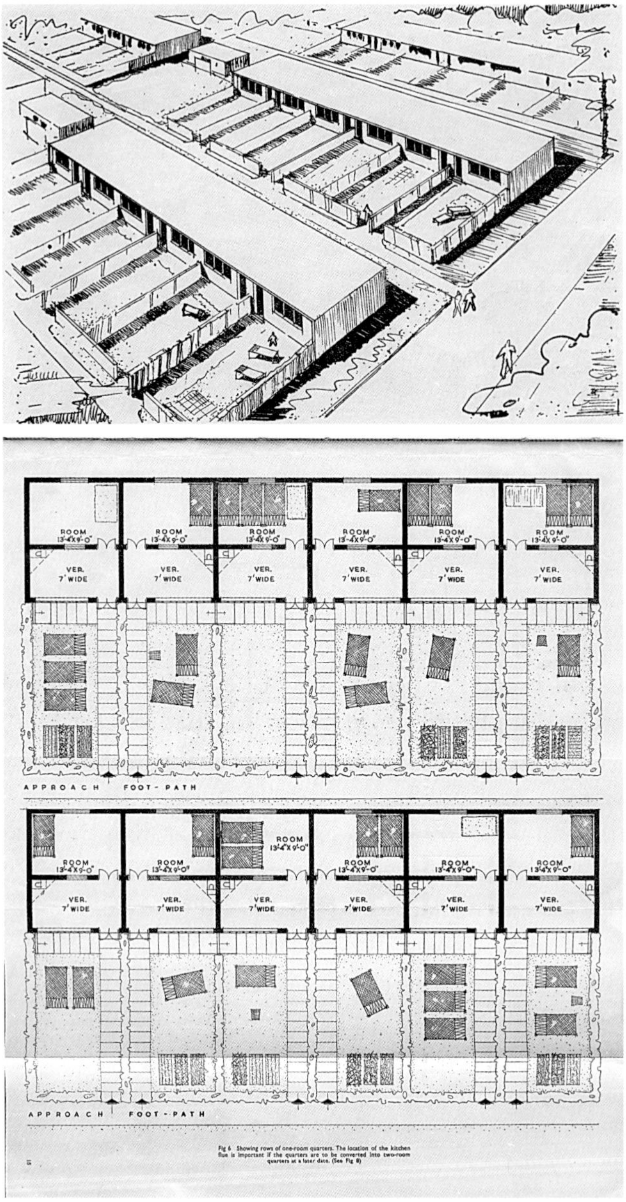

FIGURE 1.22. Dhar's proposal of an ordered life of the industrial workers in their private backyards. Source: D. N. Dhar, *Industrial Housing for the Tropics* (Bombay: Concrete Association of India, 1958): 15, 20.

class exploitation, since its characteristics had not been fully encountered or altered by colonial forces.[123] This new concept of workers as a biological species and tropical beings veneered their class and cultural identity. The discourse of ideal workers' housing as it had evolved in postcolonial India suggested that these two dimensions—biology and class—should be delicately separated.

2

Exhibiting Development

In 1954, seven years after independence, Indian vice president Sarvepalli Radhakrishnan recounted the country's condition of poverty at the first-ever United Nations International Exhibition of Low-Cost Housing in Delhi: "The hungry and homeless people are not concerned with the intricacies of economics or complexities of politics, but they ask for food, clothing, and shelter. If we are to further the interests of peace and democracy, we have to put ourselves on the inside of the poor of the world."[1] His speech captured the general sentiment of 1950s India, when the new country was grappling to escape Cold War politics and more interested in solving the problem of poverty, resource scarcity, and economic exclusion. Radhakrishnan also expressed his hope that the exhibition would resist the emerging "fascist trends" within India's domestic politics. He also added, "Wise policy consists not in opposing social revolution, which is inevitable, but in being of use to it and making use of it." His call to internalize a subjectivity produced by global poverty differs from the objectification of the poor through the philanthropic culture of sympathy. Instead, it demands a dismantling of the cultural imaginary separating the poor from activists working to eliminate poverty—just as Gandhi theatrically exercised in his personal and political life. Indian spiritual tradition rooted in asceticism not only pleads for one to empathize with the poor but also to identify as being one with the poor.

In the opening remarks of the exhibition, Prime Minister Jawaharlal Nehru reiterated the theme of emotional identification with the poor and asserted the importance of "vital spiritual values" in the design of low-cost housing.[2] Through the political rhetoric of Gandhi, among the most critical concepts for defining postcolonial subjectivity in India were spirituality and interiority.[3] Politicians and government officials deployed this idea of identification with the poor and spiritual interiority as a synthesis of spirituality with modern functionalism, which was framed as a broader project of the United Nations' global empathy-building program. For instance, in a 1951 UN report on Puerto Rico, UN consultants suggested that by losing its spiritual value, the house's collective communal value had been damaged, which led to poverty. According to the report, "The home which is supposed to provide shelter against the weather and a place for rest and recover after the daily struggles of life, weighs heavily on the spirit and the flesh of roan. The results in terms of social deterioration, frustration, and crippling of man's creative powers and of his drive to master his own destiny through his own efforts are so important to our civilization as to fully justify the deep concern which we are witnessing in the study and efforts to find a solution to the problem."[4]

The discourse of aid through self-help housing, promoted by the United Nations and the United States, configured empathy as a way to help the poor learn how to help themselves. Unconditional gifts or assistance, it was believed, would never eliminate poverty. Architectural aid projects in the Global South were characterized by a continuous confrontation, negotiation, and, sometimes, a negation of their emotional framework of empathy. Empathy, or feeling *with* the other, avoids the sentimentalism of charity, which can turn the other into an object of sympathy. For the expert advisers to the United Nations who were engaged in an empathy-building program, empathy was the emotional lingua franca that planted First World technicians on common ground with the Third World. The United Nations and Indian leaders believed that this synthesis was the only way to save architecture from the dehumanizing effects of modernism—a solution only postcolonial geopolitics could offer.[5]

The United Nations' 1954 International Exhibition of Low-Cost Housing (January 20 to March 5, 1954), which was associated with the UN Regional Seminar on Housing and Community Improvement (January 21 to February 17, 1954), organized jointly by the United Nations and the Indian government, was more than a display of architectural techniques. The exhibition worked as the platform to project a future image of the so-called developing nation's path to economic prosperity and create balance in contesting domestic powers by establishing a unified architectural vision of the future. With technical and financial assistance from the United Nations, the 1954 exhibition was among the earliest attempts to gather and showcase a wide range of prototypical model houses for the poor across India and other developing countries from South and Southeast Asia. A concerted effort by various sections of the United Nations and the US

Agency for International Development (USAID), the exhibition was eventually followed by the inception of a global project of Third World housing improvement led by Ernest Weissmann, the United Nations' chief of the Housing and Town and Country Planning Section.[6]

The objective of the United Nations' debut exhibition in Delhi was not exclusively to address the Indian housing problem. Rather, the exhibition used India as a demonstration of self-help housing as an architectural prescription to end the global problem of inadequate human shelter and ensure the path to global development. The conference speakers presented a variety of model houses in the exhibition to physically demonstrate their theoretical discussions. UN consultant Jacob Crane and planner Jaqueline Tyrwhitt organized the seminar that gathered different perspectives of UN experts and Indian architects and planners on the issues of low-cost housing, slum improvement, and urban planning. Crane was a proponent of self-help housing and the key figure to disseminating the land management policy that he drafted.[7] However, his role in the 1954 conference was mainly as an adviser and discussant. It was Tyrwhitt who organized every detail of the conference. Tyrwhitt's and her peers' interest in this exhibit and in the conference grew mainly from their personal beliefs that self-help could be the salvation of the poverty-ridden and disintegrating developing countries.

Tyrwhitt, a South African–born British landscape architect and urban planner with a diploma in horticulture, was one of the most important twentieth-century thinkers, organizers, and educators in the field, having already established her dexterity in transferring and exchanging ideas on a global scale, especially with regard to urban design and modern planning pedagogy.[8] Given her previous experiences in organizing the events of the Modern Architectural Research Group and Congrès Internationaux d'Architecture Moderne (International Congresses of Modern Architecture, CIAM), she successfully attracted a wide range of key figures in Delhi. Recalling one unique moment, Tyrwhitt wrote in an open letter: "I being more or less alone in Delhi, suddenly friends appeared from all over the world: first [Ernest] Weissman[n] from NY, then [Michel] Eccohard from Pakistan, [Arieh] Sharon from Israel, [Louis-Georges] Pineau from Vietnam, Charlie Abrams from NY to say nothing of ex-students of the School of Planning from all round India, Desai and Godbole from Bombay, Naidu from Bangalore, Gupta from Jaipur."[9]

The United Nations was the most important intergovernmental organization that believed providing low-cost housing through aided self-help programs was the key to creating an entrepreneurial attitude and thus to eradicating poverty from developing countries. The concept of the house in UN discourse was more than an architectural or engineering issue. The United Nations conceived of housing as a combined social engineering and financial system related to the production, distribution, and ownership of houses. This exhibition was among the earliest effort to use the house as a metaphor to depoliticize the production of poverty and thus define architecture for the less affluent as separate and different from its sociopolitical context. The concept of aided self-help housing became popular in the Cold War, when UN consultants considered housing inadequacy in developing countries to be a precondition for the spread of communist encroachment. In this discourse of self-help housing, family and home—instead of community—were taken as the fundamental unit of economic development. The UN consultants believed that if individual families could be firmly placed in the collective desire for development, developing nations would not be lured by communism.

The 1954 exhibition in India was presented as proof of the United Nations' hypothesis that self-help housing was adaptable to diverse regional contexts without compromising the fundamentals of the "free" world. The idea of home ownership was presented as a basic human right and the fundamental step toward economic prosperity. A house loan or a house as a loan was the preferred financial model for achieving home ownership. New financial models and the idea of home ownership formed a new aesthetic technique to address the new location of the home at the juncture of finance, power, and social engineering. Through the United Nations' discourse of self-help housing, the idea of low-cost working-class housing eventually became analogous to the norms of austerity and scarcity, which translated developmentalist modernization into images symbolizing postcolonial national identity.

The Roots of a New Aesthetic

On the opening day of the exhibition, the Indian crowd watched Canadian documentary filmmaker Douglas Wilkinson's classic short film *How to Build an Igloo* (1949) with great curiosity. The film is about two Inuit men in Alaska's far north who build an igloo in a few hours. The men choose the site amid the vast Arctic white, which, from an Indian perspective, may have appeared as an expanse of nothingness. They quickly assess the location, cut snow blocks, and finally place them to create an igloo. As the short winter day darkens, the two builders move inside to spend a snug night in the midst of the Arctic cold. One might wonder what benefit or technical knowledge this film might have to offer Indian viewers; however, this film, along with three others, was a tactical gambit to accumulate various vernacular building practices under the umbrella term of "self-help housing." The main idea was to establish that building a home is one of the most basic and natural skills a human inherits. The United Nations wanted to promote the ease of home construction: that the basic technique is so easy, anyone could master it without much effort. The pack of global transatlantic experts who gathered at the exhibition to explore the efficacy and potential of such methods in varied situations across developing nations would argue that whatever differences developing nations might have, self-help housing would be applicable in every regional context.[10]

Although the exhibition was organized under the umbrella of the United Nations, the majority of the structures were not designed exclusively for this event. Rather, they were reproductions of houses from existing projects in India and other South Asian countries, designed by local architects and engineers. However, the design methods of most non-UN consultants were compatible with the UN idea of low-cost housing. Although no detailed mandates or rules existed for designing the model houses, the selection criteria set by Tyrwhitt were based on quality, appropriately addressing particular geoclimatic conditions with the culture of less-affluent working-class populations. In judging the quality of the exhibition entries, Tyrwhitt dismissed the "inappropriate designs" presented by "big builders of India" and admired designs by different low-resourced government agencies or small offices. Analogous to the United Nations' broader philosophy, Tyrwhitt's objective in this exhibition was not to find an ideal or universal prescription but to appreciate creative manipulations of local technology that resulted in unique architectural expressions. None of the participating architects' work was in perfect ideological harmony; their responses to the question of low-cost housing were dissonant. Curating these dissonances into a cohesive view within the development discourse was important for Tyrwhitt and her colleagues.

The exhibition grounds stretched out at the foot of the Old Delhi Fort ruins. The exhibition path (fig. 2.1, fig. 2.2), dotted with information kiosks made of parabolic concrete shells, guided visitors gradually through the model house section showcasing eleven "selected ideal" designs and then across the ideal village center—bustling with "working villagers."[11] None of the structures exceeded five thousand rupees in cost, the number of Indian rupees that the housing secretary set as the Indian affordability ceiling. The show was an amalgam of aesthetic, technical, and financial approaches that displayed a nuanced understanding of Indian modernism underpinned by a concerted political and bureaucratic commitment to make housing available to the masses (fig. 2.3). This show was antithetical

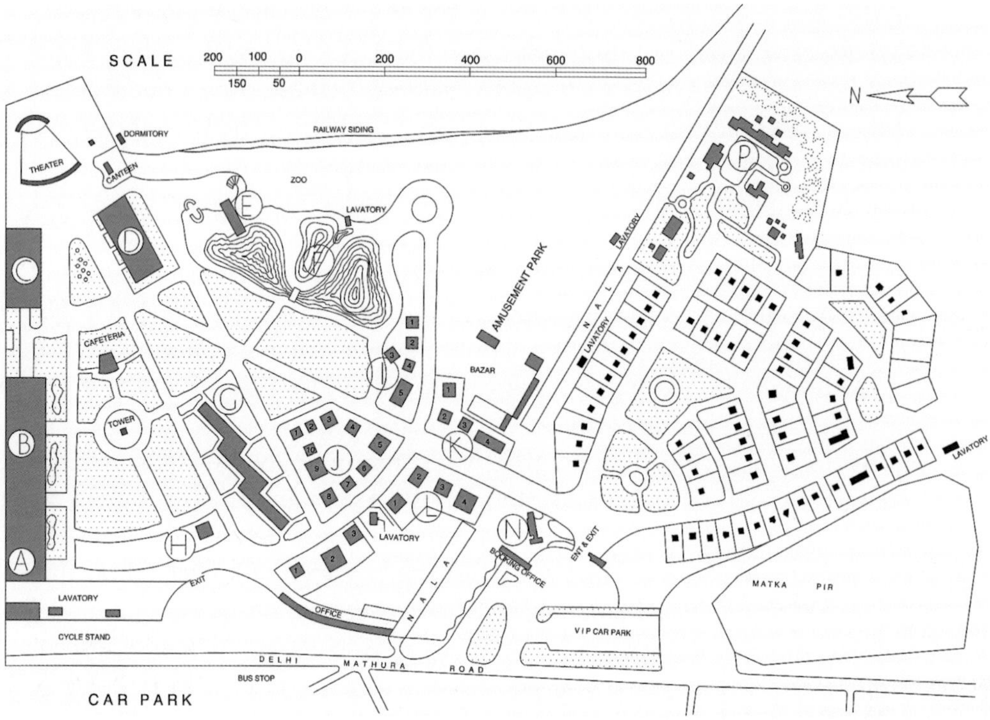

FIGURE 2.1. The Delhi exhibition site layout, 1954. Drawing by Suraiya Mymuna from the Ministry of Housing, Works and Supply, Exhibition Souvenir (New Delhi, 1954), 233.

FIGURE 2.2 A bird's eye view of the International Low-Cost Housing Exhibition in New Delhi. Source: Photo Studio, February 1954, A05m. Photo Number: 37011. © Photo division, Government of India.

FIGURE 2.3. Prime Minister Jawaharlal Nehru at the International Low-Cost Housing Exhibition Grounds in New Delhi on February 1, 1954. Source: Photo Studio/February 1954, A22a(v)/A22a(I). Photo Number: 36916. © Photo division, Government of India.

to the capitalist spectacle and consumer miracle of postwar US culture. It provided a scarcity spectacle through the display of ideal houses, formed by the rational manipulation of scant national resources, meager international loans, and technology aimed at serving the human cause.

San Francisco Bay Area architect Joseph Allen Stein captured the spirit of this exhibition with his drawing of a courtyard veranda of a two-room, low-cost urban dwelling designed on behalf of the Bengal Engineering College (fig. 2.4, fig. 2.5). This sketch embodies the representation of human labor with a newly wrought aesthetic to accommodate the scarce financial resources of developing regions. The drawing gives us a view of the house's backyard; the central figure is a woman winnowing the chaff from a small pile of unhusked grains at her side. The viewer is cast as an unbidden intruder whose piercing gaze is well represented by the sharp

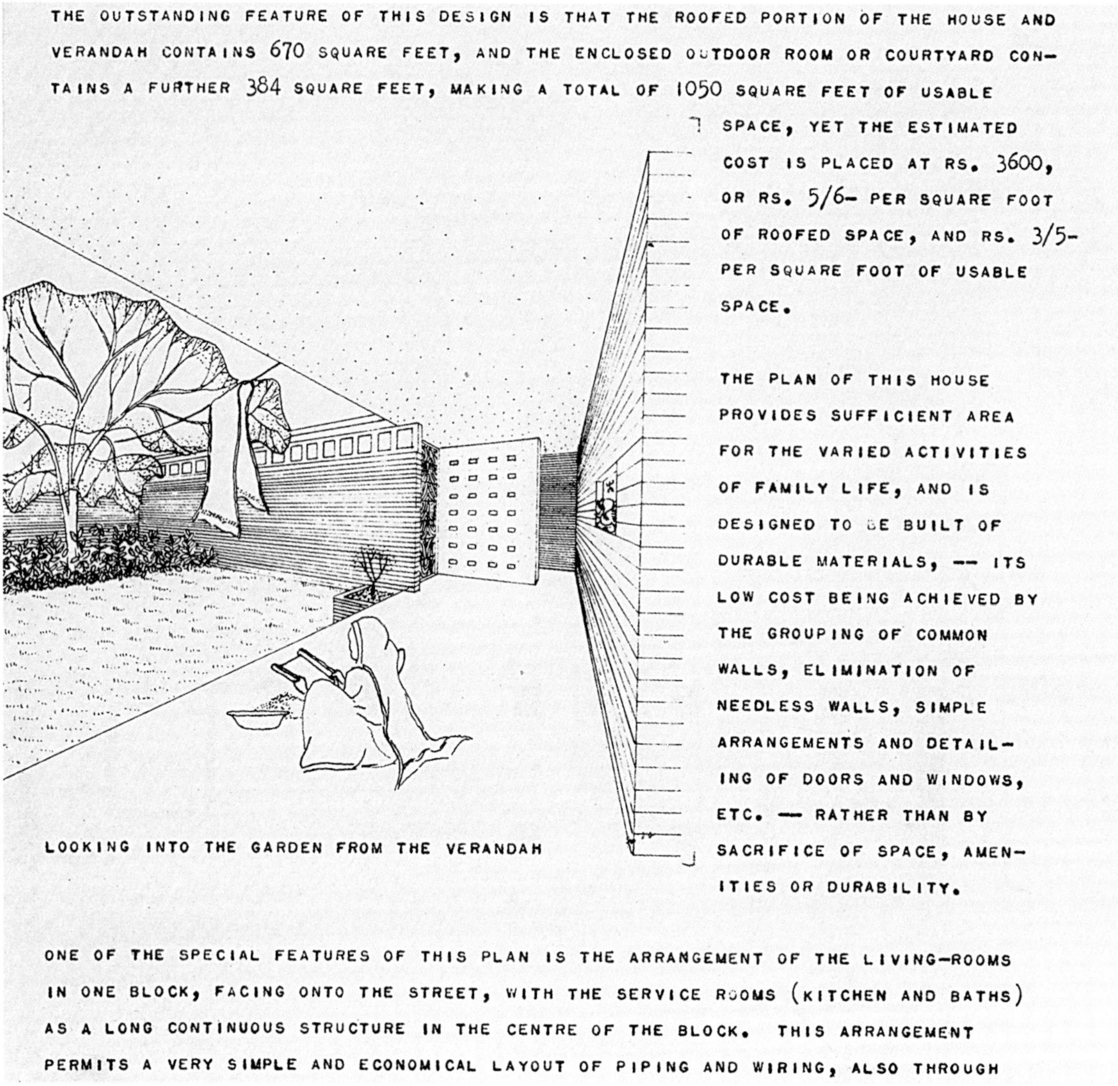

FIGURE 2.4. Annotated drawing of the courtyard and veranda of the low-cost house designed by Joseph Allen Stein and Bengal Engineering College, Calcutta, 1954. Source: S. White and J. A. Stein, *Building in the Garden: The Architecture of Joseph Allen Stein in India and California* (1993), 36.

perspective lines of the veranda and ceiling that dramatically frame the woman's working body in the disciplined order of the drawing board. Beyond the working body, a "functional" courtyard is spread out, and a drying cloth hangs next to the picturesque tree as evidence of the space's workability. The deity of Ganesh, the lord of entrepreneurship and pros-

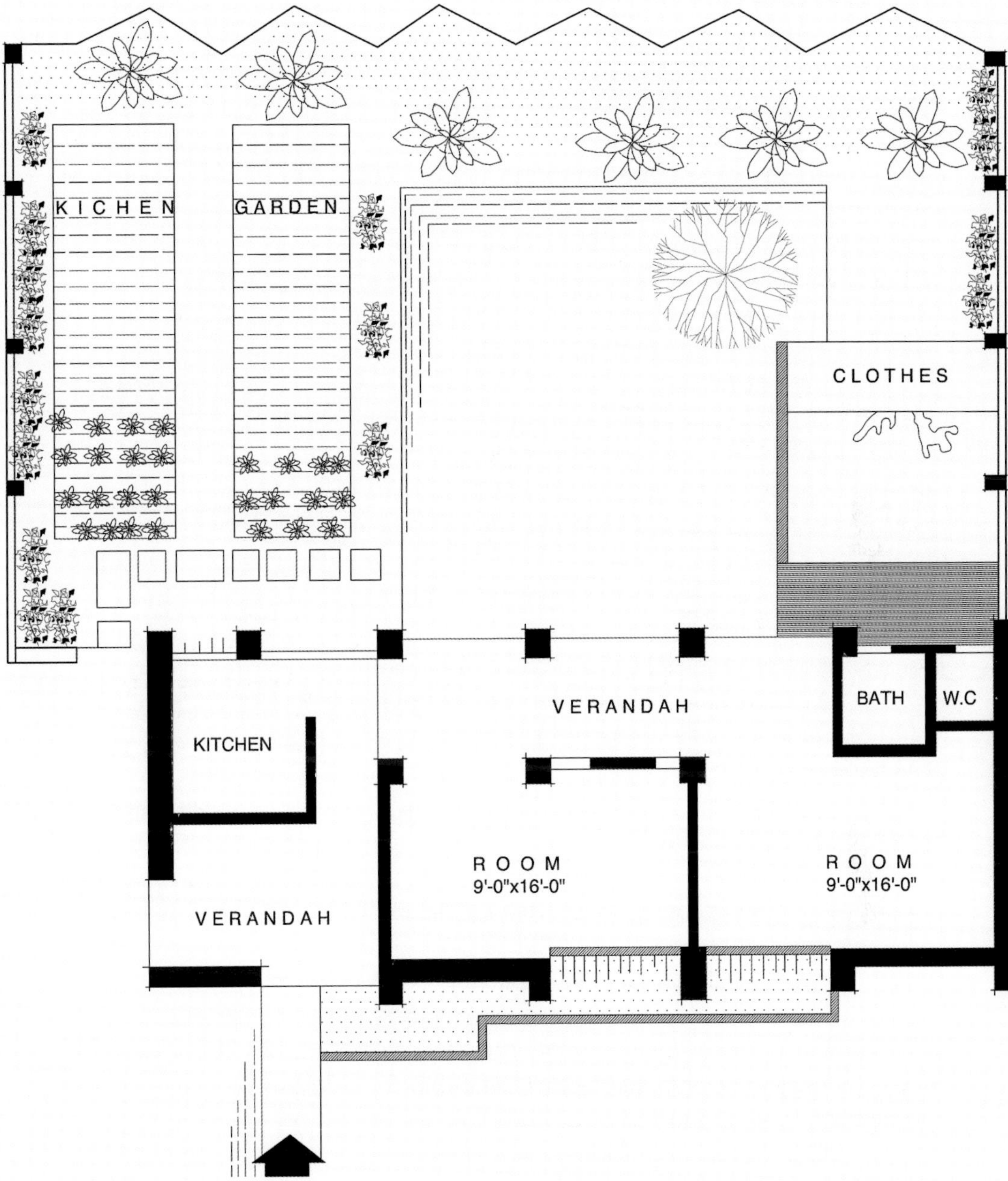

FIGURE 2.5. Plan of low-cost house designed by Joseph Allen Stein and the Bengal Engineering College, Calcutta, 1954. Source: drawing by Suraiya Mymuna from S. White and J. A. Stein, *Building in the Garden: The Architecture of Joseph Allen Stein in India and California* (1993), 39.

perity, is revered and kept high on the south wall. Everything is captured on its three adjacent planes, with an obvious vanishing point at the end of the veranda. Stein used the typical International Style slick pen-and-ink rendering to capture the spirituality of Indian daily life as a ritual performance. This is one way to understand the new version of modernism that appropriated the CIAM functionalism myth, which was the dominant axiom that had confronted Tyrwhitt and her ideological European allies.

Stein's other design for the exhibition was a low-cost rural house built in a rammed earth structure (fig. 2.6). In this design, Stein devised an ingenious way to use handwoven bamboo in movable vertical blinds instead of conventional windows. In order to enhance the barren façade of the rammed earth wall, Stein used a pattern inspired by local bamboo chick. The tactile quality of the wall underscored the haptic experience of tropical existence and its crop-growing community. In Stein's understanding, Indian postcolonial society was divided into many layers of economic classes, social feuds, and religious sectors, and no single overarching development theory could bind all of these contesting fragments together. Stein's interpretation of development sought to accommodate different economic levels of Indian society without collision or overlaps. His phrases "network democracy" and "multi-staged democracy" interpreted architects as contributors to the democratization of a society. In Stein's argument, architects should cease to produce master plans or universal principles; rather, they should introduce mechanisms to connect the multitude of small community efforts.[12] In such view, the central concern was not the principle itself but the power of the principle to spread and to be inclusive.

An ardent San Francisco Bay Area modernist, Stein moved to India in 1952 on the recommendation of his former mentor Richard Neutra to take up the position as head of the Department of Architecture, Town and Regional Planning at Bengal Engineering College, Calcutta. He eventually settled in India for the rest of his life. Stein was a prodigy of the Bay Area's ecology-conscious architecture. The two-room house he designed for the exhibition adopted a typical plan of working-class housing, one not very different from the Indian government's existing effort. He kept construction costs well below the government standard with his slick one-room, one-story structure, and he considered outdoor space to be the "most important single factor in tropical housing [that is necessary for] living as well as for food growing."[13] The British version of tropicalism, mediated by the newly formed Department of Tropical Architecture at the Architectural Association in London and the Tropical Building Division at the Building Research Station in Garston, England, reinjected colonial

FIGURE 2.6. A view from the veranda of the low-cost rural house, designed by Joseph Allen Stein and Bengal Engineering College, Calcutta, 1954. Source: S. White and J. A. Stein, *Building in the Garden: The Architecture of Joseph Allen Stein in India and California* (1993), 320.

values into the postcolonial world through "expert" knowledge of climate. Many of these experts previously disseminated modern values as neo-imperial ethics in its colonies. For instance, Jane Drew, the English tropical modernist famous for her contribution to the formation of a regionalist language of tropicalism as an alternative vein of modernism, designed a one-unit house in brick arches for this show, which might easily fit the theoretical framework of European tropicalism as the new imperialism. The US version of tropicalism, such as that of Stein, however, was rooted in the regionalism of the San Francisco Bay Area and its postwar housing reformation.

Stein started his own practice in collaboration with John Funk, who made the Second Bay Tradition popular, and the famous landscape architect Garrett Eckbo. Stein also became a member of the Telesis, a voluntary association of Bay Area architects who valued regional attributes over universal ideals and sought holistic human living through an integration of nature and the built environment.[14] While working with Richard Neutra, Stein was introduced to the idea of biorealism, which he later transformed into a social reformation project that he thought would harness the "real democracy." He spent his formative years of practice in the prewar depression, and his involvement in Roosevelt's reformation program of the Resettlement Agency and Farm Security Administration had stirred his hope for a new community-based democratic society in which architects would act as interdisciplinary agents to facilitate societal transformation. Around the same time, John Entenza, the influential Los Angeles critic and editor of *Art and Architecture* magazine, gathered leading US practitioners with his case study house program to design low-cost houses for the middle class, often with donated materials from industries. As a whole, Bay Area architecture envisioned a world as a hypothetical singularity in which the middle-class and low-income American population, nature, and architecture poised in harmony.

The theme of singularity and "One World" was further accentuated in various ways by the experience of war. Before the Second World War, many European intellectuals considered America to be a cultureless nation and a tainted offshoot of European civilization. The war alliance between the United States and Western Europe fostered the idea of a transatlantic nation in which America and Europe were now seen not as rivals but as heirs of a common civilization of Western enlightenment.[15] In addition, the Cold War world was viewed as a grand dialectical process in which the socialist and the capitalist blocs were interlinked in a confrontational yet reciprocal way. The Cold War and the vision of a Three-World Order conceptualized a unified world. In addition to this grand dialectic, the experience of atomic annihilation in the Far East brought in the possibility of world destruction with a single stroke—not just human settlement but its entire ecology. The well-founded paranoia of nuclear apocalypse set up a paradox of singularity in which the oneness of the world is approached negatively and inversely: if the world could be destroyed at once, the belief went, it could be perceived and constructed as one too.[16] Against this growing concern for One World, the inchoate visibility of the decolonized world and Third World poverty, inclined toward socialism, proved to be a potential threat for US homeland security. The Third World, the regressive and incapable portion of human civilization as it was commonly conceived in Western view, had long been intellectually invisible within the folds of colonialism. With a growing share and control of these newly decolonized countries in the world economy, the Third World gained a new intellectual focus. Moreover, in order to secure the idea of transatlantic capitalist sovereignty, it also became important to acknowledge and assimilate the notion of "poverty" and underdevelopment within global capital circulation. In doing so, the transatlantic West and the Third World had to be woven together as One World through dialogues of development.

Within the rising discourse of an integrated globe and global crisis, Bay Area architects proposed a solution from a local and regional perspective. The globe in this context could only be perceived through an endless network of local fragments. Against this backdrop, between 1939 and 1949 Stein embarked on various projects in the United States that included unrealized and unsuccessful low-cost housing prototypes for the unemployed poor (1939), war housing for the navy shipyard (1942), and an ideal community for four hundred families (1944–49). Stein's design ideology was driven during this period by what architectural historian Stephen White has termed "beauty with simplicity." Though his single-family house earned him a reputation as a prominent Bay Area architect, his failure to realize an integrated and just society through community design prompted his intellectual foray into the possibility of holistic ecological improvement of the less-affluent "tropics" of the Third World.

In 1951 while traveling in Switzerland, Stein codesigned two austere homes with sociologist Stanley White, one for a mountain region and one for the tropics (fig. 2.7, fig. 2.8, fig. 2.9, fig. 2.10). These ideas were a modern reinterpretation of primitive huts of the working-class community, anti-industrial in spirit and ascetic in philosophy. These homes, though designed to be rooted in their geoclimatic context, were consciously acontextual, since they generalized the sociopolitical reality of a region under the rubric of geography and climate—tropics and mountains. The discourse of economical inequity on the basis of interstate politics was replaced with the territoryless perennial geoclimatic condition. Yet they were contextual only in terms of a self-constructed, transcendental reality.

FIGURE 2.7. Self-Sufficient House for the Tropics, designed by Stanley White and Joseph Allen Stein. Source: Joseph Allen Stein Collection, drawing no. 15-045-111. Environmental Design Archives, University of California, Berkeley.

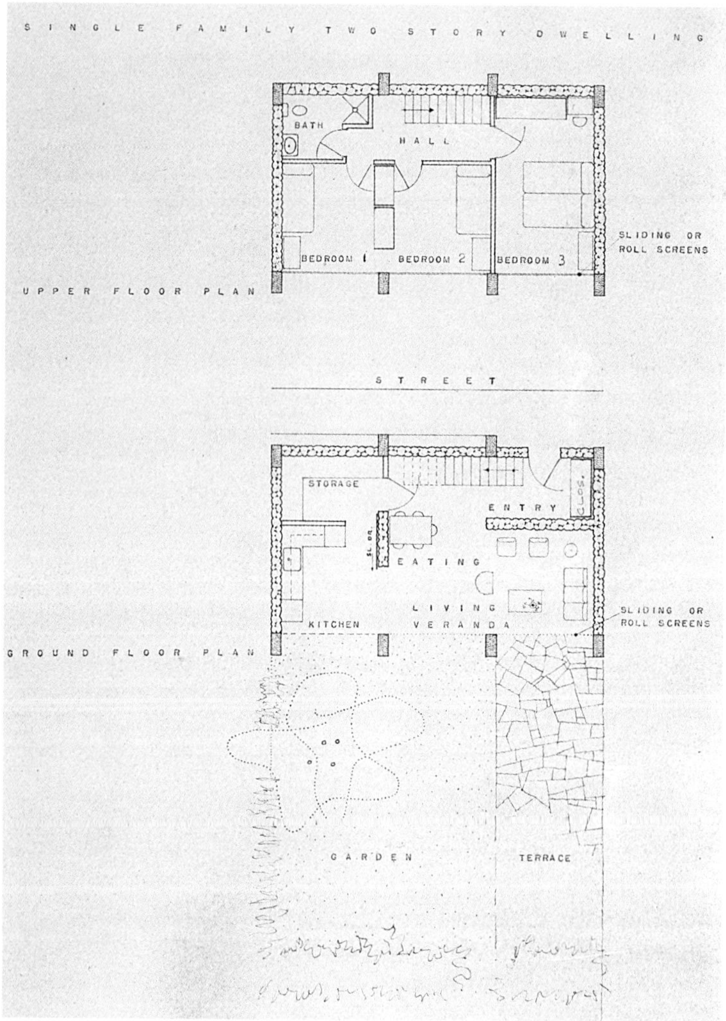

FIGURE 2.8. Prototype of a two-story self-sufficient house in the tropics designed by Stanley White and Joseph Allen Stein, 1951. Source: Joseph Allen Stein Collection, drawing no. 15-045-112. Environmental Design Archives, University of California, Berkeley.

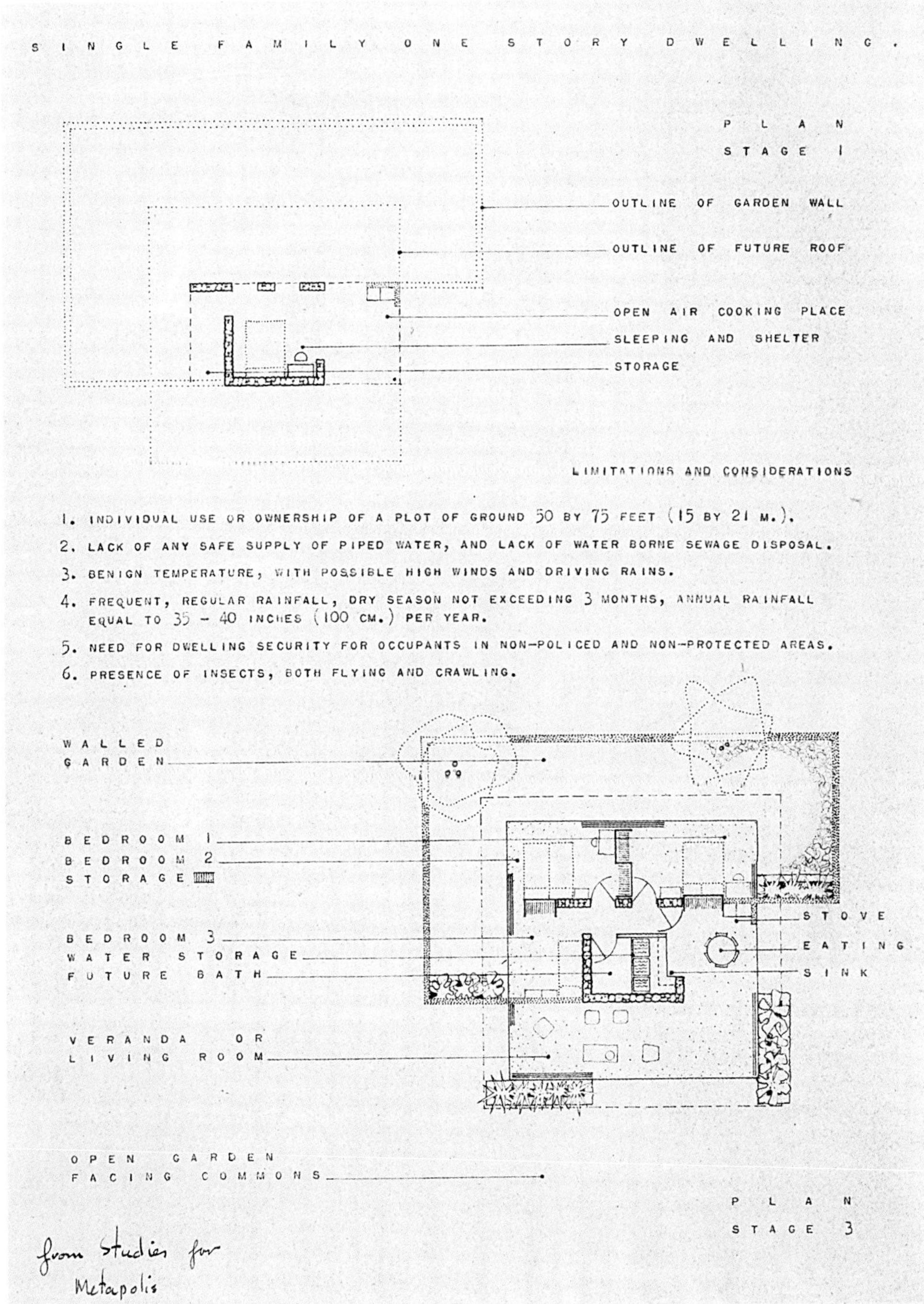

FIGURE 2.9. Annotated plan of the self-sufficient house of the tropics, showing functional zoning. Designed by Stanley White and Joseph Allen Stein, 1951. Source: Joseph Allen Stein Collection, drawing no. 15-045-113. Environmental Design Archives, University of California, Berkeley.

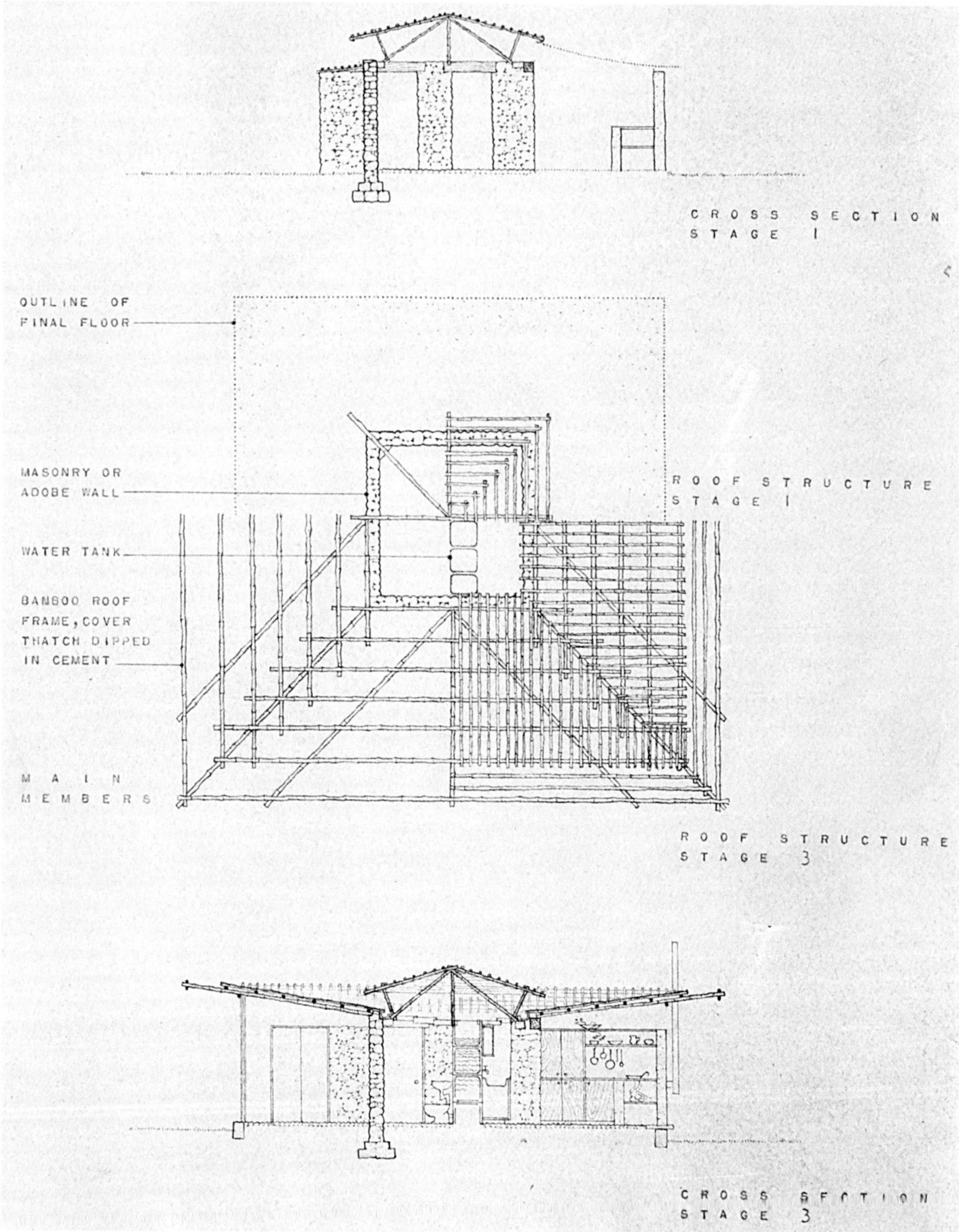

FIGURE 2.10. Roof plan and section of self-sufficient house, showing the details of rain water collection, 1951. Stanley White and Joseph Allen Stein. Source: Joseph Allen Stein Collection, drawing no. 15-045-114. Environmental Design Archives, University of California, Berkeley.

The Model House and the Mirage of a Better Life

The Indian government only partially adopted the UN- and US-promoted self-help housing program in which the state would exercise minimum power and reserve only limited scope to intervene. As opposed to the self-help method's decentralized, low-cost housing program, Nehru spearheaded the formation of state-controlled, centralized housing factories and research institutes to produce prefabricated elements for low-cost housing. A major focus of these initiatives was to explore low-cost design details and multipurpose building elements, for instance a window that could be transformed into a chai table. Two major institutions involved with designing and making low-cost housing in India were the Central Building Research Institute (CBRI), Roorkee, and the Hindustan Housing Factory, Delhi. Neither CBRI nor the Hindustan Housing Factory fully complied with the United Nations' aided self-help housing program. But because of the interest of the Indian government, the CBRI participated in the exhibition with its new experiments that utilized a parabolic concrete structure—reminiscent of Nissen huts and wartime technology—to produce low-cost housing (fig. 2.11, fig 2.12).[17] It's clear that Tyrwhitt and her colleagues at the United Nations were not against entertaining other methods, in this instance the production of housing through state-controlled factory and research institutes, even if they were contrary to the United Nations' model of self-help. It's also evident that the projects exhibited by the CBRI exemplified the Indian government's stance that developing countries ought to explore alternative state-controlled methods for providing housing for lower-income populations. From this perspective, the Chandigarh Housing Authority presented its two-room house for government officers, designed by Pierre Jeanneret, not as an example of design by famous expat architects but rather as evidence of the government's ability to control the production of low-cost housing in India.

CBRI's prototypes—odd structures hunched throughout the exhibition grounds—provided the Indian psyche with wartime technology's promise of a humane postcolonial situation. Nehru invited Kurt Billing, an American civil engineer and expert in wartime construction in precast concrete, to direct the newly established CBRI. The main objective of this institute was to invent and execute appropriate technology for the mass production of low-cost or affordable housing. Along with the newly formed Hindustan Housing Factory under the direction of Otto Koenigsberger, the famous German architect who pioneered the concept of tropical architecture, Nehru looked for a method that could mass-produce low-cost housing at a rapid pace. Billing, however, who drew on

FIGURE 2.11. G. V. Mavlankar, speaker of the House of the People is visiting a CBRI thin concrete shell house. Source: Photo Studio/February 1954, A05m. Photo Number: 37372. © Photo division Government of India.

his previous experiences in wartime construction, adapted innovative use of reinforced cement concrete shell structures as a means to supply mass housing at low cost. The majority of India's cement supply during the 1940s was reserved for large-scale development projects like dams and public buildings.[18] In order to operate within resource scarcity, the Indian government encouraged government research institutes such as CBRI to explore vernacular materials and indigenous techniques in conjunction with modern techniques.[19] Tyrwhitt and her colleagues of global experts were not enthusiastic about using labor-saving industrial technology and RCC in the developing regions. They were less likely to appreciate a sole dependency on concrete or a technology-intensive method. Rather, self-help housing advocates supported labor-intensive methods that depended less on machines and more on manual labor.

Quite contrary to the preferences of UN experts, almost all endeavors controlled by the Indian state used RCC, and the organizational behemoth

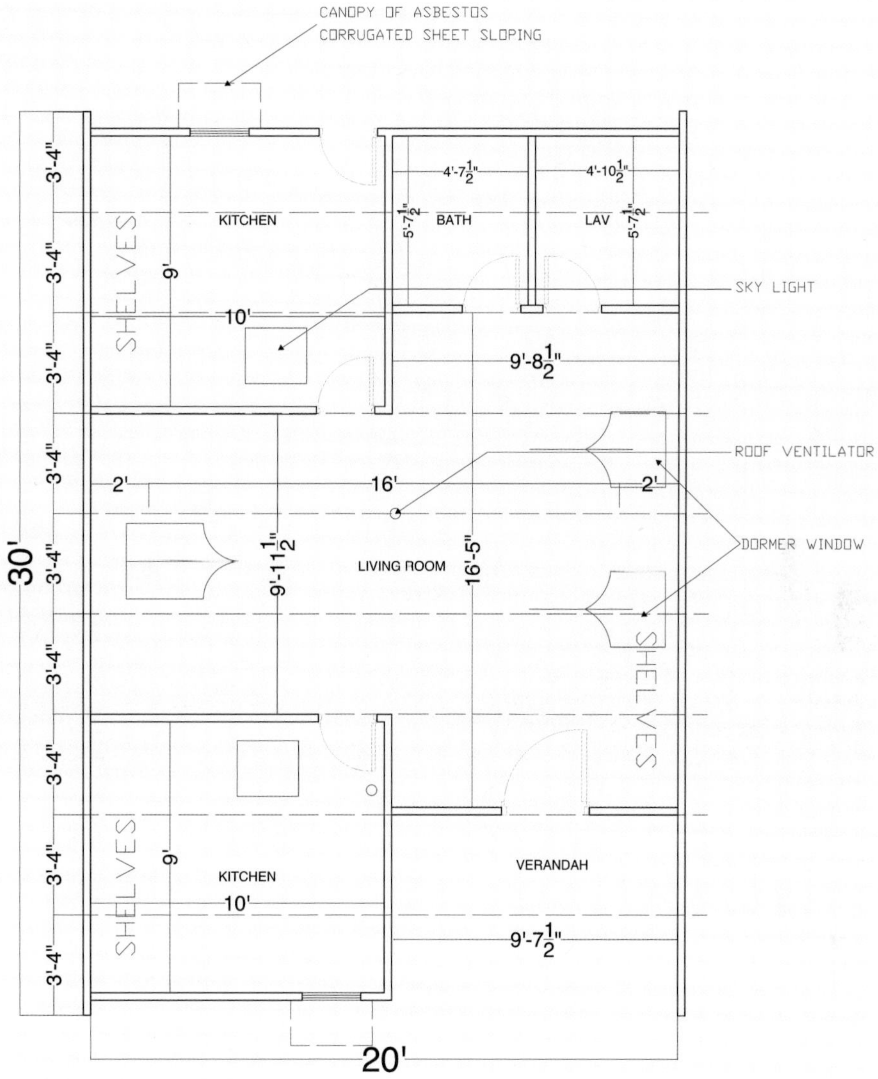

FIGURE 2.12. Plan and section of one prototype (four variations) of shell-type housing, designed by Kurt Billing and the CBRI. Source: Drawing by Suraiya Mymuna from drawings published in Ministry of Works, Housing, and Supply Exhibition Souvenir (New Delhi, 1954).

Associated Cement Companies Limited promoted RCC structures as the most technologically and economically appropriate structures for the country. Naturally, the ACC promoted Billing's project as a creative adaptation of wartime RCC parabolic structures to meet local demands.[20] The ACC argued that thin concrete shells were more appropriate in the Indian

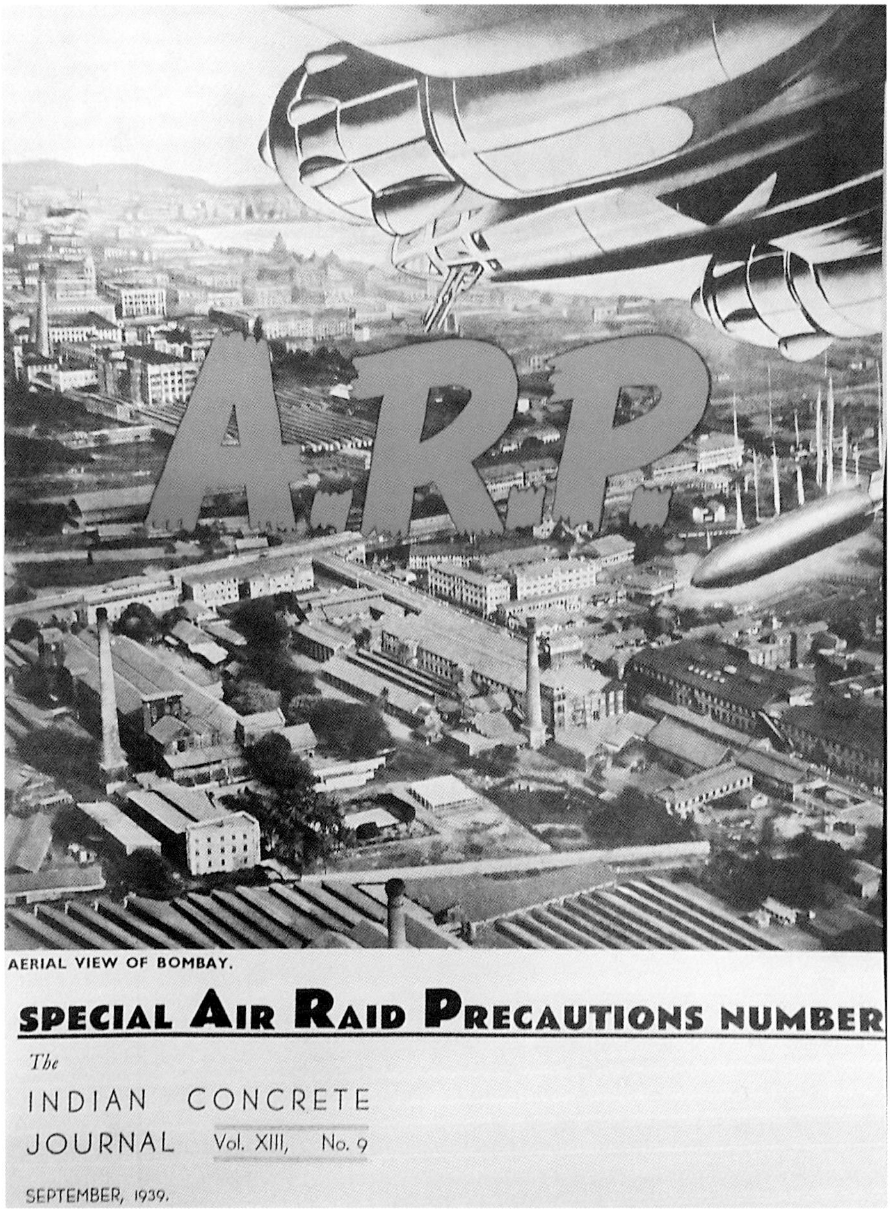

FIGURE 2.13. Cover of the "Special Air Raid Precautions" issue. Source: *Indian Concrete Journal* 13, no. 9, Special Issue on Air Raid Bombing (1939). © Associated Cement Companies.

context because they required only a minimum cubic volume of cement to create a maximum built volume. For the government, the economic use of material was a more convincing factor than the creation of a "beautiful" form. Aesthetics became a tertiary factor, eclipsed by the argument of scarcity and austerity as the main factor of design discourse. Although the shell construction technique used less material, it required a large number of skilled laborers. The labor-intensive method was considered a positive factor, as the postindependence Indian government encouraged methods that engaged its vast manpower. However, while Billing experimented with shell structures in India, the United States and Europe were recycling the predecessors of Billing's hut—the Nissen hut and other similar structures of parabolic steel or concrete—for postwar civilian use. This recycling strategy incited substantial public discontent in Europe, as wartime memories stigmatized those structures. Quite interestingly, Billing's attempt in India stirred a nation's hope and precariously persuaded the vernacular taste to accept the "spectacular half moon" structure of concrete, reminiscent of the West's prestigious wartime technology.[21]

During the 1930s and 1940s, the ACC operated in many ways to popularize concrete structures in India. Among their most effective strategies was to emphasize the material's ability to withstand air-raid bombing. The ACC's *Indian Concrete Journal* also played a major role in disseminating war propaganda and creating a positive view of the RCC through its specials issues on war.[22] Between 1944 and 1946, the ACC published articles on how builders could adapt RCC and other special techniques to make Indian houses more durable and protect lives during air raids (fig. 2.13). It also published two special issues on air-raid bombing in 1939 and 1942.[23] The ACC's publications presented an explicit survey of wartime development in building technology and expanded the connection between the new Indian domesticity and concrete.

Two themes emerged from wartime promotion of a new postwar India built in concrete: first, the concrete structure as the symbolic safe shelter from impending air-raid bombing and, for that matter, any threat caused by a mechanized, modernized world (figs. 2.14, 2.15); second, the unusual architectural form of US and European wartime architecture as an important inspiration for a permanent and stable architectural expression in India. The emergence of these two themes should be understood against the backdrop of the colonial portrayal of the Second World War as a distant imperial battleground of machines from which the Indian society could learn about technology (fig. 2.16). The war was generally considered to be a brutal technological showdown with a conceptual and institutional congruity that could benefit India's own "backwardness in technology." For instance, the Indian government's Reconstruction Committee Council recommended that the government send "senior men engaged in industry" to Germany to learn from wartime industrial development.[24] War as

FIGURE 2.14. A community air-raid bombing shelter. Source: *Indian Concrete Journal* 16, no. 5/6, Special Issue on Air Raid Bombing (1942): 123. © Associated Cement Companies.

an opportunity of economic and social change was evident in a speech delivered by Khan Bahadur Mushtaq Ahmed Gurmani, director of publicity and recruitment at the Department of Labour, at the 1943 War Services Exhibition in Bombay. In his speech, Gurmani presented the war as a cleansing mechanism, providing India with the opportunity to enrich itself with war technology.[25] The government's perception of war and development as a simultaneous dialectical couple contrived a counternarrative of the colonies' development. In Gurmani's interpretation, world war on the one hand threatened to destroy the entire world, but on the other hand it also opened up a global and networked world through wartime technology that bounded the colonies together and also boosted the morality of the people in the colony. This message of world war as a boon to the colonized population was circulated through national war exhibitions and conferences, which had the recurring theme of improvement of public morals and development of social structure.[26]

On May 29, 1945, Sir Ardeshar Dalal, member of the Viceroy's Executive Council for Planning and Development, said in a meeting of East India Association in London that "almost every great war leads to the upheaval of the existing social and political order and lays the foundation of a new one."[27] Dalal continued that India's "war on poverty" could benefit from the experience of war. War was thus stripped of its physical violence and reduced to an idea that gave India a chance to be modernized. For

FIGURE 2.15. An individual home air-raid bombing shelter. Source: *Indian Concrete Journal* 20, no. 6 (1946): 207. © Associated Cement Companies.

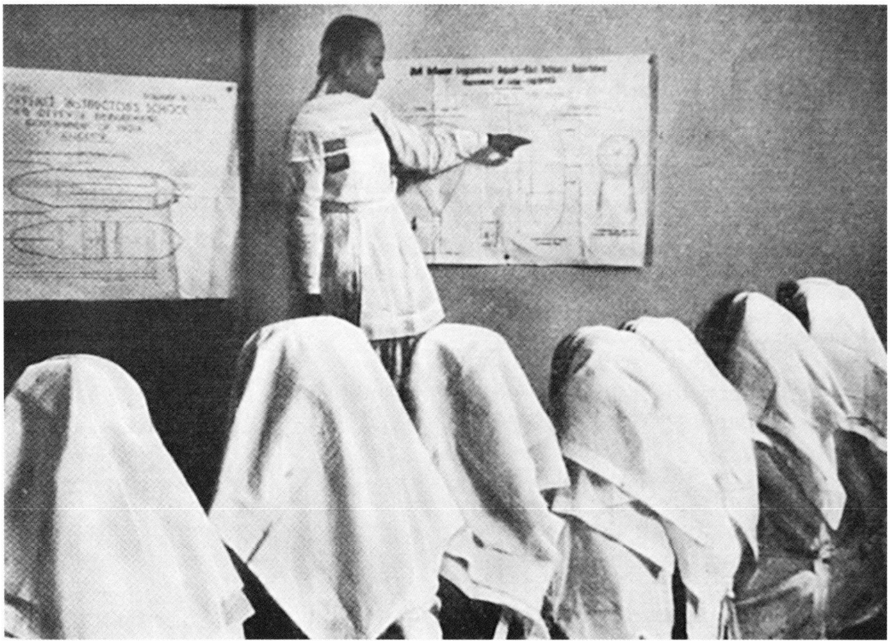

FIGURE 2.16. A government publication demonstrates that wartime knowledge could help to bolster social progress in peacetime, specifically in woman's education. Source: Bureau of Public Information, Government of India, *Post-War Planning: An Outline* (New Delhi: Government of India Press, 1945), 5.

instance, it was reported that the 2 million Indian soldiers who joined the war actually expanded their "mental horizon" because they not only acquired different technical skills but also familiarized themselves "with all kinds of machinery" as well as the need for public health and hygiene and thus would develop a more active social consciousness. They also acquired, according to Dalal, the discipline of working together with people of many religions and castes, potentially an important factor for progress in the postwar years.[28]

The Indian government circulated a series of propaganda publications advertising war as a boon to the economy and all aspects of society, from education to industrial development.[29] These publications, all published by the Bureau of Public Information, remained completely silent as to how such development would occur. By repeating the typical colonial promise for development, these materials created a reality of their own and painted a sanguine future for the country. One explained how "after complete victory," the country would achieve complete social and economic reformation.[30] Postwar housing was among the main topics of discussion at the meeting of the Reconstruction Committee Council. Most of the members warned that India was to experience a huge building boom in the immediate postwar years. They suggested that the government must take measures to ensure an increased supply of building materials, a tax benefit for the producers of those materials, and the formation of a centralized housing finance mechanism that would help the middle class and industrial workers build houses.[31] The council strongly suggested that the Indian government consider war as an opportunity for urban development, keeping in mind the socioeconomic condition of urban labor.[32] However, the council repeated the same colonial belief that despite India's great natural wealth, the country remained poor because of an unmotivated and unambitious population. According to the council, "true leadership and self-help," visible through industrialization and its built environment, was the key to developing India, and war would give the country a chance to become self-reliant.

Colonial bureaucrats created a fantasy of an affluent future in which Western cutting-edge knowledge would transform the fragile Indian home into an impregnable fortress.[33] This will to self-transformation from frailty to strength sought to distill virility from architecture as the keeper of the Indian self and to interiorize that virility. Another important theme related to RCC and war was the idea of a suburban development—dotted by detached two-story, concrete, single-family homes with "pretty cars and virile flyovers"—that at war's end would liberate returning soldiers and their families. In a 1946 war exhibition at Lahore organized by the In-

FIGURE 2.17. New suburb for returning soldiers in the model town for postwar India. Source: Indian Concrete Journal 18, no. 6 (1944): 4. © Associated Cement Companies.

dian Labour Department, the ACC built a huge model of a postwar Indian city (figs. 2.17, 2.18).[34] In this city was a combination of three zones: commercial, industrial, and residential. The ACC and the Labour Department viewed suburbia and detached residences as the most appropriate form of postwar urban living. The ACC presented its low-cost prototype of a single-family residence, costing 1,200 to 1,300 rupees, as the ideal house for returning soldiers and also for the civilian middle class.

During the 1950s, though the Indian government's emphasis on concrete was driven mainly by the economy and convenience, but its symbolism—that war might help to reform the morality of the Indian population—cannot be overlooked. Anxiety about the chaotic and vulnerable present and its subsequent transposition into a safe and ordered future was mediated successfully by the ACC's version of a concrete landscape.

FIGURE 2.18. A model town for postwar India. *Indian Concrete Journal* 18, no. 6 (1944): 5. © Associated Cement Companies.

In the 1954 exhibition Billing's concrete parabolic hut along with a similar design by the English Branch of the Vacuum Concrete Company, designed for Bogotá, Colombia, embodied the nuanced relationship between war, RCC, and the future of low-cost Indian house.

The Global Network of Architecture for the Poor

From the 1950s through the 1970s, the United Nations sent a large number of Western professionals to emerging developing countries as expert consultants to find solutions for housing problems in specific contexts—in Latin America, Africa, the Caribbean, and South and Southeast Asia. The United Nations' theory of architectural production in developing countries through self-help was associated with the politics of reducing the Third World as a general category or a field of investigation in which the modernization theory could be applied thoroughly.[35] Development thinkers and architectural consultants alike conceived an operational method in which the basic social unit to mobilize development activities was family and then community. Consequently, in the discourse of UN global experts, the idea of a single-family home with family as the basic unit of socioeconomic development gained central importance. Starting from the debut exhibition in Delhi in 1954, many subsequent exhibitions (by the UN and others) inscribed values in the design and production of detached or semidetached single-family houses. Against this backdrop of multiple ideologies, stances, and politics, the first UN exhibition in Delhi did not merely showcase the diverse architectural styles created by the UN-prescribed self-help method; it also positioned individual houses—a metaphor of family as the liberating force of socioeconomic development with minimum intervention from the state—in the center of the development discourse. To this end, the participating local and Euro-American architects used the concept of home as a common means to alleviate poverty and civilizational backwardness.

In Europe and later in the United States, self-help housing has long been promoted as an alternative to community housing.[36] After the Second World War, self-help housing became an integral part of US foreign policy in the global Cold War, especially in the Caribbean, for quick pacification of the unemployed poor and thus communism. American planner and engineer Jacob L. Crane, director of the US Housing and Home Finance Agency, first formed this political method of using aided self-help housing. UN agencies such as the Inter-American Housing and Planning Center (also called the Centro Interamericano de Vivienda) followed by the United Nations, promoted Crane's idea of aided self-help housing throughout the developing world. The first political use of self-help housing on a large scale was demonstrated in 1949 in the Aided Self-Help Housing Program in one of the unincorporated organized territories of the United States, Puerto Rico. During the early 1950s, the most significant self-help housing projects under the UN-US influence were that of Germán Riesco in Chile, the Colonia Managua in Nicaragua, the Chacra La Palma in San Gregorio, California, and the Clara Estrella projects in Guatemala.[37] The Aided Self-Help Housing Program set out preliminary programs in Latin America (Chile, Guatemala, and Nicaragua), in the Caribbean (Barbados, Jamaica, and Trinidad), and in Southeast Asia (Korea, Burma, and Taiwan). In the 1960s the program spread into Turkey and Africa (Egypt, Rhodesia [now Zimbabwe], Nyasaland [now Malawi], Mali, Zambia, and Liberia). Running concurrently, self-help programs and self-help housing quickly occupied a major position in the US Cold War theory of modernization. Together they created a case for voluntary engagement of the unemployed workforce in housing construction and promised the myth of affluence and private ownership in its impending future.

Self-help housing was not exclusively a UN or US invention; however, it was the United Nations that devised a generic version of self-help housing after the Second World War and associated it with the promise of an indefinite global development. Historically, self-help was hardly a homogenous concept and took different shapes depending on its interpretation by the state and the nature of the civil society. It is also noteworthy that the self-help method was not specifically mobilized in the developing nations but conceived for the less affluent in general—in the First and Third World alike. It was designed as an indefinite mechanism of integration, capable of mutation to suit different situations. For example, in postwar Germany, self-help was manipulated to facilitate housing reconstruction. Aided by the Marshall Plan's postwar reconstruction program, the Standing Committee of Self-Help organized German Self-Help Day in September 1950 with an intention to control the "uncontrolled and self-organized" workforce. Historian Hans Harms argued that through the self-help housing project, postwar capital restoration of Germany absorbed the vulnerability of popular insurgence. The US Marshall Plan, which aimed to rebalance the trade deficit between both sides of the Atlantic, and the US Point Four Program, which intended to close the finance gap in the Third World, continued to advocate the power of self-help to integrate the global poor into the global circulation of capital.

The United Nations' advocacy for development through self-help in the Third World was based on two fundamental hypotheses: First, self-help would be naturally and enthusiastically aided by Third World states and should be considered mainly as a state project. Second, in case Third World states failed to provide assistance to the self-help project, it should be able to bypass state authority and would appear as a self-mobilized project. From the point of view of development economists, Third World citizens are "naturally" capitalists or entrepreneurs, able to act individually in the context of almost absent or even failing states.[38] The question of home ownership thus achieved a new meaning in UN discourse that was intrinsically related to the solution of development.

In the colonial era, the main question of housing the poorer class pivoted around issues such as the nature of accommodation and standardization, appropriate construction techniques, rules of proxemics, legal responsibilities, and strategies of coordination among different stakeholders. In the postcolonial era with the involvement of the United Nations, concerns shifted to the political relationship between home ownership and the empowered individual and development. During the colonial era, the question of whether or not members of the poorer class would be considered potential homeowners was secondary. The poor were considered to be too rural and too rudimentary even to be tenants of government-built, low-cost housing, let alone home owners. Here we see a conflict between the postcolonial Indian government, which based its policy on the same colonial-era principles, and the United Nations' promotion of home ownership via financial aid and credit.

In 1950 the United Nations established a Housing and Town and Country Planning Section, headed by prominent CIAM member Ernest Weissmann. Shortly after it was founded, the section sent Jacob Crane and Otto Koenigsberger to the tropics to identify the status and causes of housing problems that crippled the newly emerging decolonized world. The report of this mission, "Low Cost Housing in South and South-East Asia:

Report of Mission of Experts," spelled out the root cause of poverty in human habitats as a managerial failure of capitalism and its workforce.[39] It also discovered housing problems at the intersection of an emerging global urbanization and the inefficiency of unskilled workers who were not part of the modernization process framed by industrial development. The report implied that the root cause of poverty lied in capitalism's internal crisis, which had gradually become a self-exclusionary process. According to the report, to fix this problem the existing system of housing finance needed to invent a new strategy for inclusion. The report was a watershed moment in US global strategy to adopt self-help as its official method to solve the housing problems of poor countries. In 1952 the Ideas and Methods Exchange series of the US Department of Housing and Urban Development presented a wide swath of self-help housing projects across the developing world, initiated in cooperation with USAID.[40]

The loan structure for self-help had two distinct parts, the visible money that came from foreign loan agencies and the invisible capital of unwaged labor from the self-helpers who invested their work hours or leisure hours to replace waged work hours. The structure was apparently straightforward: external resource funds were collected through grants and loans at reduced or concessional rates from USAID, the Inter-American Development Bank, and the World Bank. These organizations provided the loans or grants along with technical experts who safeguarded the money and trained the locals how to properly spend it; this process was known as the Technical Assistance Program. The United Nations mainly was responsible for the selection, management, and operation of the program.[41] The leading CIAM architects and planners took on their new role as UN expert consultants. They acted as a liaison between funding agencies and the underresourced private and government organizations of host countries.

The architects thus appeared in a new mediatory role, as technical experts and conveyors of information among moneylenders, policymakers, and consumers in developing countries. In this process of transference, complex knowledge of economic disparity and the culture of construction and architecture was flattened and reduced into relatively simple packages. As a result of the Technical Assistance Program, UN experts produced numerous mission reports, which produced a cartographic image of poverty and its spatial manifestations. Poverty thus attained a discursive status in the numerous UN reports, leaflets, and surveys. This discursive understanding of poverty was then relayed to the granting agencies, which engaged the next level of experts to build an array of model houses in developing countries. The First World's responsibilities were restricted to identifying problems and demonstrating model solutions. It was the host country's duty to carry on the cause.

When it came to lending seed capital to the poor to begin the construction of their self-help housing, public sources such as the government of India and the Reserve Bank of India were hesitant. Lending to individuals with limited collateral entailed considerable financial risk. What's more, the economic structures in developing countries like India, economists thought, would be made vulnerable to collapse if a large number of private loans were made to poor people without collateral. The public financiers were unwilling to lend money on a regular basis, but did grant loans for individual projects on a one-time basis. Thus, the external grant and loan agencies identified the need for continuous sources of private domestic financing, which could be supplemented where needed with limited government subsidies. The architectural experts interpreted this contingency to mean that foreign loan money should provide "model architecture"—models or prototypical buildings—with the help of foreign expert opinion. The primary function of such model homes was didactic. In financial terms, the external grant and loan agencies identified the need for continuous sources or private domestic financing, supplemented where needed with limited subsidies from governments. Private banking institutions were reluctant to lend at the income level and suggested that the meager savings of the potential beneficiaries of aided self-help housing be tapped.

In such contexts, the concept of domestic savings was crucial, and for the first time, the poor family was highlighted as a primary unit of capital production. The self-help program and the lending mechanism considered the family earnings as the fundamental unit of economic development. Successful continuation and expansion of the self-help model depended on a sustainable credit system in tandem with an individual family's domestic capital resources. Under the auspices of USAID and the Inter-American Development Bank, local governments would receive loans as "seed capital" to set up their own domestic loans and mortgage institutions to mobilize what Harold Robinson explained as a "new system of induced savings." Debt capital would then spill into society's lower stratum, which otherwise had no access to loans. To prevent major debtor defaults, several mechanisms were enacted. Among them, the single mortgage housing cooperative became popular, in which repayment would be policed by its members or by the cooperative credit union or saving institutions. By the end of the 1950s, the self-help program that had emerged in developing countries was considered inclusive because the program facilitated grassroots privatization and an expansive credit system.

Capital Credit and Architectural Aesthetes

Postcolonial South Asian architects often placed their hope in modernism's promise that an address or a dignified shelter could transform poor family into a self-dependent, dignified, and earning social class. Such hope that home ownership could bring economic prosperity at a national level and thus transform society had long been cherished by the immediate postindependence South Asian generation. The failure or success of that grand hope crafted by the self-help method as manifest in the 1954 exhibition is debatable, but in retrospect, it is possible to identify the ambiguity of the self-help program. The exhibition did not present a clear picture of the relationships between domestic income, domestic savings, human relations, and architecture. The ambiguity lay in unanswered questions about whether the process of owning a house through the self-help method could really facilitate income generation of the unemployed and low-income population or whether it was only meant to create a visible aura of progress and private ownership for families with scant income.

Architects used the new term "core-house" interchangeably with the concept of seed capital, which is the minimum capital that any lending agency will lend to users to grow their own capital through small business. Architect and planner Charles Abrams, chairman of the Urban Planning Program at Columbia University and a regular consultant to the United Nations and USAID, argued that in a development program it was necessary to understand architecture as a process rather than a ready-made product. He suggested that loans should be given only for constructing the "core" of the house—an undefined, abstract construct that indicated the bare minimum portion of a settlement considered to be sufficient for immediate occupation by the new owners.[42] The term "core" sometimes suggested a combination of roof and plinth, sometimes the vacant plot with infrastructure, and sometimes a complete single room, depending on the availability of local funds. Using the core as the base, the rest of the house should grow self-systematically. After the seeding of the core-house, the occupant family was responsible for its growth and expansion. The responsibility of architects and planners was limited mainly to the production of core. In the 1954 exhibition, the core-house was placed in the first portion of the housing section and was short-listed as the most convincing solution for varied regional situations. Built of *pucca* (burned) and *kucha* (sun-dried) bricks, the house was popularly known as the "Growing House" (fig. 2.19). Its cost was calculated at only 440 rupees (approximately eighty-eight dollars in 1954) and could be constructed by a two-person family with an annual income of around five hundred rupees.[43] The house

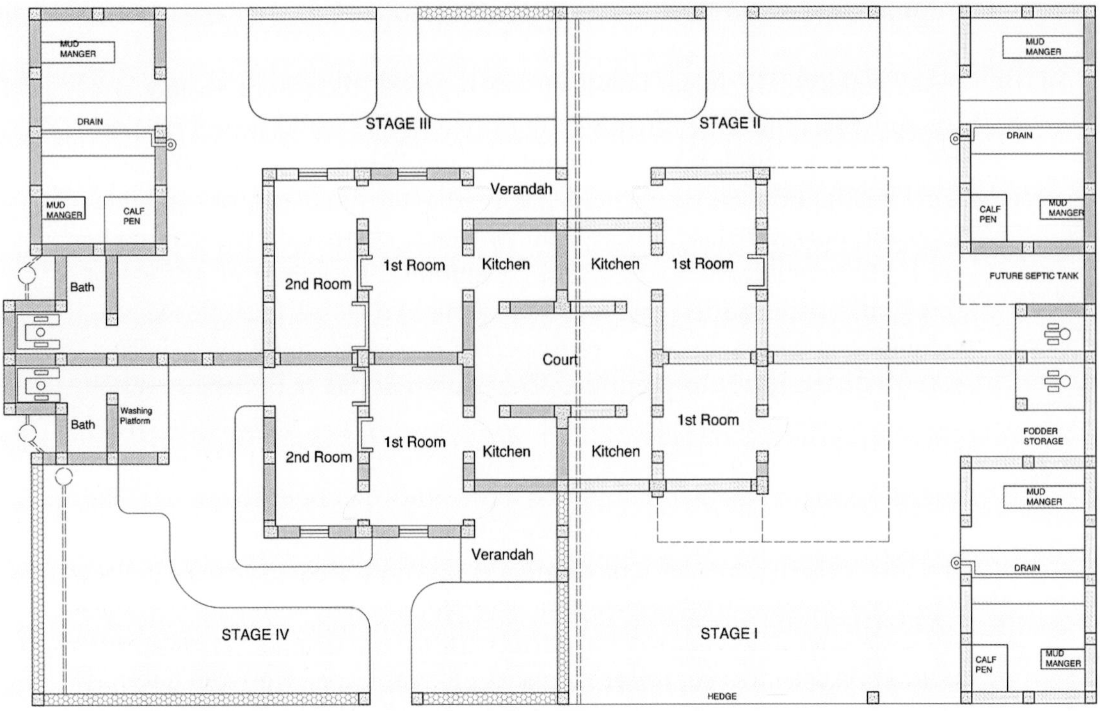

FIGURE 2.19. The Delhi "Growing House" exhibition. The first stage starts from a room, a kitchen, and a washroom, and eventually grows into two six-room units. Source: drawing by Suraiya Mymuna from a drawing published in Ministry of Works, Housing, and Supply Exhibition Souvenir (New Delhi, 1954), 105.

presented the subordination of product in preference for the process as the inevitable solution for housing in developing countries.

The core-house was the visual and managerial interpretation of the theory of development outlined by economist Sir Arthur Lewis, who explained poverty under the surplus labor model. This theory holds that the only impediment to development is the paucity of machinery, as the supply of labor is always abundant and in surplus in poor countries.[44] This theory became a classic example for ensuing development theories suggesting that new factors introduced into poor countries could be absorbed through surplus labor without affecting rural agricultural production. However, since poor countries could not afford the "rapid capital accumulation" required for building new factories, a financial gap arose. In this theory, the role of rich countries in global development is to fill this financial gap. This thesis is a direct heir of that in Russian-American economist Evsey Domar's 1946 article "Capital Expansion, Rate of Growth, and Employment"—known as the Harrod-Domar Model—and the proposition of Russian economist N. A. Kovalevsky that growth is proportional to investment.[45]

The financial gap approach drove the overall development theory of the 1950s and 1960s, in which foreign funding sought to fill the financing gap by lending and investing capital. According to this approach, foreign investment would add to the national gross domestic product to attract rapid domestic capital accumulation. Its moral imperative was to employ seed capital to breed a desire for development in the native population. Similar to the core-house theory, it was believed that the supplied money would stimulate the initial mobilization while long-term development would rely on a continuous and regular circulation of domestic capital and expansive domestic markets. The core-house succeeded in translating development rhetoric into architectural terms, in which it was assumed that there was an abundance of labor hours capable of expanding the core that was seeded by foreign money.

This new approach argued that the development process should be based on the local way of life instead of a lifestyle imposed by policymakers. However, following the social Darwinism approach to development, Cold War discourse considered underdevelopment to be an inevitable, if not necessary, stage in development.[46] It would probably not be wrong to assume that Cold War–era development theory is a descendent of the social theories of the Gilded Age and the Progressive Era, informed by Darwin's evolutionary thoughts. On the one hand, American social darwinism justifies structural inequality as the fundamental evolutionary force of civilization, similar to the struggle of existence for biological species and their urge to climb higher up the ladder. On the other hand, it also imagines the laissez-faire market economy as an organic space of ecology. Social darwinist political thinkers believed in directed human planning for the sake of political and economic development.

Acknowledging that indigenous social patterns are an inevitable stage toward development was a radical shift in attitude. Early modernization theory had considered the local context of developing countries as a recessive state, an impediment to overcome. But the technical suggestions of UN experts coherently favored working within the existing sociocultural pattern. They considered the indigenous context to be the consensual hosting body, to be used as a positive factor in establishing the new financial system. Funds from the First World were never adequate to meet the needs of developing countries. As a result, technical experts encouraged native populations to desire development, which would transform the indigenous society into a self-generating machine.[47] Loan agencies enthusiastically supported the focus on vernacular lifestyles and local aesthetics, since construction in local materials with local technology would keep building costs comparatively low. In summary, the agencies promoted the local over the universal and thus capitalized on the pride of local populations for three reasons: to keep within budget constraints, to use unskilled labor power effectively to mobilize the project, and to prove the First World's empathy for the regional identities of newly decolonized countries.

After the show in Delhi, the United Nations wanted to find ways to continue a global intervention in the housing problem of developing countries. With this vision, in November 1954 Ernest Weissmann called a joint meeting of various UN and non-UN organizations. Weissmann identified architecture and physical planning as not merely the conveyors of development benefits but as the precondition for development. This meeting included the UN Economic Commission for Latin America; the Pan-American Union in Washington, DC, for the housing, technical, and planning aspects represented by the UN Social Affairs Division (in the Housing and Town and Country Planning Section); Inter-American Housing and Planning Center in Bogotá, Colombia; and the UN Technical Assistance Administration.[48]

The 1954 exhibition model houses were examples of the United Nations' efforts to transform developing countries' resource scarcity into an advantage for economic development through systematic and institutionalized loans. Each of the projects in the exhibition had its own strategy and roots in various ideological stances, but the common motivation was to invent strategies to transform scarcity into the basic condition to attain affluence. Through myriad building techniques and strategies of self-help architecture, the United Nations prescribed a method that eschewed questions of politics and eventually transformed the problem of socioeconomic exclusion into a sequence of technological problems.

The 1954 exhibition is best understood as a multilayered dialogue among various midcentury experts and experiments. It pioneered new ways to limit the production of aesthetic modernism by imposing climatic factors, financial limitations, and resource scarcity over experiments with forms and aesthetics, a trend that would come of age in the following decades.[49] According to UN experts, the emergence of developing countries required a reformed version of modern architecture that would blend an urge for development, nationalism, and site specificity. In this regard, the Delhi exhibition's experiment with local conditions was as much an aspect of the identity discourse of developing countries as it was an investigation into understanding the capacity of modernization to make positive changes apart from the First World. The array of adaptive modern forms that dominated the Delhi exhibition reflected the spatial dimensions of India's expanding domestic market—a consumer culture that, by pushing away the Gandhian ascetic domesticity, promoted a transatlantic theory of modernization and development.

Many midcentury home exhibitions considered home an ideological battlefield of Cold War isms. But the main objective of the 1954 UN exhibition was to open up new discourses through which scarcity could be considered an inevitable ingredient of the modernism of developing countries. Although the United Nations conceived the exhibition as international (Nepal and Burma erected two houses), this was mostly an all-India show. The participants and visitors were, in fact, mostly Indian. Through the show, India subtly incited a radical social transformation of the belief in the capacity of house that would coalesce into a postindependence identity. The model homes postulated the spatial dimension of Indian identity built on the idealization and stylization of the life of idealized poor. For the Indian audience, the exhibition's novelty was the consideration of the domestic environment and family life as a culminating factor for social change, the notion of human embodiment in the social workforce. This reveals the moment when the swift global itinerary of Western experts traveling between the First and Third worlds contrived a way to present the world as a single network for the reception and production of ideas about global development, mainly through US aid and grants.

Earth Architecture

In order to satisfy foreign loan preferences for local building practice and indigenous aesthetics, Western consultants rediscovered a myriad of techniques to standardize native building practice and make local building materials mass-producible. Among them, rammed earth construction, or *pisé de terre,* caught the United Nations' attention. The technique was considered ancient and thus metaphorically linked to the ancestral home and cultural authenticity. However, since there was no official building code for stabilized rammed earth construction, the architects, construction industries, and finance organizations hardly considered including this building technique in the formal housing finance system. In addition, it was seen as incompatible with the spirit of technologically oriented modernism. Under the tutelage of the United Nations, the first large-scale earth housing effort began in 1953 when the United Nations' Department of Social Affairs engaged Australian architect George Middleton to build rammed earth houses for Israel's Ministry of Labour. This project gained substantial attention from other sections of the United Nations and development officials. Middleton included his rammed earth designs in Israel in the revised edition of *Construction with Earth* (1956)[50] and later developed a series of prototypical houses made with stabilized earth.[51]

Middleton's key argument was that the low-cost technology required for the rammed earth building was more efficient than the makeshift modern technology available in developing countries.[52] The project explored the reproducibility and streamlining of rammed earth construction techniques to create mass-producible prototypes that would not contradict the modern spirit of reproducible mass housing. Middleton focused mainly on a technical, comparative analysis of stabilized earth and concrete to prove his hypothesis that in poor countries earth is an even more effective material than concrete. He argued against the effectiveness of concrete because laborers of local construction industries were unskilled, and without adequate technical know-how of mixing, pouring, and casting concrete, concrete structures were ineffective and inferior. In the poor and developing world, Middleton argued, it was wise to upgrade existing vernacular techniques instead of investing money in modern techniques. His publication presented evidence of the low efficiency of poorly adapted modern technology in developing countries. He also justified use of the vernacular as the new means to achieve modernism via the alternative route of indigenous techniques, which Middleton argued were better than those offered at the global periphery by a pretentious pseudomodernism.

Middleton designed and built a stabilized earth-wall house for the 1954 Delhi exhibition (fig. 2.20). Middleton's project in this exhibition was a remarkable effort to combine the spirit of corporate financing and the self-help method with vernacular participation. Along with the replica of Gandhi's hut at Tyrwhitt's village center, Middleton's earth-wall house for the rural population attracted substantial public attention. For the audience, the rammed earth building designed and constructed by a trained Western architect was a harbinger of a new era that synthesizes modern technology with the Indian spirit of austere living. It became an example of the adoption of vernacular norms by foreign experts to forge a new kind of modernism of austerity. The appreciation of vernacular technology by UN experts was implicitly connected with the development theory's interest in vernacular social life. The new global order of a financial process, as envisioned by the United Nations and the United States, now included the bottom layer of economic classes and renewed interest in a vernacular aesthetic that had generally been considered regressive in the discourse of industrially oriented modern architecture.

FIGURE 2.20. George Middleton helping construction workers remove the mold he designed for rammed earth wall construction. Source: "Decent Housing at Low Cost: New Delhi's International Exhibition," *United Nations Bulletin* 16, no. 5 (1954): 187.

In his native Australia, Middleton's effort was to harmonize the problem of earth construction and private housing finance systems. Middleton sought approval for earth to be a standard, acceptable construction material for the housing finance organizations, an approach later seriously considered in the global context of UN housing finance. In the early 1950s, the Commonwealth Bank of Australia, the country's largest banking network for lending money for housing, was considering ways to broaden its customer base by including poor and aboriginal people living in rural areas. The formal financial sector rarely considered people who lived in far-flung rural areas as potential homebuyers. In order to include the distant rural population in a formal loan system, one major fact needed to be assured: that rural houses built with vernacular materials would satisfy the state's codes of practice and the risk factors set by insurance companies. Research done by the Commonwealth Scientific and Industrial Research Organisation's (CSIRO) Division of Building Research aimed to influence the Department of Local Government to advise councils that rammed earth was an acceptable form of construction, and Middleton became its earth building section's primary researcher. CSIRO eventually succeeded in convincing the trading banks to advance loans for earth-wall houses in rural areas, and insurance companies underwrote rammed earth as an acceptable risk. In the 1954 Delhi housing exhibition, Middleton demonstrated the construction method behind his rammed earth technique, which entailed several Indian government rammed earth projects, and the government eventually published his method as the most efficient earth-wall technique suitable for India.[53] Indian designers C. B. Patel, housing adviser to the Community Projects Administration, S. P. Raju of Hyderabad, and the Soil Research Institute at Karnal, Punjab, designed and built the exhibition's other rammed earth houses.

The United Nations' fascination with the rammed earth structure was not only for its seeming ingenuity; rather, it stemmed from the apparent "simple" technology's enormous potential to fight communism by providing housing at the lowest possible cost to the Third World poor. What would be more elementary, the United Nations thought, or more primitive, and easier than providing rammed earth houses to the homeless Third World?

India's Response to Developmentalist Architecture

Struggle for "development" was not new in India; colonial and nationalist powers had long fought to claim their respective authority over it.[54] The colonial notion of development was contested and challenged by nationalist power, and the nationalists' concept of development, nevertheless, was not without its internal detractors. Although the UN-US discourse of development may appear deterministic and monolithic in the official documents, the idea of development in colonial and postcolonial India was never a monolithic or unchangeable concept. As the name implies, development is an ever-incomplete process—an evolving idea that would be shaped and reshaped in future by unforeseen forces and thus would never come to an end. During colonial rule, development was considered the domain of state action and the role of individual agency was subdued. Development was also a field that defines the power relationship between the governed and the governor.

During the colonial period, the colonial and the nationalist forces had no disagreements about the attributes, methods and deliverable of development projects. Both parties also agreed that India needed development. However, the conflict between nationalist and colonial power was over the political goals. Nationalist forces argued that although colonial governance represented the technologically advanced West, colonial power would never create the right condition to incorporate the Western scientific method into national development. Nationalist power and independence was thought to be the only force that could create that right condition.

From this perspective, development was a product of a process marked by an asymmetrical power relationship between colonial governance and postcolonial nationalism.

Immediately after independence, India's development agenda oversaw rapid capital accumulation. Economic historian Vijay Seth has suggested that after 1947, Nehruvian development represents a unique socialist blend of nationalism, productivism, and universal developmentalism. Housing of industrial workers and the low-income population was also part of these state-initiated development projects. Similar to the other more pressing sectors of development, such as agriculture and industry, the problem of low-cost urban housing was also placed at the intersection of state and the structure of capital. It was generally conceived that low-cost housing in urban areas is primarily the responsibility of the government, a concept that originated in various colonial urban and housing development projects. Against this perspective, during the 1954 UN exhibition and conference that brought in self-help housing advocates, Indian administrators, planners, and designers who firmly believed in state-initiated development projects paused to rethink and reflect on their achievement so far. Self-help was a program in which the state would assist individuals and private agencies to initiate self-motivated development projects autonomously.

The self-help approach was not entirely unknown to India. Patrick Geddes proposed a self-help housing and urban development project in Indore that became widely known for its novelty but was never implemented, as it was thought to be too ambitious and acontextual for India.[55] It was not that self-help as a concept was unknown, but between the pre-independence nationalist and the postindependence government, no individual agency was deemed responsible or capable enough to take charge of development projects. In a rural context, as I will discuss in chapter 3, the decentralization of development projects of rural housing and community buildings came about without much thought. Perhaps the state was not confident enough that it would impact and control the development of the physical environment in its margin very effectively. The 1954 UN exhibition gave Indian planners, policymakers, and designers the opportunity to reinvestigate its housing programs.

In addition to the exhibition, the UN Economic Commission for Asia and the Far East planned a conference as a supporting event. The objective was to encourage development in this region by establishing a network of planners and policymakers from across Southeast Asia with the hope that solutions applicable to one country that might benefit another could be shared.[56] The conference was first slated for Singapore but later moved to India, which was

FIGURE 2.21. Sardar Swaran Singh, union minister for Works, Housing, and Supply, with Jacqueline Tyrwhitt (*second from right*) Guillaume Georges-Picot (*center*), assistant secretary general of the UN Department of Economic and Social Affairs, and others at the final meeting of the UN Seminar on Housing and Community Improvement at the International Low-Cost Housing Exhibition in New Delhi, February 17, 1954. Source: Photo Studio/February 1954, A05m/A22a(v). Photo Number: 37172. © Photo division, Government of India.

then considered one of the most important Cold War battlegrounds. India also had a rich precedence of low-cost housing and community development projects in the South and Southeast Asian regions that fell within the interest of the United Nations' housing policy in developing countries.

In 1953 the Indian government agreed to the United Nations' appointment of Tyrwhitt as project director of the show and technical adviser to the Ministry of Housing. Tyrwhitt was already a well-connected scholar, and after receiving her new appointments she rapidly expanded her network within the United Nations and visited its four specialized agencies: UNESCO, International Labour Organization, the World Health Organization, and Food and Agriculture Organization. Because of her deft administration capacity, she gathered more than 120 delegates to participate in the conference, including "experts" such as Rafael Pico, Ernest Weissmann, Jac Thijsse, Constantinos Doxiadis, Jacob Crane, and Charles Abrams, as well as delegates

FIGURE 2.22. Sardar Swaran Singh, union minister for Works, Housing, and Supply, addressing the final meeting of the UN Seminar on Housing and Community Improvement, February 17, 1954. Source: Photo Studio/February 1954, A05m/A22a(v). Photo Number: 37170. © Photo division, Government of India.

from Burma (now Myanmar), Ceylon (now Sri Lanka), Hong Kong, India, Indonesia, Laos, Pakistan, Singapore, Thailand, and Vietnam. The conference consisted of three main technical paper sessions: housing related to redevelopment, rural configuration, and planning implementation. Each session concluded with a discussion by invited delegates (figs. 2.21, 2.22).

A recurring theme in papers presented by the Indian delegates at the conference was frequent use of the word "redevelopment" instead of "development." The term also reflects the idea of "reconstruction," a term coined by Indian and US missionaries as early as 1926.[57] Implicit in this term was a conviction that India had already experienced several development phases during the British colonial period. Indian speakers unequivocally argued that the goal for Indian planners should be to pave new paths toward development, and they did not unquestionably subscribe to the view that development in their country had just begun. For example, in his paper "Housing in Relation to Redevelopment," S. V. Desai, assistant engineer of planning at Bombay Municipal Corporation, suggested that "the process of redevelopment in a city is spontaneous as there is a natural

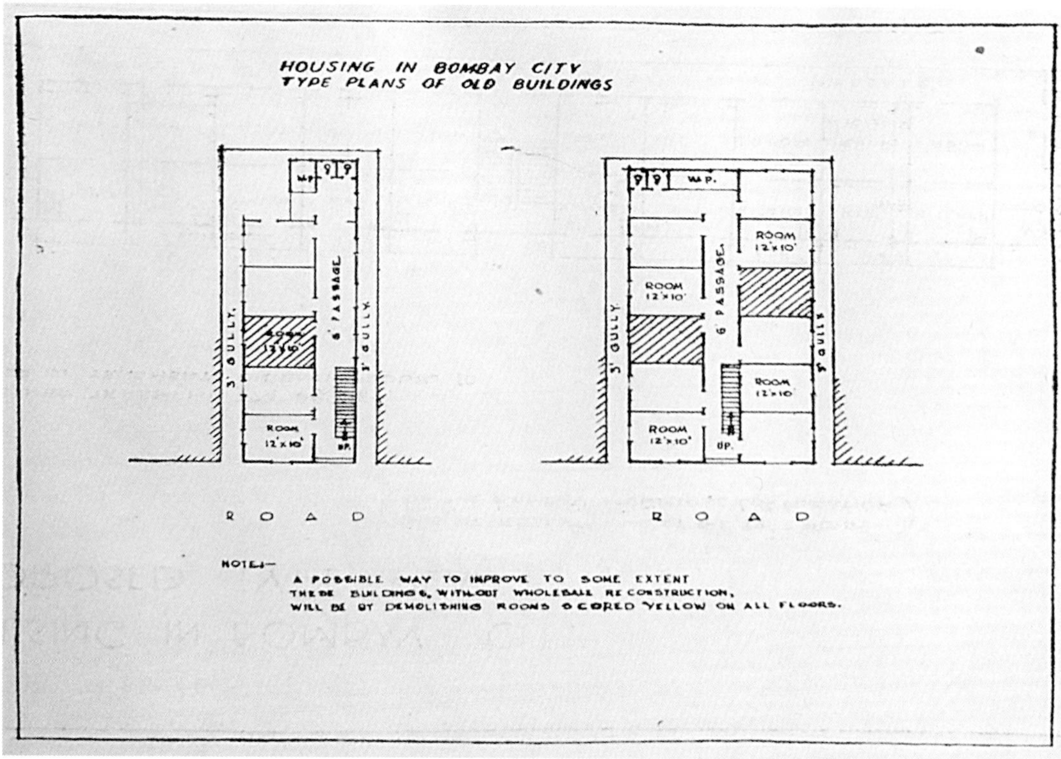

FIGURE 2.23. Prototype plan for housing for the urban poor by Bombay Improvement Trust before independence, as presented in Desai's paper "Housing in Relation to Redevelopment." Source: Proceedings of the South East Asia Regional Conference, New Delhi, February 1–7, 1954.

desire on the part of owners of land in the city to scrap, if possible, the obsolete existing development on their lands for replacing it by a better one on modern conception."[58]

Euro-American thinkers introduced "development" and "developing nations" strictly as a novel postwar event.[59] The Indian planners and policymakers, however, approached development as a continuous phenomenon that began long before UN intervention in the Cold War. In combination with the anticolonial movement, they viewed it as a continuous project vied for by colonials and nationalists but with its own life and autonomy. Perhaps this is why Indian planners in their papers for the 1954 conference took the colonial development policy as a point of departure to be expanded upon by adding new layers of the meaning to "redevelopment." The project of development as such was not a matter of intellectual scrutiny—at least not for the Indian speakers, as they believed the legitimacy and appropriateness of development ultimately depended on who executed it and how.

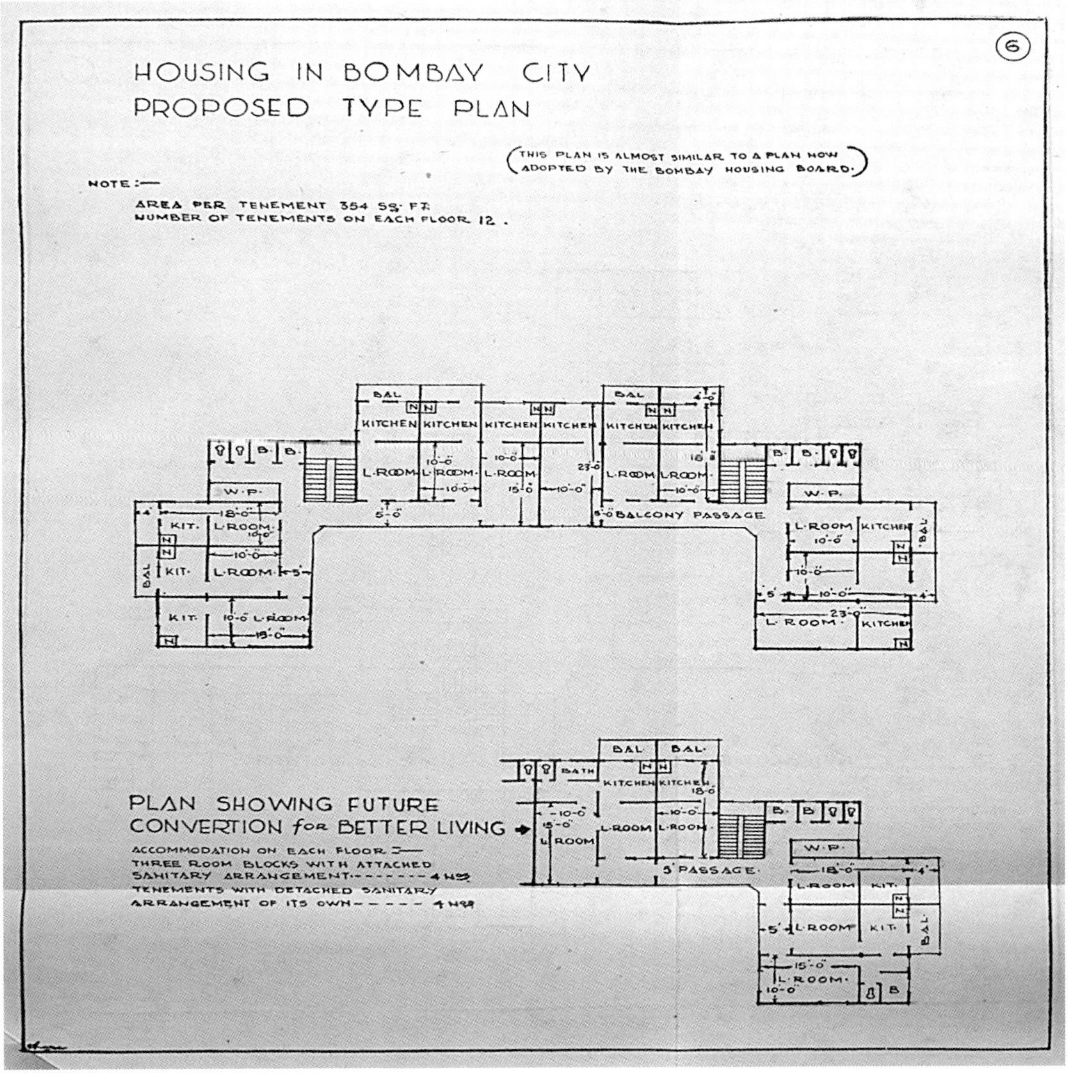

FIGURE 2.24. Desai presented this improved multistory apartment type plan developed by the Bombay Improvement Trust after independence. Source: Proceedings of the South East Asia Regional Conference, New Delhi, February 1–7, 1954.

Desai illustrated this point by showing how the Bombay City Improvement Trust was working to further develop prototypes from the colonial period.[60] The basic prototypes or type plans (fig. 2.23) designed by improvement trusts were only partially effective, he argued, because the trusts failed to understand the culture of industrial workers and as a result built spaces that were incompatible with Indian way of life. Desai then presented the improved version of colonial prototypes (fig. 2.24) that rearticulated the basic types to suit local climate and culture. The new configuration, developed by the improvement trust after independence, rearranged the basic prototype into a pinwheel configuration, or employed a push-pull concept, to eliminate central corridor space and add additional self-shade. Almost every paper from India repeated the same theme: current efforts were trying to improve from colonial mistakes.

In other words, development itself was streamlined in accordance with local cultural and climatic context. In his paper "Social Aspects of Housing Programmes," J. D. N. Versluys, a social science officer with UNESCO (New Delhi office), praised the Report of the Indian Industrial Commission (1917) for rightly pointing out the need for privacy as the bedrock of workers' housing.[61] Versluys also implied that the spatial layout should be a direct reflection of the social structure of the industrial workers' community, which may still have been deeply rooted in rural life. He also warned that urban designers may not be completely aware of the complex social ritual tied to the spaces of workers' housing. In this regard, Versluys argued that the suggestion in the 1917 report—to consider privacy in the design of workers' housing—required renewed attention in postindependence India. The report placed privacy at the center of "social aspects of housing."

Privacy in this context, however, superseded its primary function, which was to protect female members of the family who mostly stayed at home and to create a secluded enclave for married couples. Industrial workers viewed privacy as the only way to claim control over the space in which they resided. It was only through privacy that occupants with limited flexibility to alter their surroundings could arrange their house and rearticulate a dehumanized and objective space into a home. They looked upon privacy as the catalyst that would grant them a degree of power and enable them to control their spatial existence. Versluys cited Le Corbusier's design of the Swiss Student Hostel in the Cité Universitaire as an example of what not to do. In this case, he argued, Corbusier's "dictatorial interference" of designers in matters of personal taste almost fanatically tried to control every aspect of interior design and eventually attempted to control even the behavior of the occupants. However, Desai concluded, industrial workers of India must be given privacy and thus options to take responsibility and authority over the interior space. Other than this small niche of power concealed under the practice of privacy, Indian policymakers imagined no other places where occupants could exercise their autonomy.

The propositions and work of Indian planners and policymakers had little cohesion with the United Nations' idea of self-help housing. Most opposed the concept of autonomous industrial workers who would enjoy complete freedom and authority to build, though with partial aid from the state in the form of a monetary loan. The programs of low-cost workers' housing were still conceived mainly as the responsibility of the state and the industrialists. One probable reason may be the position of local experts. Deva Raj, executive officer of the Kanpur Development Board, strongly expressed his views during the 1954 conference that good housing possessed the power to transform a disorganized community into one with "clean efficient living and loyal citizenship."[62] At a time when the government was deeply concerned as to how to transform its subjects into citizens, the question of housing was treated as a strategy to legitimize people's access to the newly constructed domain of citizenship. In this process of social transformation—people into citizens—the government showed typical colonial curiosity about the potential future occupants of the houses.[63] Instead of engaging future occupants in the design and building process, policymakers and planners continued the colonial expedition of understanding working-class society as a sociological database. Government bureaucrats wanted to make sense of this database through social science devices such as surveys and quick expert observations. These techniques represented the working class as an abstract amalgamation of scientific data that, according to those who employed it, accurately portrayed the culture of the occupants.

The United Nations had neither direct control nor authority over how to impose its aided self-help policy in India at the central government level, even though it applied the same strategy in Puerto Rico in the early 1950s with relative ease. UN consultants also had major difficulties convincing Indians to ascribe to their way of thinking. Throughout the United States' and the United Nations' involvement in India's design and housing sector, consultants did not promote a stereotypical American way of life as the summit of development. Experts likely knew this would never work in India. Rather, "development" was presented as an abstract and indeterminate journey with a vague and unreachable destination—an endless trajectory, always incomplete.[64] The identity of Indian people, along with other Third World developing nations, started to crystallize in this discourse of development promoted by the UN: that being only exists in the form of becoming. This discourse was founded on the abstraction of development along with a gradual loss of government control over the actual production of space, but it did not appeal to Indian delegates at the 1954 conference, who often challenged UN views.

This conflict of ideologies unfolded in a debate between Charles Abrams and Indian planners, who argued about whether land speculation and land shortage were the prime impediments of developing an efficient housing program in India. Abrams contended that Indian administrators' land-centric thinking was an old and conservative way of looking at the problem of urbanization in the era of rapid transportation and network. Land could never be a problem for the world, he argued, since "it is estimated that the population of the world could be kept within a range, at the present density, of 75 miles of Paris—2.4 billions. Germany raised the cry of *lebensraum* and brought about a war for it. I calculated that the whole population of the world can be put within West Germany; we need not touch Russia—density 125 per acre."[65] For Abrams, land was not a problem but a new possibility, and various modes of transportation would strategically open up new habitable areas. Abrams concluded that unless Indians assimilated with the burgeoning world of intricate connection, they would not achieve real development. He also criticized the dependence of Indian planners on a so-called master plan that in his estimation impeded a comprehensive and nuanced understanding of the problem as a whole. Indian policymakers challenged Abrams's view; it was too abstract, they said, and not contextualized at all. They presented examples of India's unique sociocultural practices—its people's unique ties with ancestral land and the existing administrative structure from various parts of India. Ultimately, the United Nations' concept of development was not without scrutiny; it was challenged and investigated by those who stood to be impacted by it. While neither vision in its totality can be reduced to binary opposition, this confrontation emanated from two distinct worldviews. UN consultants operated in a networked and endlessly expandable global space, while Indian policymakers had a pragmatic, localized vision of the world in which everyday business was far more important than a larger global context.

The emergence of a global network of information and resources together with a global ecology and rapid environmental concerns, was strong enough to convince UN consultants to rely more on the value of a networked built environment. They conceived an uninterrupted global space of infinitely stretchable networks made possible through an uninterrupted flow of resources, capitals, and professionals in that space. This image of a continuous urban network at a global scale, extending beyond the geopolitical boundaries of the state and embraced by the totality of an all-encompassing ecology, was so strong in the minds of some design professionals that architectural historian Mark Wigley termed this new attitude the "network fever."[66]

UN consultants imagined that this all-encompassing network was powerful enough to include developing countries. The glaring question for developing nations, however, was how to define their position in this discourse of networked and global development. Prime Minister Nehru, while navigating the challenge to claim India's postcolonial existence in the global network, found its appropriate cultural expression in Buckminster Fuller's ecological theory of development. Fuller first met with Nehru in 1958, three years after the UN exhibition closed in Delhi. In the next few decades, Fuller maintained an enthusiastic relationship with India, Nehru, and Indira Gandhi. In his Nehru Memorial Lectures, he emphasized the postcolonial need to extend Gandhism, which could, he claimed, "feed" and "solve the problems of poverty." In his first meeting with Nehru, Fuller explained:

> I have a strategy which is other than political, and I know how extraordinarily well informed you are in the world of politics. And I explained that I had a policy where, instead of trying to solve problems by political reforms or laws, any reform of man, I was interested in reforming the environment, because the environment itself is continually reforming itself, and I said there are options and I can participate in it, and if I can bring about a favorable environment by virtue of producing artifacts I must never use words, I must actually find a tool that solves the problem makes what is going on obsolete.[67]

Fuller saw no problem in separating politics and political agency from development. Fuller's idea of development for India was indeed an ahistorical process that relied mainly on the existence of an all-powerful global network of a man-made built environment and the intertwined ecological domains of geography, animal, and plants. This sense of an undivided and continuous world was not completely absent from the model houses on display at the 1954 exhibition, but it was not the primary focus. For instance, Joseph Allen Stein through his two housing prototype designs identified his own version of development that was global in spirit but local in execution. In Stein's understanding, as Indian postcolonial society was divided into many layers of economic classes, social feuds, and religious sectors, no grand development theory could unify all of these contesting fragments. According to Stein, it was more desirable to form a strategy that considered every layer of society—contested forces and different stages—as parallel to the next. Stein's development sought to accommodate different economic stages of Indian society without collision or overlaps.

Through the 1954 exhibition, the United Nations promoted the newly devised mechanism of self-help housing development to forge a democratic balance of development economy. The Third World, which seemed to be set apart from this ideological battle, needed to be assimilated through the implementation of the self-help method. Most of the houses, with their unique aesthetic and construction techniques, were the result of a mutual self-help project between the First and Third Worlds. The interest of Tyrwhitt and other experts in this exhibition grew mainly from their personal beliefs that self-help could be the savior of the poverty-torn and disintegrated Third World.[68] However, the indigenous experience was different. "Working vernaculars" were the new paper-heroes of postcolonial Indian modernism. In light of the United Nations' self-help projects and active partnerships with First World global experts, Nehru's modernism should not be understood merely as a neo-imperial ploy to insert foreign policymakers back into its colony. Rather, the policy rationalized the existence of poverty, which was then folded into the dignified rhetoric of austerity as an inevitable step toward development.

Investigating Development

It is difficult to say what impact this 1954 exhibition had at the government policy level. But the Indian government did want a UN representative to review its research infrastructures and offer feedback on state-controlled projects currently in operation. After the exhibition, the government commissioned Greek architect and planner Constantinos Doxiadis—the most active housing and planning consultant for the United Nations and the Ford Foundation—to review India's current projects involving state-initiated low-cost housing and government-owned organizations that were researching housing issues. Doxiadis was also asked to prepare a report on disparate research cells and state-owned factories that produced prefabricated elements for low-cost housing. Doxiadis's consultancy firm, Doxiadis Associates, designed and built projects in major urban centers of the emerging Third World.[69] Doxiadis became acquainted with the UN and US interest in global development through his involvement in the Greek housing reformation program supported by the US Marshall Plan.[70] Later, he became a part of the Ford Foundation–sponsored Harvard Economic Advisory Group that contributed to Pakistan's Five-Year Plans, which is where he became acquainted with Indian subcontinent.[71] His inclusion in the specialized group of advisers on economic issues of a newly independent country was a watershed moment for USAID and the United Nations, as it acknowledged that development of housing and urban centers in the Third World was a central concern to fulfilling the United Nations' global development mission.

Doxiadis arrived in India on October 19, 1955. His main task was to offer his expertise on structural improvements that would create a more effective national housing program. Doxiadis's main subject of investigation was the National Building Organization (NBO), theoretically the center of all government activities. Doxiadis came only six months after the Bandung Conference in Indonesia (April 18 to 24, 1955), where India was one of the leading countries represented. The spirit and excitement of creating a cooperation among the newly decolonized and nonallied countries were still fresh among NBO officials. The NBO was considering creating a regional housing center in India—a concept coined during the Bandung conference to facilitate exchange of recent knowledge about housing innovation between the member countries. Doxiadis was informed by Shri N. P. Dube, undersecretary of the Ministry of Works, Housing, and Supply, Mr. Patel, housing consultant, and Sadaar Sarup Singh, director of the NBO, that the organization was exploring every means to set up a regional housing center, and the United Nations promised to appoint Massachusetts Institute of Technology (MIT) professor Boyd Radwin as its permanent adviser. Doxiadis, however, was not happy about this news, as he held firm to the belief that if the United Nations was to commission any consultant in India, it ought to be him. In addition, despite Singh's enthusiasm, the idea was no more than a hypothesis, as the NBO was not sure about the logistics required to establish and run the center.

Doxiadis met with Mr. Hay, a member of the UN Technical Cooperation Mission, who had a pessimistic view on every housing project recently undertaken by the Indian government. In Hay's mind, India was neither ready nor capable of hosting a regional center. The country, he argued, had no essential knowledge to share with other countries and was not in a position to offer in-depth and extended research on any topic related to housing. To him, the United Nations' 1954 conference was utterly pointless, and any such theoretical exercise would bring no benefit to India, since "people of India are not interested in housing. . . . [They are] much more interested in other fields of production." Hay suggested that the government was wrong to try to apply knowledge imported from a foreign context. He stressed training local experts through conferences that would emphasize how to contextualize and customize knowledge for India.[72]

Doxiadis did not fully agree with Hay's pessimistic views. Throughout his visit, Doxiadis also stressed the contextualization of knowledge. Like most other Western experts of his time working in India, he referred back to Gandhi to validate his intellectual and professional position. In a dinner with his foreign colleagues of development experts, Doxiadis explained his view of Gandhi's take on modern India:

> I am asked that if I understand why Gandhi has lived in this mud house and I say that it is my impression that he must have lived in mud houses not because he thought that all Indians should live there but because he thought that this was the starting point from which new Indian ways of living should be developed. . . . What happens today in India is the following: people in the urban areas try to build houses which they have seen abroad. Most of the people who are building them do not understand them and people who are living in them have never been used to them. . . . The right policy to follow would have been to start with a pattern known to the people and develop them gradually into forms corresponding to the modern way of living.[73]

Doxiadis also met with Shridhötra, secretary general of the Gandhi Memorial Trust, and Gandhi's associate, Polish architect Maurice Frydman (later named Swami Bharatananda), to learn about their experiment with modern rural housing. Doxiadis also met an anonymous disciple of Gandhi from the memorial trust, whom he described as "an impressive person but fanatic with her idea. . . . [She] called several of the personalities of India today . . . 'westerners' and 'non-Indians.'" Out of all the development experts in India, it seems that Doxiadis took pride in the appreciation and validation he received from such a "fanatic mind." Doxiadis also recalled her mentioning, "After all we have been confused by the west and it might be a good solution if the west is going to help us to find our own way."[74]

Doxiadis visited some of the housing estates designed by the Ministry of Works, Housing, and Supply and in his report criticized all of them for being insensitive toward the use of material, culture of the tenants, and comfort and climatic considerations (fig. 2.25). However, as historian Markus Daechsel has explained, Doxiadis's signature technique as an expert of the United Nations was to arrive at a conclusion about the culture and social use of space just by gazing briefly at the building.[75] For example, by carefully examining some representative specimens of a typical Indian house, he seemed to gain an insider's perspective on how an Indian housewife would prefer to design her home. Based on his observations and schematic surveys, Doxiadis concluded the core typological aspects of an Indian house. So when Singh was explaining the new building types developed by the NBO, Doxiadis was not at all convinced those designs would work because NBO was apparently against a core typology that only Doxiadis understood. As he wandered around various cities of India, guided or self-guided, he saw the same problem repeated everywhere: Indians did not understand their own behavior patterns, their climate, or their cultural association to space.

FIGURE 2.25. Courtyard of a government housing for peons. Photograph by Constantinos Doxiadis. Source: India vol. 5, file no. DOX-IA 10, 1956, p. 55 (Archive Files 24968), Constantinos A. Doxiadis Archives, Athens. © Constantinos and Emma Doxiadis Foundation, Athens.

Sometimes Doxiadis identified problems that the NBO did not take into account. They did not consider, for instance, how unbuilt spaces within and outside housing estates—public courtyards, parks, and squares—might improve residential neighborhoods and the overall well-being of urban life. "This is a question," he wrote, "which sooner or later, will have to be clarified, what is the types of squares, gardens that India needs." As a UN consultant, it was Doxiadis's moral imperative to bring these problems to the fore if they were not already a part of the collective consciousness. That the Third World poor lacked this consciousness was a determining factor in the United Nations' philosophy toward global development. According to Doxiadis and his colleagues in India, the people of India did not value development and thus did not cooperate with the government, especially when it came to matters of housing and personal lifestyle. Another fundamental problem in India, Patel informed Doxiadis, was people's unwillingness to repay the government-initiated housing loan.

Doxiadis's diary and draft reports on the Indian government's housing organization reveal how the NBO, CBRI, and most other government research institutes were preoccupied with finding a probable scientific solution to the production and delivery of housing units. The many publications released by various research units in the 1950s almost exclusively involved the development of building materials and construction techniques. Indian government research institutes also conducted a substantial amount of research to determine the optimum height and width of a room, mainly from the perspective of climatic comfort and material economy. Doxiadis noted in his reports that government research institutes gave little if any considerations to the social use of space. The central question raised in Doxiadis's report is why all of the government institutes took the same approach toward housing as mainly a problem of production and supply. We may add to Doxiadis's queries by asking why housing was conceived as a problem of scientific and economic technique in their research. And how does this general trend in government research relate to the concurrent discourse of development advanced by the United Nations and their allied consultants?

Indian governmental research endeavors' almost exclusive focus on numbers and techniques is best understood as an immediate if not a reflexive response to resource scarcity. Rapid industrialization was the dominant theme of postindependence development discussion. Since the 1930s Indian policymakers and planners had blamed the housing problem on the building industry's failure to proper industrialization. However, reframing housing as a problem of industrialization came with a complex set of questions. Indian policymakers and planners refined and developed their approach and argument into a single train of thought: maintaining a balance between production and supply of their end product—housing units. Government researchers held that the housing problem would have been easier to solve if only they had considered the industrialization of housing as a collection of well-synchronized industries that produced different building elements. Nehru's government wanted to establish as much authority over the initial development of housing industry as possible before it would move toward full privatization. And yet, since the Indian government wanted to achieve self-sufficiency in every sector related to the production of housing units—such as government-owned cement factories, steel factories, and so on—the scope of the task became enormous. It was also the government's intention to expand and develop other related industrial sectors through the industrial production of housing. Consequently, with housing at the crossroads of different industries, NBO's and CBRI's research activities gradually streamlined to fit the broader goal of an integrated industrialization. Doxiadis, a United Nations and Ford Foundation consultant, believed that the labor-intensive self-help was an essential step toward full industrialization. His emphasis on contextualization and low-cost technology has been informed by the enduring conflict between the United Nations' perception of the Third World and India's understanding of how the state should steer development projects.

Doxiadis's sojourn in India was distinct from his involvement in Pakistan or Iraq, where he was jointly commissioned by the United Nations and the local governments to fulfill specific missions. In both places, he had concrete projects to pursue. However, in India he was only invited, almost casually, to give experts comments from his perspective as a development consultant; the invitation did not come with any promise of future projects. Indian public administration was curious to learn about the outsiders' view of the state-initiated development plans. It seems that India, with its good number of research institutes, did not want to entirely change its development plan. Rather, Indian bureaucrats were curious to learn whether anything could done within the nation's existing capacity to expedite development activities. The NBO was established only a few months before Doxiadis arrived in India, and its administrative and legislative structure was still taking shape. The CBRI was perhaps the most active research institute at that time focused on the material investigation, and the Hindustan Housing Factory was producing various prefabricated elements. Doxiadis saw in India what he wanted to see: that India lacked an accountable centralized control over all of its different research institutes. Like any other UN expert consultant, Doxiadis had a theoretical predisposition about the problem. In addition, as a professional who persistently searched for new projects for his consultancy firm, Doxiadis approached any new problem with the intent to solve it by creating a new and concrete project his firm might pursue. In his report on India, he repeatedly stressed the fact that despite the existence of many competitive and operating research institutes, the net result was ineffective. Doxiadis advised an expert consultant's intervention to weave all of the moving parts together.

Indian low-cost housing program was ineffective, Doxiadis explained, because it lacked a central administrative body to coordinate and synchronize its disparate efforts. It did not have the specialized body of skilled experts needed to establish such a coordinated network—only an experienced consultancy firm could establish such a professional network and train the locals to sustain and advance the system once the supports from the expert consultants were removed. He substantiated his argument by arguing that local planners also saw the value of an administrative body. Without expert intervention, he said, individual research institutes failed to focus on the most urgent and relevant issues and could not always see the true nature of the problems at hand. Although at the time India had a number of well-developed research institutes, such as the Road Development Institute and the Forest Research Institute, Doxiadis explained that those institutes were not involved in architectural design or neighborhood planning. As a result, India's housing research institutes completely overlooked the fact that housing is an integral part of neighborhood units, and without a proper road system, any design efforts were destined to fail. As Doxiadis described in his notes, "There is no creation of community spirit at all. There is no interconnection of the different buildings. On the contrary they look as being thrown on a vast land with no order. There is no formation of social pyramid. No neighbourhoods, no communities."[76] The solution, he concluded, was in a central coordinating body that would link all the disparate parts of Indian government organizations together—an authority that would produce not only development per se but also new knowledge about development.

3

The Idea of an Ideal Village

From the shadow of the "romantic" ruin of the Old Delhi Fort on February 12, 1954, Jaqueline Tyrwhitt, key organizer of the United Nations' low-cost housing exhibition, had written an open letter to her extraordinary group of colleagues.[1] In that letter, Tyrwhitt described the "Ideal Indian Village" she had organized for the exhibition:

> An Indian "village" can be anything from 300 to 3000 people, almost all of whom live in the walled courtyard of small mud huts together with one or two cattle (cows, bullocks, or water buffalo), perhaps a few chickens, lots of children and a few elderly relations . . . the villages are the only "liveable" kind of places in India. In them there is a certain informal order—an accepted place for everything that goes to make up life. The Indian himself has not learned to live as a townsman: either he apes the foreigner or he tries to bring his village life into the towns (animals etc.) and the result is plain hugger.[2]

Tyrwhitt's portrayal of a rural India that is perpetually pastoral and that "apes" an urban life of western foreigners could conveniently be interpreted as one of many orientalist versions of a stereotyped and reductive conception of the other. Tyrwhitt's "apefication" of Indian villagers' behavior represents a nuanced situation in which the concept of the ideal village became politically attractive both in India and the West yet was embroiled in debates about the purity and perfection of pastoral life of the subalterns. However, Tyrwhitt's stylized and stereotyped rendition of multidimensional and complex Indian villages could not have gained traction without local endorsement. After independence, the portrayal of an ideal village in various government documents and trade advertisements

FIGURE 3.1. The president, Dr. Rajendra Prasad (*center front*), at the crafts shed at the International Low-Cost Housing Exhibition, New Delhi, from January to March 1954. Source: Photo Studio/January 1954, A05m/A22d(v). Photo Number: 37034 © Photo Division, Government of India.

was part of India's own struggle of conceiving new ways to modernize its vast rural areas and its inhabitants. During Tyrwhitt's time, the process of modernization of Indian villages was often associated with the problem of how not to disrupt the inherent austerity that designers and planners believed an "ideal" Indian village bore naturally. The portrayal, imagination, and representation of how an ideal Indian village would appear and work in the postcolonial condition is in itself a discursive formation.

The fictive Indian village that Tyrwhitt and her Indian colleagues erected beneath the shadow of Old Delhi's ruins was brought to life by an illusionary placement of Indian villagers at the heart of the Indian capital.[3] By performing daily life duties and domestic chores in fictive villages at the exhibition, they seemed to appropriate their place in Indian identity discourse (fig 3.1). The exhibit was divided into two sections—a residential zone and village center. The main spirit of the ideal village center mani-

FIGURE 3.2. The community hall at the village center. Source: United Nations News and Photo Media Division, no. 337732.

fested in its austere workability (fig 3.2). The residential zone comprised six experimental houses and two houses under construction to demonstrate the ease of techniques and the effectiveness of the self-help method from locally available materials and labor. Through the exhibition's rhetoric, the village center was transformed into a symbolic museum that stylized the lived experience of the Indian village with displayable artifacts.

The location of the exhibition site was strategic in indicating the complex entanglement of Indian history that provoked the audience to imagine the nuances of India's past and present. According to the UN general report, the selection of the site was catered to evoke an abstract sense of historical progress in Indian society: the exhibition "was laid out on a site about ¾ of a mile by ¼ mile deep. Along the Mathure road which links New Delhi with Old Delhi and lay just at the foot of the ancient fort of Purana Qila. Now in ruins. The ancient walls of Purana Qila now shelter one of the colonies of refugees from West Pakistan and beneath the mound on which it stones probably lies the earliest of all of the Delhi's, a city which may date back to the prehistoric era of Mohenjodaro."[4]

Sponsored by the Indian government, facilitated by the United Nations,[5] and codirected by Tyrwhitt, the village center most unlikely contextualized CIAM's urban core, an idea originated by European modernists to facilitate postwar development in Europe.[6] In a broadcast talk to England on January 19, 1954, Tyrwhitt said of the exhibition: "It is not only the first housing exhibition to be held in Asia—it is the first exhibition of its sort to be held in the world."[7] The uniqueness of the show, as recognized by the organizers, lies in the incommensurability between the CIAM's idea of functionalist modernism and the various prescriptions of modernization for the Third World by the UN's so-called experts and consultants. The village center in particular was not exclusively a prescription for India. Tyrwhitt approached it as an introspective moment for Western designers—a moment of self-reflection—to investigate the possibility of a new model for modernity incarnated in low-cost, nonaffluent housing in the developing world.

This show, a site of hope for the Western modernist and postcolonial Third World, was not without precedent, at least for Tyrwhitt and her CIAM colleagues. Architectural historian Ellen Shoshkes demonstrates how Tyrwhitt's India exhibition could be seen as a continuation of Tyrwhitt's three previous exhibitions for the Association for Planning and Regional Reconstruction in 1946, Modern Architectural Research Group, and the Festival of Britain in 1951. All of these efforts could be conceptually linked to the exhibition of Deutscher Werkbund in Stuttgart in 1927—one of the earliest twentieth-century shows to explore the possibility of post–world war reformation of European housing with the limited resources available at that time. The first policy document of the Werkbund exhibition stated in 1925 that "the economic circumstances of our time forbid any extravagance; they demanded that the greatest end be attained with the smallest means."[8] To strip the show of any form of abundance and reduce it to an absolute minimum was the main objective of the architects. In the wake of wartime economic construction, the immediate postwar European notion of dwelling, especially that formulated by the Werkbund and Bauhaus alumni, sought to formulate a low-consumption living pattern that would discard any notion of "false abundance." They aestheticized poverty as a form of redemption, promoting a minimal way of living furnished with ascetic objects. In postwar Germany, it was all about asceticism—a concept that was killed off by the West German economic miracle of the late 1950s.[9] The forgotten European tradition of ascetic modernity, which endured from the 1920s until the end of the 1940s, has been largely ignored in histories written in postwar times, given that those histories were written at a time of Western economic expansion and peak affluence. Walking this same line of ascetic tradition, Tyrwhitt tried to replace the trope of symbols from Indian society and culture that were vaguely associated with the idea of technological progress and modern development at a time when India was striving to form an independent, democratic, yet traditional identity with a new material culture.

Tyrwhitt personified the ideal village as a laborer with three distinct components: mind, hand, and body. To emphasize a symbiotic interdependence among the parts, she rendered the village as a living organism and made an anthropomorphic analogy in which the mind, hand, and body of the organic system work in harmony. Her analogy confronted the much-praised and prevailing view of modernism as a mechanical system à la *machine-à-habiter* (a machine to live in). This organic and anthropomorphic analogy transcribed and strengthened the colonial view of the organic village, but in a different context. The mind of the village center was the school building that would also be used as a meeting place for the Panchayati raj. The multiple uses of a single structure, according to Tyrwhitt, indicated the direct relation between the space for learning and the space of social responsibility. The main inspiration of the design came from her visit to Gandhi's ashram, where she witnessed students of various factions and caste backgrounds dining together and practicing spinning to cultivate national solidarity and harness a collective moral and physical discipline.[10] Similar to Gandhi, Tyrwhitt adopted the disciplined and selfless workers as the foundation of an ideal village society. Her school was centered on the practical lessons of horticulture and agriculture but also had a carpenter's bench and a small forge where boys could learn the elements of two basic trades in addition to their general education. With a smokeless chula instructors taught girls the principles of preparing a balanced diet for their families. The gendered separation and organization of work was not questioned but rather taken as organic and natural for an Indian village, where such separation, as seen by Tyrwhitt, was practiced for social benefits.

While the village center's mind processed the information to navigate action, the second section, the hand, transformed the action into a meaningful work that contributed to the overall social and economic development process. The hands indicate mainly the craft skills demonstrated by the village potters, blacksmiths, and carpenters, who produced elements for housing construction: pipes, chulas, cottage tiles, bolts, hooks, door latches, window frames, and doors. The emphasis on the production of building material by local craftsmen was driven, along with cost considerations, by the populist tenor that modern industrialization was destroying Indian culture and craft. This attitude has a long and complex history mediated by various nationalist politics and colonial trade interests. Tyrwhitt, nevertheless, eschewed those debates and justified her position by adopting Gandhi's idea of a self-contained village, quoting from Gandhi's popular remarks: "The revival of the village is possible only when it is no more exploited. Industrialisation on a mass scale will necessarily lead to passive or active exploitation of the villagers as the problems of occupation and marketing come in."[11]

The village center was conceived as a model of alternative development, independent of foreign and state aid, through an ingenious application of indigenous working methods. Free from any external intervention, this alternative mode of production encouraged development initiated only by local participants.[12] The third section of the village center was the body—a network of managing, disciplining, and caring for the corporeal existence and physical well-being of the village. It consisted of a small health clinic, a demonstration of a scientific latrine, and a plant operated solely by the village cooperative for generating methane gas from manure. On the exhibition grounds one could witness a village woman boiling water on two chulas with fuel from the plant and a room lit by a gas burner. Thus, in this section the circle of working villagers was complete and made a continuous loop of actions—starting with the mind, where the village girls learned to cook in a smokeless chula, and finishing with the body, where they cooked for members of the larger society.

A replica of Gandhi's hut, a stylized social space in which to practice individual and social liberty through ascetic rituals, appeared to be the most popular attraction of the village center. Gandhi's hut was not part of Tyrwhitt's initial scheme, as the exhibition focused more on new construction methods using vernacular material and adapting modern space to local demands. The center was originally intended more as a technical than an aesthetic or ideological exhibit. However, Indian organizers persuaded Tyrwhitt to include Gandhi's idea about village reconstruction as a centerpiece of the ideal village center, which sparked a subtle political row. Gandhian disciples Shrimati Mridula Sarabhai and S. N. Aggarwal, secretary of the Congress Party, were both exceedingly anxious upon learning that Gandhi's views on village improvement were not incorporated in the exhibition in any form.[13] Because Sarabhai was especially furious with the organizing committee, they sent Tyrwhitt to placate her rage, to no avail. In Tyrwhitt's words, "She practically blew my head off, because the Government of India had sent a foreigner to talk to her."[14] Finally, it was decided that Tyrwhitt would visit Wardha in December and return with a report on Gandhian ideas that could be incorporated into the exhibition. It seems that in order to avoid political acrimony, Tyrwhitt had already decided to build a replica of Gandhi's hut (fig. 3.3), which most of

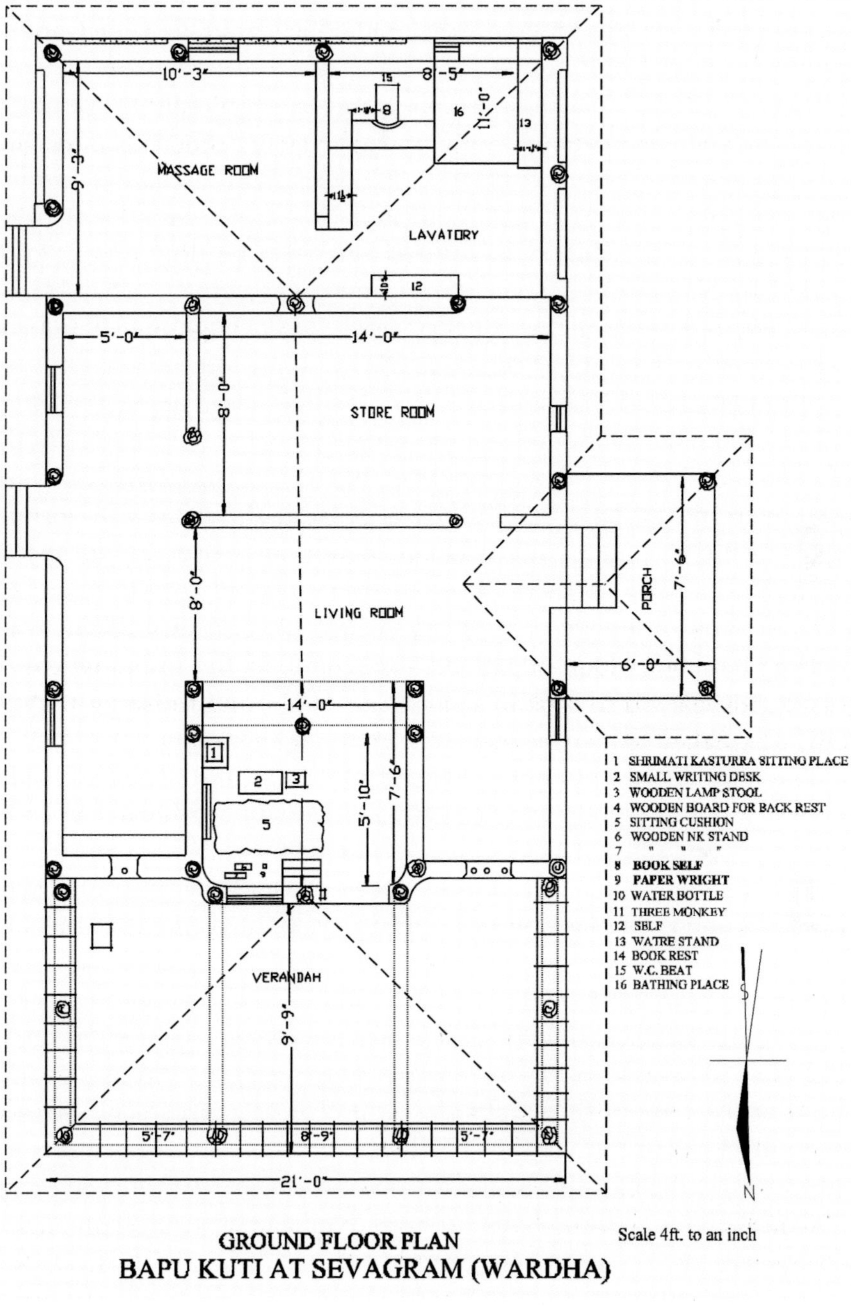

FIGURE 3.3. Plan of Gandhi's Hut (Bapu Kuti) at the Village Centre. Source: drawing by Bushra Nayeem from the plan published in *Ministry of Works, Housing, and Supply Exhibition Souvenir* (New Delhi, 1954), 41.

the designers and audiences eventually praised as the "most beautiful."[15] Shortly before December, Tyrwhitt set out for Sevagram to study Gandhi's original hut. Details of her journey, undertaken to understand pastoral India, appear in her open letter to colleagues: "We drove off to Wardha, to Sevagram where we slept on boards and sat on our haunches for hours on end, listening to endless recitals from various scriptures; eating cold porridge made from mixed cereals; contemplating in the chilly hour before the dawn amid the whirr of a hundred and fifty spinning wheels in the dim light of two hundred lanterns. . . . Gandhi was a great teacher—probably a saint. . . . His life in this 'ashram' was a sincere attempt to develop an ideal way of conducting the simple life."[16]

Although Tyrwhitt was moved by Gandhi's ideas about the Indian village, she could not appreciate the exaggeration of the ascetic life that was practiced in Gandhi's ashram. She probably considered its remaking to be instrumental only in fulfilling a political stipulation. By forming political difference and cultural uniqueness, Gandhi sought an alternative to the industrial society powered by individual consumption, and his promotion of ascetic domesticity—a hermit's life in a distant rural ashram—had major implications for the shaping of the Indian psyche in relation to postcolonial identity discourse.[17] Yet Gandhi's imagination of a new India had an equally unrealizable or utopian dimension that scholars variously identified as anarchic, conservative, and reactionary. Tyrwhitt felt that Gandhi's ashram and its practiced daily life was "phoney." In her mind, it encompassed "a natural way of life [that was] being turned into a formalised religion: inessentials have become exaggerated and codified."[18] Tyrwhitt's and many later village-based development projects extended Gandhi's concept by problematizing the utopian dimension of his ascetic domesticity. They attempted to give it a synthesized and seemingly negotiated form that would comply with India's midcentury aspirations within large-scale industrialization and a growth-oriented economy.

After the close of the exhibition, a number of government and nongovernment organizations showed their interest in erecting similar village centers in their localities with the objective of "creating a visible focus of integration for all the different phases of village life—economic, social, educational, etc."[19] The Indian government decided to erect a full-scale replica at the village of Mukhmailpur, approximately ten miles from Delhi, with a slight enlargement in view of the policy and emphasis relating to this new center. The Kasturaba Gandhi Memorial Trust has also reproduced a village center in connection with its training center for village women in Gujarat; and the National Cooperative Union of India requested to be allowed to continue the exhibition center as a model for their multipurpose cooperative village. The maharani of Jodhpur, Rajasthan, also wanted to build a model village center as a memorial to her late husband. It seems that through this exhibition Tyrwhitt was able to generate public interest in the concept of model villages.[20]

Tyrwhitt called for reconceptualizing the village center as a space of politics that would facilitate a smooth functioning of the village Panchayati raj—an autonomous village governance and judicial mechanism.[21] UN development thinkers together with the Indian government recognized Panchayati raj to be the primary political institution of rural democracy. The Indian government thus considered Panchayati raj as the first stage that would ultimately lead to a true democratic nation. Indian villages are in general driven by parapolitical systems whereby individual leadership emerges as a powerful agent among various local agencies that operate to maintain a balance between traditional and modern political mechanisms and authority.[22] In this context, a village center was not simply a pragmatic space to exhibit how a village could be redesigned more effectively; it was a sign of growing public interest in Panchayati raj. The United Nations' association with this endeavor increased its perceived global reach, a fact noted by Vice President Sarvepalli Radhakrishnan, who exclaimed during the opening ceremony of the exhibition: "The United Nations charter places before the peoples of the world the ideal of a democratic society."[23] The village center of the 1954 Delhi exhibition, and eventually its preservation as a permanent display, could be understood within the broader perspective of global politics.

The Roots of Tyrwhitt's Village Center

Tyrwhitt imagined the village center as a pragmatic and prototypical space that would instigate "development." She and her colleagues had little interest in how it would be reproduced in the real world. This raises the question of how Tyrwhitt's imagination of this pragmatic prototype can be contextualized within the nationalist discourse of the Indian village community. Although the idea of the village center was not completely absent in nationalist and colonial discourse, Tyrwhitt's had a larger and more complex genealogy, as it connected a number of diverse ideas, such as Gandhi's ashram, CIAM's core, Patrick Geddes's bioregionalism, and organic growth. The ideation of Tyrwhitt's village center also tells us about a unique historical moment when a significant number of Western architects, such as Team X, became skeptical and critical about the ongoing development trend in the United States and Europe that in their opinion overlooked human factors in design. These architects, designers, and planners were searching for an alternative model from the "East" via Geddes's idea of bioregionalism and to find inspiration and right direction for the West. In this regard, Tyrwhitt's village center was as much a pragmatic prototype for India's future as it was a form of the West's introspective self-criticism. The Indian village—despite its reputation as a site of extreme poverty, superstation, and regressive morality—eventually became an inspiration and lingua franca of the world's development thinkers.[24]

Tyrwhitt developed her initial conception of village centers by exchanging views with local and international experts. She spent a month at the UN headquarters planning the accompanied seminar of the Delhi exhibition, and then visited London and Geneva to meet consultants of different UN agencies. She also met with the International Federation for Housing and Town Planning (IFHTP) at The Hague. She then made a short trip back to India before jetting off to Paris to join the CIAM 9 meeting. On her way back, she stopped in Israel to meet Australian architect George Middleton, an expert of rammed earth building, and asked him to erect such a structure in the village center.

Tyrwhitt's idea of city and urban design was informed by diverse sources, but she regularly revisited the ideas of Geddes, who was likely her single most important inspiration.[25] Tyrwhitt claimed to be "an ardent disciple of Patrick Geddes" when she was working as the director of the Association for Planning and Regional Reconstruction. Its founding director, physicist and structural engineer Eric Anthony Ambrose Rowse,[26] had left to serve in the war and relied on Tyrwhitt to train a large number of planners for postwar reconstruction.[27] During this time, Tyrwhitt played the central role in disseminating and popularizing Geddes's ideas on a global scale by editing and reproducing his work. Geddes's ideas substantially influenced not only Tyrwhitt but also, through her efforts, the contemporary generation of architects and designers who formed the alternative strain of the CIAM's functionalist credo of modern architecture and urban design.

Tyrwhitt edited Geddes's various reports on India, then published them as a book titled *Patrick Geddes in India* in January 1947, the same year India gained independence from British rule. The book thus appeared as a guide for the built environment of the new postwar, postcolonial global order of humanism. *Patrick Geddes in India* soon captivated the enthusiasm of both Western consultants and Indian sociologists and planners and was often considered a guiding template for future development in India and abroad. Through the book, Tyrwhitt intrigued experts and renewed their enthusiasm in Geddes's work, which was significant in two ways. First,

Geddes's works and studies were done in the colony—a place many modernists believed was located outside the space of modernity and hence a pristine place in which the contamination of modernism is easily and readily visible and examinable. Second, Western scholars still largely considered Indian society as the preserver of the values of community that exhibits anthropological variations of nonmodern rituals and mysticism. As a result, India was thought to be the appropriate place to undertake delicate experiments connecting rational modernism and spiritual metaphysics. Tyrwhitt's focus on Geddes's numerous reports on India was not exclusively for Indian development; her goal was to provide guiding principles for universal application. More specifically, she intended to explore the possibility of making Geddes's bioregionalism a universally accepted ideology. It was a self-educative journey for Western observers to learn how to preserve the spirit of modernism without impairing the inner spirituality of Western civilization, which was believed to be weakened by "modernist" and "functionalist" aggression.

Tyrwhitt's reading and extrapolation of Geddes provided a framework for her design and planning philosophy. In "the diagnostic survey" section of the book *Patrick Geddes in India,* Tyrwhitt explains both her own and Geddes's view on the relationship between man and environment. She also mentioned Rabindranath Tagore, the first non-European Nobel Prize winner in literature, writing: "Tagore's criticism at the opening of his 'Sadhana' that Man and Nature in the west have come to be viewed apart is indeed answerable."[28] Tagore was a Bengali poet, musician, painter; a zamindar, or land-owner nobles; and an educator and founder of a leading liberal university in India, Sriniketan. Tagore, a monumental cultural figure representing the high culture of the colonized nations, is often criticized for his ambiguous political: being naïve to the political situation of his time, being sympathized with the morale of the colonial western liberalism, and propagating an exclusive elitist view of urban Hindu middle class. Tyrwhitt and Geddes were strongly inspired by his philosophy, and their connection to Tagore deserves some explanation.[29]

Tyrwhitt's intellectual connection to Tagore was established through her two-year stay at Dartington Hall—an establishment by British agronomist Leonard Knight Elmhirst and his famous American philanthropist wife, Dorothy Payne Whitney—to combine arts and crafts, farming and forestry. Dartington Hall was inspired by Rabindranath's Sriniketan and devised as an experimental learning place in which Elmhirst served as a founding teacher of the Department of Rural Reconstruction. He also believed that agricultural reformation would not only eliminate poverty at the personal level of the farmers but change the society as a whole through its spiritual sway. The idea came from the American farmer missionary Sam Higginbottom whom Elmhirst met in India during the First World War, when he was working as a secretary for Lionel Curtis, who was working on the Montagu-Chelmsford reforms for the Indian constitution.

Elmhirst's second important connection with India began by Rabindranath's invitation to his newly formed international university, Visva Bharati, at Santiniketan in the province of Bengal to establish and develop the Department of Rural Reconstruction and train students to carry out research on various rural issues. This department opened in February 1922, and by 1924 Elmhirst turned over the responsibility to an all-Indian staff. However, on his return to England in 1925, Leonard and his wife, Dorothy, bought the neglected fourteenth-century Dartington Estate and founded the Dartington Hall Trust to advance what became known as their Dartington Experiment, synthesizing human creativity with environment and industry. We can safely assume that Tyrwhitt was first exposed to Geddes's ideas in her two-year stay at Dartington, and it's safe to speculate that she was well acquainted with Rabindranath's vision on the environment's power to stimulate human creativity and surpass the mechanism of state-centric politics.

The second major inspiration of the village center came from the CIAM. At the IFHTP's first regional conference for Southeast Asia, the next big conference following Delhi's UN exhibition and seminar, Tyrwhitt explained her design as "based on the CIAM 'core' . . . an open space enclosed by community buildings."[30] It showed her commitment to the CIAM's postwar experiments of "core," a physical and notional meeting point of the community, both in rural and urban areas, that was meant to draw people together in public space. Core was the central theme of the CIAM's eighth conference in 1951 at the Bridgewater Arts Centre in London, organized by the British Modern Architecture Research Group, of which Tyrwhitt was a significant member. The central theme of the CIAM 8 was to reassess the functional myth of modernism and to review the CIAM's so-called fifth function, the core. Conference attendees discussed how to design new cores and reviewed older urban cores and explored the core's capacity to consolidate community by attracting people toward a spatial center. The conference promoted the idea of a postwar democratic community.[31] CIAM's eighth conference summarized the core as follows: "It is the expression of general factors of human nature and organic life" that harnessed "the possibility of new encounters and . . . a recovery of civic consciousness."[32] The CIAM's postwar meetings were increasingly focused on looking beyond the four functional aspects of the modern city first devised in CIAM's fourth conference in 1933, which later became famous as Le Corbusier's Athens Charter in 1943. The ninth conference of CIAM at Aix-en-Provence in 1953 was a point of departure; the younger architects openly confronted the fundamentals of the CIAM's authoritative older generation.[33]

In response to the dissenting younger generation, the CIAM radically turned away from the grand hope of functionalism and began exploring the built environment's capacity to produce intangible qualities like a sense of camaraderie, cultural identity, and the self. In CIAM's eighth conference, Siegfried Giedion surveyed the core's historical development as an essential and integral part of human settlement. This offered the necessary context for various aspects of the core as used by Tyrwhitt, Philip Johnson, Le Corbusier, J. L. Sert, E. N. Rogers, and J. M. Richards. Sert and Tyrwhitt edited this collective effort and published it in 1952 as *The Heart of the City: Towards the Humanisation of Urban Life*. In the book, Tyrwhitt's essay "Core within the Urban Constellation" expanded the CIAM's cumulative effort to incorporate the expressive dimensions of people within the urban environment. Tyrwhitt emphasized integrating the everyday experience of common people instead of heightening the dignity of an urban civic core. At the meeting, Tyrwhitt chaired a session titled "The Background of the Core," in which the social implication of the core was discussed, and by *social*, she meant the everyday experience of the middle- and lower-income population.[34] In Tyrwhitt's remarks, she argued that the city core's basic function was to support the "urban constellation." This new term, introduced by Tyrwhitt, described a state of the urban environment that intensified the human habitat and promoted human expression and subjective emotion that in turn generates a sense of community. It was her methodological strategy that confronted the idea of decentralization and of the garden city development and instead created new "innovative places" for people.

Tyrwhitt's idea of an urban constellation was crystallized in her visit to Hungarian-born artist and theorist György Kepes's 1950 exhibition *The New Landscape* at MIT. The exhibition showed a collection of scientific images of biological and physical matter, revealing the inner structure of matter and life through what were then cutting-edge visualization techniques: X-rays, stroboscopic photography, sonar, radar, and infrared sensors. What intrigued Tyrwhitt about the exhibition is that all of Kepes's photographs demonstrated that all organic life and inorganic material, irrespective of nature and scale, maintained one universal principle: a strong integrity toward a specific core in a way that visually and organizationally forged a point of attraction within its structure. Tyrwhitt extended this idea of a constellation to human settlement and suggested that it would solve the amorphism of alienated modern society. In designing the village center in India, Tyrwhitt pulled together all her various experiences related to the formation of the core and devised new ways to apply them in developing countries.

Geddesian philosophy, however, remains the most important inspiration for Tyrwhitt; it suggested that dispersed settlement, having no hierarchy of centers and subcenters, was symptomatic of land-based imperialism. Intricate spatial networks, however—based on well-ordered systems of centers and subcenters—were thought to open up a new physical environment suitable for an international colonial economic system. What made Geddes's theory so convincing to Tyrwhitt and her CIAM colleagues was that his philosophy was substantiated by natural sciences and natural laws. Geddes argued that the conventional understanding of separated and segmented human settlement was limited, as it did not comply with the natural laws of evolution and thus excluded "humanism."[35] Geddes's humanism was generated from his biological research on natural evolution, which holds that humanism relates to a situation in which humanity is allowed and encouraged to move up to the next level of natural evolution. Since the publication of Darwin's *On the Origin of Species* in 1859, the views of natural scientists toward the formation and history of life have radically shifted. The collective existence of a species and its variations is now defined by characteristics that survived through time because of continuous adaptations and evolution to live in a specific environment. Natural scientists have since placed more emphasis on the environmental setting of a species, in which the quintessential characteristics of the species respond and develop. According to the evolutionary point of view, environmental knowledge was indispensable to acquiring knowledge of a species. It is from this stance that the idea of a "biological region" emerged in Geddes's discourse. Geddes elaborated his biological theory to relate to efforts to design built environments according to the process of natural evolution.

The idea of bioregionalism was gradually expanded to connect a number of other abstract ideas, such as humanism and political emancipation. An important example comes from Julian Huxley, the British evolutionary biologist and first director of UNESCO, who declared that evolutionary human civilization should find its coveted emancipation in a harmonized relation between man and environment. This extended the idea of bioregionalism to, in Huxley's words, "evolutionary humanism," which set the philosophical stance of the United Nations' cultural wing. Thus, the postwar humanism of the United Nations and its allies was structured on the concept of the interdependence of people and place—an extended and adapted utopia of Victorian ecology that was holistic but evolutionary.

The book *Patrick Geddes in India* was a sign of Tyrwhitt's optimism in a postfascist democratic world in which the concept of ecology would integrate environment, people, and political institutions into one overarching structure. In relating evolutionary ecology with human settlement, Geddes argued that Western civilization's bias toward the ancient Greek model of the city-state eventually caused uncontrolled urban development.[36] Geddes contended elsewhere that the extreme consequence of such a tendency was the "German dream of a predominant World State."[37] Drawing on the laws of scientific evolution, he argued that any settlement needs to be of an optimum size. While a state's political aspirations meant that it strived to maximize its territory, ecological law tends to reduce it—that is, to minimize it. A balance of this dual if not opposing force determines the sustainability of any settlement and secures the development of political institutions that would result in better human evolution. Instead of striving for an ideal pattern of living, we may consider Geddes's evolutionary theory as a eugenic project of natural selection that was devised to improve the human condition through the built environment. Geddes hints to an all-encompassing grand theory of humanism to control state politics by engaging in a scientific and natural law of ecology.

Tyrwhitt's and Geddes's ideas could be understood as a methodological investigation of how to fit democratic polity in the grass roots of developing nations. Tyrwhitt's ideal village center as presented in the exhibition could be understood as a discourse that aimed not at finding the essence of Indian villages but at a system to conflate Indian villages with the democratic polity. Tyrwhitt's efforts in India were framed by a specific moment in the Cold War when the United Nations appeared to be a leading voice of eliminating global poverty. Mediated by the moral and technical support of the United Nations, the United States started pouring money into the newly decolonized world through various reformation and development projects. This concerted effort appeared to be a charm offensive aimed at distracting the Third World poor—an economic synonym for postcolonial vernacular subjects—from socialist propaganda. The rhetoric of vernacularism embedded in the ideas of Tyrwhitt, Geddes, and others in their cohort anointed the average village life with a new cultural status, viewing it as an intellectual idea with the power to mediate global development. Their rendition was not opposed to the ways in which Indians were rediscovering their own villages, present and future. The village in the educated urban Indian psyche appeared as a catalyst that provoked a dialectical journey of the Indian self from spirit to logic, underdevelopment to development. Both Tyrwhitt and Geddes acknowledged that it was not the pastoral life of the village that was important for postcolonial India per se, but the possibility of its rearticulation to inflict a social revolution.

Tyrwhitt's adaptation of the CIAM core to an Indian village revealed fundamental differences. The prevalent political dimension of the CIAM core, devising human liberty in a postwar European society, was transposed into a spiritual and cultural project in India. Although Panchayati raj was an essential component of Tyrwhitt's village center, its discussion remained marginal. From the Indian perspective, the village center was of course a political project related to the rural reformation of Panchayati raj, but from Tyrwhitt's perspective it was basically a spiritual quest. The dominant perspective shifted radically from perceived uninterrupted communication between individuals and the freedom of society, as evident in CIAM's various definitions of *core*, to the Gandhian spiritualization of the working body and the integration of everyday work into the very nucleus of the core. Tyrwhitt's initial conviction to transpose a westernized CIAM core to India stemmed from her belief in the power of the core to socially transform any society. She wrote: "The reason for my special interest in the village area is . . . [because] I am a town planner who is convinced that town-planning starts with the re-development of the cores of the Community rather than by concentrating all efforts upon its outer fringes."[38]

Tyrwhitt's ambiguous relationship with the CIAM is represented in the exhibit of the CIAM projects that she curated and intentionally placed close to the village center. Tyrwhitt was adamant about bringing exhibition panels of CIAM projects to Indian audiences so that they could see what a desirable development would look like. The CIAM projects arrived in the United States and Europe after much difficulty, and Tyrwhitt gave them a "significant place" at the exhibition. After considerable delays, she was able to bring a selection of CIAM projects that she saw as "most applicable to India and the South East Asian conditions." The CIAM materials were collected from its 1953 meeting in Aix-en-Provence, France, and brought to India. They included exhibits from the Dutch avant-garde magazine *de 8 en OPBOUW*; modernist architectural and urban projects in Morocco, Algiers, Holland, Sweden, Paris, England, the United States, and Italy; and Israeli architect Joseph Neufeld's idea of a community core. To counter CIAM's functionalist credo, Tyrwhitt also screened four documentary films—*Good Neighbours*, *How to Look at a Village*, *How to Look at a Town*, and *Road to Kelsht*.[39] Tyrwhitt would not uncritically subscribe to the CIAM's conceptual emphasis on static architecture and the built environment on the basis of four main components: living, working, development of mind, and body and circulation. Tyrwhitt continued to argue that principles of town planning should follow Geddesian philosophy, which viewed the city as a continuous process.

However, the physical materialization of the Indian village center did not fully align with the CIAM's definition; it sought a new kind of adaptive constellation that had its roots in Patrick Geddes's idea of ecological humanism and bioregionalism. For Tyrwhitt, CIAM core had a larger and more complex form, as she wrote: core is "signs of the humanizing process of our time[.] The natural condition exists for the organic synthesis of modern technology and the plastic arts as instruments and expression of society."[40] Perhaps Tyrwhitt wanted to capture the organic and expressive attributes of the core through live demonstration of everyday village life in the village center. The actors, who were real villagers performing their daily chores in real time at school and medical and craft centers, presented an embodied value of the work as the epitome of social transformation. Tyrwhitt wrote to N. P. Dube, deputy secretary of the Ministry of Works, Housing, and Supply, instructing that "as far as possible this village centre should be made to come alive. That is, there should be real children in the school, a nurse should be attendance at the health centre, and people should be working in the craft workshops. The impression should be given that this is the focus of active and friendly village life—simple but not drab, down to earth but full of vitality."[41] This was quite a unique situation, because this show was neither explicitly about displaying an exotic lifestyle of Indian villagers to foreign colonizers, as in many nineteenth-century colonial exhibitions, nor was it explicitly an ideological battlefield of the isms, as in midcentury Cold War exhibitions in Germany and the USSR. However, the show was a little of both—the performer of village life and the beholders were, in fact, mostly Indians, but the onlookers, despite their Indian origin, were still outsiders. The show may have appeared to the Indians as a subtle recalling of an ideal past and a reminder of the power of their villages spawning a radical social transformation and postcolonial identity.

From Colonial Typecast to Postcolonial Urban-Village Nexus

Under British rule, the village was understood through census-based studies—gazettes, district handbooks, and regional surveys—the prime goal of which was administrative and to collect revenue. This understanding was enhanced further by bureaucratic and extracultural curiosity that sought to understand the governed population, in which the Indian village was considered external to the natural process of civilization. In 1810 Sir Charles Metcalfe, the imperial sociologist, described villages as "self contained little republics," and Sir Thomas Munro also described them as "mini republics."[42] The 1812 House Commission Report gave typical representations of villages as disconnected, self-sufficient, and introverted spaces characterized by immutable economic and social reality.[43] The colonial Rural Agrarian Reformation triggered the development of new survey techniques that focused more on micro-level issues such as ethnic composition and grassroots-level economic issues. Among these, the 1901 ethnographic survey of India was the pioneering study, followed by major village-based surveys carried out by Gilbert Slater in 1916 and H. H. Mann in 1917 and 1921.[44]

Anthropologist Bernard Cohn explained that the cumulative effect of colonial surveys and quantification efforts conceptualized an image of the Indian village that was devoid of its everyday experience and rendered an "archetypal peasant community."[45] The dominant imperial perception of a village was driven by the idea of self-sufficiency and caste hierarchy. This method eschewed the existing economic and political power structure to prove that the village was an amalgamation of immutable and least-perishable institutions. The prevailing self-sufficiency myth, that villages were produced and consumed locally without any external interference, considered the village to be the perpetual retainer of pristine culture and hence a site that was ahistorical, acultural, and acivilizational. Similarly, Baden Henry Baden-Powell's 1899 study typified Indian villages by dividing the diverse village culture into two sections: those having Aryan roots and those having Dravidian roots.[46] The main limitation of the parochial perspectives of the imperial authority was the failure to recognize villagers as active agents of social change or their capacity to affect the economic and political power structure.[47] A further limitation was that the colonial studies did not acknowledge the inherent diversity and differences of villages; rather, they sought commonness among economic, political, social, and cultural structures. The schism between the lived experience of villages and the extrapolation of that experience into a discursive form transformed the village as an idea into a specific and stagnant state of human existence.

The colonial authority conceived of India exclusively as a nation made up of autonomous village republics. Historian Ronald Inden has observed that although many other countries in the East had agrarian and village-based economies, only India was exclusively stereotyped into a territory of villages and attributed fictional qualities such as perpetuity, autonomy, and self-contained tradition.[48] The numerous social surveys and reports conducted under colonial city improvement trusts and regional development authorities across the country highlight that India did not have a pedigree to any sophisticated urban culture, and thus did not preserve a natural right to be urbanized in the Western sense.[49] In these reports and in concurrent academic discourse, India was represented as a federation of village states in which villages were portrayed as the fundamental units of a large, ambiguous, organic, and decentralized system of governance.

Colonial surveys repeatedly argued that the absence of any centralized urban governance and public culture made it impossible for Indians to establish any effective democratic institutions. The essential colonial portrayal of India as an agrarian village-based nation was strategical, as explained by Bernard S. Cohn, because it implies that the rulers of India, such as the Mughals before the British, were always outsiders, and that Indian villages were never self-governed. Cohn shows that the portrayal of a rural India consisting of ahistorical villages was intended to legitimize outside rulers—India was destined, so the colonial arguments suggest, to be subjugated, and colonization of this land occurred naturally, with British domination only the most recent addition and therefore an acceptable continuation.[50] Representation of India as a federation of decentralized villages was indeed a mechanism to deploy and sustain moral justification of colonial rule in India.

The arrival of Patrick Geddes in India in 1914 caused a profound shift in the discourse of the village, at least within the circle of designers. Geddes, a Scottish urban designer, educator, and biologist, is generally discussed within the premise of urban planning and design. Geddes maintained idiosyncratic ideas about the Indian town, applying his "urban village" theory and equating cities with villages both in terms of social construct and physical fabric. His rendition of Indian villages and towns as interchangeable entities introduced a new argument that the nature of colonial governances should be identical in villages and urban areas.

While in India, Geddes was involved in various urban development projects, commissioned by princely estates and various city improvement trusts. Geddes's approach to the issue of Indian rural and urban development was quite different from existing colonial practice, which meant total demolition of the existing context, after which new construction was initiated from scratch. Geddes advocated for a new attitude, a technique he named the "surgical method," to build on the existing urban context and infrastructure with a strong theoretical emphasis on preserving the prevailing urban fabric. Geddes maintained unequivocal reliance on the normative colonial sociological view that the Indian urban environment is mainly an amalgamation of distinctly divided and divisive communities, groups, castes, and tribes. He used the concept of the urban village, first developed in his famous *Valley Section* (1909), to argue through his works, lectures, and exhibitions that one must understand Indian cities in terms of villages because the core structure of the Indian city was naturally rural. What is unique in Geddes's view was the desire to conserve a hypothetical rural culture within the urban context and thus create a new vision of the Indian city—cities devoid of any urban lineage, incapable of implementing the culture of urban metropolis. Such representation of the city in the image of the village extended and problematized existing notions of city and village and their development. This is not merely an issue of reading urban problems through the lens of the village. It marked a moment when the fictional village appeared as a perpetual inspiration, if not a template for Indian urban development.

In Geddes's discourse, the rural and urban became an entangled, intertwined, and inextricable phenomenon, representing a continuum of the same space-time and event. Like the rest of his colonial colleagues, Geddes considered India to be a large compendium of stereotyped villages, but he advocated to blur the division between urban and rural. He proposed that the India village and the urban environment are so interconnected that one must look upon all urban centers as extensions of villages, which explains why, when referring to Indian villages, Tyrwhitt used the notion of "urban core" without any reservation.

The Village as a Critique of Colonial Governance

At the age of twenty-four in 1878, Patrick Geddes moved to Paris, where his thought was deeply influenced by the social theory of French sociologist Frédéric Le Play. Le Play's sociological thesis structured on the triad of *lieu, travail,* and *famille* (place, work, and family), which Geddes extended to his ideas of city dwelling either as place, work, and folk or as environment, function, and organism. Like many of his European colleagues, Geddes adapted human labor, work, or function as the central pivoting point of his thesis. While for Thomas Carlyle labor had a quasi-religious function, William Morris and John Ruskin considered labor as the potential condition of synthesizing art and crafts or human expression and mechanization. Marx and Engels, on the other hand, emphasized the growing disconnection between human labor and self-expression, given the deep schism created by the divided and stratified production process a factory offers to its workers. However, Geddes's view of work was one of "conscious action," or a condition that helps human beings assimilate with their surrounding environment. In this regard, Geddes thought the urban environment was a material and cultural product of human labor that allowed people to retain their evolutionary existence and that bound together the other two factors of folk and place.

The other important influence on Geddes was the French philosopher

Henry Louis Bergson, after their first meeting at the Universal Exposition in Paris in 1900. Bergson was then famous for his idealistic questioning of the materialist-scientific principle of reasoning. By the time Geddes was acquainted with Bergson's philosophy, he had already established a fascination for extrascientific mystiques and metaphysics. Among late nineteenth-century natural scientists, comprehensiveness and exclusiveness were accepted as universal norms for ordering and categorizing. Mostly inspired by Le Play's sociological triads, Geddes attempted to encompass the religious or extrascientific beliefs and metaphysical practices with the natural order. Bergson's critique of natural evolution, which excluded metaphysical questions about life, was part of his argument against the mechanistic understanding of the physical world. Geddes's response to Bergson was mixed, and he tried to reconcile the two opposing human faculties—the scientific or rational and the unscientific and irrational. He introduced his idea of *genius loci*, meaning the material existence of a region and its urban environment is the condensed form of a human's work and her attempt to interact with her environment, and used this concept to define the evolutionary existence of a human and the teleological life force embedded in its space. Geddes subscribed to the spiritual attributes of human work at the intersection of man and environment.

In early 1880 Patrick Geddes became close with Fellowship of the New Life, a group of intellectuals who sought social reformation through the spiritual development and opposed the materialist perspective of science. In 1870 Geddes came to know Annie Besant, who would become an influential figure of the international theosophical movement and the movement for Indian self-governance. Besant established the Central Hindu College and later the university in Banaras in 1899. Encouraged by the spiritual connection of Indian life, Geddes moved to India in 1914 with an invitation from Lord Pentland, secretary of state for Scotland and governor of Madras, to mount his much-praised Cities and Towns Planning Exhibition. Geddes stayed in India until 1924. During his stay, he set up his exhibition in Bombay and Calcutta, was involved in many town-planning projects, and produced a number of reports on town planning and urban conservation. From 1919 he served as the chair of sociology and civics at the University of Bombay. During his stay, he was commissioned by princely states and colonial authorities, such as municipalities and town improvement trusts.

As a representative of colonial bureaucracy, Geddes had an ambivalent attitude toward colonialism. He accepted the colonial structure as an affirmative framework as long as it unified the British Commonwealth across the globe. His criticism against colonialism was reserved for its oppressive power structure and its unwillingness to pledge "development" in its colonies.[51] Development as an abstract goal was widely and uncritically adopted in various colonial policies to manage poverty, tackle civil unrest, define public health, and thus devise colonial citizenship. Instead of engaging in the debate about applying evolutionary theory to restructure the colonial power structure, Geddes chose to operate at a pragmatic level, hoping a micro-level, problem-solving attitude would alter it. In colonial discourse, development became a strong polemic that determined the trade, political, and philosophical relationship between East and West, between the colonized and the colonizers. Even as late as the Cold War, the development discourse continued its colonial legacy to experiment with the Third World poor, previously the colonized poor.

Geddes's critique of colonial development policy was two-pronged. First, Geddes argued that colonial attitudes and endeavors rested on assumptions of a passive indigenous population; second, colonialist development projects mainly emphasized visual and geometric order in the physical fabric of village or urban areas. According to Geddes, various improvement trusts and municipal engineers took little or no account of the existence of the vernacular population. In Geddes's terms, the colonial attitude of disengaging the users was fundamentally incongruous with the bioregional entity of a settlement. Disengagement or exclusion of users from colonial development projects, Geddes argued, forged the long-lasting colonial myth that the colonized poor were unaware and incapable of appreciating the potential of their own development. Geddes thought such presumptions would validate external dominance—the work of municipalities and improvement trusts—which sought to create idealistic environments for the poor. They would then learn what "development" meant and would desire "real development" as demonstrated by the government. In a 1915 report on town planning, Geddes confronted this method in favor of more engaging ways to integrate users in the development process. He wrote the following in his "Report on the Towns in the Madras Presidency": "Does this show that 'the citizens do not care for improvements'? Everywhere in the slums we see women toiling and sweeping, each struggling to maintain her poor little home above and distressingly low level of municipal paving and draining in the quarter. The fault does not lie with the people and I have no fear that the people of the cities would not respond to improvements. The immediate problem is for the municipal and central government to understand what improvements really are needed and desired, both domestic and social, spiritual and artistic."[52] While colonial authority overlooked the existence of a collective desire for development, Geddes was apparently looking for instances to prove that Indians already desired it. He argued that this coveted "desire" already existed in the Indian population but needed to be structured into a productive will that colonial rule had suppressed. As Geddes argued, when "individuals develop into citizens, ideas will become organized into personal purpose and public life, instead of being diffused and scattered—like new dust over old—as at present."[53]

Such evolutionary transformation of individuals into self-developing citizens is politically confronting to the colonial structure, which proposed the transformation of docile colonial subjects into a cooperative and desirous citizens under local leadership.[54] Geddes's confrontation of the colonial structure was conditioned by the formation of evolutionary human beings who could be developed and transformed into citizens. This concept in a different context was formed first in his 1915 book *Cities in Evolution*, which was later reprinted with a new foreword by Tyrwhitt in 1949. In this book, Geddes categorized the war-prone "old world," the colonial and fascist world, and countries with limited democracy as the "paleotechnic order," a "kakotopia" in which human energy and material resources are engaged in money wages instead of a "vital budget."[55] Similarly, Geddes wrote of human action forging political will and devising various institutions to retain that collective will with the tendency to consume natural and nutritional resources. The political will of people could only move to the next evolutionary level of the "neotechnic" order or to utopia when human and natural resources could be directed to conserve energy. This, he argued, would result in a broader evolution of social, personal, and civic well-being. Geddes proposed that ecological humanism and development theory are universally applicable principles for both towns and villages in the East and West. The proposition gained iconic status through his famous diagram of the "valley section," in which he presents the transition from wilderness to village and finally to towns, which all exist in an unbroken spatiotemporal continuum.

Geddes gave an explicit account of the application of his evolutionary theory in determining international relations among European countries and its mediatory role of retaining each country's internal regional balance. His discussion concerned mainly European metropolises, but the financial dependences of these metropolises on their colonies were absent. Tyrwhitt's selection of Geddes's text offers few hints about the relevance of evolutionary theory in the colonized worlds. Geddes's text also does not explain how one could resolve exploitive trade relations between colonizer and colonized countries or solve issues such as equal representation in governance and racial indiscrimination in state and society.

In his *Town Planning in Aden: A Report to the Government of Bombay,*

1917, Geddes elaborated on the "scientific" logic and rationale behind colonial governance. Tyrwhitt did not include this report in her compilation. This omission might have been intentional and might have indicated her disinterest in debates about colonialism at a time when some of her French CIAM colleagues were ardent supporters of French colonial policy. Aden, a port city of present-day Yemen, was part of British India. Aden was ruled from Bombay until 1937, when it was detached from India and became the Colony of Aden, a British Crown colony. Commissioned by the Aden Port Trust, Geddes and his associate H. V. Lanchester, town planner of Madras (now Chennai), submitted a framework for improving the port city. Geddes weighed in on the water supply system, the public health system, and the preservation of the city's biodiversity and local bazaars. He advocated for an urban monument around which city life could evolve, one that would symbolize the "Expression of the Imperial Situation." A network of centers around which everyday life could take place and achieve "spiritual meaning" complemented Geddes's strategy to weave an intricate urban fabric. In the case of Aden, he proposed a monument of imperial spirit that would bind the life of the city together, emphasizing his model of an unified global colonial order in which colonizers and colonized, universalism and regionalism complement each other.

The old world order, in Geddes's view, was maintained through an imperial system of terrestrial continuity and the annexation of more land via military prowess. Empires like Rome, Russia, Germany, and Austria-Hungary were based on regions connected mainly by land routes. These land-centric empires were limited because they encouraged a rigid centralization of closed metropolises, hindering the natural evolution of the human race as it consumed more resources than it preserved. The British Empire, which was developed through naval power, connected distant landmasses by indivisible and invisible sea routes, "along the ship furrows which we plough through the seven seas," as Geddes wrote. An absence of physical proximity and detachability through land, and thus the restriction of ground movement, gave the British Empire a framework within which a "unison of states and kingdoms, races and languages" was possible. The British Empire, through its abstract line of rule and control, was free from the disadvantages of centralization and autocratic rule as seen by Geddes. Rather, it generated a "tolerant humanism, if not yet of essential Christianity." In describing the suggested nature of the urban monument that represented imperial spirit in Aden, Geddes further elaborated the colonial structure as a positive force to harness collective political will within the framework of colonial governance. As stated in the report, "The fitting Expression of our imperial solidarity is thus not any memorial of militancy, . . . for the British Empire is not an Empire in these ancient or modern Germanic senses, of militancy and of centralisation. It is also more than 'England' even at its very best. It is a great and growing Federation of increasingly self-governing communities and peoples."[56]

Geddes's discussion of colonial structure, which apparently excluded the existence of colonizers, was rooted in his experience during the First World War. He argued that in a time of great crisis and war, colonial structure provided an effective framework for an elevated humanism in which the erasure of any racial boundary would find an "antistatic form." Two years before he published the Aden report, Geddes and Gilbert Slater, an economist and former head of Ruskin College in Oxford, organized a meeting on the consequences of and reason for the war. Their position was "objective" and "neutral," as they claimed they were simply using scientific methods to understand the biological root cause of the war. In a way, they tried to withdraw subjective engagement in politics for the sake of understanding the war's scientific nature and its implication in creating one unified world.

The question of regionalism only arises in Geddesian philosophy when we agree that colonialism can nurture "humanity" and sustain a long-distance, decentralized globe and world society. Aden, equidistant from Bombay, the Suez Canal, and Zanzibar, strategically occupied the central location along the route from Britain to the East. Though the term *globalization* had not yet been invented, historian Peter Hoffenberg showed that many British intellectuals of that time were optimistic of a new integrated and humane world of "commonwealth" through British rule—and the series of colonial trade exhibitions bore the mark of that optimism.[57] In a global urban design perspective, Geddes considered the invisible imperial network of key seaports and port cities: Dover, Gibraltar, Malta, Aden, the Cape, Singapore, and Hong Kong. It was a cross-regional framework that accommodated, connected, and gathered various and distant regional spots. The network's sustainability depended on its strategic dialectics—to enhance regional identities and align those regional bodies with an imperial morality. Geddes saw it as an opportunity to break through the older world order of intense regionalism that failed to achieve a universal stance. The British Empire created a decentralized world of fragmented and internally centralized regions. In Geddes's proposition, Aden and similar port cities needed a symbolic expression of this new spirit of universalism, an architectural expression of synthesized regional interest and universal morality. Lanchester and Geddes proposed an Arch of Empire (figs. 3.4, 3.5) that would adopt a local Arabian style and details. The arch would express an imperial universalism but with distinctly re-

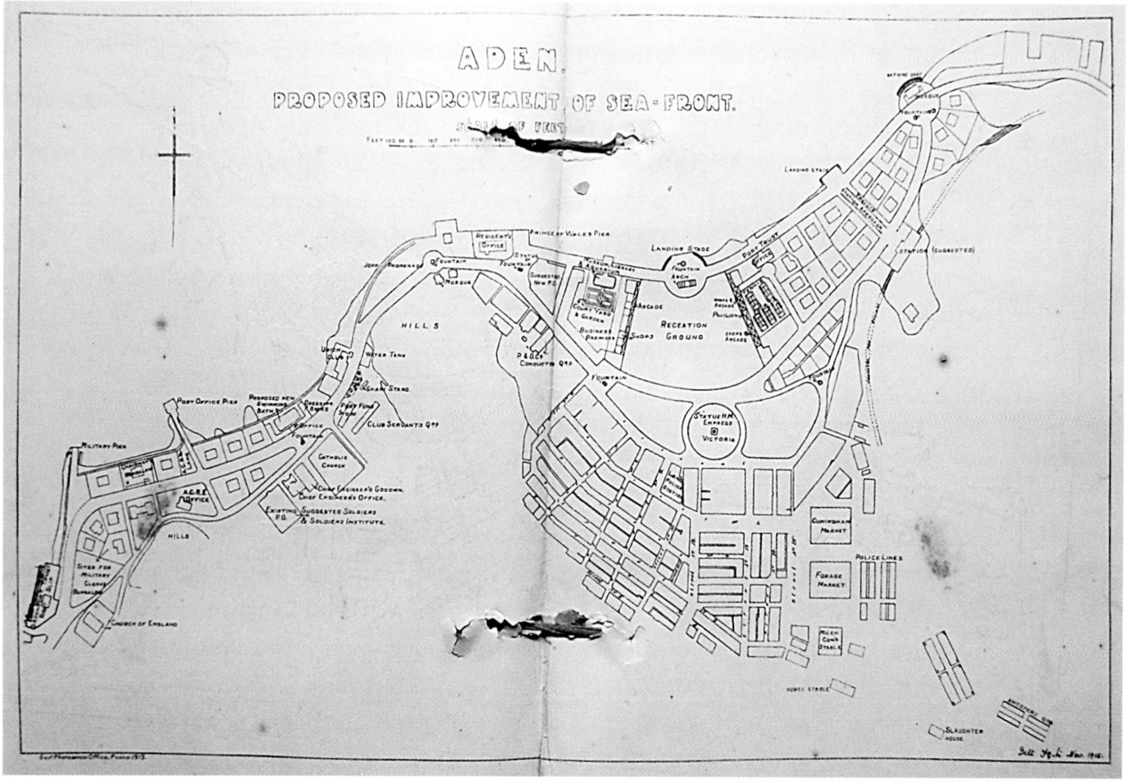

FIGURE 3.4. H. V. Lanchester and Patrick Geddes's proposal for an Arch of Empire in Aden. Source: Patrick Geddes, *Town Planning in Aden: A Report of the Government of Bombay* (Bombay: Government Central Press, 1919), 12. Maharashtra State Archives, General Department 1919, box 26, file 726.

gional visual details; thus, regionalism must maintain a close connection with its host structure, which is inevitably colonial.

Geddes tried to overcome the colonial "paleotechnic" mindset that sought to create a superficial and mere optical order by transforming winding and organic lanes and plots of a traditional Indian settlement into perfect orthogonal lines. In his "Reports on the Towns in the Madras Presidency, 1915: Madurai," Geddes provided an example in which a beautiful old house was demolished not to widen the adjacent lane but rather to bring the edge of the lane sixteen degrees closer to the draftsman's drawing. Common sense would dictate this activity as mindless, but Geddes explained it as part of a larger culture that he termed the "principle of functional substitution" in his evolutionary theory of settlement. This action was driven neither by functional need nor by improving an existing use or program. It was intended to satisfy a professional adaptation—such as the

FIGURE 3.5. Rendered presentation of H. V. Lanchester and Patrick Geddes's proposal for an Arch of Empire in Aden. Source: Patrick Geddes, *Town Planning in Aden: A Report of the Government of Bombay* (Bombay: Government Central Press, 1919), 12. Maharashtra State Archives, General Department 1919, box 26, file 726.

draftsman's interest of visual clarity—of an abstract set of rules set by another group of professionals, such as sanitary engineers and their bylaws or in Geddes's terms, an "uncritical functional substitute." The central interest of such an attitude, Geddes explained, was to adhere to the unconditional and uncritical dependence on the professional's "work" itself. However, on an evolutionary ladder, this action belongs to the lowest level. The next step of this uncritical functional substitute is what Geddes called "conservative surgery," a strategy that improves by conserving the existing character of a place, or the *genius loci*.[58] Geddes's criticism of "functional substitution" was renewed in a post–Second World War context, when mindless craftsmanship, in which a specific work is approached and done uncritically and without a clear idea of its impact, received widespread criticism.

The Ideal Village in Romantic Nationalism

At a time when the colonial intellectual tradition was adamant about proving the backwardness of village societies, Gandhi conceptualized the village as the cardinal space of a superior human civilization. He confronted the colonial exclusion of the lived experience of villagers from census data. His portrayal was of an industrious and disciplined village life framed by ritualized daily chores in ashrams, which capitalized on the myth of the self-sufficient village. Inspired by John Ruskin's theory of a craft-oriented, pseudomedieval society, Gandhi took a unique position that sought communal liberalism (communalism) within the hermetic and controlled demonstration of an ideal village life in his ashram.[59]

Gandhi established his first ashram in India on his arrival from South Africa in 1915, a few months after Geddes arrived in India. In the following decades, Gandhi's ashram served as the utopian space of Indian independence, a postcolonial ideal mode of rural living.[60] Ashram members abandoned their old lives of industrial modernism, at least symbolically, and lived the physical equivalent of a metaphorical everyday life of working villagers.[61] The performance of disciplined everyday life involved spatial rituals in which villagers' interactions with the material world were employed to reach a universal harmony beyond the rigid caste system. The projection of Gandhi's bodily images—a working villager poised calmly in a utopian space—was a strategy to combine the space and body to forge an ideal postcolonial subjecthood.

In the daily life of the ashram, Gandhi exhibited a rigorous practice of physical and environmental hygiene in combination with a strict diet and celibacy. Gandhi meticulously choreographed his everyday life to create a counternarrative to Eurocentric modernism. However, in doing so, he formed an idiosyncratic rationale that symptomized a complex collation of myths of science with a set of ritualistic performances in space, such as spinning. Hand-spinning was one of the strongest metaphors created by Gandhi that worked at the intersection of body, space, and economy. Gandhi's mythic new Indian citizen was the working common villager who possessed total control over consumerist and libidinal desire. This metaphorical self was perpetuated through the didactical space of his ashram to teach potent citizens of a new India. A constant exposure of the Gandhian self in public discourse and its active presence in his ashram became part of the process of constructing a new Indian self-image. The circulation of his new form of action through various public media thus transformed his ashram from a place of dwelling to a place of teaching and exhibition. A physical manifestation of this pedagogical space, the new body together with the new landscape of material culture, offered a context for the new architecture.

Historian Dipesh Chakrabarty argues that in colonial India, colonized society constructed a different form of public sphere that was not compatible with the definition of contemporary political science.[62] The continuous display of Gandhi's experiment with his personal life in the ashram through varied media was central to his project of forging the public sphere through modern media.[63] Creating political awareness among Indian people would bring social agency, he believed. Nevertheless, Gandhi succeeded in raising political awareness through the construction of sociopolitical myths, but his performance as a rural ascetic in an ideal village setting was of little help to Indian physical planners. They did not have the institutional and organizational infrastructure necessary to replicate Gandhi's model in a mass scale across India. Gandhi's ascetic model was characterized by inherent impossibility. Although it was a romantic utopian ideal, it was nevertheless effective in creating strong nationalist zeal.

Several nationalist architects approached the Gandhian utopia with optimism, attempting to reconstruct it into an applicable form within the existing social, economic, and political system. Among them, the prominent Calcutta-based architect and planner Sris Chandra Chatterjee attempted to translate the Gandhian didactic or exhibitionary ashram into a universal "Indian architecture and human planning."[64] Among Chatterjee's other polemical proposals was an ideal village for three thousand inhabitants, which added to the contemporary debate about appropriate village life in postcolonial India (fig. 3.6).[65] The architectural style of the buildings was eclectic and freely borrowed and juxtaposed elements from various precolonial pasts—ranging from the Vedic age to the Gupta Empire. Chatterjee's proposal was not a literal but an interpretive translation of Gandhi's ashram in a modern setting, which was of course oxymoronic. His proposition hardly strayed from Gandhian stylized rural space and was difficult to accommodate within Prime Minister Nehru's socialist development-oriented strategy.

During the 1930s and 1940s, in his early career, Chatterjee worked on several renovation projects in Bikaner as a civil engineer, and his work was closely related to the Indo-Saracenic style of British army officer, engineer, and architect Samuel Swinton Jacob.[66] Jacob advocated for creating a hybrid new style by combining Hindu (Indo) and Islamic (Saracenic) architectural elements and embellishments. This style, he argued, would appropriately create the myth of a unified India under British rule. Influenced by Jacob, Chatterjee became interested in the power of ornaments and thus the ancient crafts of building. He eventually advocated for the

PLATE II

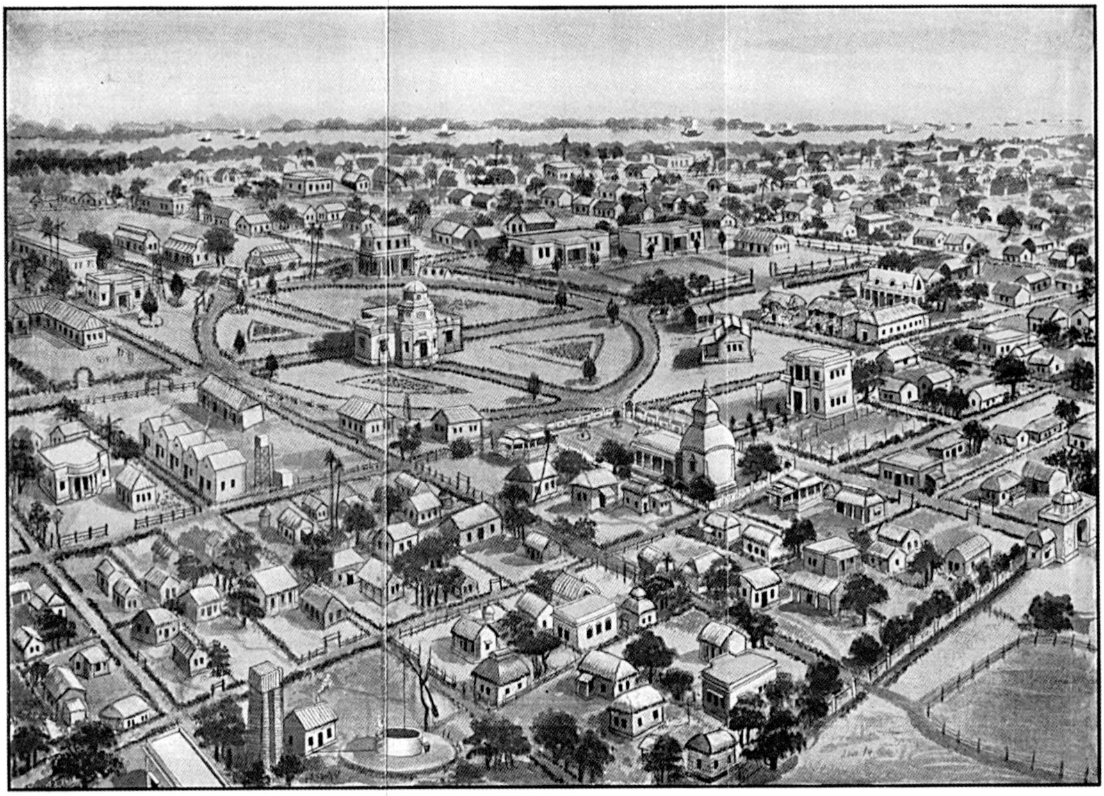

Drawn by Panchugopal Banerjee INDIAN VILLAGE OF TO-MORROW Architect : Sris Chandra Chatterjee

FIGURE 3.6. "Indian Village of Tomorrow." Sris Chandra Chatterjee's proposition for an ideal Indian village, drawn by Panchugopal Banerjee. Source: Sris Chandra Chatterjee, *India and New Order: An Essay on Human Planning* (Calcutta: University of Calcutta, 1949).

promotion of a national architecture through a "renaissance of old building techniques and metaphoric visual images."[67] Chatterjee conceived of architecture as a monolithic scheme based on visual symbols freely taken from India's Hindu core, which according to Chatterjee is the pre-British and pre-Muslim time. The political ambition of forging Chatterjee's version of a precolonial past of absolute independence aimed to seek ideological refuge within an ahistorical process. Chatterjee's enthusiasm for making up prehistory to assimilate a timeless past with an ideal future was stirred by significant archaeological discoveries of its time. In 1920 archaeologist and historian Rakhaldas Bandyopadhyay identified Buddhist Stupa in the site of today's Mohenjodaro, which led to an elaborate excavation of Harappa and Mohenjodaro during the 1930s and 1940s. The archaeological discovery of pre-British, pre-Mughal urban centers had created vigor for imagining an alternative to the present: utopian cities and village centers of the future.

Chatterjee's precolonial utopia and ideal village excluded the diversity of contemporary Indian society in favor of a monolithic Hindu society, thus cleansing and purifying the Hindu core of India. This aesthetic position, which was purgative in its tone, was not uncommon during the time. The preference for an ahistorical process by going back to an ideal past was the reverse of development or future-oriented anticolonial movement. Idealization of an ideal Hindu past resulted in aesthetic violence—ruthless exclusion and pruning of the British and Muslim past. Although Chatterjee's ideas did not attract much professional attention, they attracted serious attention in various educational institutes, including Calcutta University, the Bengal Engineering College, and Andhra State University. However, as an Indian National Congress member, a member of the National Planning Commission, and the Bengal Post-War Reconstruction Committee, Chatterjee was able to present his ideas to various government bodies to challenge the government's nascent interest in a modern aesthetic, modern technology, and large-scale industrialization.

Chatterjee's utopia was initially structured on Gandhi's alternative modernity, which conceptualized a nonconsumerist economy, subaltern empowerment, a decentralized state, spirituality, and a liberal scientific method. Translation of these ideologies into architecture, however, was problematic. Chatterjee's strategic reformulation of tradition to serve a revolutionary end was a response to the expanding home market and middle-class attraction to a modernist aesthetic. Chatterjee's utopia pleaded for a homogeneous Indian space to transpose its postcolonial subjects in the precolonial past. In his many unrealized urban and rural projects, he proposed a Gandhian and nationalist space. But ironically, instead of forming a nonhierarchical space like Gandhi's ashram, his utopia eventually codified Indians into parenthetical entities governed by an ambiguous bureaucracy, which differed little from the colonial myth of self-sufficiency.

In Chatterjee's view, architectural elements from the ancient ruins of Magadha, Harappa, and Mohenjodaro did not bear the colonial scar. So he pled to contemporary architects to select freely from those elements and juxtapose them eclectically to create a hybrid yet pure nationalist form. In this method, free association and free selection were more important than an exact rendition of historical process. This reduced architecture to an infinite variation of assemblage and malleability, a process that architectural historian Andrzej Piotrowski has described in a different context as the sumptuous accumulation of value-free objects from the market without resistance or restraint.[68] This version of Gandhi's utopia was well appreciated by Chatterjee's political coterie but failed to attract support for its practical application. However, Chatterjee's drawings and writings gave little indication of the institutional framework required to produce such architecture and eventually failed to propose a realistic solution.

Chatterjee's failure to produce a convincing nationalist utopia coincided with a transatlantic endeavor to frame a new utopia in postindependence India. The symbolism of the dissenting vernacular man was central to Gandhi's political rhetoric. Entangled in a self-referential cultural code, the Gandhian man lost his ability to address his location in the global market economy and in Cold War cultural dynamics. The utopian space of the Gandhian village that romanticized an eternal Hindu India and thus inverted the colonial stereotyping of the Indian village seemed to be inoperable in the realpolitik framed by an emerging global economy.

Anti-Utopian Nationalism and Modernism

The concept of the village as a site of postcolonial development demanded a rearticulation that is not self-sufficient but rather part of the larger socioeconomic context. Scholars such as Milton Singer and McKim Marriott confronted this imperial perception to prove that "introverted" Indian villages in fact had deep connections to the outside world, thus challenging the notion that previously conceptualized villages were not affected by external forces.[69] After independence, the new wave of scholarship in sociology and anthropology by William and Charlotte Wiser, Ruth and Stanley Freed, M. N. Srinivas, and A. M. Shah and I. P. Desai described the space of the village as a dialectical result of a caste-based, introverted economic system combined with an open system of intricate networks that connected the inner space with the wider outside. To comply with this paradigm shift, Nehru attempted to give the Gandhian ascetic and apolitical subjects a critical edge by assimilating villages with a global capital flow and endorsing their cultural visibility and spatial existence. The spatial transformation would thus be mobilized as a natural consequence of desire.

Various representations of ideal villages and village development projects initiated during postindependence showed a major epistemological shift—from Gandhian utopia to a more pragmatic reality—elaborated in a different context by sociologist André Béteille as an anti-utopia.[70] Béteille's anti-utopian stance stemmed from an inspiration similar to that of the ideal village projects of postindependence, which hoped to produce democratic social institutions at a grassroots level. Béteille argues that a utopian erasure of inequality will either fail as a social project or will transform into an autocratic system. An anti-utopian society acknowledges a host of natural inequalities and values universal social policy as its foundation.[71] Béteille's philosophical emphasis was on the creation of de Tocqueville's notion of public institutions that mediate the state and its citizens.[72] This particular emphasis on mediating institutions disputed the model of development that is exclusively based on nongovernment organizations (NGOs). In scholarship of postcolonial India, an ideological skirmish developed around whether nonstate organizations should dominate the process of anti-utopia. For people to grow from individuals to citizens capable of desiring and effecting further development requires slow-paced evolution mediated by public institutions.

During the 1930s and 1940s, the Associate Cement Companies directed a substantial anti-utopian stance at a time when contemporary professional architects were struggling to define their disciplinary and professional existence. Architects had limited scope to get involved in debates related to political emancipation and social reformation. Issues like affordable housing and rural reformation were of secondary importance to the Indian Institute of Architects. On the other hand, the government mainly concentrated its efforts on industrial housing schemes. Against this context, it was the ACC's trade interest that, with the help of the Institution of Engineers India, produced a large number of ideal design prototypes and disseminated information about low-cost or affordable buildings for Indian villages. We can assume that professional architects created those designs, though the names of the designers were never recorded in the publications. So it is now difficult to fully understand how the ACC worked in collaboration with professional architects.

Through relentless efforts by the ACC, the notion of a developed and modernized village claimed its location in a liberal development process without being allied with any political party. This desire fed off the populist demand for development—indifferent to the origin, locality, or religion of the population. The desire to overcome poverty without disrupting the existing power structure was more important than forging any radical political movement. The ACC attempted to initiate a rural development program through strengthening private ownership, expanding private entrepreneurship, and creating a desire for development through private enterprises. The ACC nevertheless did not confront the tenet of the anti-utopia theme: that formation of participatory institutions should be the instigation point of any development project. In contrast to prevailing views—that built structures are natural and automated consequences of institutions and should therefore be built by institutions—the ACC preferred to give those

FIGURE 3.7. Associated Cement Companies' proposal for an ideal village at Virar. Source: Associated Cement Companies, *Our Villages of Tomorrow: How Shall We Build Them?* (Bombay: Associated Cement Companies, 1932; reprint, 1949). © Associated Cement Companies.

institutions a visible form through architecture. The main argument of the ACC presumably derived from its interest in promoting privatization and developing new trade avenues. However, as a trade organization, the ACC primarily sought to create a tangible expression of development through an array of architectural projects, a clearly defined site to contain citizens' mediating institutions for development. It is important to note here that although the proponents of anti-utopia argued for a society mediated by public institutions, it was trade organizations that took the initiative.

One of the ACC's earliest efforts was to erect an ideal village at Virar, near Bombay, in January 1945 (fig. 3.7). In this project, the ACC built a few cement concrete structures for village residences and various public structures that included cattle sheds, water wells, temples, and community rooms. ACC carefully constructed an alternative modernism of austerity in which creating beautiful buildings was not of primary interest and the scarcity of economic resources was an essential component of a clean modern look. The ACC's efforts complemented state efforts to motivate its citizens to pursue their personal goals for development with their own private resources. Guests at the opening day of the ACC's ideal village project at Virar included advisers to the governor of Bombay, G. F. S. Collins and Sir Charles Bristow; Mr. Bedekar, collector of Thane; engineers from the Municipal and Public Works Department; and members of the District

FIGURE 3.8. Associated Cement Companies' proposal for a universal ideal village. Source: Associated Cement Companies, *Our Villages of Tomorrow: How Shall We Build Them?* (Bombay: Associated Cement Companies, 1932; reprint, 1949). © Associated Cement Companies.

Local Board. The guests were in sound agreement on the central theme of the ideal village project: that the self-help approach and private trade's intervention into the state's development effort were timely steps toward a holistic development program. Tellingly, Collins, the keynote speaker, announced that in "these days of scarcity of practically everything the appropriate thing to do was to encourage private intervention."[73] Private initiatives and trade organizations were considered to be complementary to state-initiated rural development projects. The colonial rural development effort located at the juncture of a Gandhian and an imperial utopia was thus substantiated by the ACC through the privatization of development.

One of the most successful and widely circulated ACC publications of 1949, *Our Villages of Tomorrow: How Shall We Build Them?*, was produced in a series along with other publications on ideal modern living and low-cost houses (fig 3.8).[74] We can safely assume that the public imagination of rural development in India in the 1950s was largely informed by images the ACC presented in the aforementioned booklet. The modern structures of this new village, all built in reinforced cement concrete, and the introduction of new building types such as a village cinema hall and clubhouse, absent from the Gandhian ashram-based model village, appeared to be more appropriate, modern, and practical. Compatible with global trade relations, the ACC's new village replaced the Gandhian ascetic utopia of self-reliance. Two themes underpinned the ACC's anti-utopian proposition: first, coveted rural sanitation, which symptomized the visual evidence of an absence of poverty, and second, a challenge to the normative relationship between the Indian village and indigenous material culture, evinced by a pragmatic image of a future village built with modern materials, such as concrete, and techniques.

In the ACC's proposition, all vernacular materials were to be abandoned outright to keep with the modern zeitgeist. The practice of vernacular techniques and aesthetics, as suggested by the ACC, were only to be practiced at a moral level; their presence in material culture was no longer requisite. By advocating for the local production of hollow concrete blocks—the prescribed material for constructing the ACC's two-room modern prototype, described in chapter 1—the ACC intended to shorten the time between the production of construction materials and their consumption on local sites. The ACC also advocated for the integration of the villagers' unskilled workforce with the construction of the development project under the rubric of self-help. It seems that the ACC adopted the United Nations' institutionalized method of self-help as its main philosophy for development. And yet because of a paucity of information, we do not know precisely how much of the ACC's philosophy was driven by the United Nations' promotional documents.

Nevertheless, the ACC embraced self-help as its preferred substitute for skilled construction labor as much as possible. By emphasizing a reliance on unskilled labor at the local level, the organization probably unknowingly complied with the United Nations' global development goal. However, the ACC version of self-help had maintained crucial differences with the United Nations' version by silencing about how to utilize local labor in the construction process. UN's program prescribed to engage the villagers in an intense construction program through the self-help method. The United Nations did not take into account that, since the first profession of villagers most likely involves menial labor, they might have little interest in engaging in voluntary construction that required heavy physical work. In hindsight, many scholars criticized the United Nations' strategy to make poor villagers donate their labor.[75] The United Nations consultants, however, defended itself by arguing that self-help would only claim the work hours of the unemployed population, or that the time was to be carved out solely from their leisure hours.[76] It is unclear if the ACC was aware of the debates around the concurrent self-help rural housing prescribed by the United Nations. But it took ingenious tactics to motivate villagers. The workers illustrated in the ACC publication were dressed as congress workers, suggesting that the voluntary donation of labor not only helped to build their villages but was also an act of nationalist service to one's own country (fig. 3.9).

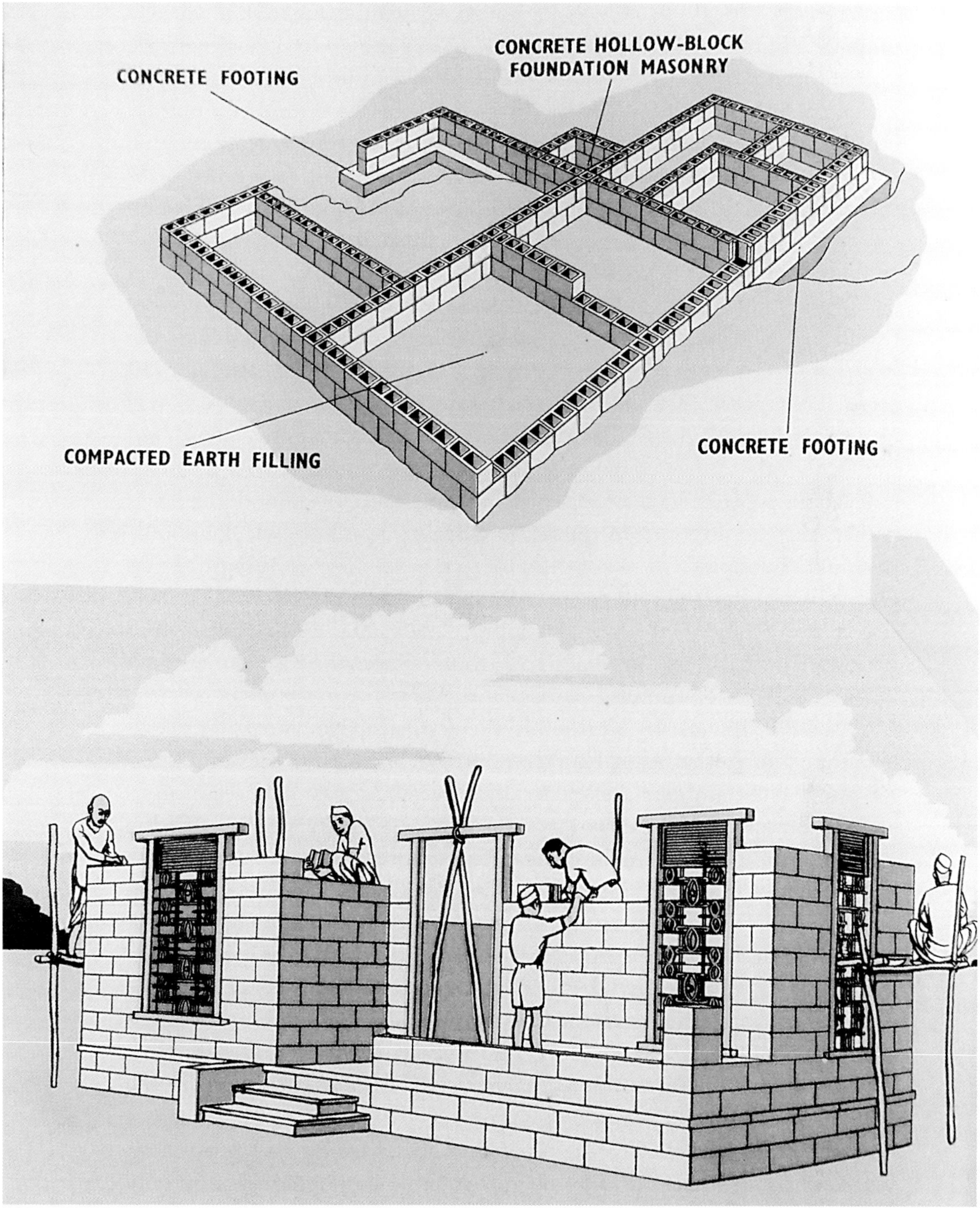

FIGURE 3.9. Local villagers construct rural houses by the self-help method. Source: Associated Cement Companies, *Our Villages of Tomorrow: How Shall We Build Them?* (Bombay: Associated Cement Companies, 1932; reprint, 1949). © Associated Cement Companies.

The ACC's ideal village was conceived as an amalgamation of various public institutions, institutions that in Béteille's mind would facilitate the formation of citizens. The village was laid out around a central core in which the main building was the village hall or the central community building. From this center, pathways radiated outward to create a radial system of residential plots. Along with the village hall, two other institutions occupied the central core, the village school and the rural health center. The ACC proposed that the village hall should be the higher order civil institution, and that it was only to be built in rural communities that had already entered a "developed civic and social life." The difference between such a proposition and the colonial imagination of rural civic life was that ACC did not presume a socially and culturally degenerated rural population; rather, ACC assumed an absence of civic sense. The ACC was optimistic that an ideal village space would create that civic sense and thus gather disconnected actions into a common arena. The ACC village hall would provide such a space, as "its appearance of quiet dignity and good taste, can do much to rouse the villagers' spirit of civic consciousness and civic pride." It is not difficult to see the echo of Tyrwhitt's and Geddes's idea that the root cause of Indian underdevelopment is the lack of community and civic sense. An appropriate spatial framework such as the core, village center, or village hall would induce the formation of that lacking sense of community.

The other interesting addition to the ACC's village core was the cinema (fig. 3.10). In the 1940s, rural community cinema that was only used for public entertainment was generally considered to be a space of moral degeneration. The ACC, however, created a different narration of the positive benefits of cinema in village life, and presented cinema as a new didactic space that could be used to disseminate essential public knowledge. Cinema was therefore a very timely and effective instrument for mass communication. According to the ACC booklet: "Not only has it [cinema] brought with it a new world of entertainment but it has placed in the hands of the rural reformer a most potent weapon of education. By means of the cinema the rural population can be reached easily and effectively . . . which would surely work a change for the better in the habits of the rural population."

With concern growing for a rapid modernization and integration with the global economy, the power of cinema to communicate directly with the wider population was a unique opportunity to inform society at large. The ACC proposed a rural cinema hall as one of the village's new pedagogical and civic spaces. This reflected the belief that cinema halls were powerful spaces that could draw large assemblies and not only mold

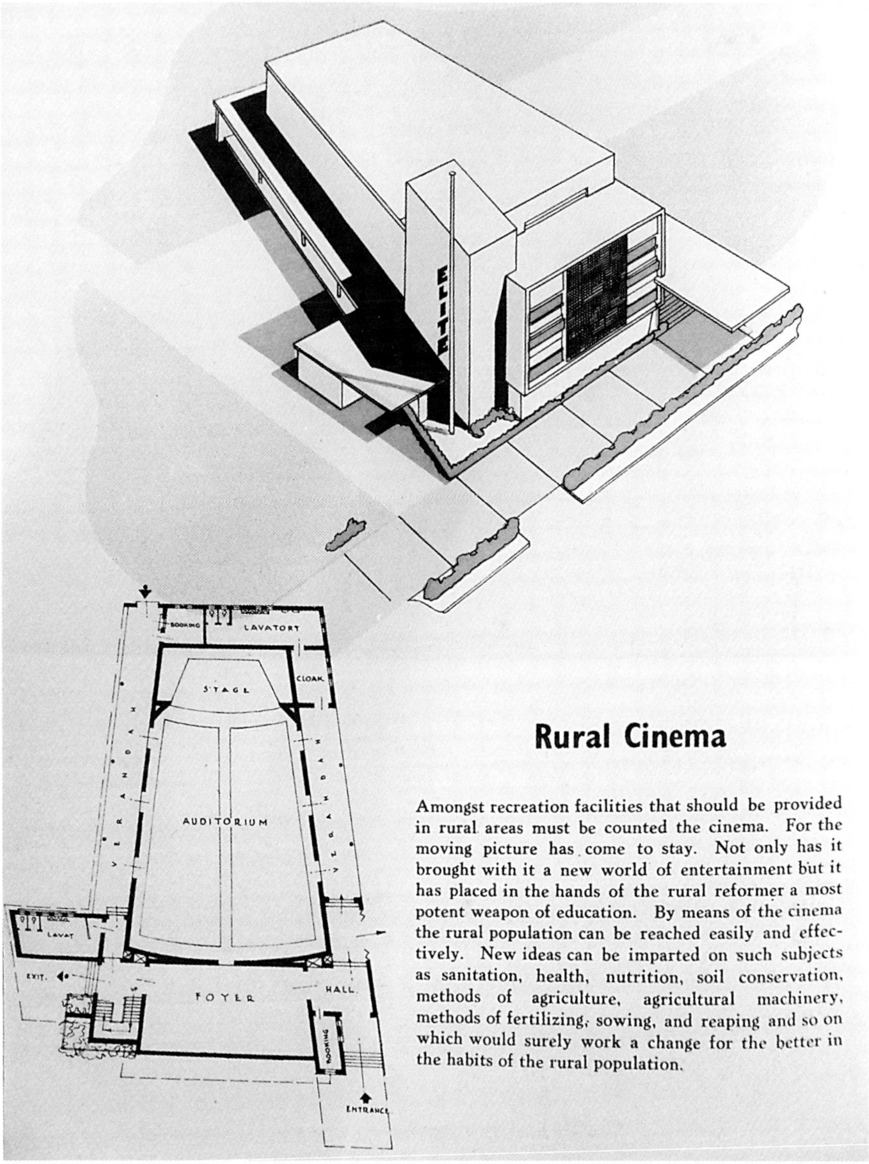

FIGURE 3.10. The rural cinema at the Associated Cement Companies' ideal village. Source: Associated Cement Companies, *Our Villages of Tomorrow: How Shall We Build Them?* (Bombay: Associated Cement Companies, 1932; reprint, 1949). © Associated Cement Companies.

popular taste and opinion but also forge a sense of community. Historian Prem Chowdhry discussed how, during the making of nationalist cinemas in the 1930s and 1940s, many nationalist cinemas acted as catalysts to create a strong and univocal public opinion. This phenomenon was a

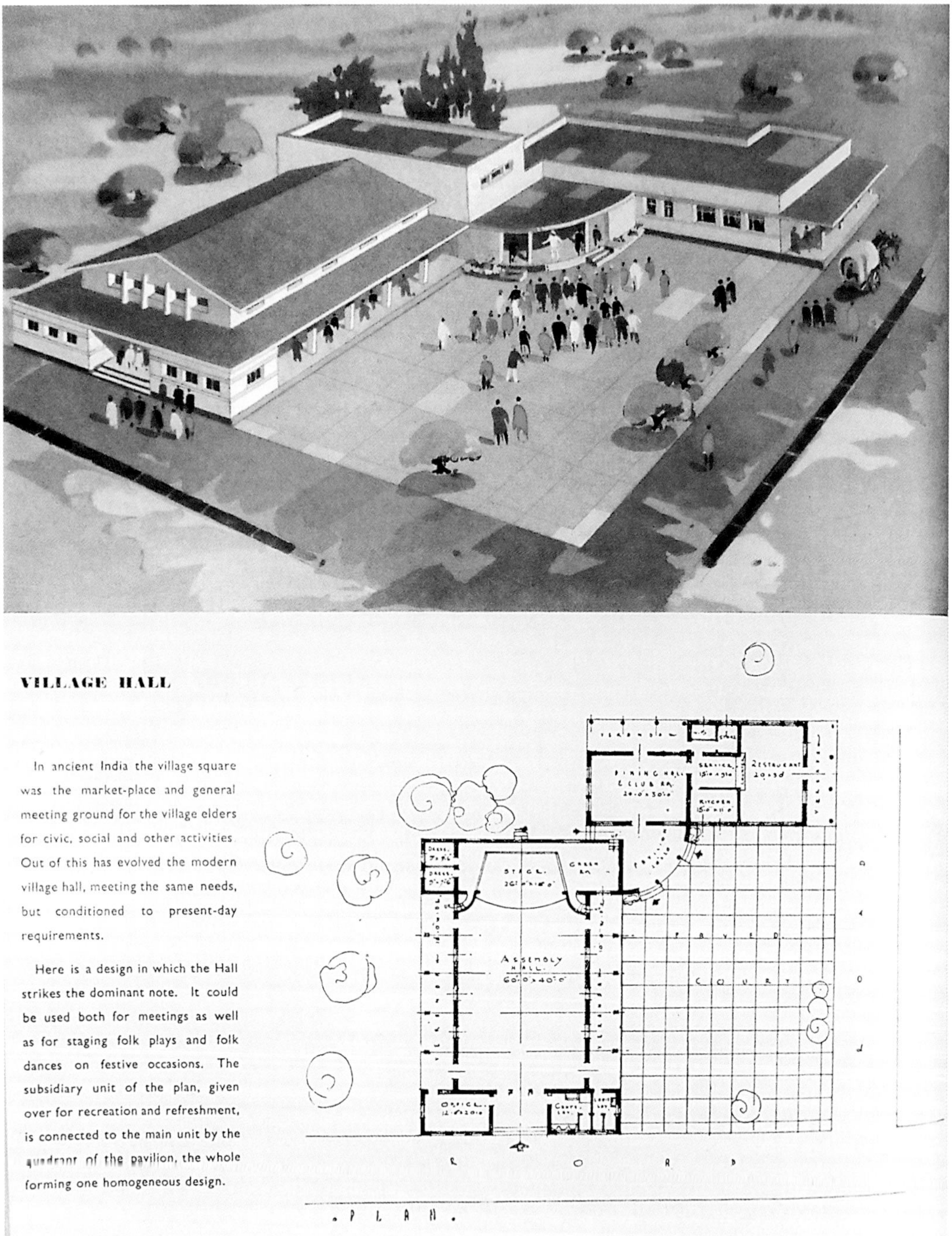

FIGURE 3.11. Village hall at Associated Cement Companies' ideal village. Source: Associated Cement Companies, *Our Villages of Tomorrow: How Shall We Build Them?* (Bombay: Associated Cement Companies, 1932; reprint, 1949). © Associated Cement Companies.

rarity in colonial India and challenged the validity and ethical ground of imperial rule.[77] Besides parks and promenades in British Bombay, cinema halls were one of the earliest popular urban public entertainment spaces. Cinema halls were a new form of urban space symbolizing uninterrupted right of access to entertainment culture and concurrent formation of the egalitarian public sphere. The ACC, a Bombay-based organization, must have drawn its inspirations from urban cinemas to replicate rural cinema as the civic center of village life. In addition, at a time of stratified urban society, entry into an urban cinema hall, at least hypothetically, was not typically restricted by a spectator's class, gender, religion, caste, or race. As a result, the cinema hall was a metaphor of egalitarian modern space. Cinema halls represented a collective space of urban entertainment to spark nationalism. The space of the cinema hall was thus assumed to be a novel social space where people could practice liberty just by being physically present and passively appropriating the narration of nationalist cinemas.

The other two civic spaces that the ACC had proposed were a club for small towns, reminiscent of colonial elitist culture (fig. 3.11), and a makeshift ladies' club formed by rearranging the village well. The village club was considered the culmination of rural life's evolution into a mature civic society. The idea of the clubhouse, modeled on the expatriate British officials' community space in India, was regarded as a token of civility and sophistication. Within it, rural society supposedly could not only overcome ingrained gender prejudices but could also possibly forge a local leadership and civic society. In describing the club's character, the ACC wrote, "In small towns where social life is developed in a different way from that in villages, a club is a necessity. Here men and woman could spend their evening together playing games or cards, dancing, or just sitting out on the lawns to relax after a hard day's work."

These clubs were at the ideological threshold of the colonial self, the liberal bourgeoisie, and the working class. Since the idea of a clubhouse was imagined on the colonial model, it could not escape an inherent contradiction. On the one hand, the clubhouse was supposed to be used by average people. But on the other hand, the rosy portrayal of its members doing leisurely activities in the evening implicitly assumed the presence of a large cohort of domestic servants. Without their support, taking over everyday domestic drudgery and liberating civic society, the hardworking men and women could not indulge in this kind of evening leisure.

In addition to the clubhouse, the ACC's other proposition of transforming the village well into a ladies' club (fig. 3.12) assumed a natural gendered conception of human grouping attached to rural spaces. Specu-

FIGURE 3.12. The village well and makeshift ladies' club. Source: Associated Cement Companies, Our Villages of Tomorrow: How Shall We Build Them? (Bombay: Associated Cement Companies, 1932; reprint, 1949). © Associated Cement Companies.

lation on the romantic vision of such a gendered conception of collective spirit cantered on a village well is not uncommon even in today's architecture. Accompanied by the following caption, the ACC provided a design to show how the village well could be transformed into a ladies' club: "It has from time immemorial been a centre around which the village wives meet and relax for a short half hour from the drudgery of their existence. It should then be more than a bare utilitarian structure. Without erring on the side of over-elaboration, its design should be such as to please and attract, a sort of informal 'Ladies' Club.'" The idea of village ladies' club appears in many contemporary government documents. For example, a village well being transformed into a "Village Gossip Center" was suggested in one government publication, marking the well as the central social or public place for women.[78]

The organized sequence of the cinema hall, clubhouse, and ladies' club could be seen as a hierarchy of public space, from more public to less public, in which the ladies' club offers the women more privacy. Although representing an imagined gendered space contradicted the open civic society, such spaces nevertheless were incongruent with the reality of Indian village life. As Tyrwhitt explained, "Social life for the woman is at the well, and for the men at the panchayat," a comment that clearly confronts Tyrwhitt's liberal Western pedigree.[79]

The ACC publication *Our Villages of Tomorrow* alludes only to a small part of the complex debates on development and design of the rural environment, the look and meaning of modern architecture in rural India. The book represents a discourse that both supplemented and confronted Tyrwhitt's discourse of rural development, as showcased in the Delhi exhibition of 1954. She was adamant about evincing her understanding of a true and authentic indigenous picture of developing the Indian village, one embedded in vernacular material culture and the everyday lived experience of villagers. The ACC did not confront this view but argued that the objective of development is not to seek and replicate authenticity but to upgrade it. The ACC also argued that development did not mean blindly limiting the new India according to Gandhian vernacularism. We can get a sense of this ideological confrontation from one of Tyrwhitt's letters to Marcel Schwob, acting chief of Economic Commission for Asia and Far East. Tyrwhitt opposed the PWD's proposition to build an "urban type house" in the village center. She contended that "unless the buildings are genuinely made in a manner, and using materials that are normally available to villagers, the whole centre makes no sense. It has been pain and grief to the PWD, but they have come round at last."[80]

The debate of development was not limited to the selection of building material and the look of the building; it went deeper into the kind of lifestyle the space should cultivate and how much consumer culture one should allow in the village to keep it authentic. The PWD wanted to display certain modern household appliances and fixtures, such as washing machines and fluorescent lighting, in both urban and rural sections. Tyrwhitt strongly opposed the idea, referring to these objects as "luxury items" and "trade material" not suitable for real village life.[81] The PWD on the other hand identified these objects as fundamental amenities of modern life required for the comfort of people with low income. During the 1954 exhibition and conference in Delhi, Indian representatives argued for domestic comfort. As S. P. Raju of Hyderabad explained, "Another big problem in the village house is the absence of special arrangements for [the] preservation of food, so we have tried to evolve, along scientific principles of cooling and evaporation, and from simple materials, a sort of village refrigerator that can be made by the village potter; then there is scientific ventilation and a hygienic latrine." R. B. Gupta of the Planning Commission, India, added, "It is most important that the poorer people of India should have comfort. This does not only mean accommodation but also water, drainage, light."[82]

Tyrwhitt was not convinced that incorporating new appliances and features into the physical design was a good idea. Tyrwhitt's idea of authenticity was challenged by her Western colleagues, including the British architect Jane Drew, who worked on low-cost housing at Chandigarh. Drew contended that Western drive to protect authenticity was flawed and unrealistic. In a discussion with J. D. N. Versluys of UNESCO, Drew explained:

> You should think directly of people's possibilities of their requirements of their comforts and take every possible opportunity to have full discussion with them, but the last thing you should do is to try and follow or copy what was done by their parents and grandparents before them. There are several things which we have innovated in Chandigarh—the high level chulas [cooking stoves] and so on, but which we did not [text missing] poorest quarters because we were afraid of altering their tradition. We have since been castigated for this. They have said "Why have you given these comfortable things to Clerk's wives and not to us? Why do we still have to sit on the floor?" And they were quite right: we had been too timid to think of their real needs and way of living. Of course you have to have the closest contact with your client, and to watch the reactions all the time, but you should only think of their true way of life, and not at all of what was done by their grandparents.[83]

A good deal of the seminar's discussion and debate pivoted around the conflict between traditional practices and modern ways. The speakers had varied understandings of modernity—they disagreed about what was still valid and living, what was out of date, or what was no longer serving a useful purpose and needing to be discarded or improved. Development discourse was thus challenged by a growing confusion among consultants about the idealization of the subject—the village poor.

Tyrwhitt mentioned several times in the Rural Reconfiguration session of the conference that Indians had not learned how to live in the city. "I do not think the Eastern World had yet learned to live in towns. It knows how to live in the countryside. Living in towns is something which takes long time," Tyrwhitt said in response to Shri G. B. Deolalikar.[84] Indian participants agreed with Tyrwhitt's view. They concluded that the overall development goal of Indian villages was not to transfer villages into mini-towns, since they are mutually exclusive, but to allow the villages to develop according to their own standards. The emphasis on decentralized village-based communities, in conjunction with a rejection of established urban centers and their associated cultures, instigated a nationalist imagination of the village and its development that continues to this day. The influence of these representations of agrarian India was far-reaching, affecting the views of policymakers and designers even in the postcolonial era.

Speculation about the village and its everyday life underpinned the majority of thematic discussions that occurred in two sessions of the Delhi conference: one on Rural Reconfiguration and another on Social and Economic Development of the Village Community Organisation. The physical and social structure of the village as presented by speakers and discussants ultimately depended on their interpretation and observation of village life. There was not much debate about what constituted the village, as it seemed that all speakers agreed on that point, though all of them had diverse backgrounds and diverse personal and professional connections with Indian villages. However, the ways in which villages were imagined, portrayed, and internalized by the policymakers guided their recommendations for future village development. The four speakers in the first session—G. B. Deolalikar, S. H. Godbole, V. K. Bakre, and Tyrwhitt—expressed that "community life hardly exists in the typical village." Although it is not clear from the discussion how the experts came to such a decision, we at least understand that lack of community life was the single most important assumption that shaped the representation and conceptualization of the Indian villagers as a fragmented and politically unconscious society. Based on this assumption, most of the experts' propositions on physical improvement were directed at the community development project. However, Tyrwhitt and the experts' conception of community was exclusively an idea that the ways in which they wanted to see the villages and the villagers.

The village continued to represent the whole of India. It provided a mental framework that often transformed into an aesthetic background used to assess any development program in India. The nationalist movement against British rule was a decisive moment. For the first time, the village appeared widely as a symbol of national solidarity and the fundamental unit of a new Indian nationalism. Historian Surinder Jodhka shows that the initial knowledge of middle-class leaders of nationalist movements about Indian village and society were based primarily on colonial scholarship.[85] The distorted colonial knowledge of the village, which represented India as an ancient civilization operating through various social divisions and hierarchy, was later revised by the firsthand experience of the sociologists and politicians who worked with the villagers at the local level. The nationalist imagination of village life was never a homogenous construct, as shown by Jodhka. Gandhi, Nehru, and Ambedkar, the three main leaders of the nationalist movement, had their own perspectives on the village, its future, and its instrumental use in nationalist politics. While Gandhi's approach to the village was more ideological, Nehru's philosophy was more aligned with 1950s development theory initiated by the sociology of modernization in the United States. Despite these differences, the village, along with its perceived austerity and spatial practice, was perhaps deployed as the most important allegory in the nationalist imagination of a sovereign India.

Village or City?

In early twentieth-century India, rural and urban society have been conceptualized in relationship to each another, the village always conceived as totally disconnected from the city. However, in the mid-twentieth century, as architectural historian William Glover observes, rapid urbanization destabilized that conception of radical separation. A new sociological category then emerged in which the village and city are entangled.[86] Geddes's work in India nevertheless provided a unique opportunity to Western observers to champion this approach: a symbiotic modernization and development process that appropriated the apparent irrationality of traditional societies. Geddes's ideas, of course, share many typical colonial attitudes toward the development of colonized regions. And yet his ingenious philosophical arguments convinced the group of Western consultants who worked in postcolonial India to unequivocally accept the village as an emblematic symbol to valorize their work.

Geddes identified urban India with its rural origin, proposing in various renovation projects to transform and reduce the urban context into a mosaic of hidden rural environments. During the 1950s and 1960s, Geddes's idea attracted tremendous interest among foreign consultants commissioned to advise on various urban and rural development projects in India. As Andrew Friedman shows, consultants such as American architect and planner Albert Mayer, who worked on several major urban design projects and a massive rural development project in India, argued that the Geddesian model of urban village should be applied to the planning of new urban development in America.[87] Anthropologist Mathew Hull notes how in postindependence the idea of urban-village entanglement was carried over into the urban neighborhood development project. The challenge for American consultants was then to convert the migrant villagers into urban citizens.[88]

After independence, it was because of American interest and initiative that community development eventually became the lingua franca of the Indian built environment connecting the rural with the urban. One of the earliest major urban community development projects originated in Delhi in 1958 with assistance from the Ford Foundation. The project was followed by Ahmedabad in 1962, Baroda in 1965, and Calcutta in 1966.[89] When the United States reintroduced Geddesian community development was reintroduced to India, it was repackaged to fit with the recent development of American social thinking; that is, community development equals democratic society. In his seminal book *Social Organization* (1909), the sociologist Charles Horton Cooley, a student of John Dewey, convincingly pitched the equation "community equals democracy" for the first time.[90] Cooley's conception of community differed from Geddes's urban village. Cooley believed the true nature of the modern community is an unstructured assemblage of informal human interactions in everyday encounters. Daily face-to-face interaction, he argued, enables some inexplicable sense of morality that binds the modern community and gives rise to social participation and consequently social agency. The American consultants who worked in postindependence India more or less believed in Cooley's central theme. As part of the United Nations' Technical Assistance Program in India, in 1966 the Rural-Urban Relationship Committee of Indian Ministry of Health and Family Planning produced a report that recommended a nationwide urban community development project to cultivate a new sense of democracy. The concept of urban community was used to realign the conceptual relationship between India's village and city. It also connected in one strand a number of other issues, such as responsibility of state and citizen participation, rural-urban migration, and the political nature of society. According to the report:

> It is generally agreed that Community Development seeks to mobilize people and to create [in] them an urge to change and improve their conditions of living by their own efforts and resources supplemented by utilizing all the opportunities and assistance offered by Governmental or other agencies. This concept of Community Development is of prime importance to the building up of a healthy

> democratic base for our welfare state, which far from being a purely paternal benevolent entity, must depend for its subsistence and growth on the active participation of the people who must be stimulated to think, decide and act for themselves and utilize fully the opportunities offered by the national plans.[91]

The overall philosophy of the United Nations' postwar development mission in the Third World was deeply rooted in Geddes's idea of development through the urban-village nexus. The abstracted and idealized village poor were considered the inception point of Third World development in both rural and urban areas.

4

Architecture of the New Villages

In 1945, amid the tumultuous time of the Second World War and the final days of the Indian independence movement, Albert Mayer, the American architect and planner, met the would-be first Indian prime minister, Jawaharlal Nehru, with a unique proposal: a sweeping program of village-based, bottom-up development intended not only to modernize the national economy but also to cultivate new subjects of Indian democracy. Mayer proposed that the postcolonial state take the responsibility of turning the populist image of an ideal village, such as the Gandhian ashram, into reality. His proposal suggested that an important premise of an impending postcolonial state lies in its capacity to intervene, coordinate, and mediate rural development programs. Nehru agreed to Mayer's idea, and thus the Indian state embarked to materialize the myth of an ideal village.

The project's crucial modernization initiatives attempted to reconfigure the nation's rural spaces, seen as symptomatic and symbolic of an archaic colonial India. The main objective of the project was to produce a blueprint for modernization through rural settlement planning and economic infrastructure. Mayer's project was later handed over to the Ford Foundation. The foundation's project was one of the earliest strategies of US postcolonial intervention in which physical planning was promoted as one of the catalysts for a democratic society. It also revealed how American expertise was employed to imagine a rural Indian landscape. Home and village were transformed from the artifacts of colonial heritage to the harbingers of postcolonial inevitabilities in order to achieve industrialism, a liberalized economic structure, and a stable democratic state.

Village experiments, or ideal village construction, was not entirely unknown to India: before independence and Mayer's proposal, Gandhi, the

Rockefeller Foundation, and several American missionaries and philanthropists embarked on various ideal village projects to teach Indians how to develop their villages. Although all of the rural and community development projects seem to have similar objectives—that is, to modernize the village community—the projects actually had different cultural and political contexts and thus different agendas and objectives.[1] Mayer's proposal, however, differed even more from earlier efforts, as he proposed the need for a large-scale state intervention to create a decentralized, institutionalized, rationalized, and systematized program that would ensure a continuous production of the discourse of "rural development." The target was not exclusively to produce the ideal village per se but to foster the promise of rural development. As historian Nicole Sackley observes, Mayer's emphasis for the pilot project was less on bringing actual development and more on establishing an experimental methodology to discuss development.[2]

A major focus of the idea of Mayer and Nehru was to bolster the existing power structure of the village society and consolidate power at the hands of rural elites in the form of Panchayati raj. From this perspective, Mayer's proposal to use centralized state power for decentralizing state bureaucracy in rural areas might sound oxymoronic. However, community developers unknowingly desired this contradiction. The other unique feature of Mayer's proposal was that he offered his service as a professional consultant exclusively to the Indian state. Unlike all other key figures of ideal village projects preceded Mayer who operated mainly out of humanistic interest or to represent an NGO, Mayer did not see his role exclusively as an empathetic volunteer. Instead, he proposed to bring ideal village projects, and any such projects that aimed to alleviate poverty and develop grassroot economics through design and planning, into the fold of his professional service. Although Mayer praised American missionaries' programs in India to uplift village life, he contended that a voluntary and humanistic approach to the problem was unsustainable unless design professionals could find a way to conflate the humanistic intention with stark professionalism.[3]

Mayer arrived in India as an army engineer to serve on the China-Burma-India border and build airfields in Bengal. By the time he joined the US army, he was already an established architect in New York and was among the key proponents of public housing and the regional planning movement in the United States. Mayer also served as a consultant to the US government on public housing issues. His experience as an activist in innovative governmental policy in the United States and his concern for the improvement of human living conditions drew him to the idea of modernizing and developing Indian villages. It opened a decade-long intimate relationship with Indian people, politicians, bureaucrats, and design professionals.

Mayer's longtime hypothesis—that design could cause significant change in human life—would be tested in an emerging Third World context.

Taking Gandhism as the point of theoretical inception, Mayer's working methods relied on physical transformation through the accumulation of capital from local sources, the engagement of local materials, and the employment of local labor. Nehru introduced Mayer to Gandhi on his second visit in 1947, when they had a closed-door meeting that lasted several hours. The details of the meeting were never documented, but we know Gandhi fully supported the working method of Mayer's community development project. Mayer admired Gandhi's saint-like appearance and ascetic lifestyle.[4] He accepted that Gandhi's approach to the village-based micro-development scheme was a proper starting point, but he was critical of Gandhi's operational method, as he believed it lacked practical insight.[5]

Mayer's rural development project conceptualized rural community as the basic unit of power and was supposed to work almost independently from the influence of the central state. This community-centrism and decentralization problematize many of our normative concepts about the role of the postcolonial Indian state, especially the ways in which the state imagined its role to develop and modernize the physical environment of its villages and the ways in which foreign designers contributed to the modernization discourse against the stringent economic backdrop of India. While Mayer's project was taken as an experimental pilot project, Nehru created a parallel new agency, the Community Projects Administration, and made S. K. Dey an engineer to lead it. Dey and Mayer became rivals. Dey launched his first pilot project Nilokheri, a settlement for the partition refugees, and established an elaborate monthly journal *Kurukshetra*. Nehru was very much aware of Etawah's image as a project led by a foreign consultant and was more supportive of the Community Projects Administration and its nationalist sentiment. The administration continuously criticized the foreign origin of Etawah through essays and cartoons in *Kurukshetra*.[6]

It's important to remember that at the beginning, Mayer was not a representative of any US-government-controlled aid agency or NGO; those had very specific goals during the Cold War era. When Mayer approached Nehru for the first time with his idea of a large-scale and state-controlled village redevelopment program, he conceived that project as a typical professional project with social agendas. Nehru was attracted to Mayer's proposal for obvious reasons. The postcolonial Indian government was bound to do something with the development and modernization of Indian villages, an issue everyone felt was important but had little idea how to execute in practical terms. Mayer proposed a solid outline of that desire to do *something* about Indian villages in practical and professional terms.

And the good thing about Mayer was that he was seen as a professional man who did not come with ideological baggage.

The Indian government hired Mayer as a moral mercenary to contribute to the nourishment of vernacular modernism. However, in 1960, after handing over the project to the Ford Foundation, the government reduced Mayer's capacity to a powerless adviser, at the start of a decade when village improvement programs worldwide were increasingly related to Cold War cultural politics.[7] Mayer always took pride in his autonomy and his distance from US Cold War politics. He understood himself strictly as an independent consultant to the government of India, which wanted to apply his professional knowledge and experience to a professional project. He hardly considered his village development project to be any different from his other consultancy work in India, such as the master plans for Bombay and New Delhi and the planning of Chandigarh.

Can Mayer's proposition of Indian village development projects be understood as a process of Americanization—aimed to spur growth and development, the path through which all developing nations would have to pass in order to join an imminent industrial and global modernity?[8] Do community development programs offer an alternative to the dominant narration of state-controlled modernization, as famously discussed by James Scott in his book *Seeing Like a State*? Or was the idea of decentralized power and community development nothing but a deception of modernization—a way to exert centralized power on its countryside under the guise of community participation? Is Mayer a symbol of the imposition of American thought, of how it wanted to modernize Indian villages in a specific way so that poor villagers could escape the lure of communism? Or was Mayer excluded completely from Cold War power politics and working solely as a self-contained professional to the best interest of his client? And what was the intention of his clients anyway? There is no simple answer to any of these questions because all of these assumptions are partially true and entangled in such a way that we cannot paint a simple black-and-white picture. Nehru's perception of the modernization of the poor villages was not exclusively a national project, nor was Mayer's strict professionalism completely disconnected from the politics of an imagined utopian society rooted in American pragmatist culture.

How the limited physical and economic resources of the Third World could be used most prudently to create an elementary and austere modernism was the most fascinating and exciting political fiction of the 1950s. Nevertheless, the making of this political fiction had no single or fixed locus. It took various shapes in various political and economic contexts and fed on ideas from different countries, agencies, and individuals.[9]

However, if we consider the making of this political myth—the modernization of the rural poor—as the result of a transnational network, then Nehru and Mayer could be understood as nodes who not only borrowed ideas from each other but also generated their own ideas to suit respective national contexts. The conventional idea of modernization as being linear, with a monodirectional flow of power from the developed to the developing countries and then from state to village, promoted in the guise of cultural transference, is subject to scrutiny. Discussion of Mayer's project in this chapter demonstrates that even before the mobilization of US grants through a technical assistance program, India crystallized its own demands for development and hired independent foreign consultants. These included Albert Mayer, who was not representative of the typical American Dream, but, giving at least as much comfort to US politicians and Indian nationalists, he was also not communist.[10]

Therefore, the discourse of development of the Indian village was not entirely an American product. Rather, it was an entangled postcolonial situation in which American intervention came as an inevitable historical condition. Official US Cold War warriors had paid attention to India after a long quiescence, only when US foreign policy made a bulwark against the spread of communism in Asia and the Middle East. It was not before the mid-1950s when US diplomacy invested formidably to increase the distance between India and communism, tinged with the faint hope of making India compliant enough to draw the American Dream near. By this time, the community development projects of Mayer and Nehru had set foot firmly in India.[11] India's own postwar aspirations favored a mixed economy: a blend of capitalism and socialism that made Chester Bowles, the US ambassador to India, and his allies uncomfortable because of its idealist "impurity."[12] The mixed-state policy made for an ambivalent mix of community-based micro-development and state-controlled urban macro-development. The winding trajectory of Mayer's village development project started without any US influence. But after a decade it received a major allotment of US aid, revealing that the import and export factors in any transnational exchange of ideas do not always work exclusively. An idea can be imported and exported by different stakeholders at different periods, and the importer and the exporter can even share exchangeable positions.

Parables of Mayer: Nehru's Community Development Project

As early as the 1930s, Albert Mayer became skeptical of modernism's promise for an egalitarian society. By that time, he had become acquainted with several other architects and planners who were likewise striving to address the issue of social inadequacies of modern housing.[13] During his early career, Mayer shared a revisionist attitude—with Frederick Ackerman, Catherine Bauer, Robert Kohn, Lewis Mumford, Clarence Stein, and Henry Wright, among others—that modern physical designing as a method is impaired by its inherent reluctance to foster environments that are conducive to community life.[14] In 1933 Mayer, together with Lewis Mumford and Henry Wright, founded the Housing Study Guild with a vision to bridge the gap between architecture and regional planning.[15] The guild, supported by the Lavanburg Foundation and the Housing Association of New York, was devoted to researching technical, social, and economic aspects of housing and to training personnel for the nascent limited dividend and public housing programs.[16]

Mayer's commitment to micro-level design and planning efforts brought him closer to the Regional Planning Association of America, and in 1933 this group assisted Franklin D. Roosevelt's New Deal in drafting a new federal housing policy that brought about the US Housing Authority in 1937. This extraordinary group of architects, planners, and thinkers had conflicting views on public housing. However, they all unequivocally believed one thing: that the root cause of the decaying social fabric in America was caused by the loss of a sense of community in urban environments, especially in residential areas. Through their housing design, planning, and writing, this group advocated for a new community-oriented, relatively introverted and self-contained if not idealized design. When some members of the group were hired to work offshore, this design became popular as a "neighborhood unit" and was later exported beyond the United States.[17]

Albert Mayer was a strong supporter of the neighborhood unit. He picked up design techniques of a typical 1930s neighborhood across the United States when he worked with Stein and Wright on the seminal neighborhood unit at Redbarn. Clarence Stein—an École des Beaux-Arts–trained architect who was deeply influenced by the early twentieth-century pragmatist philosophical culture of the University of Columbia—formulated the idea of the neighborhood unit based on Ebenezer Howard's Garden City.[18] Stein's unit was a midsized, car-free neighborhood. Around two hundred residential units, a public school, and a library constituted its physical and ideological center. In Stein's ideal neighborhood, every major part of the unit was accessible by foot without crossing any major streets. Walkability in a pedestrian-friendly space was central to his vision. Stein's inspiration stemmed from the anxiety that the overarching and homogenizing force of industrial modernism would destroy regional varieties and community bonding in American society. Stein also believed that the disintegration of community was responsible for the loss of political consciousness and the critical body of civic institutions. Stein offered his neighborhood as the basic urban unit that would harness political institutions by fixing a socially disorganized community while restoring regional diversities of society.

Mayer was initially commissioned by Nehru to develop a pilot project in the Uttar Pradesh to erect model villages to demonstrate the end result of developed and modernized villages. The commission brought an excellent opportunity for Mayer to test his idea of the neighborhood unit in a developing nation. Mayer did not see any contradiction between the contexts of American cities and Indian villages. He believed that the essence of the neighborhood unit was so basic that it could be applied to any built environment. Mayer was also convinced that the main cause of underdevelopment in Indian villages, similar to America, was the absence of a strong sense of community, which, according to him, was the foundation of a self-motivated and politically conscious modern society. Mayer believed the relationship between community and political emancipation was reciprocal, and this lack of community made America and India commensurable. Although he and his colleagues at housing guilds never clearly defined what they meant by "community" in sociological terms, they envisioned an ideal physical context to wield community bonding.

Mayer and Nehru's hypothesis of creating a network of ideal villages was outlined in August 1946 in a letter to Uttar Pradesh Premier Govind Ballabh Pant.[19] These ideal villages were conceived as a prototype of development, expandable through reproduction, and repeatable with adequate provision of self-adjustments as required in different settings. Their conception was not at odds with the state-controlled development goal that had been germinating during the 1940s through the 1960s.[20] These projects assumed the presence of a potential and motivated native population that, as believed by the state bureaucracy, was desperately looking for opportunities to change its economic and social status. The postcolonial Indian state believed new citizens of India were naturally willing to accept its leadership and would receive top-down models of development as prescribed by its authority. However, the initial proposition of Nehru and Mayer changed radically when Mayer returned to India in the fall of 1946 as an adviser to the United Provinces government at a site that was selected for implementing the very first pilot project.[21]

Soon after his first exploratory trip throughout the United Provinces countryside, Mayer concluded that without a social and economic base for self-sustaining development and without external supports, the earlier top-down developmental efforts of government, missionaries, and even Gandhian "constructive workers" failed.[22] Following this logic, he abandoned his initial suggestion of a program to build model villages, proposing instead to organize an "integrated" rural development program that would focus more on developing rural infrastructure and villagers' attitudes, personalities, and thinking processes. After four months, in December 1946, Mayer outlined physical planning as the final stage of his working plan. In his revised proposal, he presented a three-tiered plan. The first phase focused on a large-scale, grassroots publicity campaign for economic development that would encourage a proactive desire among villagers. The second phase involved convincing them of their need for "betterment."[23] Mayer was convinced that, in the Indian context, sustainable physical change would occur only when the target population itself felt the need for change. In a newsletter to his Indian colleagues, he emphasized that "a visible and noticeable physical improvement is required in the village, which will lift the habits and the 'sights' of the villager." In Mayer's view, planning and design was only a framing apparatus for materializing this collective desire in the people.[24]

Mayer's rejection of the idea of erecting an ideal built example to teach the villagers, and his new proposal to develop a system that would continuously work to produce a desired environment—his preference of process over product—might well have been influenced by pragmatism, an American philosophical movement that holds there is no single or ideal truth. Pragmatists contend that truth is variable, ever-changing, and always in the making. Stein and his colleagues were well informed and convinced by the pragmatist view. In his new proposal, Mayer argued that village reconstruction demanded a new sense of temporality, just as a dedicated pragmatist would. The present had to be experienced not as a moment in a uniform continuum but as radically transient: a work in progress.

Nehru granted and supported Mayer's revised proposal. Seven months before independence, he appointed Mayer as planning adviser to the government of the United Province. His proposal suggested the initiation of experimental schemes, not merely for improving the material quality of villages but also for structuring the existential values of the community and nurturing a desire for self-improvement. The plan soon became known as the Etawah Project, named for the district where it all started.

A perfectionist and assiduous organizer, Mayer personally recruited key Indian and American staff, including Horace Holmes as agricultural extension adviser, Eldon Cullins as agricultural engineer, and Dudley Trudgett from his own firm, Mayer and Whittlesey, as town and village planner.[25] He established his workplace at a government own Bungalow in Lucknow about three hundred miles away from the project site. His team worked closely with Pant and Krishna Behari Bhatia, United Provinces development commissioner. Mayer offered himself solely as an occasional guide who, by providing overall supervision and setting the principles of the project, would help to develop the program. Indian officials had to tackle everyday administrative issues, the immediate program, and operational challenges. Over the next eight years, the pilot project spread to seventy-eight other villages. During the first few years (1947–1950), Mayer's team devoted its strengths to preparing appropriate contexts that could mobilize, contain, and sustain the physical transformation of rural life. This was demonstrated at two levels: by introducing techniques to improve agricultural production to increase the purchasing power of villagers, and by educating them both socially and morally about a lifestyle that was more hygienic, rational, dignified, and thus desirable. Development as defined by Mayer had to follow a slow, integrated process that would systematically prepare the villagers for a changed life.[26] Architecture and any material effort would be a natural consequence of this changed life.

A Theory of Self-Development

In January 1947, a few months before the Etawah Project became fully operational, Mayer visited an ashram run by Gandhian worker Dhiren Majumder and visited a model village at Faizabad that was set up by the former Congress Party government.[27] When Mayer's team arrived, the short winter day had already rolled into dusk, sinking the entire village into darkness—the uninhabited prototypes did not merit lighting. Mayer satirized this Indian Potemkin village as disconnected from the realities of the rural economy and its patterns of living. He believed that, as a new template for village life, it was destined for failure. Such exclusive efforts were incapable of producing a sustainable and self-generating "model" for village life.

While unimpressed by the formal imperatives of model buildings, Mayer was far more interested in his guide who guided them around the village with a fickle hurricane lamp.[28] Mayer's guide, a local schoolteacher whom he described as the "lady teacher," represented a new generation of rural Indian women. He was fascinated by the intellectual and emotional architecture of her novel subjectivity, which would become a focus of his work in India. Mayer was less curious about the material design of the village; rather, he was interested in the school (Faizabad School for Adult Literacy) that had shaped the personality of this female teacher who, it appeared to Mayer, had liberated herself from the rigid taboos of rural society in India. Mayer later argued that architecture for rural India ought to be a consequential byproduct and an end result of a larger social proj-

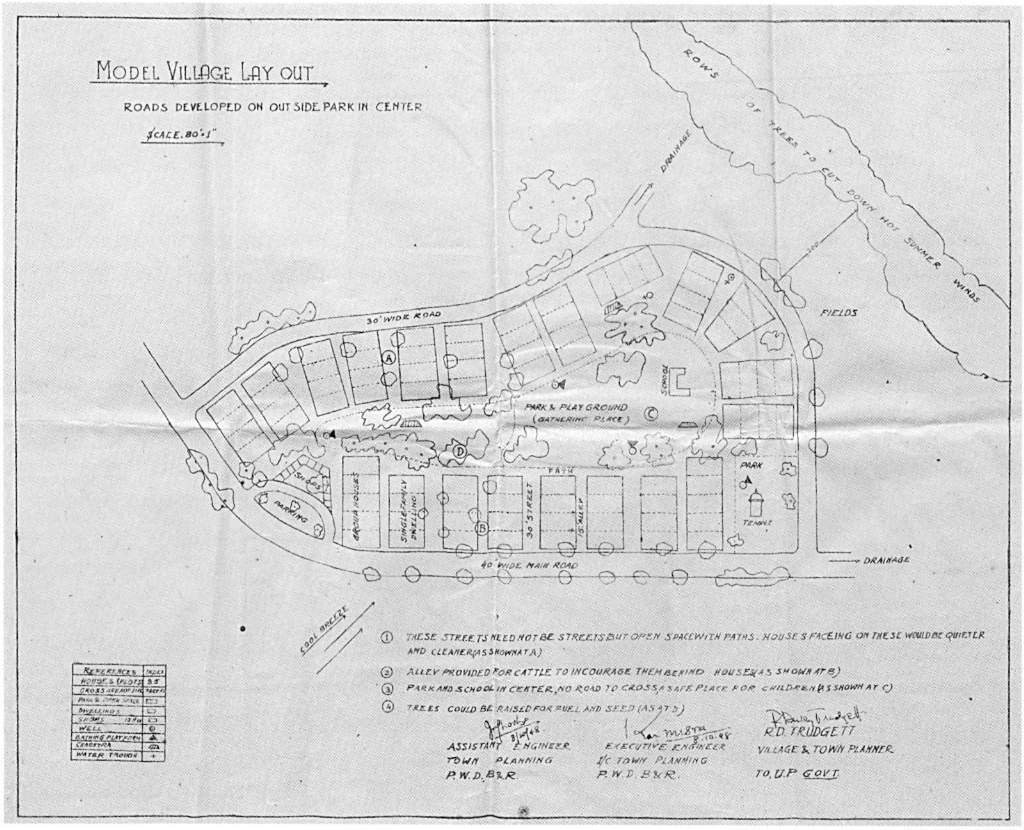

FIGURE 4.1. Trudgett team's proposal for a prototype model of a circular village. Source: Albert Mayer Papers, box 6, folder 7, University of Chicago Library.

ect.[29] He also contended that design must function within an institutional framework of rural economy and politics and must not perpetuate a systematic hierarchy of class-based social relations. Instead of imposing top-down development ideas, he suggested a political reordering of the former feudal system of colonial India and supported the populist political opinion that power be consolidated in the hands of the village panchayat. Mayer's supervision worked to forge an indigenous willingness to clear away hindrances to India's own path toward postcolonial prosperity.

By 1949 Indian politicians became impatient to see physical results of development efforts, but Mayer's team was still struggling to prepare the villagers for the imminent change. A few months later, during the heavy monsoon of September 1949, the incessant torrents washed away hundreds of houses built of unbaked mud bricks. Mayer considered the natural disaster the appropriate opportunity to test the readiness of the villagers to bring in a physical transformation of their homes. Mayer and

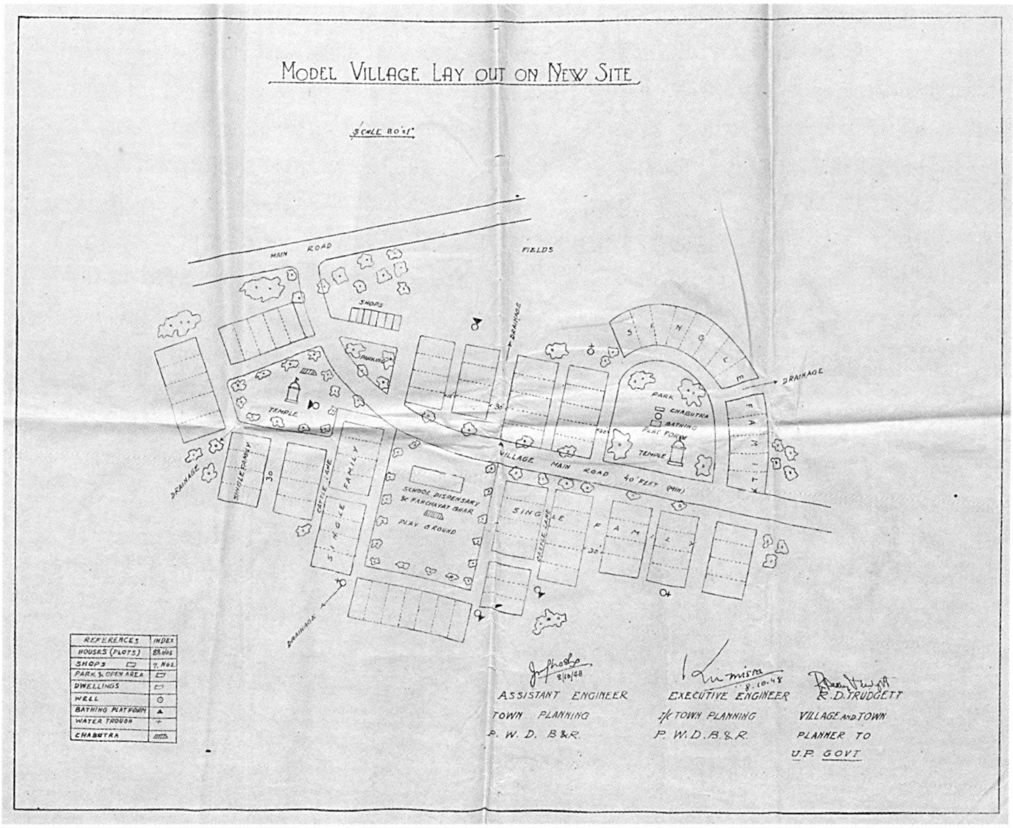

FIGURE 4.2. Trudgett team's proposal for a prototype model of a linear village. Source: Albert Mayer Papers, box 6, folder 7, University of Chicago Library.

Dudley Trudgett, the town and village planner of Mayer's team, sketched layouts for the damaged villages and plans for village houses. The Indian staff at the Provincial Town and Village Planning Office in Lucknow, set up by Trudgett, produced the working details of his and Mayer's ideas.[30] Trudgett served as an occasional consultant to matters pertaining to planning and design issues, and Eldon Collins, the agricultural engineer, worked as a chief engineer of the operations section of the rural work and was responsible for implementing ideas.[31]

Mayer and Trudgett considered three different layouts as prototypes. The first was the cellular type (fig. 4.1), a concentric interiorized layout of rectilinear plots, organized around a nucleus of public functions. The continuous peripheral road gave it an introvert character and was considered appropriate for a small community. The second was the linear type (fig. 4.2), in which a central thoroughfare connected recurring and alternating public and private spaces. Public spaces created secondary cellular organization, often surrounded by residential plots. This type suggested a linear development with future provisions for the addition of subsequent residential plots and new public cores. In the case of the village Hari-Ka-Pura, the public core was on the western end of the neighborhood, thus creating a clear distinction between it and the residential zone. The community core included a cottage industry, Gandhi Chabutra (a Gandhi plinth is a raised platform to hold community gathering), *akhra* (open-air gymnasium), a community flower garden or orchard, a children's playground, and finally a school that would also be used for panchayat meetings. These elements are present in all seven designs recorded in the Albert Mayer Collection of the University of Chicago Library.

It is noteworthy that Clarence's original neighborhood theory often argues for a central position for the community core, but Trudgett's design preferred a peripheral location. Only one of Trudgett's "model village layouts," probably for a new site designed in 1948, had a central community core that included a school, playground, and an open "gather space." This central core was linked with trees on the west side to the commercial core, including shops and parking spaces, and to its east to the spiritual core: a temple nestled in an open space. A note on the drawing read: "Park and school in center, no road to cross. A safe place for children."[32] The public school, following Stein's basic scheme, was the focus of the community, and the building itself was loaded with meaning: it was a symbol of education and future and also of participatory governance.

Trudgett's last design was the deformed grid (fig. 4.3), in which a single central public space was organized along the main road and the residential plots arranged in a rectilinear pattern around the central public core that allowed development in all directions. An example of this type was explored in a more dynamic way in another model village layout in which the four cores—commercial, spiritual, school-panchayat, and park—were all arranged along a forty-foot-wide central main road. Residential areas surrounded all four cores. Similar principles were applied in another model village for a new town that was accompanied by explanatory notes. Shops in the commercial core were built away from the main road to provide more room for public gatherings, probably an effort to create privacy and a sense of community. It was also explained in the drawing that a layer of back alleys was added to encourage the villagers to keep their cattle in the rear of the house, probably the main reason Trudgett preferred a linear development.

Besides the single-family house, Trudgett also introduced the group dwelling. There is no clear indication as to the nature or intention of "low-income group housing" in his master plan. However, based on the

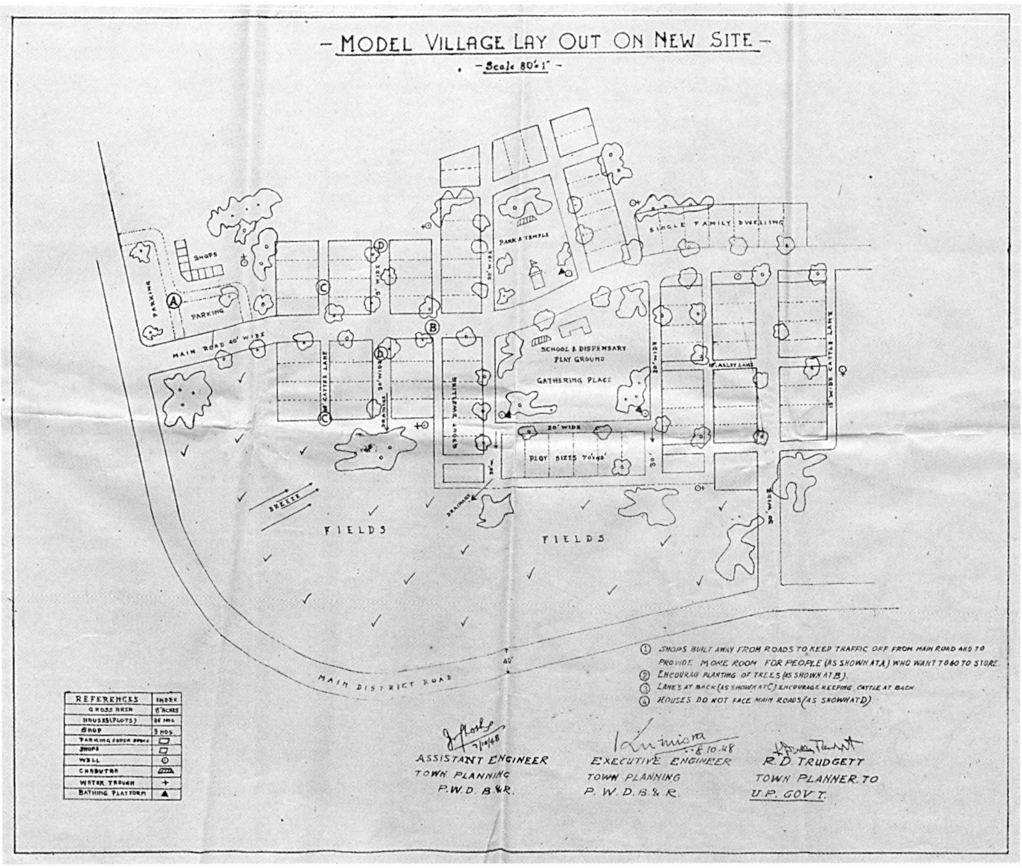

FIGURE 4.3. Trudgett team's proposal for a prototype model of a deformed grid village. Source: Albert Mayer Papers, box 6, folder 7, University of Chicago Library.

1958 design for the Bombay Municipality, on which Mayer served as a consultant (fig. 4.4), we can assume that it would be a shared dwelling for three to four people with one bedroom, kitchen, bath, water closet, and veranda. While the designers substantiated the necessity of such a group dwelling in the context of Bombay, where many single male and female workers needed to share a home, so far I have not uncovered any studies or documents that explain the rationale behind group housing in villages.

Mayer and Trudgett opened up lanes, roads, and pathways to make the existing village fabric more accessible, which had both pragmatic and transcendental objectives. The pragmatic objective was to improve environmental sanitation by decreasing the density and increasing ventilation and sunlight inside individual households. The transcendental objective was to elevate the sense of camaraderie and solidarity among villagers, as it demanded a mutual sacrifice while removing and clearing off verandas

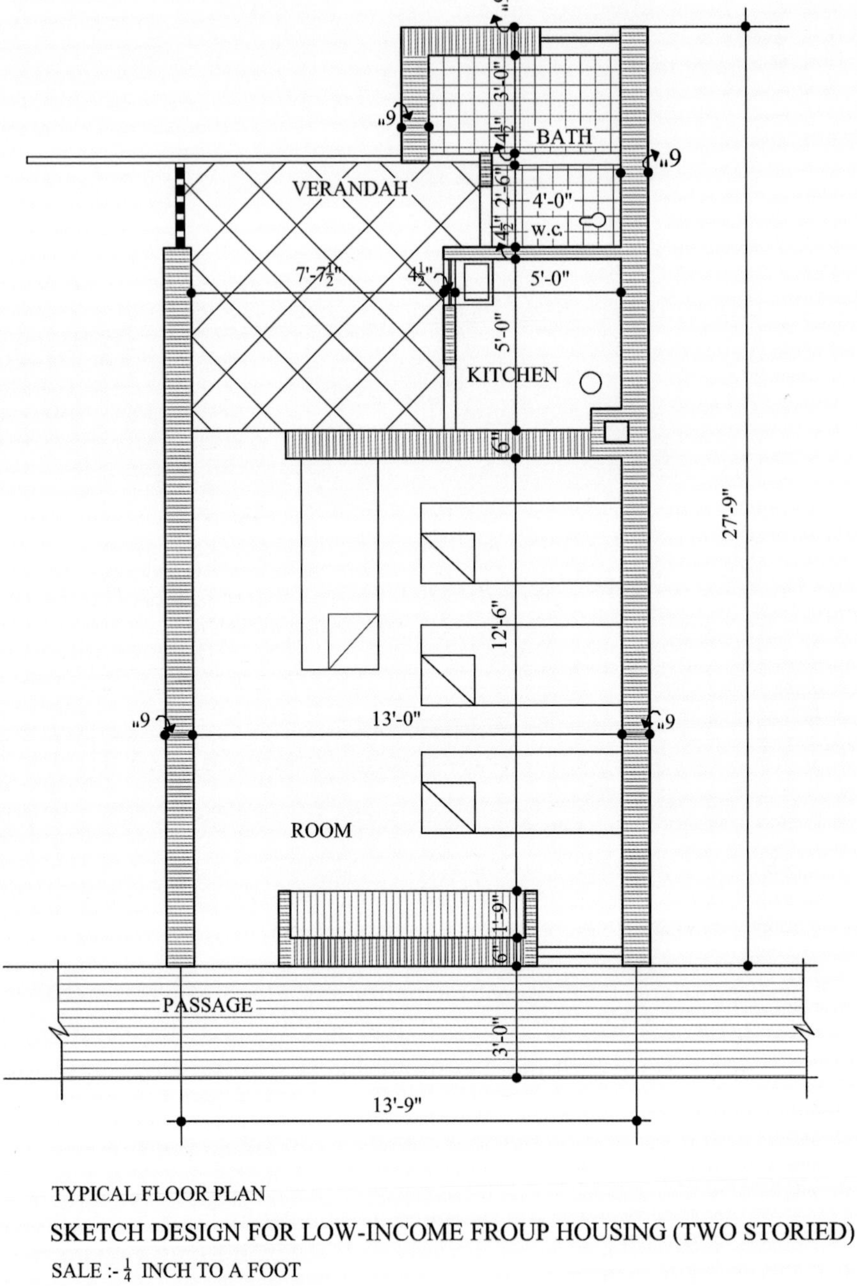

FIGURE 4.4. Low-income group housing designed by Albert Mayer for the Bombay Municipality. Drawing by Bushra Nayeem. Source: Albert Mayer Papers, box 29, folder 18, University of Chicago Library.

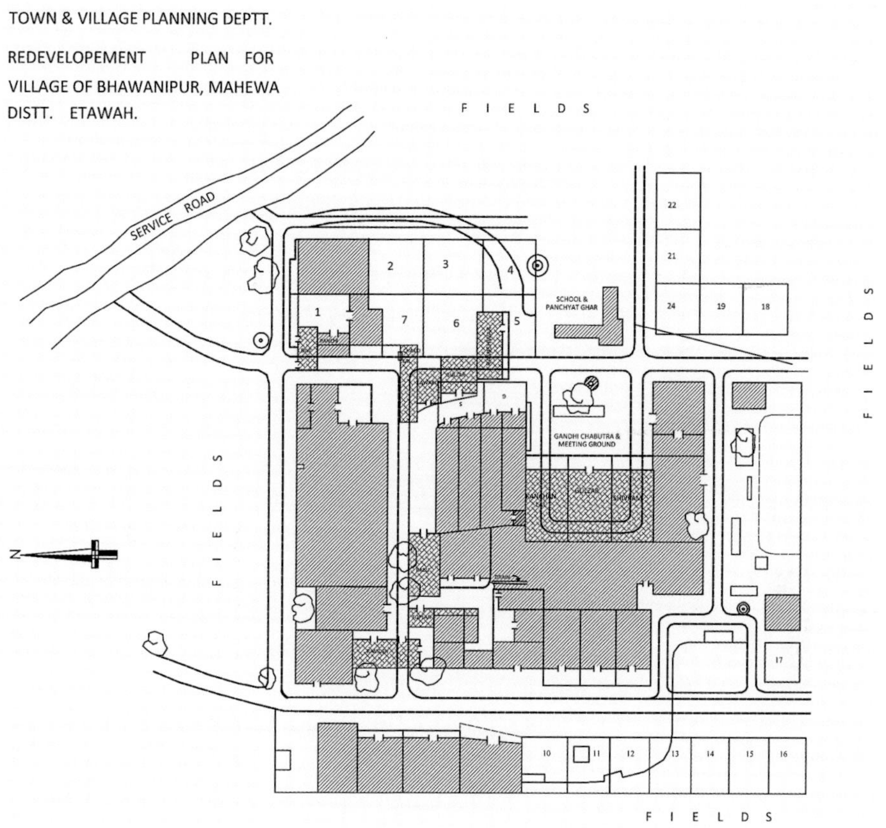

FIGURE 4.5. A development plan for village Bhawanipur, Mahewa, that requires some change in land ownership. Drawing by Bushra Nayeem. Source: Albert Mayer Papers, box 6, folder 7, University of Chicago Library.

or sitting platforms along roads and lanes. Mayer's team hoped the project would generate local leadership that would then channel a collective drive for betterment. However, redesigning an existing village was not without limitations, as any substantial improvements of road networks and zoning were extremely challenging.[33] In order to successfully implement Trudgett's layout of an improved village, a radical change in the ownership of land (fig. 4.5) was essential.

The village development authority could not simply acquire land in villages. Mayer and Trudgett relied on their hypothesis that if the heads of the Panchayati raj could explain the benefits of the new scheme to villagers, those villagers would willingly cooperate to materialize the plan. In the process, if any individual had to make personal sacrifices, she would do so altruistically, for the benefit of others. Through this collective sacrifice, villagers would gradually create a sense of community—something rural people did not possess, according to Mayer and his Indian colleagues. If a village did not have strong community ties, they believed it would collectively create a physical environment and therefore a collective memory; in their minds, the two were directly linked.

Mayer and his colleagues believed that in villages the communal harmony and balance of power naturally existed through the empathetic and benevolent love of the powerful for the powerless, echoing a stereotyped Gandhian vision.[34] This process is a hybrid one in which the state performs the mediatory role that apparently encourages and facilitates individuals to act as agents of social change. The community-centrism of Mayer and Trudgett involved multiple factors: Mayer's personal commitment to conflating socialist ideals with the values of consumerism in New Deal America; his roots in the neighborhood planning movement that imagined a small government with minimum intervention in public life; and finally, India's experiments with a bottom-up approach of development that sought examples from the United States and hoped that the state could foster grassroots development with minimum intervention. One thing was for certain—individuals, neighborhoods, and communities were seen as the space where the individuals or the agents could apply their power. And against this scenario, the state had little control. For this community-centric model of development, the willpower of poor villagers was the central driving force behind development. State-level centralized planning or structural determinacy was only conceived as a complementary and mediatory force.

This interpretation of the community development project challenges the conventional history of postindependence India. Sociologist Subir Sinha argues that the concept of community in sociological scholarship is problematic as a binary opposite to the concept of state. And yet the theoretical framework of prominent subaltern historian Partha Chatterjee, Sinha argues, further bolsters this conceptual binary by arguing that community is the last space unaffected by colonial dominance.[35] Chatterjee's explanation inhibits intellectual inquiry into the possible relationship between state and community. The partnership of Mayer and Nehru, or the states interested in harnessing a decentralized governing body, tells a different story. American designers deployed the community-centrism and neighborhood-ism that would alter the political power relationship within the community, which is essentially linked to the state. Community as perceived by Mayer and Nehru was not the polar opposite of state but rather complementary.

In Mayer's and Trudgett's proposals for improved new villages, they explicitly showed their preference for a gradual altering of the existing village layout. They conceived of a village as a palimpsest and thus conceptualized rural development as a natural evolution from a lower to higher level of planning. They reclaimed the public core of the village, composed of temples, parks, schools, and shops. These were already present in the existing layout but hidden behind cramped houses and less integrated with the overall village because of "narrow and crooked" roads. Their main priority was to form and enhance the concept of a "public" rural life, as the public sphere associated with public space was considered the foundation of any democratic system. The proposed layout was arranged around a central public area accessible through relatively straight and wide roads: a deformed radial pattern that accommodated the rectilinear plots. The ultimate goal of such order, as stated by the designers, was to provide a space where "everyone is healthier, stronger and happier—no sick days when farmers can't work, he can now work more because he is stronger."[36]

Implicit in the idea of a participatory public space was the conviction that it would cultivate a successful, industrious, and more productive society through design. A strong emphasis was placed on the working male body. The akhra, or an open-air gymnasium, was located in the central public core of the village so that it could continuously display the development of virile male bodies. The akhra in a typical village had multiple symbolic values. It was of course a place to exercise, build strong physical bodies, and practice wrestling. But the strong physical body was not meant to exercise dominance over society. Anthropologist Joseph Altar explained that the mission of Indian vernacular wrestlers was similar to the personal and cultural mission of a sannyasi—to acquire greater control over one's libidinal desire and hedonistic pleasure and thus to challenge the structural dominance of society.

In classical Greek townships, a wrestler's body symbolized an anthropomorphic worldview; it was the idealized embodiment of civilizational achievement, a concept probably not unknown to Mayer. Vernacular Indian wrestlers strengthened their physical bodies only to control and subdue sensual and libidinal pleasure. In this context, the akhra promoted a nullification of the self: increasing a man's strength and virility increased his capacity to work and to produce for the benefit of the community. We cannot tell for sure whether Mayer and Trudgett were fully aware of this meaning of Indian wrestlers. But for Mayer and his Indo-American colleagues, the akhra would promote producing a physically strong, happier, more virile, and more industrious generation that would facilitate postcolonial nation building and economic development.

The akhra, in conjunction with the public school, thus created a symbolic core the village to fight against "cow-dung psychology," a derogatory perception of the effects of rural life. According to an anonymous discussant at the All India Technical-cum-Promotion Program for Planning and Rebuilding the Villages in 1957, "Today village people live in crowded, dirty villages which in and of themselves produce a 'cow-dung' psychology." Mayer and Trudgett's approach to rural development was not an aberration; they advocated a prevailing public opinion among the middle class that Indian villagers ought to improve their physical strength and uplift the morale of their minds to successfully harness the boons of social development. A promotional quote from the same all-India conference better portrays this mindset:

> In the building of New India village people must be educated to have a new outlook and assisted in achieving in higher level of living. They must see themselves as self-respecting citizens, capable of planning for their future, and must learn through experience that they possess within themselves the resources to solve most of their problems. . . . What is needed is national program. . . . Such a program will go long way toward creating the "new village" outlook that is so essential in making village development a continuous dynamic force. In this new outlook, which can flow the physical rebuilding of the villages of India, two new values—Orderliness and Cleanliness—can be expected to emerge.[37]

The Natural Villagers

About the same time when Mayer was working in India, German architect Otto Koenigsberger extensively used the neighborhood unit concept in his planning projects in India and argued to apply the principal not only in India but also in other developing countries.[38] Like many other Western professionals of his time, Koenigsberger looked upon developing countries as a homogenous construct; they shared one "traditional" social structure and had similar aspirations and interests. According to Koenigsberger, the neighborhood unit "has special appeal to the people of underdeveloped countries . . . and people are used to thinking in terms of village communities. For them the neighborhood units of the new town form the best possible links with the type of community life they know from their villages."[39] He was convinced that the neighborhood unit would preserve the essence of a community-based village life within a new urban fabric. His thesis was based on the conviction that the majority of people in new Indian cities, having recently migrated from rural villages, would look for affinity with their known world. These urban villagers would naturally feel at home and thrive in their new neighborhood units. Mayer was also confident that Indian city dwellers who had originated in villages would be much happier living in a neighborhood unit, explaining, "However useful the neighborhood concept is here [in the United States], it is more valid in India, where most people are still villagers and small community people at heart, and fairly recently by origin."[40]

For Western designers, India was a microcosm of the entire swath of "underdeveloped" countries and a natural fit for the neighborhood unit. The people, irrespective of their national and regional identity, were naturally members of an abstract idealized village. This abstraction was helpful for the designers who packaged and conflated the United Nations' self-help housing with the neighborhood unit. While the neighborhood unit presented a top-down approach to development or an idealized environment designed by an authoritative architect, self-help housing offered a technique to materialize that idealized vision with a bottom-up approach.

In the wake of the global Cold War, Mayer's team sought to explore the novel method of self-help in management, finance, and building technology to fight back against resource scarcity and poverty. Mayer and Nehru's project emerged at a time when poverty gained a discursive status in UN and US foreign policy, which identified poverty and the loss of communal consensus as the root cause for the spread of communism in developing countries. Over a few years, a great wave of UN experts lined the shores of the emerging Third World to facilitate the urge for development and almost unequivocally accepted self-help as the most effective method to achieve it.[41] This method, conceived as part of the Cold War take-off economic model, espoused that financial and intellectual aid to the Third World would "fill the gap" in its path toward coveted economic growth.

UN experts thought the moral dimension of the self-help economic model would make the "common people" aware of their own needs and disadvantages. They believed that the self-realization of the native population, in tandem with limited First World aid, would motivate Third World societies to help themselves. In 1951 Mayer prepared a draft pamphlet of the self-help method for the United Nations that outlined five consecutive steps toward development for developing countries with the help of external technical assistance and action groups. For these countries, the pamphlet recommended the following: "In what they lacked and what they have, the background had to be developed, leadership applied and activated, the productive base improved, the great resource of idle manpower is to be fully harnessed."[42] In Mayer's explanation, the root cause of India's troubled disadvantage was the absence of an institutionalized mechanism that might harness community sense and convert the unwieldy population into an effective workforce or into an exchangeable product.

Mayer's team split the process of housing construction into two distinct sections. The first section dealt with the portion of a house that could be built by nonskilled laborers: a team composed of the would-be homeowner's family members. The second section involved the residual part of a house that required skilled laborers for its construction. Skilled labor had to be procured outside the villages and required a cash subsidy. This split-off notion shifted the traditional connotation of a house from a hereditary possession and a shelter of multiple generations to a matter of material fabrication and therefore an exchangeable product that could be produced and end within a single generation. The transformation of house to exchangeable product was the basis of Mayer's model of modern housing and was beneficial as long as the exchange value of the house did not surpass its use value. However, Mayer's attempt to reform the concept of rural housing in India was an effort to enhance the use value of a house, and thus the house was valued only in terms of its material content and the labor-days required to build it. As Mayer recounted, "Two hundred and sixty-five labor days were required per house, of which the occupier, his wife, and his family put in 225 days, and 40 days were put in by skilled workers."[43]

The transformation of a house exclusively into an exchangeable product eventually proved convenient for circulating housing ideas among Third World contexts. This tenet was recycled in the United Nations' 1964 publication *Manual on Self-Help Housing,* which defined self-help as "with or without aid, technical assistance, hidden or direct subsidies, government support, tools or machines, etc."[44] The United Nations offered an open definition of self-help housing that was flexible enough to incorporate contested ideas of various First World–Third World relations. The inbuilt contingency of the definition increased its potential to fit into various cultural contexts of developing countries. It nevertheless engulfed the precapitalist mode of housing production or the actual self-built house and reorganized it into a product of a more complex division of labor. The organized self-help housing program exercised an integrated global financial system that further advanced a unique mode of production in which a product was supposed to be consumed only by the producers.[45] The new proposition of self-help housing rather emphasized that a house as a product should not be exclusively consumed by its producers. The new role of producers was that of service providers from whom houses should be purchased on the basis of their exchange value. For the rural Indian community, this was rather a new consciousness in which the relation between producers and users was determined in terms of the exchange value of the product.

The above hypothesis of aided self-help housing—as an assimilating apparatus to conflate precapitalist modes of production with the developed capitalist mode—was problematized by Mayer's conception of cooperative factories to produce building materials, mainly bricks, the principal building material for an improved rural house. Mayer's team encouraged the villagers to establish a brick factory, run almost entirely by unskilled laborers. The initial idea behind the cooperative factory was to reduce the villagers' dependence on external supplies and enable them to produce their own bricks. These factories bestowed multiple identities upon the villagers—a farmer assumed a dual role as a food and brick producer. Even the schoolchildren donated voluntary labor to produce bricks for their own school. Implicit in Mayer's conception of self-help housing was an obliteration of the social and economic division of labor in an idealized romantic way.

His effort also reduced the duration of the production process by providing social agents with multiple capacities to produce. The first cooperative brick kiln industry of the Etawah project opened in 1948 under the auspices of Dhyan Pal Singh, Etawah's district planning officer. What was initially conceived as a secure and immediate source of bricks grew into a profitable community business venture for the next four years. The first brick kiln was established at Mahewa with initial funds from the Mahewa Cooperative Union. As stated by D. P. Singh, it was more "the child of necessity than of deliberate planning."[46] Since Etawah was not meant to produce sporadic shows of model buildings but to germinate a consistent physical development across the district, it was necessary for the city to secure a continuous local supply of construction materials at a lower cost. A congenial environment of voluntary village laborers was the central inspiration for running such a cooperative brick kiln.

The objective of establishing small self-help factories was to produce low-cost materials by cutting down transportation costs and eliminating as much wage labor as possible. Around this same time, Phool Singh, the deputy minister of planning in Uttar Pradesh, circulated the idea of the voluntary gift of labor as *shramdan*, or the labor-gift movement, which also added enthusiasm to voluntary community development projects.[47] However, the first brick kiln at Mahewa incurred a significant loss due to inexperienced management and eventually closed down. Coincidentally, in 1949, the following year, a heavy monsoon damaged hundreds of houses, encouraging D. P. Singh to restart another cooperative kiln at Mahewa, this time with a generous supply of fuel from the Indian government. The venture eventually made a fortune by providing a large supply of bricks to rebuild recently damaged houses. Singh described this success as the "permanent, self-paying, self-perpetuating, and self-generating relief measure."[48] This endeavor developed the concept of a sustainable model of community business that supported incomes and local building industries in a symbiotic way.

FIGURE 4.6. Albert Mayer (center) visiting a brick kiln, talking to D. P. Singh. Source: Albert Mayer Papers, box 41, folder 23, University of Chicago Library.

The initial success of the cooperative brick kiln created extensive interest in the villages for their capacity to generate employment during agricultural slack seasons. The kiln became a symbol of progress: by resourcing affordable construction materials, it helped to sustain consistent development. From the perspective of designers and administrators, homegrown bricks unified the division between urban and rural housing. The bricks were thought to free the local builders from mud wall, or *kucha*, construction, and gave them the opportunity to produce a standard, reproducible rural housing scheme (fig. 4.6). Modernist discourse has long deemed rural housing incapable of expressing modern principles, since a negotiation between rural organics and scientific modernism was thought to be absurd. The brick kiln of the community development project was in this sense an effort to incorporate rural housing within the jurisdiction of modernism. Rural adobe houses represent the preindustrial culture of handicrafts and an extreme decentralized pattern of housing construction because the materials used in such houses were locally gathered and locally constructed. Brick houses not only give the impression of order and geometry but also represent an industrial culture. Brick embodies the idea of centralized production and tailored manufacturing, and locally produced brick also stands for a homogenous material culture. Although rural brick factories manually controlled every step of production, the idea of centralized production, distribution, and supply differentiated brick construction from adobe.

In the Indian context of the 1940s, the concept of the homegrown had connections with the swadeshi zeal of Congress and Gandhi's political symbolism of consumer liberty, autonomy, and economic self-sufficiency. Over the decades of the 1930s and 1940s, the Indian psyche was articulated around the showcased body of Gandhi as a working man, a hand spinner, a destitute man who, despite having a fragile appearance, took extreme pride in his self-sufficiency: satisfying his material needs through self-production. But the Gandhian material culture of austerity that had spurred on anticolonial zeal was later denounced, much to the chagrin of many Gandhians, as ineffective in a postcolonial context that vied to enter an industrial and tech economy.[49] The project of Nehru and Mayer was in this context an effort to negotiate between opposite poles: it offered a pragmatic solution for village development with scant aid without causing a radical transformation of existing economic patterns and power structures. However, the need to utilize limited and inadequate government money compelled Mayer to conceive of an operational strategy that learned to fend for itself, ignore outside assistance, and achieve a self-directed definition of development.

One of the earliest houses built under Mayer's team's supervision was located in the Gorakhpur district in the village of Bhathat. One of the reasons for choosing this site was its advantageous central location; neighboring villagers could easily come and see the construction of the house. In a way, the demonstration process was designed as a large-scale exhibition, an event of "sightseeing," according to Mayer: "The chances of success for later efforts can be much enhanced by sight-seeing, that is, by bringing people from other villages both to see the work in progress and again to see the completed work. The systematic sightseeing is indispensable for spreading such work in any reasonable time."[50] One reason for conceiving the pilot project as a summation of sporadic demonstrations was an acute shortage of domestic funds for development. As time passed, Indian bureaucrats became more convinced that external funding assistance was required. Whatever development efforts India's resources could offer to village housing were still trapped in resource scarcity, or an inchoate path to the final destination that required a significant input of technology, transport, and finance.

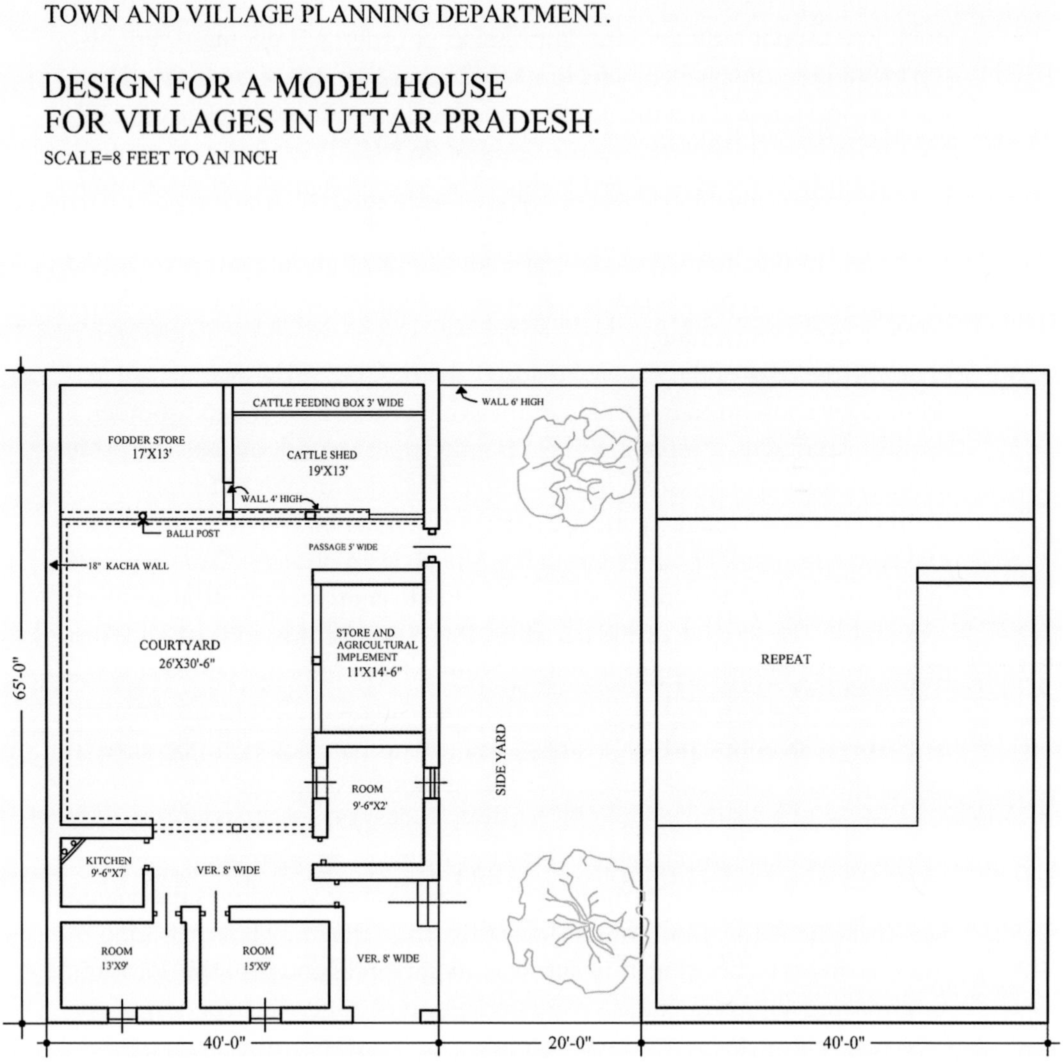

FIGURE 4.7. Trudgett team's proposal for a prototype of a rural house for Uttar Pradesh. Drawing by Bushra Nayeem. Albert Mayer Papers, box 6, folder 5, University of Chicago Library.

With a secured supply of locally produced bricks, the Town and Village Planning Office designed a group of clean cubic spaces, hierarchically adjacent to each other around a central courtyard (figs. 4.7, 4.8). The different segments of the house were composed to form a 2 to 1 or 1.5 to 1 rectangle. The size of the individual house was designed in a way that it could be well fitted into the proposed rectangular plots of the village layout. At the center of the prototype was the courtyard: a place where the

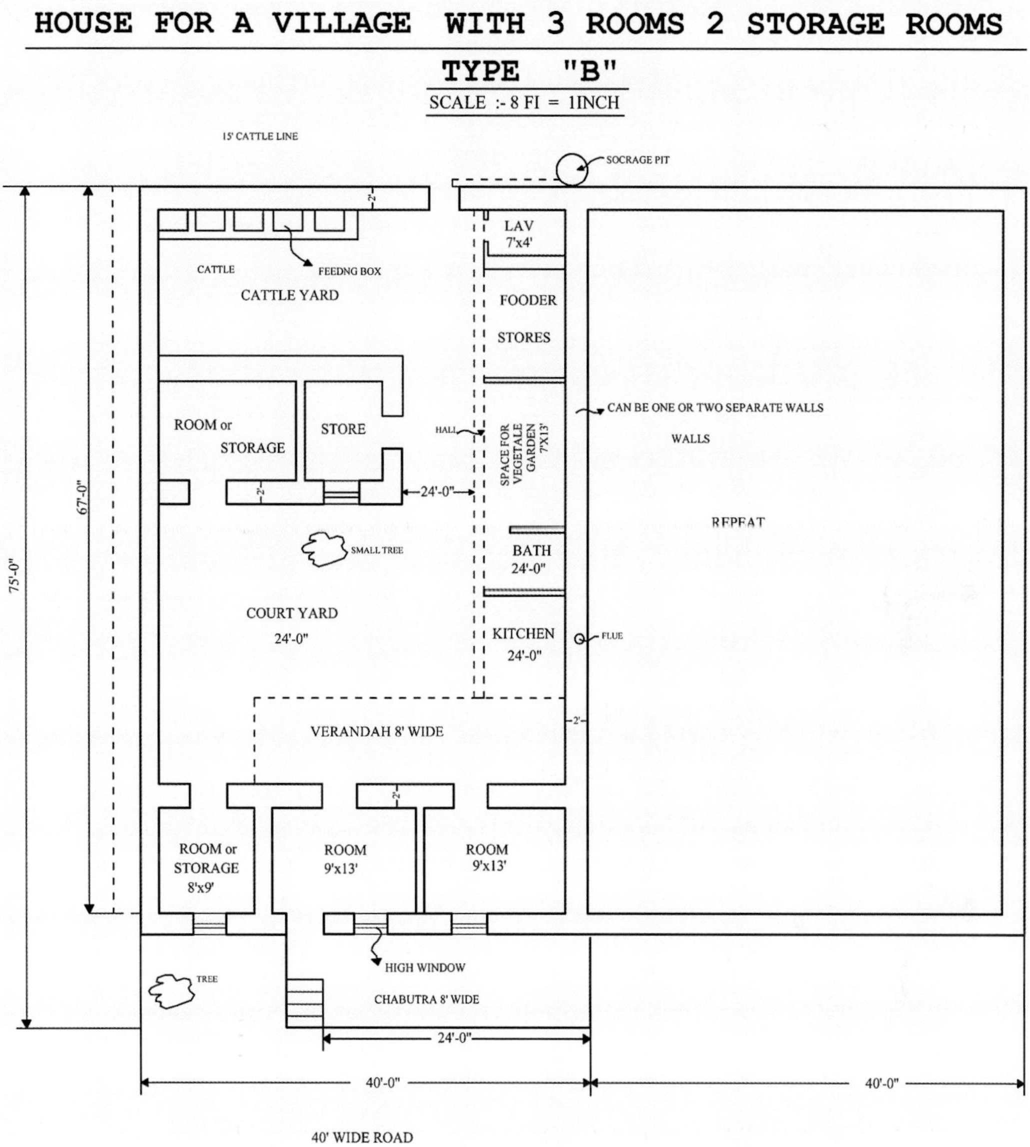

FIGURE 4.8. Trudgett team's proposal for a prototype of a three-room rural house with two storage rooms for Uttar Pradesh. Drawing by Bushra Nayeem. Source: Albert Mayer Papers, box 6, folder 5, University of Chicago Library.

entire gamut of rural work-life from after-harvest processing to sewing was performed, was dominated mainly by female members of the family. The surrounding anonymous rooms, labeled just as "rooms," rejected the idea of spatial divisions of an urban home: the bedroom, drawing room, and so on. These spaces were conceived as flexible and indefinite, not for private refuge, not for savoring domestic comfort, but rather as essential components to the work zone of the house. If the courtyard stands for the embedded work hours of its dwellers, then the surrounding spaces were for pause, helping to rejuvenate those within before they resumed their work. The daily work cycle of the dwellers was punctuated by these anonymous places. These punctuations contracted the increasing distance between human labor and material artifacts and their Cold War dispersal through modernization. According to Mayer:

> But to anyone who has spent the four hot months in Indian villages the question has always seem to be not why people work so little and listlessly, why are they so lethargic, but rather the contrary one: where do these people find the energy to work this hard in this relentless scorching heat? Why should there not some day be enough power created in India cheaply enough so that every village can afford at least one air conditioned room where each person can spend say, a half hour to relax and refresh. It would do wonders; it would be a daily rebirth. This would indeed be a modernized people's version of what in India is called the Rest House, now a travel convenience for the Sahib.[51]

Despite adopting the modern rhetoric of crisp clean lines, the kind of life suggested by these houses more closely resembled preindustrial culture, in which dwelling and working coexisted. The two-foot-thick mud walls of these homes could be replaced with brick walls when bricks became readily available from local industries. In both cases, the construction method was entirely dependent upon the advice of local craftspeople and builders. Local construction experts supervised the building construction and helped to make the walls more permanent and hygienic by using new techniques. It was a combined effort of urban experts and village specialists. These houses were built by a team of nonspecialized rural workers and supplied for immediate consumption on the production site. Thus, it is possible to identify these dwellings as modern handicrafts: marked by the visible traces of their work history and the recognition of the exchange value of personalized labor.

Mayer's message was received in multiple ways by different stakeholders, often in contradictory ways. What his model did not encourage was stripping the social meaning of housing in the interest of delivering rural housing as a product, purchasable through a long-term loan or credit system—even though the United Nations and the Ford Foundation later took this as its operational method. Housing was used as a tool to include the poor within the existing system of global capital and was thus tied to the First World by means of small loans, a concept that later matured into a microfinance system. Leftist scholars confronted the United Nations' strategy of aided self-help housing. They argued that the method was a capitalist ploy to assimilate and integrate the poor as an economical category within global capital flow (see chapter 2). In this context, aided self-help housing was instrumental solely in providing the scope to increase capital investment to comply with certain coded rules. Whatever initial intentions Mayer had, his model of self-help housing set the non-institutionalized precedent for the United Nations' official aided self-help housing program throughout the 1950s to the 1970s. As one of the pioneers of self-help in India, Mayer was able to demonstrate both to the United States and to India that, with minimal expert guidance, the poor would find their own way to survive within their own traditional economic patterns. The efficacy of his method in economic policy in the Third World provided sufficient confirmation for the benefactors of Rostow's take-off theory.[52]

Cultivating the New Indian "Man"

Mayer coined the term "inner democratization" or "inner administrative democracy," which has several meanings at administrative, operational, and philosophical levels. The main concept of inner democratization is that if one cannot change the participants of the development programs into empathetic individuals, no administrative reformation is possible. True democratization of bureaucracy demanded profound shifts in subjectivity. As stated by Mayer, inner democracy involved "joint planning and this feeling of participation and of personal value [that] is, I believe, the biggest single discovery of our thinking and work."[53] For Mayer, Indian rural development engaged multiple emotional regimes, among which empathy—the capacity to see oneself in the situation of others, or the poor—was the most powerful. Empathy, in addition to structuring the relationship between local citizens and foreign experts, would create the foundation for an emotional community uniting Indians of different castes in a new postcolonial intersubjectivity that transcended the bounds of traditional identities. Mayer believed poor villagers were not equipped to create any legitimate structure of political opposition against the socioeconomic suppression caused by the caste system.[54] He concluded that the political entity of the village poor could not be formed by top-down state authority but would only be defined within the structure of Panchayati raj. Apparently, Mayer's process of inner democratization called for the eradication of the submissive subject to make way for productive engagement and individual agency. The concept's main objective was to make subaltern agents emerge as a community by cultivating empathy. By propelling rural India toward its promised future, Mayer prescribed an institutionalized culture of optimism.

In the booklet *What This Pilot Project Is and What It Is Not,* Mayer hoped to build a "New Deal atmosphere" in to Indian villages where Indians would become as enthusiastic as Americans had been in the New Deal era: "Just as in the New Deal days in our country people of the greatest ability, energy and capacity trooped in to our projects to participate in what they believed in and had been waiting for. We hope and expect to build up that kind of excitement and reputation."[55] Mayer's work with Lewis Mumford and Henry Wright in the New Deal Housing Study group instilled in him the highly politicized emotional culture of the Great Depression and its resulting government. The New Deal used empathy—a compassionate feeling for one's fellow countrymen—to unify classes, professions, and regional populations in common goals and values. New Deal propaganda fostered a novel national identity founded in empathy for the distressed and the underprivileged. It also wielded optimism as the motive force behind economic reconstruction. Mayer's experience in devising America's New Deal housing policy suggested empathy and optimism as the emotional foundation for Indian rural development. He envisioned Indian independence as a moment especially conducive to a new culture of enthusiasm.

The emotion of optimism, hope, and empathy was further coated with martial determinism and aggression, with Mayer drawing from military rhetoric in his depiction of home as a weapon to fight the unjust. In his 1940s essay "Homes: Front Line of Defense in American Life," architects were depicted as sacrificing soldiers on the frontline, individual professionals as the bearers of the civilizing mission.[56] Mayer's description of the Indian experience was laden with a poignant tone of perceiving his role as a connector of the developing and developed part of the world. As he stated: "Many of us who served in the American Army overseas gained an education in ways we least anticipated. . . . [Now as] sadder and wiser men, we have clung to the hope that we can explain our discoveries vividly enough so that they may help effect changes in what are all but standardized viewpoints at home."[57]

Mayer's infrastructural design proposals began with altering Indian subjectivities and worked outward toward settlement and dwellings. He refused to become a complete cynic and never lost hope for the power of the built environment to motivate people to do something for the well-being of the broader public. According to Mayer, the success of the incipient democracy of India depended on the reformation of grassroots administration—a belief echoed by Indian politicians and bureaucrats. In Mayer's observation, Indian government officials by and large indulged in the comfort of the colonial bureaucratic order and thus preferred to work in sterile environments at a central office. This distance and disconnect between government officials and real villages, he argued, constructed a superficial mental image of reality. To overcome this challenge and comply with the new democratic order, his project suggested a fundamental reconfiguration of the existing public administration and a consolidation of power to Panchayati raj. He presented inner democratization as an administrative reform within the Etawah project to give the public administrators the opportunity to know the villagers in a face-to-face situation.

In Mayer's new model, officers would receive suggestions directly from the affected population and would thus review the outcome of their work firsthand. Mayer stated how this method had transformed the conceit of Indian government officials into a patriotic enthusiasm. He concluded that officers who were working in the new administrative hierarchy found a "new meaning" in their profession, as they now had the opportunity to understand and work for the "real India."[58] That is, inner democratization provided a communicative interface between service providers (government officers) and beneficiaries (villagers) in which both parties could communicate freely and raise their concerns. According to Mayer, the conception of this communicative enterprise would bind both parties "spiritually and professionally [into] a sort of closed fraternity."[59]

Mayer's theory of inner democratization presupposed that the Indigenous population's potential had been held in abeyance because of colonial rule. And this barrier, according to Mayer, had to be removed fully by means of external stimulation by expert consultants. He described development as a mutagenic process, arguing that both the First and Third Worlds would benefit equally from community development programs. But in Mayer's opinion, every agent's role must be limited to providing a platform for the exchange of ideas between experts and the Indigenous population.[60]

Mayer's team selected representatives from the villages to serve as village-level workers: Mayer's famous and widely copied concept stemming from his observations on the wartime implications of medical corpsmen in the US Army, an idea that also had roots in Gandhism.[61] Village-level workers' duty was mainly to coordinate information between US experts and Indian officers (fig. 4.9). The workers then disseminated this information at a grassroots level. But they were also supposed to make improvisations and alterations to address real situations in the field. The information they received from experts was only a framework without

FIGURE 4.9. Village workers going to work. Source: Albert Mayer Papers, box 40, folder 14, University of Chicago Library.

specific details.[62] However, once a village-level worker received brief training, they promoted development programs within a territory of four villages. Similar to medical corpsmen, village-level workers were not experts; for advice they relied on specialists at the central office. Their success was measured by their ability to evoke interest in villagers for new development agendas. Mayer's concept suggests that the framing, dissemination, and implementation of the development discourse in India relied profoundly on active participation of Indian agency. Through the involvement of village level workers, experts were optimistic about creating a new Indian generation with a strong will for development. The program's ultimate objective was to transform the former concept of the Gandhian ascetic person, someone with restrained desire, to a compassionate Indian subject who was empowered by desire and committed to action.

The Pitfalls of Inner Democratization

Mayer's project relied heavily on the Indigenous agency that eventually demanded Indian agents—such as village level workers and other development officers—to be extremely enthusiastic and motivated without fail. However, as sociologist Richard L. Park argued, "Dedications has its limits." Consequently, when the initial charm of the project faded out, the enthusiasm of indigenous agents dwindled.[63] The missionary zeal with which village -level workers started their work was not sustained throughout their professional careers. As a result, the villagers began to view the workers as having "mercenary motives" and doubted their good intentions.[64] Mayer assumed that accountability to the local authority, such as Panchayati raj, would help the workers to identify the actual needs of the village. But Mayer's assumption did not work. The accountability to Panchayati raj actually encouraged the village-level workers to see themselves as an integral part of the existing hierarchy of power. Because they only acted in the interest of village elites, they often did not represent the opinion or demand of common villagers. Mayer's emphasis on the personal agency also inhibited the institutionalization of organized activities. Mayer was in favor of a flexible administration, which actually did nothing but further consolidate the power of village elites. The result was eventually self-destructive.

In the autumn of 1952, Baij Nath Singh, a sociologist from the Etawah project, conducted a public opinion survey that revealed the bitter truth: villagers no longer held faith in village-level workers or in the capacity of any other development officers to bring about economic and social change. In addition, the officers had been steadily losing their spirit and commitment toward the development program.[65] Sociologist Gerald Sussman showed that although Mayer conceptualized village-level workers as enthusiastic patriots, for the workers themselves the role barely went beyond "a job." Limited opportunities for advancement and a weak salary structure made them really frustrated about their future.[66] A decade after the pilot project finally closed down in 1955, Douglas Ensminger, the long-time Ford Foundation director in India, articulated the problem: "After 10 years of experience with community development, it is entirely clear that this group of men cannot look forward with real hope to promotion within the hierarchy."[67]

The project of making a cohort of new Indian workers, an enthusiastic group of self-sacrificing officers, thus turned into a fiasco. A weak administration structure, together with few motivational incentives, rapidly reduced the efficacy of the program and eventually provided sufficient rationale for both bureaucrats and politicians to cut off the program. Foreign experts and local bureaucrats alike believed that the failure of the program was due to the personal failure and moral plunging of village-level workers. For contemporary observers, it was the result of their inability to carry out instructions. But as historian Daniel Immerwahr argued, from the beginning, the seed of failure was embedded in the very idea of community development projects, which eventually strengthened and validated the hegemony of an elite village institute that was incapable and unwilling to propel any radical change.[68] Failure was an inevitable consequence of the workers' position in the political structure. They were programmed to fail.

Instead of giving a voice to the demands of common villagers, village-level workers gradually become more inclined to create stronger ties with rural elites and landlords; they wanted to be part of the vertical power structure. Singh reported in 1952 that the workers confined their services only to middle- and upper-middle-class peasantry and showed less patience in hearing lower economic groups and landless peasants. The urbanized attire of the workers gradually distanced them socially from common villagers. The community development project eventually reified a rigid bureaucratic structure of village panchayat comprised of a body of village elites who had little interest in engaging common villagers in any decision-making process.

The heart of Mayer's proposition was the idealization of village bureaucracy, not unlike many other efforts that idealized and romanticized villages, as discussed in chapter 3. Mayer hypothesized that the democratic political institution already in place in Indian villages just needed to be revamped because villagers were crippled by colonial rule. It was also around this time when important Indian ethnographers such as Datt Singh, D. N. Majumdar, M. N. Srinivas and US anthropologists such as Robert Redfield challenged one of the main tenets of mainstream US modernization theory that the Indian village and its society was in a transitory phase on the way to modernity. They argued that Indian villages had stabilized socially and politically and were modern on their own terms.[69] Following advice from Clarence Stein and Lewis Mumford, Mayer gathered views of Western anthropologists and sociologists. Stein advised Mayer that designing an ideal village would not solve India's problem; he had to approach the problem from a sociological perspective.[70] Mayer met with communitarians from the Roosevelt administration, rural sociologists from the US Department of Agriculture, and eminent sociologists M. L. Wilson and Carl C. Taylor.[71] He finally proposed that the existing sociopolitical structure of Indian villages would be the best institute to implement postcolonial development programs, and thus experts must not alter in that structure. In this sense, the idea of community had a specific meaning to Mayer and others; it was hardly an all-encompassing idea but rather a system that depended on an existing vertical structure in which the access and participation of the marginal and powerless population was exclusively controlled by village elites.

Marginalizing the Woman

At the outset of the community development program, Mayer advocated for the direct participation of women. Their assumed role was to guide society through the enlightenment of their families and neighborhoods. Although Mayer's effort succeeded in drawing a substantial number of women to the program, the Panchayati raj disapproved of incorporating women into village governance or any development project whatsoever (fig. 4.10). The existing patriarchal authority of the village panchayat feared that female empowerment would challenge their establishment, and Mayer had no intention of upsetting the existing power structure. He eventually abandoned the project and deferred to the patriarchy without the slightest resistance.

Mayer not only withdrew from empowering women villagers; he subscribed to patriarchal norms to such an extent that he declared that women showed little interest in breaking prevailing social taboos to work as development workers. The pilot project, he said, had to move forward without them.[72] He substantiated his new position by explaining that women were traditionally secluded from the political life of the village.[73] Mayer told his colleagues that his efforts did not yield much success other than the sporadic and uneven participation of women in village fairs and adult literacy programs.[74] But the reality was different than he described. Women in Etawah held meetings and even protested against their exclusion from the project. Mayer simply overlooked their demands, and even

FIGURE 4.10. Village women in the Etawah pilot project doing needlework. Source: Albert Mayer Papers, box 40, folder 14, University of Chicago Library.

more strikingly, he approved the remarks of his coauthor McKim Marriott, who said such protests resembled nothing more than the "hysteroid or hysterical-like psychodynamics behind much feminine behaviour."[75]

Women were purged from the actual decision-making process, but they continued to appear as apolitical, ahistorical, and abstract subjects in Mayer's development discourse. They were portrayed primarily as tool users and domestic workers and discussed mainly in that context, where they were thought to exist in the utilitarian material world of stove and broom. After submitting to the patriarchal norms of the community, development experts argued that improving the utilitarian material world would contribute to the self-development of the users of its materials or tools, in other words: women. In this sense, women were seen as intricately bound to and entangled in their domestic material world, if not the

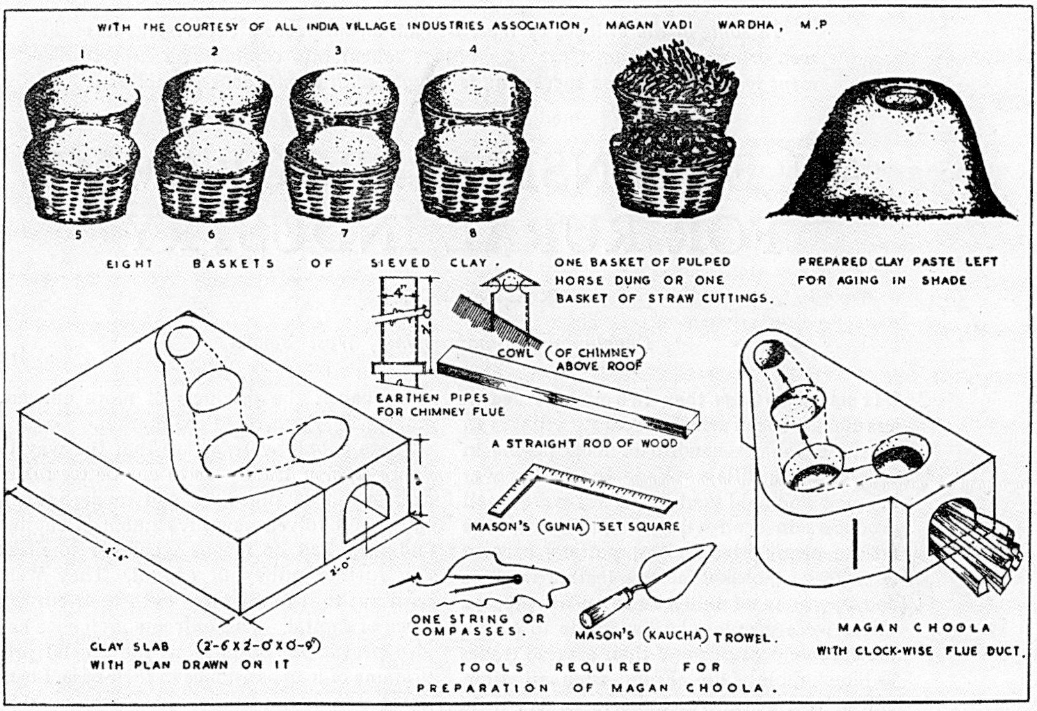

FIGURE 4.11. The Magan Choola. Source: Barkat Narain, "Housing and Health," *Kurukshetra* (April 1955): 16–17. University of Chicago Library.

embodiment of that world. Thus the question of their sociopolitical empowerment became less important than fixing their daily tools in order to reduce domestic drudgery.

Mayer thought the improvement of women's domestic work environments, such as the kitchen, was a precondition for improving their sociopolitical condition. His views might have been informed by Progressive-era urban and white American women, who called for a modernized domestic workspace. At the turn of the millennium, a substantial number of urban and working American women demanded modern housing to facilitate political, social, economic, and sexual freedom. While in the United States these progressive "new women" sought a new material world to harness their changed and changing social and economic role, in India it was quite different.

For Mayer's team enhancing the material world of village women in India came almost exclusively in the form of a new and improved wood and cow dung stove.[76] Mayer's team observed a significant amount of village women's time was wasted in the kitchen because of a primitive

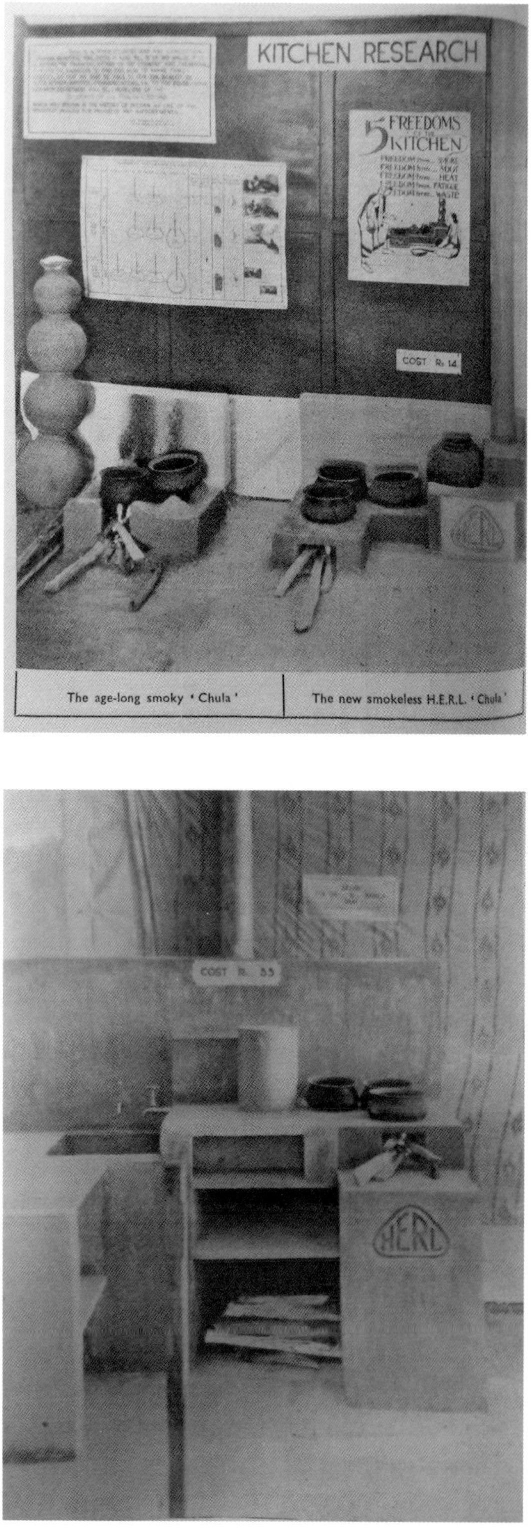

FIGURE 4.12. (*top*) The results of Hyderabad Engineering Research Laboratory's "Kitchen Research," with the smokeless chula (*top, far right*). The demonstration presents the "5 Freedoms of the Kitchen" and describes how this new kitchen could help liberate the village woman from menial household tasks. (*Bottom*) The design presented a Western-style kitchen top for affluent rural families. The original caption reads "Cooking range for Begum and Rani Sahibas." Source: S. P. Raju, '"Priority of Building Research in Post-War Planning," *Indian Concrete Journal* 21, no. 11 (1947): n.p.

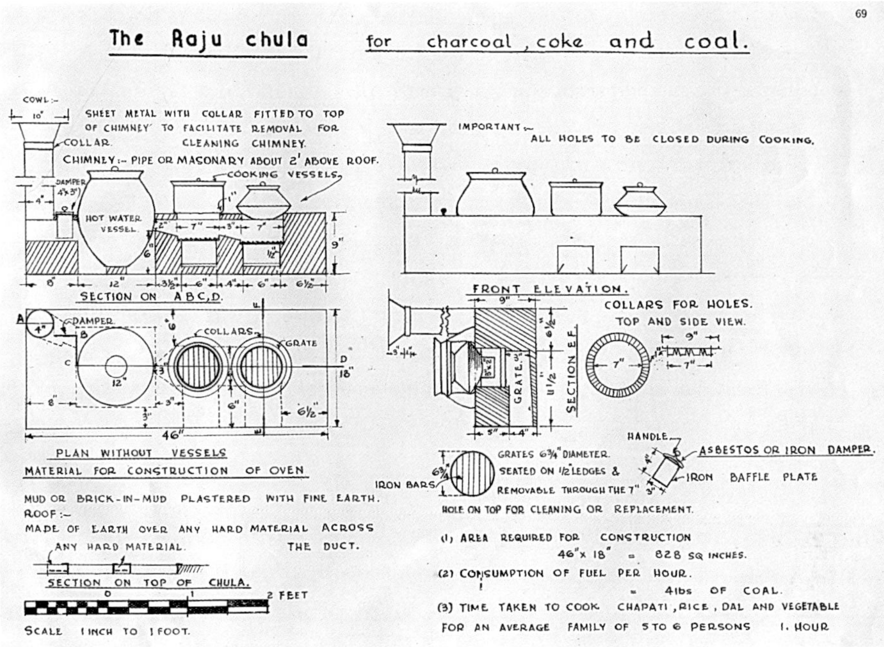

FIGURE 4.13. A smokeless chula developed by S. P. Raju and popularly known as the Raju chula. Source: Office of the Chief Adviser of Factories, *Low-Cost Housing for Industrial Workers* (New Delhi: Government of India, Ministry of Labour, 1954), 69.

stove (chula), which also wasted formidable amount of fuel.[77] In 1951 B. P. Sinha, assistant development officer for sanitation, introduced the "Magan Choola": the Etawah project's invention of a smokeless rural stove, which claimed to solve 10 percent of public health problems and also to provide "the lady of the house full facility to run a healthy and happy home" (fig. 4.11).[78] The Magan Choola attracted interest from designers and policymakers when it was presented at Delhi's first low-cost housing exhibition in 1954. It also spurred a lengthy discussion between Maxwell Fry, Jane Drew, Constantinos Doxiadis, and Jaqueline Tyrwhitt over the issue of increased household comfort and the means to liberate women from household tasks.[79] In that meeting, S. P. Raju, the former director of engineering research of the Nizam government of Hyderabad, presented his version of a smokeless chula built with concrete. Raju had been working on that project since the late 1940s, and the Associate Cement Companies was a contributing partner (figs. 4.12, 4.13). Raju described his efforts at meeting during the 1954 UN low-cost-housing exhibition:

> We have been trying to study design of village house from the point of view of human comfort. As you all know, the kitchen is the most neglected factor in our village. The kitchen smoke irrigates her eyes, nose and lungs of the housewife, and naturally also irritate her temper and her tongue. And very little has been done to relieve her. In addition to that there is a colossal waste of fuel on account of the unscientific design of the chulas that we have been using for last 500 years. Therefore, we have tried to evolve a simple smokeless Chula. We hoped by this to free the woman of the Far East from smoke, soot, heat waste and fire risks. Another big problem in the village house is the absence of special arrangements for preservation of food, so we have tried to evolve, along scientific principles of cooling and evaporation, and from simple materials, a sort of village refrigerator that can be made by the village potter.[80]

By the mid-1950s, the smokeless chula became the material artifact on which the argument over the liberation of rural women took place. Mayer's team was also a significant contribution to that discussion and argument. As his community development project depended largely on the mobilization of individual households, his team had been encouraging women to participate in conversations about sanitation, nutrition, and public health.

The Ford Foundation Takes Over

Four years after the inception of the pilot project, a widespread skirmish over the tenets and future directions of the project became evident. Soon acerbic criticism by Sudhir Ghosh, the director of the Faridabad Development Board, reached Mayer's desk. Ghosh accused the community development project of irresponsibly superimposing the American Dream on Indian rural life. He noted the basic problem: "Instead of laying emphasis on making available to the villagers adequate organized credit on easy terms and reliable supplies, the Planning Commission is busy building, a project of 300 villages, 600 miles of mud roads, 80 lower schools and 5 secondary schools, 3 health centers and one small 10-bed hospital; but nobody knows who will pay for the engineers, the teachers, the doctors, nurses and the equipment and maintenances of these services."[81]

Mayer was sensitive to the issue of keeping the pilot project outside the influence of US intervention so that the Indians could not spurn the community development project as a new imperial ploy. In addition, he also tried to minimize his authority as a US representative.[82] In reality, Mayer and US authority became synonymous and were categorized under the same neo-imperial rubric. Indian discontent with the community development program became even worse when the press demanded to know how long the national fund would support it, and Mayer sarcastically replied, "For ever and ever."[83] Convinced by the opinions of farm and agricultural experts, the press took an anti-American stance, underpinning this US design as "neither a plan of the people, nor for the people, nor by the people, but something imposed from above having no secure foundation."[84]

In 1955 the Uttar Pradesh government came to the conclusion that it no longer required the services of Albert Mayer, and thus his eventful career as a rural developer in India came to an end, though his involvement in city planning continued. The departure of Mayer from the community project marked an important phase in the progressive withdrawal of American experts from development projects. American journalist George Weller alleged that "most of [the experts] had not proved very helpful . . . [and were] of little use."[85]

The anti-American sentiment was also the result of the ways in which images of the United States and India had been communicated to each other through various cultural media. The question of the American and English perception of postcolonial India and how those perceptions might affect the bilateral political and trade relationship has been an enduring question since independence. To alter this cultural politics of perception, India has organized several "India festivals" in the United Kingdom and the United States. A glimpse of these cultural politics can be seen in Louis A. Jacob's collection of academic papers from a symposium that accompanied one such festival in 1985–1986. The last section of Jacob's *American Understanding of India* collection was titled "Cultural Interchange and American Perceptions of Indian Art."[86]

For postwar Americans, as explained by historian Harold Isaac, there were only four kinds of Indians: (1) the fabulous Indians, the maharajas and magicians in tandem with their exotic animals; (2) the mystics and religionists, a people who were "deep, contemplative, tranquil, profound"; (3) the benighted heathens, who venerated animals and worshiped many-headed gods; and (4) the lesser breed, trampled by poverty and crippling disease—"shriveled bellies, corpses, children with fly-encircled eyes, with swollen stomachs, children dying in the streets, rivers choked with bodies."[87] In contrast, the Indian perspective of the United States was one of "war-mongers and so on and so forth," as mourned by Secretary of State John Foster Dulles during the visit of leading Indian industrialist Birla to the United States in October 1954. India-US relations had long been afflicted by mutual distrust, suspicion, and acrimony. Such mutual misinterpretation ought to have been obliterated by both parties, said John Dulles.[88]

In the wake of global transference of Western modernity as a particular way of perceiving economic development, domesticity, consumer goods, and visual culture, the community development project was often considered a negotiable third space from which both countries could benefit reciprocally. Such a mutual benefit was thought to operate on a global scale—between the newly decolonized receiver, who received modernity and adapted it to its specific context, and the maker of modernity, who spawned it in the new world and claimed it within its ideological bloc. Mayer nevertheless believed that by working in the Third World context, American consultants could actually bring some wisdom of the East back home. Mayer explained this hope in his speech at the American Institute of Architects Convention in 1950: "The classic case of this is in anthropology, which when I was in college dealt with primitive Central Americans, Samoans, Fiji Islanders, but whose discovery in those remote areas and civilizations are now applied with new insight to examination of ourselves. . . . If President Truman's Point 4 ever eventuates, we will find we are not the giving and instructing end, but that if we are sensitive we shall get as good as we give."[89]

Despite Mayer's confidence in importing ideas from India, it is not clear how the experience of American designers in the Third World might possibly affect the planning and design culture of America. It was at best Mayer's wish that American consultants be portrayed not as imposers of ideas but as agents of transnational exchange. To imagine them this way comforted Mayer's ego, morally validated the UN Technical Assistance Program, and distanced American consultants from colonial planners.

The post-Mayer phase of community development is known as the rapid expansion phase, which emphasized physical development with larger financial assistance from the Indian and US governments. The urge for speed was generated by both internal public pressure and external pressure from the US government to strip the futile shell of Mayer's pilot project and make it permeate the entire nation. Both the Indian people and the US government were then eager to see the community development project cover the whole of India, not just the three hundred villages covered by Mayer's pilot project. The story of Etawah was nevertheless considered and promoted as a precedent for the capacity of foreign aid to change the Third World. In an international traveling photography exhibition, Mahewa, a village from the Etawah project, was presented as the new hope for US aid in India. According to the catalog of that exhibition, "A street in Mahewa . . . where great increases in crop production have brought a greater general prosperity to the people. New Houses and Schools are being built. Co-operative stores and banks have been opened, making it possible for residents to obtain seed, tools, basic supplies, home medicine and other commodities that raise health and living standards. Sanitation is stressed in construction of new buildings."[90]

Such optimism for foreign aid also provided Indian policymakers with the hope that India could learn valuable lessons from the first phase of the community development project's apparent failure. For US grant agencies, this kind of learning would be required to guide and manage their impending substantial grants and aid to the Third World. Nevertheless, whatever progress Albert Mayer might have made in the pilot projects eventually convinced the US government that further investment in India would prove inexorably that democracy was the only mechanism that could fight poverty in newly decolonized countries. Foreign technical and financial assistance thus transformed Indian villages as representative symbols of emerging Third World democracy. It is interesting to note here that the Ford Foundation knew this fact but continued the same faulty model by strengthening the Panchayati raj–based community development. However, hindsight reveals that the Ford Foundation's main objective was not to propel economic development but to intensify elite grassroots institutions in order to prevent the greatest fear of its time: a communist revolution of the organized village poor.

Around the same time that Mao Zedong proclaimed the People's Republic in October 1949 and the Sino-American Joint Commission on Rural Reconstruction failed, US liberals argued that the United States failed in China because the American government overlooked the emerging global peasant insurgency. Journalist Arthur Goodfriend coined the term "at the rice roots" and warned that the US government must tackle the rural reconstruction problem with its full capacity.[91] The most enthusiastic person to advocate an extension of community development in India was the new American ambassador, Chester Bowles, a New Deal democrat dedicated to public service and imbued with compassion and humanitarianism who was popular among his colleagues as the "big picture man." John Prior Lewis called him the "buoyant humanitarian who personified the Point 4 approach."[92] In 1951, on his first meeting with Nehru, Bowles stated that "one of the most crucial questions was whether Asian democracy could compete with Asian communism unless it too organized its village efforts on a massive scale." In reply, Nehru said, "History had selected India as one of democracy's chief testing grounds."[93] A devotee of President Franklin Roosevelt and a fervent exponent of the Point Four Program, Bowles wrote in support of an extension of the locality-based pilot project to a national scale development project: "Long before coming to India, I had welcomed Point 4 as an exciting opportunity for America to associate her ideals and resources with the efforts of more than a billion people to secure a better life. . . . The time has passed for 'pilot plans.' We have pilot studied Asia almost to death." Bowles was desperate to take over Mayer's pilot project and to expand the project faster than colleagues such as Ensminger or even Nehru. He wrote, "It was necessary to touch as many people as quickly as possible. . . . shake the villages out of their lethargy and arouse their people to an understanding of what they themselves could accomplish."[94]

The prevailing political environment supported the growth of the community development program.[95] The first five-year plan emphasized a rapid expansion of rural development programs based on the Etawah pilot project. Because of Etawah, Ambassador Bowles was convinced that the community development project could successfully handle the self-help approach that would require minimal state funding and resources for its expansion.[96] However, he was critical of Mayer's approach and described him as a "perfectionist who wanted model utopias." He argued that Mayer's approach would not produce anything but sporadic "show places" or "gold plated demonstration centers," and that "the impact on India's 350 million people would be minimal."[97] Bowles argued that it was time to allow the pilot project to expand freely and thus to cover the entire rural area of India.

In August 1951 at Prime Minister Nehru's invitation, Paul Hoffman, president of the newly formed Ford Foundation; John Cowles, trustee of the foundation; Chester Davis, its vice president; and John Howard, director of the Overseas Development, International Training, and Research Office, visited India. In November of the same year, Hoffman convinced Ensminger to visit as the foundation representative. In December, the first foundation grant of $1.2 million was approved to the government of India for assistance on fifteen area projects, five extension training centers, and facilities in Gujarat, Madhya Pradesh, Mysore, Uttar Pradesh, and West Bengal. From 1951 the US fund was made available for India. The Point Four Technical Assistance Program was just starting, and on October 31, 1951, US Congress voted for an appropriation of $50 million.

The Technical Cooperation Program Agreement signed by the two governments on January 5, 1952, was spelled out in detail in Operational Agreement No. 8. On February 1, 1952, a central committee was named to provide direction. The community development program was signed in New Delhi on May 31, 1952, and a supplement was added on December 6. This program dared to take up fifteen area projects of three hundred villages each, one in each of the major states. Although the Ford Foundation and USAID contributed significant financial assistance, the cumulative amount was rather scanty in comparison to India's own contribution. India funded approximately five-sixths of the money for the first fifty-five community projects with funding delineated under the Supplement to Operational Agreement No. 8, in which the Indian government invested seven times more than the United States.[98] The first fifty-five national scale projects were officially launched on October 2, 1955, Gandhi's birthday, to pay homage to his emphasis on rural development. However, the official beginning had occurred four years before, in 1951, when the second phase of the community development program, or the National Extension Program, was theoretically conceived.

For India it was not the financial aid from the United States but the psychological and moral support that came along with it that was more desired and helpful. As S. K. Dey recounted, "Although direct US assistance for community development was small. . . . The association of the American Government with the programme served the positive value of giving it respectability and dignity."[99] US involvement deeply affected the psyche of Indians, as it symbolized a friendly willingness of the American people to support India's development and created a psychological bond between the two countries.

The American Image

The international image of the United States in the eraly 1950s, far from that of an imperialistic great power, was a super economy of capitalism that engaged in propping up destabilized regimes in smaller and poorer states. Britain was still seen as the center of empire, the weight of which was yet to be lifted from India's back. The United States, by contrast, was a young nation that had won its independence from the British crown and liberated Cuba and the Philippines after taking them over from the Spanish. Although India was reluctant to align with the United States as its Cold War ally, Indian politicians and the press appreciated Americans as practical, pragmatic, and friendly. Being aware of the general sentiment about the United States, Mayer had also capitalized on American industriousness, technology, and informality in work relationships. He believed, in fact, that this injection of Americanism was exactly what India needed: "Americans, if properly chosen, are the best people in the world to help in the initiation and follow-through of development work. Our respect for the specific, our flair for knowing how to do a job and exactly what it takes to do it, our love for doing work ourselves or at least being able to do it before telling others—these are as of now indispensably complementary to Indian characteristics."[100] The image of America as the effective and friendly savior of the Third World was further developed by Ambassador Bowles, who sought to bind the two countries through emotional bondage.

As soon as US funds and moral support were made available to Indians, Mayer was sidelined. He was confined to the Etawah pilot project, which at that time was causing much public agitation due to its slow and ineffective performance rate. The role of Mayer in this second phase was described by Marriott and Park as that of "an observer and as a friendly and outspoken internal critic."[101] In contrast, Mayer continued to argue that the necessary human resources and community support for such a large-scale expansion as dreamed of by US experts and the Indian government would require a much longer extension than experts had anticipated. He argued that the targeted growth rate would be incompatible with local leadership's capacity to absorb it.[102] In his view, the expansion rate would fail to produce adequate and dedicated personnel to support an effective operational management to sustain new values and relations that the projects intended to generate. He further blamed US and Indian politicians for their aspirations to rapidly expand, arguing that the urge for quick results was the expression of a mentality of despair.[103] Mayer, the ousted leader, being aware of his "personal inability to affect seriously," made a final personal appeal to some of his old associates on the Etawah project to limit and control the rapid growth at its new stage.[104] His Indian associates, who were grim about the prospects of his slow-paced development, never replied to his appeal.

Although Bowles intended to proceed as fast as possible and to make rapid changes to the built environment, during the first few years, the Ford Foundation realized that the kind of "development image" it wanted to create was impossible to produce in the given culture. In a report, Ensminger wrote, "One of the most striking facts when observing these villages is the lack of maintenance of public areas. Even when a road is made pucca, after sometime it again becomes kutcha, because nobody maintains it. The same could be said of public drains, which, when they exist, very soon are obstructed, either with the garbage thrown out from the houses or mud collected during the rains. Cow dung cakes used as fuel, are piled in every vacant space or, simply, in front of the houses. Cattle are frequently found obstructing the narrow lane."[105]

The above passage describes the despair the foundation experienced when its planning principles proved ineffective in Indian contexts. Although the foundation wanted its development efforts to be expressed through picturesque settings of ideal villages, in reality, it claims to have encountered an "irrational and irresponsible" attitude in villagers. Its failed effort gradually became a struggle to change the newfound cultural regression of India's rural population, which the foundation thought had been accumulating over the long colonial history of poverty.[106] As a result, a significant portion of its rural development strategy focused on creating an educational wing and disseminating materials to raise public consciousness. Despite an extreme scarcity of resources, among the six issues the foundation identified as problematic for rural housing in India, "economic resources" came last, while the problem of quality, functional efficiency, habits, and attitude came first. According to the Ford Foundation's definition, development also appeared to be a social mission to disseminate enlightenment ideas.

The nature of US grants was not as homogenous as it might appear in various public and academic critiques. Sources of money were diverse and did not always comply with American modernization theory. For instance, in India, in terms of institutional operation, the Ford Foundation maintained strong independence from the US government's aid program, preferring to collaborate with Indian government organizations. Different funding bodies, though they shared some fundamental ideologies, were diverse in their focus. The personal beliefs of leaders such as Bowles and Ensminger overlapped with those of Nehru on a wide range of issues. The political beliefs they shared proffered a common ground from which various funding bodies and Indian receivers could be synchronized and negotiated. They agreed on the extent and nature of US involvement in Indian development issues, which was strictly held as a domestic concern. As Ensminger explained, "The Americans didn't talk the Indians into programs. They already wanted the programs. We only came along at the right time and our assistance was not to tell them what needed to be done but to help them do what they wanted."

Ensminger's philosophy was not to have a philosophy: "I don't have any programs, the Indians do and we are here to help them." This was translated into instructions to his staff "to keep quiet during the discussion and let the Indians make points."[107] While the Ford Foundation encouraged the active participation of Indian agencies, it perceived integrated development as achievable only through the mass transmission of US technical expertise, mainly in the form of grants that would essentially emphasize US achievements in technology and progress.

Unlike its Marshall Plan in the European context, the United States was never eager to sell the American way of life in India; rather, it sought to yield an expanded domestic market and production that would increase the purchasing power of the local population. This enhanced power and expanding domestic market would provide the working class with "more leisure time," and thus would harness a desire for privately produced consumer goods, as Bowles predicted: "radios, bicycles, sewing machines, and apparel."[108] The consequence, Bowles's administration projected, would be a self-repeating cycle in which the desire to acquire consumer goods would drive the villagers to maximize food production, which in turn would stimulate a new, dynamic, and sustainable consumer industry and vice versa. It was indeed a model to include the traditional food-growing population in the expanding market economy.

Under Bowles's billion-dollar project, the US government decided to spend money through the Ford Foundation on Indian farm improvements—nearly one-third of the cost of India's own five-year plan. The foundation, with its extravagant grants and team of experts, took over the project's second rapid extension phase. Such an excess of US interest in the Indian economy created suspicion among some economists and sociologists, who were convinced that US money had become a new form of colonization that sought to establish authority under the guise of friendship. Journalist George Weller wrote that the future of the project was "dark and ominous" and "its extension will prove all the more ruinous."[109] In addition, the community development project caused formidable public outrage when a group of researchers—three Indians and one American from a joint endeavor of the Indo-American Cornell-Lucknow Research Center—posed sensitive questions to villagers, such as: "Do you prefer Communists to the Congress? Would you rather have the British back? Would you rather be friendly with the British, the Americans or the Russians?"[110] The team was accused of foreign espionage by the press, and local academics expressed their extreme discontent in the government's policy of engaging foreign researchers and experts in domestic matters. During the 1960s, the opposition camp, especially the Communist Party of India and radical Gandhists, interpreted this methodical deployment of dollars and intellects as a new cultural imperialism: an obvious pathogen pervading the world by spreading the disease of capitalism through a brazen display of consumer culture. Global trade mobilization, perhaps the central interest of the United States in the twentieth century, cast a pall of skepticism over the regime.

The End of Community Development

In 1959 two significant studies on community development projects in India conducted by the United Nations and the Ford Foundation pointed out that the pressing concern in India was not community development per se but the sharp decrease of harvests. The foundation declared that

India must make the production of food its top priority.[111] The United Nations also warned about the impending food crisis and advised India to invest its forces against looming starvation at the national level.[112] In the following years of rapid expansion, as US Cold War policy began to change in India and more broadly across Asia, its focus shifted from an integrated community development strategy to a "green revolution" initiated by scientific advancement in food production technology. In 1960 the Ministry of Community Development asked village-level workers to invest 80 percent of their time in agricultural development.[113] Following the Malthusian model of famine, this policy determined a direct relationship between the scarcity of food (or hunger), political instability in the Third World, and the spread of communism in Asia, and thus moved away from Mayer's holistic development approach, in which human development culminated in its built environment. The new cold warriors focused more on altering food habits and changing food production in rural India to transform rural "peasants" into educated citizens with scientific attitudes and democratic morality.[114] The spectacular showcasing of US achievement in helping the Third World to overcome its poverty was staged after four years, in 1959, with the announcement of President Eisenhower's visit to New Delhi to open the US exhibit at the First World Agricultural Fair.

After Nehru's death in 1964, the new prime minister, Lal Bahadur Shastri, drastically reduced the scope of the community development project. Shastri's view toward community development was cynical, and he was skeptical about Nehru's precarious juggling with decentralization, the consolidation of power at Panchayati raj, and modernization on the basis of centralized state authority.[115] When Indira Gandhi became prime minister in 1966, she brutally reduced the community development program into nothing more than an idea with almost no operational power or resources. She abolished the ministry of community development and all related projects were taken under the Ministry of Agriculture. The training centers for Panchayati raj officials and for village workers were either abolished or transferred to the state.

Why did the community project fail? Or did it fail at all? Does this failure mean the Indian government lost interest in the decentralization of power? Or did community developers have no intention of actually empowering the lower economic class? Scholars such as Partha Chatterjee contended that the community development project was never intended to nurture a true decentralization or empowerment of the poor. In Chatterjee's view, the promise of grassroots empowerment actually deceived village elites and made them allies in India's large-scale industrialization. Community development, Chatterjee argued, was nothing more than a tool of modernization, an instrument to allow the state to intervene in the countryside.[116] It is unclear whether the whole community project was a ploy, but we can tell with certainty that its policymakers were well aware of the fact that there existed a fundamental conflict between community-based participatory democracy and the existing vertical hierarchy of rural political power. Instead of changing its course, community developers doubled their investment in that faulty model. Why? Likely because, historian Daniel Immerwahr answered, Mayer and Indian policymakers did not view the hegemony and dominance of local elites as a problem, but rather as an expected outcome.

Surinder Kumar Dey, the first union cabinet minister for cooperation and Panchayati raj, argued in favor of strengthening the power of local elites, explaining that history "was made not by representatives of the poor sections of the community but by members of the richer and privileged strata of society." Dey was not at all hesitant to dismiss any authority of the poor in development activity. According to Dey, a poor person "does not fight, nor can he provide the leadership. He can line up for a cause. It is only the middle-class or the richer class that can champion . . . a cause."[117] The community developers' view of community was not based on equal participation from all economic and social classes; their vision of community was hierarchized and ordered through the dominance of elites disguised in the democratic idioms of leadership. Because landowning elites monopolized leadership positions, and community developers avoided upsetting the existing social hierarchy, fundamental issues pertaining to overall economic development—such as the abolition of caste or new land reformation policies to ensure equal land distribution—were overlooked in development agendas. Development experts imagined that the participation of poor villagers must be realized in everyday practices of daily life. But the diffusion of power in everyday practices made that power meaningless and ineffective. As Dudley Trudgett explained in an interim report:

> "Village Participation" and "Widening Villagers' Horizon," embrace all activities directed toward study of the village, preparation of the village for activities to be undertaken, toward their later management and extension by the villagers themselves, toward creating an atmosphere of alertness and confidence out of which initiative grows. . . . We must remember that it is the daily activities and attitudes of our Village Level Workers and officers at all levels, the close discussions, the intimate leisurely night halts, in short our own daily sustained participation, that constitute the very fabric of this work. Less spectacular than the special activities, they are more basic.[118]

Development programs were only limited to the development of roads, village wells, community halls, houses, and other such architectural establishments that would create a visual experience or evidence of development. Even in 1952, when Nehru opened the national program for community development, he lauded these programs "not so much for the material achievement they would bring about but much more so because they seem to build up the community."[119] This is paradoxical to Mayer, who argued against focusing on the built environment. But in the end, all activities hardly went beyond creating a visual experience of development. Rather tragically, community development projects had become the same "Potemkin village" that Mayer denounced at the beginning of his involvement in the project.[120]

Mayer repeatedly blamed the national program and its rapid growth phase for reducing the project into a gigantic but ineffective bureaucratic machine over which the poor had no authority. Mayer, Dey, and other advocates believed that their steady and focused support of slow-paced community development was eventually marred and corrupted by state intervention. However, Mayer's accusation was not convincing, as his teams could not supply any evidence, and their efforts did not foster a structural condition that would bring about a total change in the rural economy. The community development project as a program or philosophy intended to encourage decentralization, but its advocates did not rely on the "uneducated and less motivated" village poor, and thus worked to boost the authority of the Panchayati raj. Eventually the whole project fell prey to the interest of the elites and became a partnership between the rural elites and the government. This did not pose a problem for development crusaders in the United States because it seems that they were far more interested in using the saga of rural development to tackle the peasant rebellion and insurgency that for them was the first step in resisting communist revolution.

After the End

Despite organizational change and dwindling state interest in community development, architects' conviction in political decentralization and raising poor people's motivational level to mobilize development was not totally abolished. The rural housing wing of the School of Planning and Architecture, established in New Delhi in 1959, is a case in point. The wing offered courses, professional training, and research service on rural development in Delhi and Rajasthan. The Ford Foundation continued to offer minor technical advice, but the main source of technical assistance was the National Building Organization of the Ministry of Works, Housing, and Supply, which conducted rural development planning.

The students and teachers of the Delhi School of Architecture and Planning orchestrated a development plan in which 110 new houses were built in Lalgarh—a remote village in Rajasthan. The construction works were administered by the Development Department of the Rajasthan government. For the school this was an experiment intended to prove the main mantra of any community development project: "that improved physical conditions can result in motivating people for higher standard of living, which in is bound turn to contribute to the general economic development." The main working method was almost identical to Mayer's pilot project. The published report makes the same call to urban designers for an "adventure" to become one of the villagers.[121]

The report reveals how researchers gathered social data as well as the underlying social order through a laborious door-to-door survey. The knowledge gathered wielded so much communal empathy and shared interest in development that the villagers were willing to exchange plots or even sacrifice some portion of their land to yield greater good for their community. The ultimate success of the project, according to the Delhi school, was its success in fostering the Panchayat Samiti (similar to Panchayat raj) as an active political organization. The development and redevelopment of the built environment, of which rural housing was among the most important factors, brought in a new political consciousness. As reported by the development team, "The political propaganda that had followed decentralisation of administration has resulted in the creation of a political and educational awakening amongst the villagers."[122] And finally, the report recommended depending on the existing social hierarchy to implement the development program instead of challenging or altering that hierarchy. So in the end, the difference between Mayer's community development project and the Delhi school's revision is probably inconsequential: the same development agendas and institutionalized visions of rural poverty operated in different organizational contexts.

5

Appropriating Global Norms of Austerity

With a vision to create modern domestic space using local resources and knowledge bases, the Indian Ministry of Commerce and Industry set up twelve different regional design centers across the country. These centers designed, manufactured, and publicized prototypes of various everyday utilitarian objects that had a "national" outlook but were devoid of traditional embellishments.[1] During the early 1960s, different bureaucracies—including the India Office of the Development Commissioner of small-scale industry, the All-India Handicrafts Board, and the India Central Small Industries Organization—disseminated similar publications (fig. 5.1). The Central Small Industries Organization published a number of model schemes, technical bulletins, and papers and booklets on small-scale industries, mainly those that produced household and domestic craft objects. In addition to the its general scheme for manufacturing, the Central Small Industries Organization introduced a new series, the Impact Program Scheme, which was designed to attract the attention of potential entrepreneurs in an attempt to broaden the immediate scope of the consumer market.[2] The cumulative efforts of these government organizations resulted in a general plea for a novel material culture—that is, a synthesis of the local and the modern.[3] For instance, a model interior from Indian government publications presented a hybrid modern chair made from vernacular materials together with a traditional stool. The center table in this model interior is an noteworthy example of placing a traditional basket on a steel frame to arrive at a second utility, a table (fig. 5.2).

Indian government design cells continued to produce economic furniture and domestic essentials—such as fans, switches, and door latches—

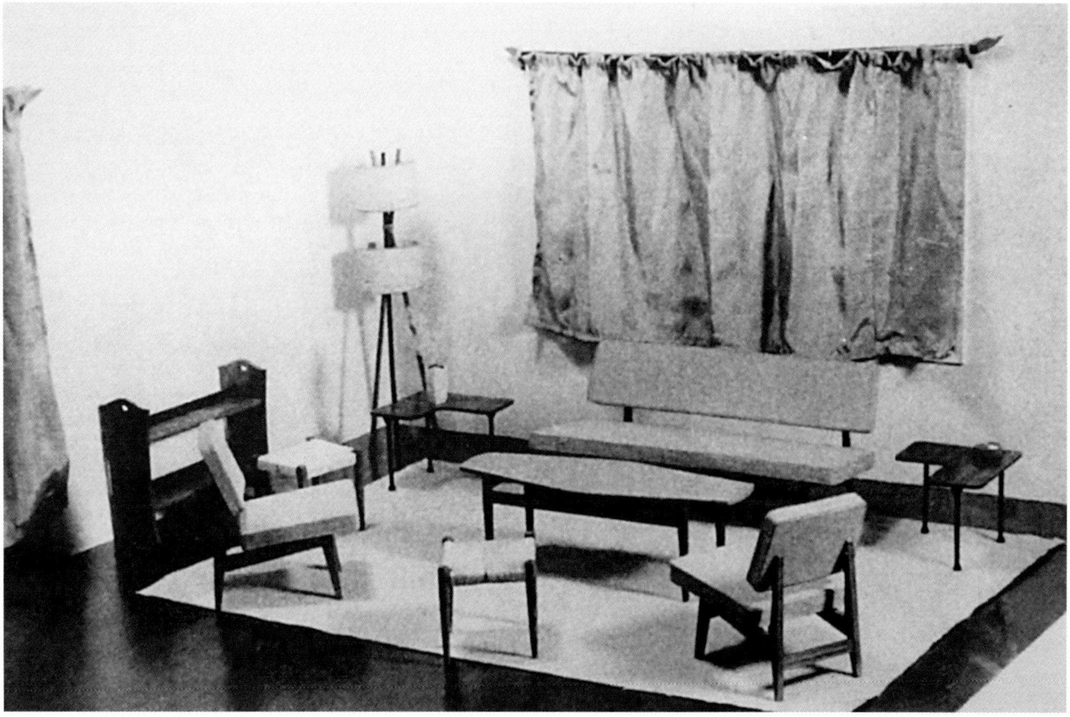

FIGURE 5.1. Modern domestic office for the emerging middle class, designed by the government during the late 1950s. Source: Ministry of Commerce and Industry, *Design for Industry* (New Delhi: Government of India, Ministry of Commerce and Industry, 1960).

compatible with the budgets of middle-class consumers (fig. 5.3). Instead of trying to establish avant-garde design philosophies to express Indian identity, design cells were mainly concerned with ensuring quick mass production. The rapid industrialization of the design sector, the Indian government believed, would testify to the rigor of India's industrial capacity and thus contribute to the construction of a postcolonial national identity. To add to this effort, the Indian government invited Swiss architect Pierre Jeanneret to design a model domestic environment for low-income semi-urban and rural houses. Jeanneret, who was then working on the Chandigarh project with Le Corbusier, explored a subdued hybrid tradition in Indian culture. His bamboo chair and rattan bench experiment attempted to devise a postcolonial aesthetic rooted in Gandhi's ascetic tradition (fig. 5.4). Jeanneret's design of a series of mock-up rooms were included in a 1959 government publication, *Simple Furniture and Interior Decoration*, along with the work of local designers who employed traditional forms. In this publication, Jeanneret's designs were accompanied by provocative slogans such as "Even inexpensive things can have an

FIGURE 5.2. "Cane and bamboo furniture"—modern Indian domestic hybrid design that employ a traditional stool and bamboo and rattan chair and table. Designed by Regional Design Centre, Calcutta. Source: D. N. Anand, *Simple Furniture and Interior Decoration* (New Delhi: Directorate of Extension and Training, Ministry of Food and Agriculture, 1959), n.p.

enchantment all their own," "Art is everywhere but the right spirit is necessary to discover it," and—most famously—"Poverty can sometimes give an impression of greater dignity than riches."[4]

The model interior design was only a marginal project for Jeanneret; his main mission in India was to oversee the construction of the monuments designed by Corbusier and to design low-cost housing for class-two and class-three government officials of the newly established capital of Punjab province, Chandigarh. Unlike Le Corbusier, Jeanneret became closely related to the native population. Subsequently, at his home studio in Chandigarh, he designed a number of furnishings in which he employed bamboo for the structural frame and a naturally woven surface as upholstery. The chair he designed, crafty in appearance yet standardized and producible

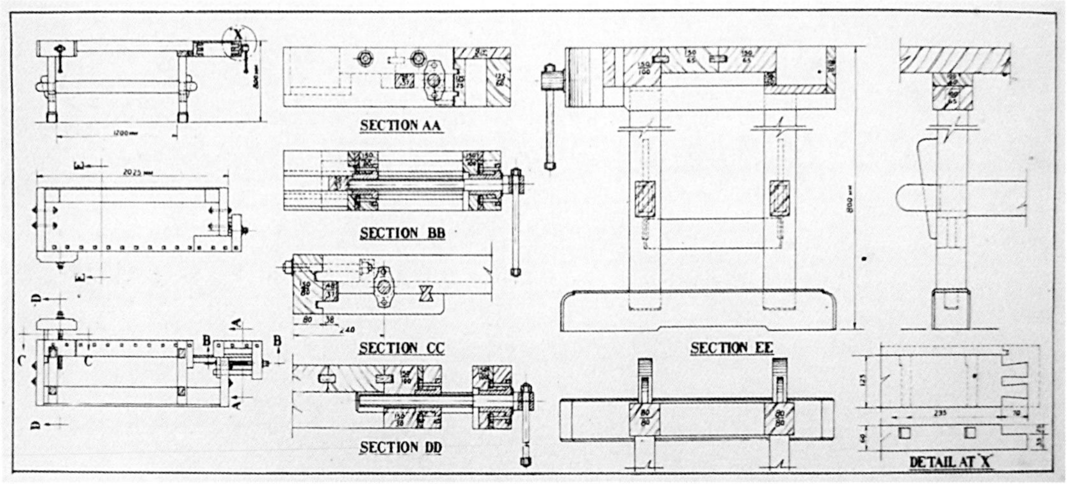

FIGURE 5.3. Design of an industrially produced carpenter's bench. Source: India Central Small Industries Organisation, "Small Scale Industry Impact Scheme No. 117," ed. Ministry of Commerce and Industry (New Delhi: Government of India, 1962).

on a mass scale, could be taken as a counterdiscourse to the dominant image of modern design composed of industrial materials such as steel, plywood, or industrial textiles. The woven surface and use of a natural element in its natural state suggest that the chair allows a certain degree of human error that is natural in any human production. At the same time, its standard fabrication suggests that it is reproducible on a mass scale and might prove consumable on a mass scale. For Jeanneret, in the unique postcolonial Indian context, absolute dependence on labor-saving mass production and mechanically reproducible objects would be less affordable. Describing his experience working in India, Jeanneret wrote: "My greatest concern now is to employ as many men as possible on the work sites which I supervise. After having for years tried my hardest to find ways of replicating human labor with machinery for economic reasons, I never thought I would, one day, be reconsidering the problem from a different angle: that of trying to give work to the greatest possible number of men."[5]

By providing an alternative vision to postwar modernism, Jeanneret calibrated to a Gandhian political economy, which championed austerity, asceticism, poverty, and the spiritual importance of physical labor. Jeanneret's connection to the ascetic mood of objects can be traced back to his early career during 1927, when he jointly designed three houses with Le Corbusier for the Deutscher Werkbund in Stuttgart. This particular exhibition explored the possibility of a post–world war reformation of European housing using the limited resources afforded by Europe at that

FIGURE 5.4. Pierre Jeanneret experimented with designing domestic furniture using nonindustrial materials. Photograph by Jeet Malhotra. A collection of his experiment appeared in D. N. Anand, *Simple Furniture and Interior Decoration* (New Delhi: Directorate of Extension and Training, Ministry of Food and Agriculture, 1959). Source: ARCH279618, Pierre Jeanneret fonds, Canadian Centre for Architecture. Gift of Jacqueline Jeanneret.

time.[6] Jeanneret's design exemplified an effort implicit in different state initiatives that tried to find a middle ground to reconcile radical Gandhian material culture with the culture of industrial modernity.

Destigmatizing the Aura of Indian Objects

In 1955 Pupul Jayakar, a prominent cultural activist, writer, and promoter of Indian craft industry, organized an exhibition at the Museum of Modern Art in conjunction with Edgar Kaufmann Jr., MoMA's director of industrial design. Kaufmann, director of the famous *Good Design* exhibition series (1950–1955), conceived the India exhibition to be a gesture to appreciate the difference of "other" cultures and seek commonality in differences. This perspective was congruent with MoMA's Cold War role, which began with the establishment of its international program in 1952, as the disseminator of the images and material culture of American domestic lifestyle, proclaiming the benefits of democracy over other forms of political ideology.[7] However, against this context, Pupul Jayakar used the 1955 exhibition to solicit assistance from the Ford Foundation to make a plan for developing a design industry to serve the burgeoning domestic markets and match global demand. In conjunction with parallel events using classical music, dance, and feature films, this show was the first large-scale international exhibition in a foreign land that displayed products of Indian art and design, especially India's handloom culture, clothing, and textiles, as profitable global commodities rather than exotic artifacts with limited marketability.

The show lasted from April 13 to September 25, 1955, and created tremendous curiosity and interest about Indian culture in the American psyche.[8] Far from conventional tropes of Orientalism, the show was an ardent effort to explain India through its material culture. In a press release for the show, Monroe Wheeler (director of MoMA's exhibitions and publications), expressed her hope that "this exhibition, in furtherance of the ideals of the Museum's International Exhibitions Program and its International Council, will enrich the American esthetic experience, and at the same time give recognition and stimulus to the great crafts of India."[9] This was a show to inform the American public—indeed, intellectuals in general—about the potential of the newly decolonized part of the world that seemingly could be expropriated within the ideological jurisdiction of a consumer society. This show moved to ameliorate mutual misinterpretation, and to broaden the possibilities of postwar cultural exchange. In doing so, MoMA explored ways in which to revive tropes of a fabulous, dazzling Orient. MoMA's representation, capitalized upon the quixotic image of the Orient, was mainly motivated by trade interest, and it put both the countries—the United States and India—in a win-win situation.

A significant number of exhibits came from private collections in India, England, and the United States. These included the collection of Edgar Kaufmann Jr. and Alexander Girard. The partnership of these two key figures of American high modernity proved successful in constructing an Indian image in a Western land. Kaufmann and Girard embarked upon a six-week tour of Great Britain and India to collect exhibit artifacts ranging from Indian textiles to various craft objects, creating a "prototype" for the exhibition.[10] Sir Leigh Ashton and John Irwin of London's Victoria and Albert Museum, helped Kaufmann and Girard to select from the museum's vast range of Indian objects to build an authentic version of Indian material culture to present in the United States.

The show was conceived of as "a celebration of the revival under India's new commonwealth status of some of her oldest native crafts."[11] The physical installation of the show was devised to invite the audience to conjure up the lost world of fantastic objects of the East. Alexander Girard, a renowned architect, textile designer, and famous folk art collector, designed the exhibition in the form of an "imaginary bazaar," a prototype of an Indian marketplace that he hoped would provide a self-explanatory of its .[12] The exhibition site included three consecutive rooms. A fifty-foot-long pool surrounded by twelve towering golden columns embellished the main exhibition hall. Over the pool, a dazzling array of saris hung from the ceiling, creating a sky canopy resembling those in Indian fables of rich gold and silver brocades, intricately handwoven and tie-dyed silks, Kashmir shawls, gossamer cottons, vigorous muslins, feathery wools, and patterned embroideries. However, the objects of everyday use presented in this show were somewhat understated since the main objective of the exhibition was to emphasize the quality of the ornaments, the vibrant colors and patterns, all of which—in relation to Indian objects—are historically regarded only as embellishments exclusive to their use-value.[13]

Elsewhere, Girard expressed his notion that an exhibition of objects exclusive to their context drains their meaning. As design historian Kate P. Kent argues, it is imperative to construct a context for the objects that creates a certain theatricality of presentation instead of forcing viewers to infer objects' true place of origin. Girard's proposal in this respect was to construct a "fantasy setting based on relationships . . . between it and certain other objects, perhaps from other parts of the world."[14] Notwithstanding the faux pas as constructed by Girard, the intention of the installation was to introduce the myth of Indian exoticism and to spur the curiosity of both public and press. To this end, it was an "out-and-out success." As noted by journalist Betty Pepis in the *New York Times*, "Glitter and gilt dazzle the eye as one enters the native Indian bazaar just installed on the first floor of the Museum of Modern Art."[15] Lester Gaba, writing in *Woman's Wear Daily*, implored his reader to "Go west, young displayman, go west on 53rd Street to see the town's most exciting display."[16] The 1955 MoMA exhibition was effectively contrived to convey the spectacle of Indian craft, a magical setting for equally exotic and mysterious objects amid the concrete "jungle" of Manhattan's modernity.

While it was difficult to determine the impact the show made on the American mind, one could suggest that India appeared as a piece of fantasy amid the modernity of American life. According to Alice Hughes in the *Times*, "The American beholder is swept up with admiration for the 'fantasy' now displayed in the 'Arts of India' show." The exhibition drew more than three hundred thousand visitors. Public demand prolonged the exhibition for five months, during which time the press became aware of the increasing news value of the show. Optimistic comments expressed in a MoMA press release, echoed the American image: "The arts and crafts of India are already influencing both fashions and home furnishing in this country. . . . What's important to American eyes in viewing this handsome exhibit is the shadow of the future its casts on our latest fashion for living." The show reflected the postwar faith in a future of open exchange—an avenue that would make cultural transference possible among the seemingly asymmetric segments of the world. MoMA saw the trade potential of this show as its highest stake. As Wheeler maintained, "Its purpose is to guide the millions of skilled native craftsmen in the way of traditional design and to publicize and market those folk arts in India and other countries."[17]

India's postindependence international trade potential was an important consideration for the National Planning Committee's pre-independence scheme. Apropos of the historical fracture of sovereign trade over two centuries, when India was preparing to make an independent trade debut with the West and embrace the notion of a modern democratic nation-state, the issue at hand was the formation of a rhetoric of *Indianness*, the semantic construction of a free India within a free market of consumer goods. When it came to the *Indian object*, in the world's eyes, postwar India wanted to retain an exotic persona.[18] The Indian magazine *Life*, in describing this exhibition, declared with immense pride that "the East has been inching up on the US for several years."[19]

From an Indian perspective, it was the superiority of India's long tradition of crafts and art that would take over the world design market. K. Balaram, an eminent journalist, wrote a series of articles in the *Hindu* (Madras), the *Nagpur Times*, and the *Capital* (Calcutta) about the potential of India's trade with the United States. She used the sari as an example, as it had been transforming into a global dress or "saree-dress" and found its position in the global market.[20] Although India issued periodic statements of the intent of progressive socialization, and some industries were reserved only for the public sector, the government of India tried to attract American capital by promising equal treatment, full remittance of profit, and fair compensation in case of eventual nationalization.[21] During the late 1950s and early 1960s, the United States, which had previously regarded India as little more than "a scratch on our minds," started to promote India as a democratic counterweight to communist China.[22] In the view of the US State Department: "South Asia became a testing ground for the free world; in this will be determined whether nations can surmount tremendous economic and social problems, can achieve far reaching changes in their entire pattern of life without resorting to the totalitarian system of communism."[23] In a bid to prove the triumph of the free market and the free world over the communist bloc, US assistance toward making India a consumer society reached its peak between 1954 and 1964, when US aid totaled $10 billion.[24] This signaled an attempt to assuage the negative mindset that the United States and India had long held toward each other. It also provided an opportunity to explore their potential mutual relationship in the future free market, a possibility to sample the blessings of a consumer society in which America had long imbibed and India had yet to relish.

At the closing of the exhibition, the Ford Foundation, emissary of American Cold War cultural politics, welcomed Pupul Jayakar's invitation to assist in modernizing India's design industry. For the foundation, it was an opportunity to foster enduring relationships among American designers and promoters and Indian designers, cultural brokers, bureaucrats, and trade organizations—relationships that it considered to be a precondition for open trade and a free market.

Alexander Girard requested that Charles Eames film MoMA's 1955 exhibition, and we can assume that this was the first time that Ray and Charles Eames came into close contact with Indian crafts and with Jayakar. After two years, the Eameses were commissioned by the Indian government and the Ford Foundation, on Jayakar's recommendation, to survey and critique the development program of Indian industrial design and to develop a set of recommendations to establish a new design school. They visited India in 1957, stayed for about three months, traveled extensively through major Indigenous craft centers, and eventually submitted the celebrated yet argumentative "India Report" in April 1958.[25] Instead of presenting any details of the anticipated new institute or ways to develop the mechanisms to market Indian products, in the report the Eameses greatly emphasized the "value of work" in the production process. They sought the meaning and purpose of work and its value and significance in the Indian context, and they began the report with a quote from the Bhagavad Gita: "You have the right to Work, but for the work's sake only;

you have no right to the fruits of work. Desire for the fruits of work must never be your motive in working."[26]

Rather than suggesting rigorous technical details, which is what the Indian bureaucrats and the Ford Foundation were expecting, the report sought to reconcile the ideological binary of the East and West and to mediate and position the new Indian "object" between these two realms. The report argued that the production of material artifacts in 1948 operated in a dialectical pattern—on the one hand, modern "communication society" mass-produced industrial objects, the design of which was determined by conscious decisions of individual designers. On the other hand, the design of craft objects, produced personally as a result of a "tradition oriented society," was driven by the subconscious decisions of successive generations. Although one may see the Eameses' argument as a continuation of the nineteenth- and early twentieth-century debate around the division of objects into mass-produced quotidian objects and handmade craft objects, their position differed significantly from that of the reformist cultural policies headed by colonial aesthetes such as Henry Cole. Unlike Cole and others in the nineteenth century, who advocated for a museum-like preservation of craft objects collected across the colonized East as a didactic means for the degenerated industrial design of the West, the Eameses' suggestion in the "India Report" was to reconcile the realms of industry and handicraft as a coherent whole. In a way, the report suggests the Eameses' desire to conflate the luxury that the American consumer paradigm offered—of which the Eameses were directly related as designers, promoters, and agents—and the asceticism that Gandhi would propose.

Charles Eames's fascination with Indian asceticism, which perhaps started during his first Indian tour, was alive nearly two decades later. In 1972 he started making a short film for his *Mathematica*, a social commentary exhibition, entitled *Banana Leaf: Something about Transformation and Rediscovery*.[27] One year before he started this project, in December 1971, Charles had told the story of this film in his lecture to the American Association for the Advancement of Science: "The very poor man [in India] eats his meal off a banana leaf. A little higher in the scale is a low-fired earthenware dish, a *tali*. Then a glazed *tali*, then brass, then bell bronze, or polished marble, which are both very handsome—then to show you can do better than that, you get into things that are rather questionable: silver plate, solid silver—presumably even gold. But there are some superior men—with not only means but understanding, and probably some spiritual training as well—who will go a step further, and eat off a banana leaf."[28]

In the Eameses' rhetoric, an expression of asceticism marked the uniqueness of India in both the anticolonial nationalist struggle and Indian culture in general. The Gandhian ideal of Indians living traditionally, measured against the ascetic lifestyle of the sannyasi (who renounced worldly possessions) and the Yogi, was perceived as critical to the very fundamentals of human necessity or to the requisite conditions of human existence and what is extraneous to it. The concept of *nissaya* (minimal earthly possessions) was even more applicable to the traditional wrestler, who in general symbolized an abundance of physical strength and the source of an equal abundance of physical pleasure.[29] However, the Eameses' role cannot be understood simply through the lenses of Orientalism, which might wrongly present them as orientalists who came to a reductive conclusion that India's highest achievement lay in embracing a stylized asceticism and a rejection of technology and industrialization. Both Eameses were indeed avowed supporters of India's design industrialization, and after the establishment of the National Institute of Design in 1961, they actively took part in the assessment of its progress. What I point out here is that the Eameses' implicit argument in the "India Report" goes beyond the structural coercion of Cold War cultural politics and India's planning for rapid national development. The report is a testament to the complex interaction in the Eameses' personal definition of design as an apolitical, if not ahistorical, action for the betterment of the human condition.

Influential Western agents of modernity such as the Eameses and Girard seem to have been poised to place asceticism and austerity within postwar American consumerism. They advocated for the coexistence of craft and noncraft as a spectacle that emerged from the binary opposition of incompatible sets of worldviews. The MoMA exhibition in New York brought Indian craft materials to the United States as elements of what at first glance seemed to be a typical Orientalist fantasy, the "glitter and gilt " of ethnographic spectacle. However, this show was contextualized in the broader set of design practices forged by Girard and Eames as postwar American innovations. Girard's intention regarding museum and exhibition design was not to set up displays that were culturally consistent—he would mix Mexican and Indian objects in a single museum installation—rather, his aim was to be aesthetically evocative.[30]

The same mixture of craft artifacts undertaken by the Eameses in their home, which was one of the most influential modernist villas of the postwar era, was called "functional decoration" by Ray Eames.[31] This term revealed that the practice was not meant to be an archaic form of Victorian displays of decorative relics; instead, it was intended as a legitimate contribution to modernist functionalism. Design historian Pat Kirkham

FIGURE 5.5. A modern Eames chair inside the Girard House, Santa Fe. The chair contrasts with Girard's collection of folk objects. Source: Robert Mayer, "The Grand Master of Santa Fé," *Metropolitan Home* (December 1982): 64.

analyzed it as an attempt to humanize modernism, to inject psychological comfort and the warmth of auratic craft objects into the emotionally cold environment of modernist physical comfort.[32] A reverse situation occurred in Girard's house, which could be considered the antithesis of the Eameses' case study house, as it accommodated museum-like collections of folk and ethnographic crafts collected from all over the world, expressing a preference for the nonmodern and for folk culture.[33] Girard sporadically and delicately placed the Eameses' modern chairs as "decoration" among his vast collections of craft, not to prove that modern design is equally extraneous to a large "nonmodern" population but to strengthen the modern project by marking the fissure and contrast between nonmodern and modern (fig. 5.5)

The juxtaposition can be termed a lumpy aggregate in which machine-crafted and handcrafted objects were mixed together as equally important ingredients of a postwar global culture. As Kirkham notes, in the Eameses' house there were two Indian craft chairs in the living room right next to the Eameses' incredibly expensive, elegant couches. In the classic photo of Ray and Charles Eames in the living room, they are sitting on *Indian* chairs—not on furniture of their own iconic design (fig. 5.6)—which would have offered a very uncomfortable posture from a Western point of view. They seem almost to be sitting on the floor. Kirkham's thesis argues that the Eameses' design had the goal of "humanizing modernism"—relieving it of its machine-age coldness and injecting warmth as a form of *psychological* comfort—through the addition of craft objects collected from all over the world. That they would include such furniture in their home and even be photographed sitting on such uncomfortable Indian chairs suggests that their broader, humanist notion of comfort was able to encompass and accept some degree of physiological *dis*comfort, a quality that they would never have designed into their own chairs. It may be suggested that the kind of humanized modernism envisioned by both the Eameses and Girard was categorically *not* the product of design hybridization—that is, the harmonization of thesis and antithesis in a new, uniform synthesis. Rather, it was a lumpy cultural aggregate in which sleek, comfortable, mass-produced, machine-crafted modernist objects were interspersed with rougher, auratic handcrafted artifacts of other traditions of making.[34] The sampling of "archaic" material cultures by the Eameses and Girard repudiated a fundamental trope of modernism. Rather than using the "otherness" of this jumble of folk objects to induce the alienation effect so beloved by modernists like Bertolt Brecht and Walter Benjamin, the Eameses and Girard aimed to harness the collision of aesthetic realms to create an *un*alienated modernity, or what Kirkham calls a humanized modernism.[35]

FIGURE 5.6. Charles and Ray Eames in their living room, 1958. Photograph by Julius Shulman. Source: Julius Shulman Photography Archive, 1936–1997, Series III: Projects, 1936–1997; Series III.A, Case Study Houses, 1945–2002. ID/Accession Number: 2004.R.10 (Job 2717) © J. Paul Getty Trust.

The spectacle of Indian craft that the 1955 MoMA show presented in a "fantasy setting" was accompanied by a museum-like displacement or disembodiment of human labor from the production of objects. It is worth noting here that throughout colonial rule, Indian crafts had their own history of such displacement at their place of origin. To succeed in the postindependence industrial reformation efforts, the Indian government determined that the most important task for design was to enhance the aesthetic of products to manipulate consumer demand. According to A. S. E. Iyer, the development commissioner of the Indian Office of the Development, "Consumer goods production has many a problem—the most important factor, however, is to give a product a welcome look, which easily satisfies the aesthetic demand of the consumers. This factor determines the saleable quality of product by catching the consumers' eyes immediately. The other factors such as utility, durability and price have also to be well considered."[36] Industrialists' call for an instrumental use of design as a tool to manipulate public taste is not uncommon in design history. However, the visual manifestation of this instrumental usage entailed a disembodiment of product and was well demonstrated in a poster design competition of 1946 launched by the commercial art section of the annual *Art in Industry Exhibition* in Calcutta to promote the theme "Buy Indian Textiles."[37] The common rhetoric of most of the entries tended to replace the emaciated working male bodies of weavers and craftsmen, as typified by Gandhi, with alluring female figures as the central cast, showing a fictitious attachment to work and reducing it to the task of a hobby. This new portrayal depicted production and design as a means to an end, devoid of human effort, and with commercial advantages.

In order to gain greater access to the German market, between 1957 and 1959 Indian trade organizations such as the All-India Handicrafts Board, the Indian Cooperative Union, and the National Small Industry Corporation participated in various trade fairs in places like Frankfurt, Munich, West Berlin, and Essen at the residence of Alfred Krupp von Bohlen und Halbach. He was one of the most powerful German industrialists, as well as a former military economic leader of the Nazi regime and chairman of the board of the Adolf Hitler Fund of German Trade and Industry.[38] In these exhibitions, handcrafted decorative and utilitarian objects were one of the central exhibits, and Indian trade organizations wanted to retain the exotic persona and aura of the Indian object. Such representation could easily be misinterpreted as similar to the colonial preservationist attitude. One thing the colonial and postcolonial attitude had in common regarding handicrafts was the emphasis on rarity. The experience of the British predecessors reduced the significance of the production of local crafts to that of objects to be capitalized upon for their rarity.[39] As was well known, an exotic India was more readily marketable than a modern India. The main theme of *Textile and Ornamental Arts of India*, a dual exhibition in 1955 by MoMA and the All-India Handicrafts Board, was "Buy Indian Textiles." This slogan was an eternal source of fantasy in that it submerged the tremendous workforce employed to create such fantasy and concealed the history and meaning of human engagement in the process of production.

The 1959 Museum of Modern Art Exhibition

In 1959 the office of George Nelson, one of the progenitors of modern industrial design in the United States, mounted the epochal *American National Exhibition* in Moscow on the behalf of the Museum of Modern Art. The National Small Industry Corporation—a group of Indian businessmen that was part of the Ministry of Commerce of India—requested that MoMA open a similar show in India.[40] The exhibit was sponsored by the Ford Foundation and the US Information Agency and displayed objects selected by MoMA's associate curator Greta Daniel, who also curated the widely acclaimed exhibition *20th Century Design from the Museum Collection, 1958–59*. MoMA engaged the same design team as the Nelson office to mount its first-ever and largest show in South Asia.[41] Lasting about two years, from 1959 to 1961, the show traveled through nine major cities—New Delhi, Chennai, Bangalore, Cuttack, Hyderabad, Ahmedabad, Bombay, Calcutta, and Kanpur—and drew more than a million visitors (fig. 5.7). Even though MoMA used the same design team and the same geodesic dome in Moscow and in India, the two exhibitions were fundamentally different: One was produced by the US Information Agency as a way of undermining the Soviet state by depicting the United States as a consumer paradise. The other, which was generated in response to a request by local businessmen operating under the umbrella of government bureaucracy, aimed to spur the development of the national economy.

The National Small Industry Corporation expected the show to channel local artisans' and designers' tastes into producing objects that by virtue of having a modern appearance would heighten the taste of the Indian consumer class, resulting in a concomitant expansion of the Indian home market for certain consumer goods.[42] In effect, local entrepreneurs interpreted MoMA's aesthetic mission as having significant trade potential. Thus, the 1959 Indian show was not solely an American diplomatic push but also an Indian economic pull. On the one hand, the United States seized the oppor-

Figure 5.7. A long queue outside the Museum of Modern Art exhibition, Delhi, 1959. Source: International Council and International Program Records, I.B. 226. Museum of Modern Art Archives. © Museum of Modern Art/Licensed by SCALA/Art Resource, NY.

tunity to explore India as a "testing ground" for the promotion of an American lifestyle as a gesture of democratic practice. On the other, it sought to harness the potential of India as a future consumer of modern material culture.[43] In a MoMA press release, this endeavor was expressed as "a result of [a] unique venture in international cooperation by public and private agencies."[44] The show proved to be exemplary of the symbiotic transference of midcentury modernity from one part of the globe to another.

The general setting of the exhibition was intended to portray an image of Western progress as well as to illuminate the neutral appearance of the machine-made modern product that stood in opposition to vivid and colorful Indian objects.[45] Housed in Buckminster Fuller's geodesic dome, the entire site was conceived by the architect Gordon O. Chadwick of the Nelson and Chadwick Office as having a monochrome backdrop, with the exception of the bright orange letters at the entrance depicting the title of the exhibition, *Design Today in America and Europe*. The Fuller dome was installed by the US Information Agency, which used Fuller's domes for erecting exhibition pavilions within short periods of time and as symbols of US engineering marvels.[46] Upon entering the dome, the viewer saw an Indian-style brick courtyard: in the center were variously shaped coco-matted wooden platforms on which the exhibit materials were placed, each tagged with a general number signifying its catalog entry. The four hundred household objects included chairs, lamps, glassware, kitchen utensils, textiles, and tools from New York, all representative of a time span from the eighteenth century to contemporary times and ranging in origin from Europe to the United States.

As an exhibition press release by Pupul Jayakar suggested, the objective was to draw the attention of the visitor to the place of materials and tools and their function in the creation of objects for daily use—not to replicate the objects directly as part of Indian life or to adapt to the way of life that the objects demanded.[47] The brown-stained deodar beams and white plywood panels, illuminated by the diffused ambient light that streamed through the dome, created a live domestic setting for modern Western goods. This was MoMA's aim, to draw a hard line between Eastern and Western modes of conceiving everyday objects. At the inauguration ceremony, Douglas Ensminger, the Ford Foundation representative in India, commented to Susan Cable Senior, associate director of the international program, and architect Gordon Chadwick, that "this show is absolutely going to stand this country right on its ear—which is precisely what we want."[48] Much like the presentation style adopted at the 1959 Indian show of good design, MoMA opted not to exhibit household objects by live demonstration in a virtual ideal American home, a style they had followed in Europe. Rather than attempting to sell the American way of life in India, MoMA's project in India seemed to dissolve the modern object and its aesthetic into Indian culture of production and consumption. The museum assumed that India would find ways to produce and accommodate these modern objects into everyday life (figs. 5.8, 5.9). It counted on the active participation of Indian agency—traders, industrialists, cultural activists, and designers—for the transference of modern design principles to India. Nevertheless, the internal dissonance of these two catalysts vis-à-vis transnational dissemination of modernity questioned the overdetermined portrayal of the Americanization effort, attacked afterward as an irredeemably American cultural scourge.[49]

The involvement of the Ford Foundation as a sponsor of the exhibition should be understood within the foundation's broader Cold War–era role as a transnational catalyst transferring American ideology to the developing regions of the world.[50] Historian Kathleen McCarthy shows that, in addition to its development efforts regarding technology, health, agriculture, and education, the foundation disseminated a total of $10 million between 1950 and 1980 in its cultural projects over the globe.[51] However, as a rising

FIGURE 5.8. Inside the MoMA exhibition dome. Source: International Council and International Program Records, I.B. 227. Museum of Modern Art Archives. © Museum of Modern Art/Licensed by SCALA/Art Resource, NY.

economic force, India won American attention during the 1950s. C. Douglas Dillon, secretary of state for economic affairs, described the problem of India's future development as the "most important economic project we have anywhere in the world."[52] The Ford Foundation advised the Indian government of its new development strategy, the advancing of its small-scale industries on the basis of an outline proposed by an American expert

FIGURE 5.9. The MoMA exhibition at Amritsar in 1959. One of the major objectives of this show was to evoke demand for modern household goods. The installation was considered to be a site for virtual consumption. Source: International Council and International Program Records, I.B. 228. Museum of Modern Art Archives. © Museum of Modern Art/Licensed by SCALA/Art Resource, NY.

team.[53] During their visit to India in 1953, the team identified the scope for Indian goods to create a quality market as soon as modern requirements of production and supplies were met. Taking as its point of departure the setting up of a national school of design and fashion, the team called for integrating India into a culture of mass production and mass consumption.

Integrated development, as perceived by the foundation, was achievable only through the deployment of US technical expertise and foundation grants. These funds were used to demonstrate American achievements in technology and progress in the developing regions through public exhibitions or similar demonstrations that disseminated prototypes and models.[54] With the establishment of the Ford Foundation in India in 1952, the foundation steadily developed its relationship with the Indian government and various nongovernment organizations. This contact convinced Indian businesses that there was a pressing need to apply the Ford Foundation's prescribed development strategy to the new design sector. Both the National Institute of Small Industry and the foundation predicted that future development initiated by harnessing small-sector industry would lead to perceived integrated development. Placing it in a broader context, the 1959 MoMA design show exemplified the pull factor generated by local demand pairing up with the global rise of consumerism to become part of global technical development.

Arthur Drexler, the influential midcentury design critic and longtime director of architecture and design at MoMA, wrote in the exhibition catalog that "in the Western world there is one object in which all problems of design come to a sharp focus: Chair."[55] In midcentury cultural politics of visual display that were performed at various design exhibitions, the chair became an agent to define the human subject by framing its body in it, just as the kitchen became the site of defining postwar consumer domesticity.[56] In the 1959 show, chairs were central to demonstrating the notion of physical comfort, that is, of working or resting the body paradoxically at a time when the chair—in MoMA's sense, the epitome of design—was a relatively novel product for India and was even less known by the masses. For MoMA the Western pursuit of understanding the methodology of any system directed inquiry into how humanity's life on Earth could be made ever more comfortable.[57] This inquiry would ultimately equip humanity with the novel tool of technology.[58] By presenting a survey of the evolution of Western design, MoMA's exhibition in India served to showcase the means by which the contemporary West could make life more enjoyable on Earth.

MoMA offered to turn the Victorian construct of individual comfort into something for mass consumption. In India MoMA presented Western civilization as a progressive spirit seeking a methodological formation of the physical world by asking the question, *How?* And the answer it offered was the narrative of comfort as a public discourse. The eighteenth-century consumer revolution in Europe and America recast the meaning of comfort by synthesizing its new physical dimensions with the previous form of comfort as moral support.[59] Since then, comfort has primarily become a concern of cultural progress, not merely a physical concern. At the beginning of the twentieth century, in an attempt to explain the notion of comfort in a contemporary machine-age situation, edgar Kaufmann Jr., the curator of MoMA's 1955 exhibition in New York, wrote, "The truly comfortable person was the one reclining. The attitude gradually became the model of general comfort in public."[60] Describing the interior design of William Morris as the origin of comfortable modern living, Kaufmann noted, "This room speaks to the eye of relaxation, of pampering the individual, and of friendly association between individuals who share its atmosphere."[61]

MoMA's modernity related the culture of comfort with the consumption patterns of domesticity that required households to increase their technological specialization and to lessen their primary production for subsistence. This was so that within the newer "modern" environment, domestic activities and their associated patterns of consumption could take place free from traditional elemental constraints. The vision of modernist design showcased by the 1959 show is one that used physical comfort and advanced technology as icons of a vision of postwar modernity defined by Western middle-class leisure and consumption. In other words, these artifacts prescribed a specific vision of postwar modern life, of which America was at the cutting edge in 1959.

MoMA's show in India established that mass submission to comfort and pleasure was achievable through a methodological change of the production of objects—that is, a change from craft to industry. But for Indian conditions, the mechanical reproducibility of an object carried a meaning different from simply a loss of aura in Walter Benjamin's sense; it was also a source of skepticism. This apparent passport to a utopia of comfort had the potential to erode the bedrock of their traditional relationship with the material world and its associated domesticity. In the exhibition catalog supplement, Pupul Jayakar maintained that the exhibition had been requested because recent years had witnessed a transformation in the socioeconomic life of India: "Improved communications, the breakdown of caste barriers, the carrying of an urban civilization . . . to the small towns and distant villages . . . have led to a breakdown of the traditional pattern of production, altered the relationship between producer and consumer, and posed a challenge to the forms that underlie production and distribution in the country."[62]

René d'Harnoncourt, an American-Czech art curator and director of MoMA from 1949 to 1967, noted in the foreword of the *Design Today in America and Europe* exhibition catalog that "the purpose of the exhibition is to bring to the attention of the Indian public the aesthetic values of the West in largely machine-made, mass produced objects."[63] The domesticity these objects evoked contested the idea that their own domestic objects tended to enhance social associations by articulating the relations between man and his material surroundings. Drexler further stated: "Western artifacts have come more and more to bear the mark of the machine. . . . Such machine-made objects themselves developed not only through social events and pressures, but like handicrafts no less often derive their general style from the example of work by a few great artists."[64]

Sociologist Richard Sennett argued that the advent of machine production in the nineteenth century made the artisan ever less a mediator and ever more an enemy of the machine, becoming an emblem of human individuality, imposing positive values on variation, flaws, and irregularity. Nevertheless, in describing the exhibition sections that consisted of household, office, and kitchen utensils as well as laboratory equipment and tools, the catalog emphasized that Western culture had traditionally held geometric shapes to have a superior beauty because they called into play the rational mind. Drawing on Plato's notion of the ideal and Thomas Aquinas's notion of perfection, MoMA claimed that the newly invented "art form" presented solutions that the West had evolved to accommodate mechanical production, new materials, and energy potentials that scientific research had made available, as well as the new consumer demands that had arisen in the last fifty years. By discarding the relevance of the nonindustrial, the domestic working body of the artisan was rendered subterranean amid a mass of reproducible objects. In MoMA's words: "Since [the] middle of the nineteenth century, Western handicrafts have steadily diminished in importance until they are no longer the chief source of our common implements. . . . The craftsman has found a new role in the useful arts. The prototypes for many machine-made objects are first developed by the individual crafts man, particularly in such fields as textiles and glass."[65] Two points of conjecture marked the MoMA show. First, mass-produced objects do not lose their artistic quality, and they are still representative of Western verity, irrefutable fundamentals of classical purity and ideals. Second, modern living is essentially an artistic task because individual crafts have been replaced by mass artistic proliferation, reproduced on the factory line and recycled in consumer houses. Living in a modern era is essentially practicing art amid comfort, not practicing austere life to its bitter end.

The new role of mass-produced, machine-made household objects as producers of everyday domestic experience contested the Indian notion of domesticity as a personalized and contextualized experience that had profound connections with Gandhi's alternative form of domesticity in ashram life. The exhibited objects heralded a way of life forged on comfort, the lessening of human labor on daily household tasks by means of the machine. This was quite different from Gandhi's stylized ascetic way of life, which emphasized the incorporation of gender-unspecified human labor as much as possible into all aspects of household work. Gandhi's choreographed domestic life in his ashram had a political objective of forming Indian nationalism, but it was also an antithesis to the image of a picturesque home, widely circulated by women's magazines and newspapers, in which Indian women served a dual role of Indian and Western housewife at the same time.[66] In nineteenth-century colonial exhibitions, machines were displayed as single animated forces bent upon producing a new phase of civilization: modernity.[67] Working bodies were almost erased from the scene, remaining only as a depiction of the "human exotic." Art historian Tim Barringer describes this as a "fantasy of production without labour, a world without a working class."[68]

Throughout the first half of the twentieth century, Gandhi assiduously promoted a material culture that was perhaps impossible to realize in a consumer society, but it was one that at least sounded more ethical to the Indian ear. It took effort to retain the value system imbedded in objects, a value system that the capitalist market reduced to exchange values and free-floating independent, value-free commodities.[69] Gandhi's challenge to the material culture of the modern West soon became a challenge for the people in his own country, when postindependence India rejected his ascetic way of living as being unrealistic. Gandhi, with his ascetic material culture, criticized independent India's pragmatic objective to become modern. After a decade of independence, the century-long debate surrounding craft versus industrial production transformed into a debate over accepting a form of domesticity forged in a different material culture.[70] As Jayakar wrote in the flier circulated at the 1959 exhibition: "It is a challenge to democracy and an industrial society whether or not within its contours a great artisan tradition can flourish."[71] By 1959 it was well established in India that the old way of producing objects, representative of a bygone political order, was no longer acceptable. However, the fundamental incompatibility of the two forms of domesticity led to a fantasy of juxtaposition, a soft form of modernity or a lumpy aggregate that would allow certain reminiscences of a bygone culture that India had shown in Manhattan four years earlier and for which Girard and the Eameses continued to strive.

Indian bureaucratic expectations of this exhibition, as described by Manubhai Shah, union minister of industry, were to learn how the visual appearance of Indian objects could be made more appealing as mass-consumption goods.[72] The Indian bureaucracy's major concern was that the primary task of design should be to make the objects more presentable on the global market. Such a pragmatic role of design was closely linked to the synthesis of India's home market of consumer goods with its global dispersion. Shah, writing in the introduction of the exhibition catalog, stated: "The degree of success in making a product depends greatly on the extent to which a fusion of technical quality, functional excellence and visual design is achieved. . . . [Design must create] an immediate and overwhelming appeal to a buyer."[73] Shah continued to urge, advise, and warn manufacturers that "a manufacturer must, therefore, look ahead to produce goods that are pleasing to eyes and satisfying its function." At the opening ceremony of the exhibition in New Delhi, he praised American and European design and pointed out the lessons for India: "This does not mean that we in India should produce the exact replica of these. . . . We have to produce simple, artistic and beautiful designs for articles consistent with our way of life and suitable to our genius. . . . We welcome this because an exhibition of this kind would serve the purpose of a visual demonstration of the effect of good industrial designing."

Vice President S. Radhakrishnan, in his opening remarks of the exhibition, beseeched the industrialists and craftsmen of India to adopt "quality above cheapness," calling on local manufacturers, designers, and artisans to act under the rubric "Blend Beauty with Utility" (1959). This was an approach notoriously similar to the Victorian revivalist attitude toward industrial products. The immediate, postindependence Indian bureaucracy was troubled by its bid to locate itself among global cultural politics and trade interests. While on the one hand the nation's collective memory was still enthralled by the Gandhian spirit of asceticism, on the other, Nehru's sympathy for Soviet-style socialism and (paradoxically) his longing for America's promised land of consumer goods created a complex situation. Consequently, the concept of free transference of global consumer objects was not very popular. In 1954 a Bombay economist named A. D. Shroff began a forum for free enterprise and consumer goods, an idea complemented the Planning Commission of India that had yet to develop a detailed plan of the future of Indian design industry. At the same time, a journalist and communist from Cambridge, Philip Spratt, wrote that the consequences of the Soviet model of economy would be the "smothering of free enterprise, a famine of consumer goods."[74] The theme of producing consumer goods occupied a significant position in Indian economic discourse, and consequently a demand for a well-articulated planning was growing at a slow but constant pace. This changing socioeconomic scenario is reflected in the Indian small industrialists' predilection for Euro-American state-of-the art design artifacts. MoMA's show was a careful medley of industrially produced, transatlantic consumer goods that would inform both vernacular artisans and community-based small industries.

In the global transference of midcentury modernity, while modernism was championed by MoMA for its aesthetic superiority, Indian culture brokers imported the idea of comfort in mass-produced objects as a potential business asset. As I have shown elsewhere, comfort was a key trope of this particular iteration of postwar modernism. But more often the promotion mechanism used only the myth of comfort, far from its actual realization. Mass-produced domestic comforts were an important aspect in the discussion about India's new modern house. The Indian adaptation of a comfortable, scientific, and modern Indian home can be traced back to 1926 when engineer Raghunath Shripad Deshpande published two books on the modern home for India.[75] During the 1950s, Indian newspapers circulated news of the "equality of living" as promised by American consumer society.[76] A global notion of affluence with a preference for individual domestic comfort was considered the basis of democratic equality. India's emerging middle class welcomed the promotion of "better living," circulated as an inevitable consequence of democratic capitalism. It put before Indian society the ultimate image of an ideal living environment within a consumerist society that rested and pampered the human body—that is, until it morphed into a phantasmagoria of consuming cutting-edge material culture.

Considering that MoMA's survey of Western design in India was conceptually a part of Edgar Kaufmann Jr.'s *Good Design* exhibitions, it becomes clear that mass consumption was encoded in MoMA's culturally constructed notion of comfort. Its collection of canonical objects of "good design" was shipped by the US Information Agency throughout Western Europe, intended to convince postwar Europeans that the United States was not just an uncultivated land of vulgar consumption. *Good Design* presented a transatlantic portrait of modernism in which the United States was the tradition's most recent and accomplished heir. A similar vision of modernism, presented as the domestic material culture of transatlantic capitalism to Indian entrepreneurs, became the driving force behind bringing this style to India as a springboard for the development of the nation's manufacturing and trade capacities.[77]

The objective of the exhibition was to create taste and desire for modern household goods and to demonstrate an ideal domestic environment for industrial society. From MoMA's perspective, this exhibition was part of the US promotion of the "good society" circulated worldwide to East Germany, Soviet Russia, and Eastern European countries as an inevitable consequence of democratic and capitalist society. From an Indian perspective, it was part of a broader state aspiration to form a mixed-model industrial society, both socialist and capitalist. Taking this exhibition as a point of departure, the National Institute of Small Industry, a trade organization, and the Indian government sought to establish a design institute that could produce its own version of modernism.

In India, the show was extremely popular, and over a three-week period, more than one hundred thousand people in New Delhi visited the exhibition. Between 1959 and 1961, the exhibition traveled through nine cities, and while the enthusiastic response of the Indian press was partially responsible for the large attendances, it is difficult to reflect on the nature of the people's reaction to the exhibition. The *Hindustani Times* called the show "a really fine exhibition," while the *Times of India* commented that "the western world has combined utility with beauty."[78] Commenting more directly on the economic purpose of the show, the *Statesman* reported that "human hands and sweat can produce only a small fraction of the things that people need to live decently. Only machinery can satisfy the needs of the millions who inhabit the earth." In a statement distributed along with the exhibition catalog, Jayakar (as a representative and member of the All-India Handicrafts Board) pointed out that India was on the fringe of a technological revolution that had the potential to result in a loss of pride in craftsmanship and in traditional design standards unless attention was refocused on problems such as the nature of new materials and tools. Furthermore, some of the objects in the exhibition, such as the chair and the china teacup, were unknown in India outside of its large cities just a few decades before. The solutions developed by the Western world, she wrote, should not be imitated but could serve as a guide and might stimulate the imagination of Indian designers and manufacturers.

From MoMA's perspective, mounting such an exhibition was part of the American response to India's own will to become modern, to become visible in the world market, to become worthy of participating in the global politics of modernity. The museum's director of exhibitions and publications, Monroe Wheeler, who conceived of such an exhibition of the Indian object during her visit to India in 1953, wrote about its scope: "Although I had first visited India twenty years ago, I felt when I returned last year that a country which had then been mysteriously somnolent and apathetic had, since its independence, come amazingly to life. I encountered everywhere an enthusiastic desire to improve living standards and provide better educational facilities."[79] After the MoMA show ended in 1961, the objects were presented to the Indian government to form the nucleus of a permanent collection so that the people of India could benefit from access to them over a longer period. After the establishment of India's first design school, the National Institute of Design, at Ahmedabad in 1961, these objects were handed over to NID for presentation to students as examples of what could be the point of departure for creating a new Indian modernity. For more than five decades, these objects have been a source of inspiration for generations of Indian designers.

The National Institute of Design's Pedagogical Turn toward Europe

Ashoke Chatterjee—a celebrated design thinker, educator, and longtime director of the National Institute of Design in Ahmedabad—tells that, despite being ambiguous, the Eameses' "near mystified report" of 1958 served as a source of philosophical inspiration for generations of Indian designers; however, their recommendations were considered inadequate for setting up a design school.[80] Pupul Jayakar also suggested that the Eameses' report was meant mainly to define or to understand Indian design and was not detailed enough to address the demands of the Ford Foundation and the Indian Ministry, which had expected structural guidance to establish a design institute to serve small industries.[81] In 1960, two years after the report, the foundation hired a Danish architect, Vilhelm Wohlert, and a Swiss photographer, Ernst Scheidegger, as consultants to develop a working plan for a design institute based on the Eameses' report. The following year, Wohlert and Scheidegger came up with an executive proposal that was predicated on workshop-based design learning to train and prepare India's "human resources" to provide the country with the necessary means for a comprehensive design solution.[82] The basic approach of their proposal, learning through doing, was the reflection of the Bauhaus commitment to the philosophy of the German psychologist Martin Hildebrand-Nilshon, the German educational theorist Georg Kerschensteiner, the Italian educator Maria Montessori, and the American philosopher and educational reformer John Dewey. This approach was later altered by Gautam Sarabhai, a leading industrialist and the first chairman of the governing councils at NID (1961–1974), to "learning to do and learning to know," a radical shift that shaped the pedagogical philosophy of the future design school.[83] However, on the basis of the Wohlert-Scheidegger report and with the technical assistance of the Ford Foundation, the government of India established the National Institute for Industrial Design, as it was originally named in September 1961. In 1963 it was renamed the National Institute of Design. The first grant of $200,000 was made in 1961. Over the following nine years, the foundation donated $120,000 each year.[84]

The moral framework for the institution may have derived from the Eameses' "India Report," but it was the NID's connection with the Hochschule für Gestaltung (HfG) at Ulm, Germany, that had a profound impact on the formation and evolution of its pedagogical philosophy, specifically in the sector of household product design, which some scholars argue did not sufficiently consider the Indian context.[85] Design historian Saloni Mathur offers us a critical perspective to understand this situation. Mathur discusses that the Eameses' work in India was not simply a phase in their career but rather resembles influences that India used for its own mission. India framed the Eameses within its postcolonial effort to establish design institutes and to reform small-scale industries.[86] Similarly, I propose that the partnership of the Ford Foundation with Indian government bureaucrats—as well as the HfG's connection with the NID—while correlating with many external parameters, was primarily advanced by Indian academics and more specifically by prospective NID faculty members. It was H. Kumar Vyas, who was selected to attend a ten-month training program at the HfG, who started the product design program at the NID in 1966. Sudhakar Nadkarni was a graduate of the HfG who later joined the product design course at NID as a faculty member in 1967. Through Vyas and Nadkarni, the NID enjoyed a sustained connection in Ulm with professionals such as Gui Bonsiepe, Kohei Sugiura, Herbert Lindinger (Institut für Umweltgestaltung, Frankfurt), Christian Staub, Hans Gugelot, and Ernst Reichl (director of the Institut für Produktentwicklung, Neu Ulm), who were among the most prominent.

But why HfG? Was it not expected that since it was started through the Ford Foundation and through Eames that the following phase should have sought a deeper connection with US designers and design schools? Interestingly, although the Eameses had been venerated as intellectual gurus ever since, the NID, as soon as it acquired autonomous footing, sought inspiration from the HfG and similar German experiments. How did this shift fit within the broader Indian perspective—a country that had just won its independence and was struggling to find its place in the global market? The celebrated US designers of the 1950s and 1960s, such as George Nelson, Ray and Charles Eames, Harry Bertoia, Richard Schultz, Donald Knorr, and Isamu Noguchi, were all commissioned and supported by business giants such as Herman Miller. By responding to American consumer demands, they served an exuberant and affluent postwar market.[87] The HfG experiment, on the other hand, had very different roots. What particularly attracted Indian interest in Ulm was its effort in postfascist cultural regeneration and political reformation toward a democratic end.[88]

Inge Scholl, the daughter of Robert Scholl, the mayor of Forchtenberg, Germany, took a risky initiative to establish a new "democratic" school together with her husband, Otl Aicher, a graphic artist and Nazi resister, and Max Bill, a former Bauhaus student. The original motivation behind Scholl's initiatives was to honor the memory of her siblings, Hans and Sophie Scholl, slain by the fascist regime for their active involvement in the White Rose, an anti-Nazi group.[89] However, the school soon became an experimental ground for reconciling and mediating the growing schism between German *Kultur* and *Zivilisation* through design and technological education.[90] For many postwar German scholars, the horrors of war, including industrialized death, and the destruction and historic collapse of German nationalism into militant Nazism, was the ultimate failure of the Enlightenment based on rationalism. This was obvious proof of both the ideological power and demise of technology.[91] Joachim Radkau described this collective antipathy toward technology and people involved in technology: "That technology no longer served as the central trope of [West] German liberation was nowhere more evident than in the fact that West German engineers never recouped their pre-1945 authority as anointed cultural heroes."[92] The Ulmers contested this antimodern aversion and the post-Nazi apocalyptic vision for technology through the redemptive power of rationalism, attempting to retain harmony and consonance among humanism, technology, and efficiency. In the prewar context, the Bauhaus's harmonization attempt was to combine the artist-architect into a cosmic whole.[93] However, in the postwar context, the Ulmers' mission was to forge a postfascist *Industriekultur* by rescuing it from Nazi corruption and by repositioning it within the humanist tradition of social responsibility and moral education.[94] Although Scholl's vision was to establish a more radical institute to train students in progressive political and social sciences, since the appointment of Max Bill, art-oriented industrial design had been adopted as its main curriculum.[95]

Max Bill's Werkbund philosophy, combined with inspiration for democratic reformation, directed HfG's initial activity in two significant ways. First, in Bill's language, this combination set its pedagogical foundation to educate "citizens with working careers who think politically."[96] Bill argued that instead of imposing a forced political education, an institute should reconstitute the social and cultural space and its everyday material culture if it was to contribute any social reformation project. The second major effort was to abolish *gemütlichkeit*—to erase any sign of homeliness, domesticity and comfort—from every aspect of living. This was pronounced in the new Ulm building designed by Bill. It abolished all difference between the modernist exterior façade and the interior. Any sign of the unwanted German past in the form of auratic cultural artifacts or extraneous details were removed, and decorative furniture was to be replaced by simple built-in furniture—a symbol of a pure environment and rational order. This Puritanism represented a cleansing effort to remove the epistemological error of fascism and was manifested dramatically in the classic design of the Ulm stool (*Ulm Hocker*) by Max Bill, Hans Gugelot, and Paul Hildinger. It was a simple, cost-effective, and easy-to-produce multipurpose piece of furniture that could be used as a chair, night table, workbench, step stool, and even a food-carrying tray in the school canteen.[97] The stool became the quintessence of Ulm's design philosophy, as it consciously broke down the binary opposition of human repose and activity and expressed the condition of a postfascist object in flux. The physical and notional discomfort it offered to its users was believed to be a metonymic virtue that provoked users to movement and activity.[98] It is worth remembering Eames's uncomfortable Indian chair that supplemented the American comfort-based design discourse of the 1950s and 1960s.

The American military government took great interest in the Ulm project, as Scholl succeeded to convince the American High Command of Germany that Ulm was a crucial Cold War project. Further, Scholl suggested that by pursuing its "dual containment policy," Soviet expansion could be resisted at one end of the spectrum and German Nationalism could be suppressed at the other. John J. McCloy, director of the American High Command of Germany who reestablished the Frankfurt School of Social Research after the war, considered Ulm a "spiritual Marshall Plan" and granted DM 1 million in 1953 for its establishment.[99] American endorsement of Ulm as a cultural reeducator could not win over the Ulmers' internal aversion toward American streamline design. Scholl, in her famous 1962 chapter, treated with disdain the "Nierentisch (kidney-shaped table) nightmare" as the "bastard child" of designers and merchants.[100] Likewise, Max Bill's efforts to combine art and technology into a unified harmonic reality faced tremendous criticism from academics who wanted to shift pedagogical focus from art to science. Discontent first surfaced through Tomás Maldonado, an Argentine artist and art journal editor who joined the Ulm faculty in 1954. It was Maldonado who had the deepest influence on Indian designers both directly and indirectly. However, Maldonado rejected Bill's Werkbund-Bauhaus ideology outright and argued for a more scientific method. Maldonado put his argument boldly in the 1958 Brussels World Fair, where most of the representatives concurred with Bill on the old Bauhaus ideology and similar colonial ideologies—that education that was more aesthetic and design oriented, together with the dissemination of "good form," could "fix cultural kitsch."[101]

Maldonado, on the other hand, argued that the preference for the aesthetic in modern design was an outcome of trade interest in the depression years in which aesthetic design served as a manipulative strategy to exploit human needs and the desire to reinvigorate the consumer market. This was the basic resistive tenet that framed the uneasy designer-market relations within Ulm, which was, in historian Heiner Jacob's terms, "utterly schizophrenic."[102] As a consequence of this conflict, Bill resigned in 1956 and Maldonado was appointed as the new rector in the same year. Bill continued to teach but finally left the HfG in 1957. The theoretical effort to keep market-driven industrial interest away from educational institutes eventually trapped the Ulmers in a self-contradictory and hermetic intellectual cell.[103] The NID's own uneasy relationship with the profit-driven market was largely informed by this Ulm philosophy.

After Maldonado's proposition, the HfG post-Bill pursued a radical rationalization and push toward using science in the design process, in which the principal role of the designer was determined only to "coordinate, in close collaboration with a large number of specialists, the most varied requirements of product fabrication and usage."[104] Unlike Bill's autonomous designers, whose responsibility was limited only in distant stylization of an object, Maldonado's new designers had been imbedded in the production process. While Bill's designer was "mystical and indefinable," Maldonado's designer was a specialist in mass production and industrial automation, ceaselessly demystifying the industrial production process through coordinating our "objective and communicative world."[105] He termed this process "scientific operationalism"—a critical design praxis based on separating the conventional relationship between aesthetics and design.[106] This new materiality, by refuting an object's role as the container or signifier of moral idealism and cultural values, considered an "object" to be the result of socially managed and scientifically coordinated industrial resources.[107] This changed role of designers caused an epistemological shift where the question of production of knowledge was removed by the operational capacity or manipulability of knowledge.[108] Of his method, Maldonado wrote: "By scientific operationalism I intend then a model of action oriented toward overcoming the dichotomy between theory and practice. Later on, following Kotarbinsky, I preferred to call it 'praxology'—and even more recently, 'the philosophy of praxis,' as seen in Gramsci."[109] Architectural historian Kenneth Frampton shows that Maldonado's scientific operationalism was basically rooted in Anatol Rapoport's philosophical ideas, published in 1953 under the title *Operational Philosophy*, which had expanded John Dewey's pragmatic instrumentalism.[110] The central effort of this idea was to push philosophy more toward an analytical method of mathematics and to provide a system to evaluate, examine, and measure alternative courses of action.

In the penultimate issue of the journal *Ulm*, Claude Schnaidt, a French-German Marxist and architectural historian who took on the role of director at the HfG after Max Bill and served until its closure in 1968, discussed at length the crisis of functionalism and the future direction of developing world's development in a long quotation that deserves to be reproduced here:

> Finally, we have our duties towards the under-developed countries. The habitat situation in these countries is catastrophic. . . . And since these countries also have to solve the problems of hunger, disease, ignorance and the creation of means of production, they must appeal to foreign countries for aid. Unfortunately, this barely covers the losses they suffer as a result of their economic dependence. These losses are incurred by the repatriation of the profits of foreign firms and the growing gap between the prices of raw materials and the process of manufactured products. . . . The under-developed countries must tackle their problems by their own means and make the countries that dominate them today treat them as equals. But in the meantime we must help all those organized groups who, in the "third world," are fighting against external and internal oppression. At home we must demand a foreign policy of balanced development: a development depending not on licence agreements, car exports, and wastage but on the utilization of natural and human resources.[111]

The Hochschule für Gestaltung Ulm finally came to an end in November 1968 after a long, winding, and uncompromising struggle against insatiable consumerism and parochial market interests.[112]

Against the context of the birth and executive strategy of the Ulm school, H. Kumar Vyas and Sudhakar Nadkarni worked at the HfG from 1962 to 1966. The ideas of Tomás Maldonado—who served at Ulm as rector and prorector between 1954 and 1966—for finding a balance between technology and design through systems thinking, were in decline, though he was still among the most influential thinkers there. However, in 1966 the HfG's basic philosophy was experiencing difficulties due to conflicting views among the faculty, and the school closed down in February 1968. Vyas, on his return to the NID in 1966, started the new industrial design section just two years before the cessation of the HfG; Nadkarni had joined the NID just a year before that. The industrial design section at the NID thus began at the historical threshold between the HfG's final years in West Germany and the inception of a new initiative in another part of the globe—both entangled in a postcolonial and Cold War situation. In this regard, two sets of issues need to be addressed. The first is how the NID faculty returning from the HfG, such as Vyas and Nadkarni, intended to reconceptualize and reframe the HfG's philosophy in a Third World context and subsequently to overcome the apparent incompatibility of the Ulm model in current market situations. Vyas and Nadkarni, through their teaching and practice, proposed mechanisms for contextualizing, adopting, reengineering, and assimilating the Ulm ideology in India. The second set of issues concerns the ways in which the former Ulm faculty considered how the Ulm ideology could succeed in a Third World context. They anticipated that as a

FIGURE 5.10. The India lounge designed by Hans Gugelot, 1965. Source: Private collection of Guus Gugelot. © Guus Gugelot.

sustained result of the HfG's ideology, the core essence of Ulm theory could be regenerated even after the school's closure and would therefore disseminate globally and flourish in a variety of regional situations.

In 1965 the NID invited Hans Gugelot, a few months before he died of a heart attack, to help develop the course curriculum of the Product Design Department. Gugelot was a longtime faculty member at Ulm, famous for his invention of system design. His brief stay and his works at the NID traversed through the HfG's interpretation of Third World development and Indian aspirations to devise a system of mass-producible and affordable modernism in material culture. According to Vyas, Gugelot's empathy with India was perhaps the result of his childhood connection with Indonesia, and it allowed Gugelot to think beyond the usual dependency theory. He suggested that Third World development should be free from direct involvement of the First World.[113] Gugelot's design at the NID included a domestic lounge chair and a matching table in collaboration with Gajanan Upadhyaya, an architect who joined the NID faculty in the summer of 1965 (fig. 5.10). The main design objectives were to devise a system of mass-producible and standardized elements made of local material and capable of manufacture by local skills. Standardized elements needed to be designed in such a way that they could be used as multiple furniture pieces, such as stools, tables, and chairs.

Multiplicity of function and employment of the same elements for different designs had a profound connection to Ulm's democratization effort, but for India, designing chairs in the 1940s and 1950s, there were other questions to address. The sitting posture in a chair was unprecedented and culturally unfamiliar to general Indian perceptions. The various sitting postures (*asana*) on the ground were analogs to those of the Yogi and sannyasi and the traditional grid and space division system (*Vastu*), which is also symbolized by a sitting man. When designing for the general population, Indian designers preferred to accommodate the traditional asana or sometimes the squatting position of the Indian body rather than to elevate them over a raised platform—what has been known as the "chair" in Western culture. In western perceptions, a chair is the means to elevate the body from the earth and thus to distinguish the two different spheres of bodily movement, the space of the earth and the space of work.

For Western modernists, the design of a "chair" has been considered to be among the most sensitive technical decisions and highest achievement of Western design, since no other design could possibly visually define its user's image and symbolize a work-repose dialectic. One possible negotiation in designing an Indian chair was to make it low in height to make the body posture looked more familiar with traditional squatting positions, or asana, while working bodies in an office unquestionably followed the universal corporate environment during the 1950s. The Indian chair—quintessentially Indian in culture and character—was predominantly the lounge within the domestic environment, mostly representing the reposing body at home. The Indian chair was a late development, mostly within academia's experimental sphere. It was designed when the vast swath of working bodies outside the corporate world, who did not use chairs as such but performed their work from a sitting position, were identified in the design realm, but it was possibly never produced by industry on a mass scale. However, Gugelot seems to have been inspired by a similar tenet about low height. He used Indian teak in his design, which was the most suitable wood for the Indian climate, easily procurable and traditionally considered to be the most elegant. Gugelot and Upadhyaya developed a system of members and joints, and the result was a unique structural system of standardized elements of identical cross sections that could be used both inside and outside.

The essence of a Gugelot and Upadhyaya's system design of interchangeable and standardized elements assembled in many ways to suit various functions for various spaces was an effort to dissolve the irreconcilable fragments of the disparate spaces of work and home. Through a system of visual hygiene, it attempted to gather all the fragmented parts of the disintegrated spaces and fuse them into a single visual system, reflecting use-value rationality.[114] Their system design confronted the market invention of "personalized design" and offered to nourish users' individual expressions through flexible rearrangements of modular elements. When Gugelot suddenly died in 1965, his task at the NID was continued by Herbert Lindinger and H. Kumar Vyas.

Gajanan Upadhyaya, Gugelot's associate at the NID, was then a young faculty member of the industrial design section. He was a graduate in architecture from Maharaja Sayajirao University at Baroda, a blue-collar worker at a metal workshop, and a graduate of the Royal Danish Academy of Fine Arts at Copenhagen in 1966. Between 1962 and 1965, Upadhyaya was also an associate of Charles and Ray Eames in designing round stick furniture, and of George Nakashima in designing lounges, also at the NID. Gugelot's system of knock-down furniture made of standardized elements had a deep influence on Upadhyaya's design philosophy. His 1964 design of 24/42 furniture took Gugelot's recommendation of 24-by-42-millimeter standardized German wood sections as a guiding module, which could be used to design easy chairs, low tables, work tables, beds, and storage spaces. The easy chair, which had a reinforced seat and back made of wood slats, and the bed, also made with wood slats, seemed to have been influenced by Gugelot's use of prestressed wooden slats in the Ulm bed and at the back of his famous armchair gs1076. In 1974, on his return from Denmark, where he worked with Poul Kjærholm and Nils Fagerholt, among others, Upadhyaya rejoined the NID and further advanced the idea of mass-producible knock-down furniture in teak. He opened his own practice in Denmark with Dan Svart and Peter Hjoert Lorenzen on Lille Strandstraede in Copenhagen. On different occasions he also worked with Vibeke Klint, Dorte Raaschou, Børge Mogensen, Bo Bonfils, Jens Moeller Jensen, Rigmor Andersen, and museum inspector Werner Jacobsen. His design of a semi-knock-downable chair—the "classic chair" of 1978—used teak as the basic structural material and a relatively narrow strip (four centimeters) of canvas that was used locally to make bags for pack animals. This four-centimeter strip then became the guiding scale that set the width and other proportions of the chair (fig. 5.11).[115]

In his other significant experiment of the early 1980s, low-cost furniture for the NID's residential purposes, Upadhyaya used mango and pine wood, which were rarely used for designing elegant furniture because of their low strength and natural instability. Upadhyaya used these woods

FIGURE 5.11. Low-cost furniture designed by Gajanan Upadhyaya. © Gajanan Upadhyaya and HCP Design, Planning and Management.

for cost-effectiveness; he designed standardized short lengths to accommodate their low strength and instability and used connectors to provide more resilient joints. This furniture was also a semi-knock-downable type, capable of being reassembled several times without losing strength in its members and joints. When Upadhyaya did not use the knock-down principle, his drawings used an exploded axonometric method. The buoyant elements demonstrated coherent agreement with other elements in the system, yet they retained their individualism within a structure, which was reminiscent of De Stijl, Bauhaus, and the system design that was passed down to the NID in many forms.

The "Postponable Luxury"

In November 1969 Charles Eames was again appointed as a Ford Foundation consultant, albeit for a brief period of time, to visit the NID and report on the progress of the institution. The appointment coincided with the NID's application for a new grant proposal to the Ford Foundation and the imminent departure of Douglas Ensminger from the foundation.[116] Although the Eameses' office had maintained a continuing relationship with the NID, including a commission in 1964 to put up the famous traveling exhibition on Nehru's life, Charles Eames's reappointment as a consultant ten years after the production of the "India Report," indicated that the NID's development was probably not completely aligned with the Ford Foundation's expectations. During the decade between the "India Report" and Charles Eames's visit to reassess it, the NID had grown in multiple directions, with faculty having developed varied interests in different educational philosophies and design ideologies. But even with these changes, the Ford Foundation and the Eames Office's approach remained the moral backbone of the institute. An unsigned letter from the NID to Harry E. Wilhelm, Ensminger's successor, stated that "the institute and our feelings about it have been much in our thoughts—we look on it rather as our grandchild, with Douglas Ensminger as godfather. . . . More than ever, it would seem terribly important that the Ford Foundation share the responsibility with the Indian Government for this national institution—(1) to guard its autonomy and guide its direction, (2) to make it function at the highest possible level for the good of the country . . . , (3) all that we hoped for when the first report was put together."[117] The authority of the Ford Foundation and Charles Eames was not without challenge. As art historian Saloni Mathur describes, when during the late 1960s a widespread disillusionment and dissatisfaction grew toward the official modernization effort by the Nehru government, it also brought into question the design trends at the NID, which contemporaries saw as dangerous and exclusive.[118] At the NID substantial effort had been given to rationalizing or modernizing vernacular practices without realistically considering their actual applicability or users' perceptions of them—this tendency reminds us of the romanticized design for the rural poor in pre-independence time. It is not difficult to find similar approaches, such as the colonial attitude of rationalizing indigenous design with scientific measures, or various projects undertaken by home economics colleges in the early 1960s and 1970s that tried to find out how one could improve the efficiency of sweeping in the home by altering a woman's body posture as she swept or the scientific improvement of a traditional domestic stove run by wood or coal (fig. 5.12).[119] All of these examples showed that designers were genuinely interested in improving the lives of the poor and marginalized by means of design, but none of these efforts had any real impact on reality. J. S. Sandhu, a research associate at the Industrial Design (Engineering) Research Unit at the Royal College of Art, London, sent Charles Eames a long unpublished self-written essay titled "Design Education in India."[120]

The essay was a result of a discussion between Sandhu on his return from a visit to the NID and Leonard Bruce Archer, the famous British mechanical engineer and professor of design research at the Royal College of Art. The report accused the NID of being too elitist and emulating foreign models such as Bauhaus, HfG Ulm, and Eames without paying adequate attention to the real socioeconomic situation of the economically and socially marginal population. Concurrently, at home in the United States in the midst of the civil rights movement, the Eameses were under attack, accused of being passive and apolitical and acting only on behalf of corporate profit. Under these circumstances, Charles Eames did not have a specific answer as to the future of the NID, and his last report to the Ford Foundation on the NID's progress suggested several fundamental changes. On the basis of his report, the foundation decided to remove its financial support to the NID, providing mostly moral support.[121]

The establishment of the NID reflected the policy in the immediate postcolonial decade of accelerating development through supporting India's technical capacity—design being one aspect of it. The evolving design trends accompanying this technical optimism aligned the discourse critically with market forces that considered design a tool for raising consumer demand.[122] As Mathur argues, at a time when a designer's role transitioned from being a Cold War savior of humanity to being a creative instrument for facilitating market competition, the relevance of the early import of Western ideas regarding the empowerment of the vernacular design effort needed to be revisited.[123] Indian contemporary design discourse, which adopted the approach of the Hochschule für Gestaltung Ulm and many other Western institutions in a myriad of ways, was now considering a new use of design for strengthening the presence of Indian products in the global market in tandem with recontextualization of the "barefoot designers"—designers who work for the best interest of the disenfranchised population in the contemporary scene.[124]

Regardless of the NID's affection for avant-garde sensibilities, this organization brought the nonaffluent consumers from the realm of uncharted vernacular population into the thinking sphere of urban designers. In this context, scarcity often appeared as a virtue rather than an impediment.[125] Ulm had been struggling in the context of the economic miracle of Marshall Plan Europe to limit vicissitudes and to realign consumer demand and searched for a model to sustain relationships between perverse consumerism and efforts to moralize industrial production.[126] The HfG eventually blamed the countries that were outside strict market capitalism but did not fully explore the possibility of that exteriority. In one instance Maldonado accused Soviet designers of complacency in response to claims made by Yuri Soloviev at an Aspen design conference in 1961. The Soviets were not critical enough to explore the privileges they had been enjoying as members of a noncompetitive market structure.[127]

The NID discourse was predicated on the effort to empower the nonaffluent Indian market. Through a mixed economic policy and centralized planning strategy, India had strict control on its market to protect it from global competition to encourage local imports and to discourage competition from external imports. This relatively uncompetitive market was not initially favorable for the design profession. The advocacy of designers for qualitative excellence seemed paradoxical when their designated operation in a mixed-market economy was informed by deliberately limited consumer choice. Not surprisingly, the first generation of NID graduates during the 1970s were generally considered by the business community as a "postponable luxury."[128] Although following two very different trajectories, Ulm and the NID confronted similar situations of resolving the tension between competitive and noncompetitive markets, and were often misinterpreted or misrepresented by the market as avoidable appendages.

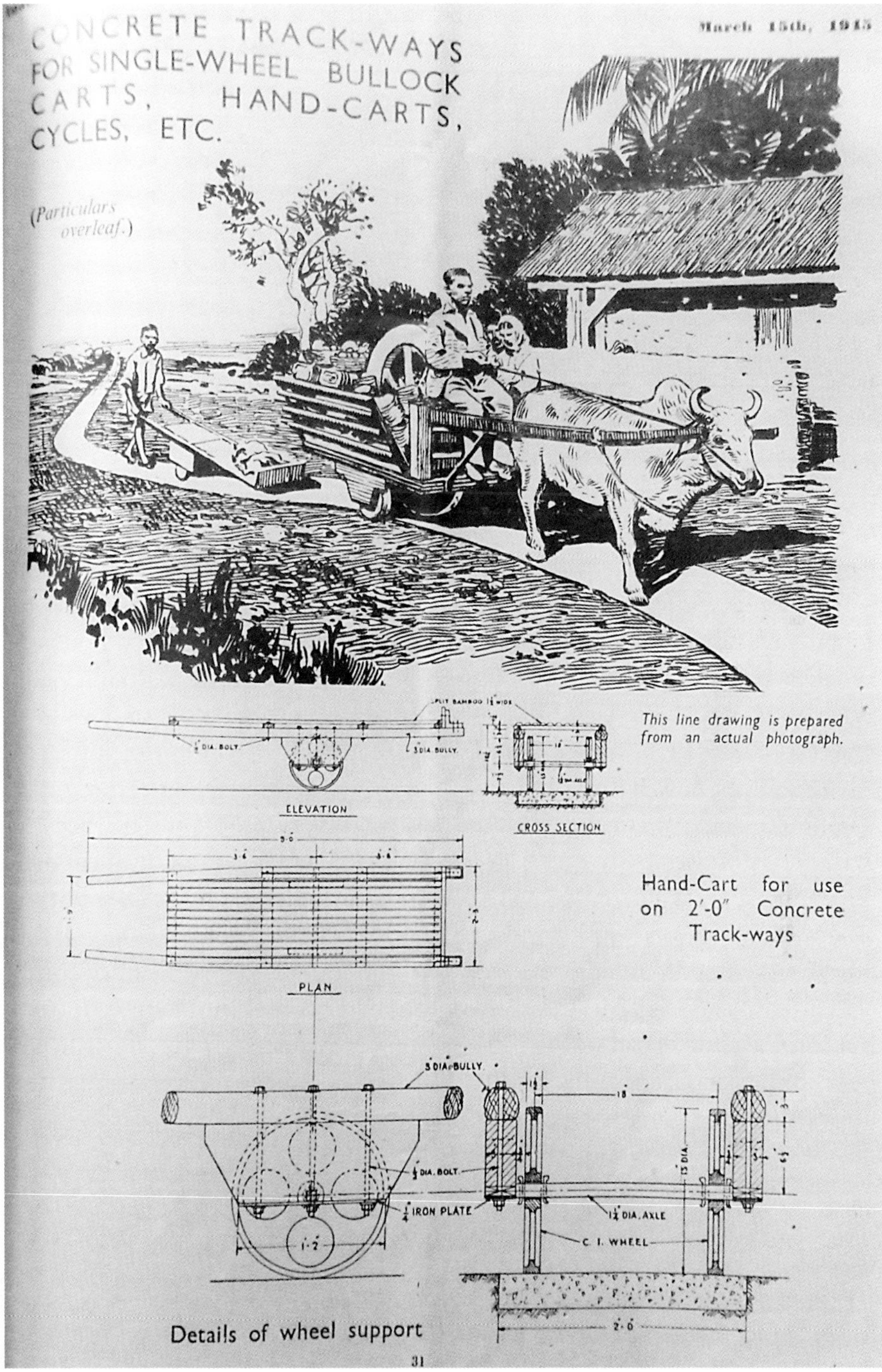

FIGURE 5.12. An oxcart with one reinforced cement concrete wheel, designed for narrow rural roads. Source: Indian Concrete Journal, March 15, 1945. © Associated Cement Companies.

CONCLUSION

In the 1972 documentary film *Housing for the People* produced by the Films Division of India, a man narrates with a dramatic zest while the camera pans over the busy everyday activities of a government-owned housing research institute: "The Central Building Research institute at Roorkee has been continuously engaged in evolving cheaper building techniques and materials, training engineers and architects in new concept of low-cost housing. Low cost houses must of course be quick to build. They must combine austerity of design with the basic needs of comfort and privacy.... A nation is known by the way its people live, a people living in a neat and clean house are a clean neat people."[1] The use of the word *austerity* in this cinematic narration might appear to be a passing fad or at best a pompous adjective. The odd analogy between clean people and a well-functioning state might also sound like nothing more than another Indian melodrama. But these characterizations are inaccurate. In this book I have argued that beneath its casual tone, the word *austerity* carries a deeper meaning. The apparent melodramatic and relaxed usage of the concept of scarcity and austerity has been entangled in realpolitik at a global scale.

In the late 2010s, austerity discourse is once again in vogue—resulting in multiple trajectories of community development, socially engaged architecture, and participatory urban development projects. I have suggested that the fundamental premises of these recent developments remain remarkably consistent with aspirations from the early twentieth century. Development in postcolonial India promised to create an architecture of emancipation that would provide the poor with a dignified dwelling. By virtue of home ownership, they would also gain political agency and economic freedom. The conviction in the power of the community to resist structural injustice and state-driven corruption and thus empower individual authority is still a much-cherished concept. The anticorruption movement of Anna Hazare (Shri Baburao Hazare, b. 1937) against the Indian government is an interesting example of the recent incarnation of modernism of austerity. Hazare, a social worker who prefers to stay outside the mainstream political world, argues that his apolitical stance would facilitate development work for the rural society. The Ralegan Siddhi, Hazare's ideal village project, started in 1975. It has many overlapping traits with Gandhi's utopian model in that it considers moral imperatives as the central locus of development, and also with the Mayer-Nehruvian anti-utopian model, as it emphasizes developing democratic institutions rather than indulging solely in Gandhian metaphysical metaphors.[2] Through his ideal village, Hazare repeats the mantra of being austere, local, community oriented, and even exclusive in order to foster empowered individuals. For him, cultivating empathetic community space and home ownership is central to a fair and just India. Hazare also added a spin to the myth of the self-sufficient and austere community by suggesting that villagers should assume full control over the ecological system of their village. Referring to villagers as "ecosystem people," he argues that claiming authority over ecology would bring substantial political agency to Indian villages that at present have no political authority whatsoever. Assuming the poor are capable of making political decisions because they have full command of their ecological system is one way to reform, the austerity discourse and open up new avenues for the development discourse in the age of environmental crisis.

Influenced by the booklet *Call to the Youth for Nation Building* by Swami Vivekenanda, Hazare, a retired army officer, devoted his personal wealth and time to transform the village of Ralegan Siddhi. He intended to demonstrate that rural development could be done internally—without any foreign and state assistance or assistance from private and microbanking—solely through natural resource management. Hazare's effort was mediated by claiming greater authority and supporting ingenious management of natural resources in the village. His two well-known projects involved catching rainwater for harvest and resisting land erosion to boost agriculture. This simple resource management brought a rise in income that was later used to develop institutional buildings or establish a visible presence of development. His ideal village renewed debate over the relevance of the utopian village as a powerful instigator of the political movement.

The Indian press vigorously supported Hazare's Ralegan Siddhi project as the most effective post-Nehruvian development model adopted in India. In 2011 The Maharashtra State Government started the Adarsh Gaon Yojana (Ideal Village Program) under Hazare's leadership; it initially applied his model to four hundred villages.[3] The basic idea was to assimilate and manage the ecosystem—to change human status without leaving any negative impact on the existing ecology—which was mediated by the local and decentralized governance of Gram Panchayat.[4] Panchayat would lead the village and its "ecosystem people" to acquire more access to their local natural resources, which would reduce the risk of omnivores, with their capitalist aspirations, transforming those resources into man-made capital.[5] Hazare's ideal village tried to repair and improve Gandhi's model by recasting it from utopia to a real political and economic system. Gandhi's rural development withdrew from the conventional capitalist world. As a result, in postcolonial development mission, Gandhi's approach was only adopted as a conceptual tokenism; it did not cause a deep physical change. The resurrection of Gandhian ideal village in Anna Hazare's politics operated as an internal critique of that system, which, through continuous scrutiny, dissent, and feedback, was thought to repair and enhance the existing system. Unlike Gandhi's ideal village, in principle the Adarsh Gaon Yojana could function within the existing political and bureaucratic system. However, as soon as Hazare started to work on the Adarsh Gaon Yojana project, he realized how that system was impaired by corruption in public administration: uncommitted agencies hindered operation and growth of the system through internal contradictions.[6]

Hazare followed Gandhi's prevalence for nonviolence and civil disobedience through a series of fasting episodes to compel the government to solve its internal corruption problem. Fasting as civil disobedience started in November 28, 1989, and culminated in 2011 when Hazare demanded radical administrative reformation in order to end corruption. The outcome of this nonviolent demonstration and Hazareh's reference to Gandhian politics that often relies on exclusive Hindu nationalism, partisan identity, and religion has been explained differently by different stakeholders. I have no intention to study the success or failure of Hazare's project, but it is important to point out that the discourse of austerity is not closed yet. From Hazare's example what is clear to us is that village and rural development received a new ideological status as the primary instigator of the "postpolitical" movement.[7] In Hazare's rhetoric of social activism, rural development is an extrapolitical issue and thus Hazare himself was reluctant to be part of any political party. Hazare's village claims its location in a new liberal development process but without refereeing to political process. In this sense, the village is Kantian as its existence and success would rely solely on the empathy and collective actions of commoners—indifferent to their origin, locality, and religion—for a new liberal democratic development. The driving force of Hazare's ideal village was a desire to overcome poverty, which is apolitical and purely social. By engaging with the idea of the village, its space of ecology, and its people, Gandhi succeeded in questioning the existing colonial system but failed to instill lasting change. Hazare wanted to give Gandhi's idea an applicable form and thus opened up new potential to assimilate the village within the political and economic system.

Anna Hazare's ideal village project is but one example of how one can utilize the landscape and built environment in a changing political and economic environment. Professional architects have also embraced this new social consciousness of benevolence. The place-bounded nature of architecture stimulates the drive of architects and designers to bring about social change. Architecture could instigate tacit social revolution by engaging the local population to create a stronger community. Put simply, this logic represents deductive syllogism in the following ways: 1) architecture and product design are primarily concerned with the production of space and material culture, 2) a strong and empathetic community, constructed around place and within the framework of a specific material culture, could overcome social and economic injustice; and henceforth 3) architecture and product design inherently and naturally produce social and political justice. This syllogism capitalized on architecture's essential attachment to place and environment. The discourse of low-cost housing, community development and associated development agendas goes very well with this location-centrism. *Of Greater Dignity than Riches* argues that this location-based discourse of development helps to harness austerity as one of its main theoretical premises, as we have seen in the idealized vision of industrial workers' housing in chapter 1 and in the rural development projects in chapter 4.

It is essential to understand the austerity discourse as part of a broader cultural politics driven by many local and global actors ranging from the United Nations to anonymous village-level workers in distant rural areas. India's resource scarcity and associated cultural plea to form a discourse of austere material culture is not exclusively a local phenomenon. Global stakeholders have been significant contributors to the cause of scarcity and have also performed as agents of austerity. There is no way to sever global and local actors that are entangled in a larger structure of cultural politics. In recent decades, historical and social studies have called for the imagination of an increasingly global world in terms of networks and linkages. Such inquiries have problematized the normative worldview of a center and periphery and have rearticulated the relationships between architectural space and social space, or between fragments and the whole. The preoccupation of a rigid dichotomy between center and periphery impedes the study of the transnational development of Third World design discourse. This ideological preoccupation downplays the role of linkage and entanglement in theories of global systems and thus obfuscates the interrelation of agency and network.[8] When it comes to the history of design, a new perspective of the world as an entangled matrix of ideas would reform how we view the disconnection, segmentation, and segregation of a global spatial hierarchy.[9] It would allow us to interpret the production of architecture in terms of distance, both spatial and ideological, as well as about relatedness, an effort to contract the distance by engaging social capital. *Of Greater Dignity than Riches* suggests perceiving the world in terms of different scales, local and global, around which flows of ideas are taking place. This model is helpful to understand the world in which resources are unequally distributed at different scales.[10]

Through a discussion of the formation of austerity discourse, I have attempted to paint a bigger picture: that modernism, the institutionalized system of Eurocentric ideologies, was never exclusively exported outside the West; rather, the adaptation of modernist norms was primarily a result of importing efforts of the "other." That is, transposition and transmutation mainly occurs during the movement of various contesting ideas and conflicting agencies that constitute a global network of ideas.[11] I have also argued that the "other," or Third World modernism, was created in this process of importing; it was not the imported content but the process itself that delimited the formation of the modernism of austerity.

This book claims that we could better understand the process of modernization in terms of conflicts and negotiations among various local and global stakeholders. Overarching structures, including the government of India and the United Nations, which operate with other stakeholders, such as the Ford Foundation, in a conflictual and negotiating way, conceived austerity as a system of interactive institutions in which values were developed through random combinations of piecemeal ideas. However, one thing that was never lost in the process is the invocation that the Third World should get closer to an ideal value complex by developing similar institutions that could harness similar value systems. For example, as described in chapter 4, the Ford Foundation was convinced that villages of Uttar Pradesh could be drawn closer to the First World if the Indian village community could be strengthened by the theory of community as developed by Clarence Stein. However, it is true that Mayer, experts at the foundation, and Nehru never explicitly mentioned the concept's American roots because every agent believed they were implementing their own ideas and thus acted freely. This contradiction suggests that they were neither solely governed by existing structures nor acted with absolute autonomy. The examples in this book demonstrate that actors were no longer the primary unit for historical analysis. Instead, they should be studied as part of an integrated system, meaning action and structure should be perceived as complementary phenomena. Society and history could not be explained as complete or autonomous and isolated entities, as the perennial existence of exogenous factors always impairs society's purity and singularity. Societies are interconnected to alien societies through trade, conflict, and communication. Therefore, society should not be analyzed in terms of equilibrium or as being a stabilized form of many subsystems. It should be conceived of as an assemblage of microstructures or the bearer of power in conflicts. *Of Greater Dignity than Riches* indicates the need for addressing the increasingly transnational integration of society and analyzes social actions mainly as a result of conflicting microstructures.

Institutionalization usually refers to an effort that legalizes a set of values and is conceived of as an unchallenged construct. This idea is convenient when making simple claims, such as that the United States imposed its cultural values over India by exhibiting its industrial goods, as discussed in chapter 5. However, while free will, autonomy, and the capacity of the agents involved—such as the National Small Scale Industries of India, Pupul Jayakar, and Charles Eames—was gradually becoming visible in our analysis, it was no longer possible to think of the process of institutionalization, such as the UN in relationship to the metastructure of global cold war, as an unchallenged phenomenon. Many instances, as in the case of UN experts who suggested institutionalization, were challenged and contested by local participants. Ultimately, the drive for institutionalization was not at the core of modernization. This understanding of history as an agent-structure complex asks to review the apparent ease and equilibrium that was expected in the study of modernization mainly as a process of institutionalizing social values, such as housing for industrial workers as a result of city improvement trusts. As long as values were considered amenable to subjective interpretation, different collective agencies were also looked upon as conflicting and could therefore institutionalize different values. From this perspective, institutionalization reflects conflict instead of equilibrium. There was no guarantee that the institutionalization of values and society, when rooted in conflict, would be the same in every context.

This book analyzes the formation of a modernism of austerity in India by showing that various private and public agencies created an entanglement of internal and transnational connections on the basis of social capital. The primary objective of the agencies involved in the making of this discourse of austerity was to acquire benefits or profits for their representative social groups and thus to form and reform social capital by creating connections within that entanglement, and subsequently to extend and condense existing networks. Architecture or any other design endeavor is thus the manifestation of that social intention that architecture is produced to forge and mediate specific social connections to accumulate social capital. I suggest that the production of austerity discourse was a profit-making endeavor of contesting agencies in a social network. Here, profit does not mean monetary surpluses generated from trades but the production of nonmaterial ideological situations that help to advance the interest of a social group within the network.

From the perspective of nonmaterial profit, this book suggests that a major objective of modernism of austerity was to create greater control over the poor community's locus and fate so that there could be greater productive autonomy within networks. I have explored the effects of nonmaterial profit on the construction of austerity through colonial efforts to supply healthy homes, rural housing reformation, working-class housing bylaws, and the first design school in India. In the case of Indian village reformation projects, as discussed in chapter 5, while major financial aid came through the Indian government, bureaucrats and administrators sought psychological assistance from the United States to boost Indian motivation. They achieved their goal by nourishing and maintaining long-term, long-distance networks between American architects, farm experts, diplomats, designers, administrators and local funding bodies. At the local level, interest in creating a transnational network stemmed from wanting to enable modernization in the villages. The main objective was to create an autonomous social class through accumulating social capital, which would lead to more control of local economic activity and income, and to integrate social networks, which would empower the locality.[12]

The other kind of profit that social capital yields is the further consolidation and enrichment of existing networks. The capacity of social capital to yield more connections in networks adds to individual or collective resources. It consequently creates more networks to generate more resources and to disseminate ideological values associated with this capital, such as modernity. In chapter 5 I explain the formation of the National Institute of Design at Ahmedabad as an outcome of social capital that gradually widened interrelations between the Ford Foundation, the Indian government, and various local and American designers and trade people. The interest of the National Small Scale Industries Committee in developing its domestic consumer industry developed the preliminary network with

MoMA and the Ford Foundation that eventually created the National Institute of Design. Depending on this initial social capital, once the NID was established, it autonomously continued to yield new networks such as its alliance with the HfG at Ulm.

For a special interest group to prefer the modernism of austerity—a profit-making endeavor and its preferred tool to achieve development—means a specific networking possibility. The network empowers collective agencies to mobilize their value complex, which in turn forms social capital through the advancement of organizational projects, by fostering a like-minded professional and occupational cohort.[13] By turning our attention to these varied occupational positions throughout a dispersed network, we can begin to understand the formation of austerity discourse as multidimensional links across various stakeholders. The 1953 UN exhibitions discussed in chapters 4 and 5 reveal how an international exhibition and conference was used to broaden a network between professionals of the First World and the Third World, and also among professionals of the Third World itself. Such a networking effort was envisioned not only to question a fixed material expression of modernism but also to establish an amorphous and free-flowing concept that emerges and exists within that network.

By considering the conflict embedded in the formation and deployment of modernism of austerity, this book suggests that modernization as a project for development and progress along the lines of the secular and scientific method may not be considered coherent or even deterministic. The process of modernization through the institutionalization of an idea such as austerity consists of many opposing views of different interest groups and stakeholders and ultimately raises the following questions: What contesting notions of development are imbedded in the forces of modernization, and how are they conceived in multiple ways by various government organizations, grant agencies, designers, and consumers? Which collective agencies in India pursued the modernization of design and architecture? Engineers? Architects? Bureaucrats or diplomats? Can professional bodies and policymakers, politicians and international observers be conceived as homogenously structured groups, or were they internally fragmented with many conflicting groups feuding over issues of social change and the modernization of society and architecture? Although we often tend to summarize these variations to create a coherent narrative, what if there is no coherent narrative at all?

I have considered how different stakeholders imagined an ideal lifestyle for the poor, how the modernism of austerity might fulfill its prophecy, and how local and global elite intellectuals, administrators, and professionals imagined the poor would eventually gain political agency and learn to help themselves and fight their way out of spatial injustice. But this book does not speak for the poor because the discourse of austerity was about them, not with them. The gigantic imaginations discussed in this book spawned exclusively from a body of intellects that have little if any connection to the actual people affected—the poor in postcolonial India whose desire for breaking away poverty were usurped by elites who stripped them of agency in an idealized quest to emancipate them.

NOTES

Introduction

1. D. N. Anand, *Simple Furniture and Interior Decoration* (New Delhi: Directorate of Extension and Training, Ministry of Food and Agriculture, 1959), n.p.

2. For a review of the ethical perspective of poverty in different societies see William A. Galston and Peter H. Hoffenberg, eds., *Poverty and Morality: Religious and Secular Perspectives* (New York: Cambridge University Press, 2010). However, the moral dimension of poverty discourse in modern India is discussed in various places but a complete book on this matter is yet to write. For a social debate of poverty and poor in modern India see Oliver Mendelsohn and Marika Vicziany, *The Untouchables: Subordination, Poverty and the State in Modern India* (Cambridge: Cambridge University Press, 1998).

3. Kenneth Frampton, *Le Corbusier* (New York: Thames and Hudson, 2001), 187.

4. Rebecca Bramall, *The Cultural Politics of Austerity: Past and Present in Austere Times* (New York: Palgrave Macmillan, 2013).

5. Paul Betts, *The Authority of Everyday Objects: A Cultural History of West German Industrial Design* (Berkeley: University of California Press, 2004).

6. Eric Rauchway, *The Money Makers: How Roosevelt and Keynes Ended the Depression, Defeated Fascism, and Secured a Prosperous Peace* (New York: Basic Books, 2015).

7. Duanfang Lu, *Remaking Chinese Urban Form: Modernity, Scarcity and Space, 1949–2005* (London: Taylor and Francis, 2006).

8. Lu, *Remaking Chinese Urban Form.*

9. Partha Chatterjee, *The Nation and Its Fragments: Colonial and Postcolonial Histories* (Princeton: Princeton University Press, 1993).

10. Antoinette Burton, "House/Daughter/Nation: Interiority, Architecture, and Historical Imagination in Janaki Majumdar's 'Family History,'" *Journal of Asian Studies* 56, no. 4 (1997): 921–46.

11. Alison Blunt, "Imperial Geographies of Home: British Domesticity in India, 1886–1925," *Transactions of the Institute of British Geographers* 24, no. 4 (December 1999): 421–40.

12. Mary Hancock, "Home Science and the Nationalization of Domesticity in Colonial India," *Modern Asian Studies* 35, no. 4 (2001): 874.

13. Chatterjee, *Nation and Its Fragments*, 6.

14. Subir Sinha argues that Chatterjee's dichotomy of community/home and state/outside is misleading, as it implies that these two concepts are mutually exclusive. This dichotomy, as Sinha argues, inhibits the inclusion of community or an inner domain of Indian society in the broader politics of state-initiated modernization. See Subir Sinha, "Lineages of the Developmentalist State: Transnationality and Village India," *Comparative Studies in Society and History* 50, no. 1 (2008): 59.

15. P. P. Kapadia et al., "The Ideal Home Exhibition," *Journal of the Indian Institute of Architects* 7, no. 3 (1938): 319–27.

16. Kapadia et al., "Ideal Home Exhibition," 320; Frantz Fanon, *Black Skin, White Masks*, trans. R. Philcox (New York: Grove Press, 1952), 64–88; Arthur Herman, *Gandhi and Churchill: The Epic Rivalry That Destroyed an Empire and Forged Our Age* (London: Hutchinson, 2008), 402–26.

17. Kapadia et al., "Ideal Home Exhibition," 319.

18. Introductory speech by P. P. Kapadia, president of the Indian Institute of Architects, in "Ideal Home Exhibition," 320.

19. Kapadia et al., "Ideal Home Exhibition," 321.

20. P. P. Kapadia, "Presidential Address," *Journal of the Indian Institute of Architects* 5, no. 1 (1938): 5.

21. *Art in Industry*, a Calcutta-based design magazine popularized the design discourse of the "minimum" (minimal); they claimed to prove "ingenuity can make of a minimum of the most unpromising material" to those who complain that shortage of material is an impediment. In newly independent India, a paucity of resources led the designer to seek an alternative way to achieve the modern look since modernity was still measured against the extent of technical progress and affluence in resource. See Michael Inchbald, "Furnishing Ferozepur," *Art in Industry Magazine* 1, no. 1 (1947): 69–73.

22. Editorial, *Journal of the Indian Institute of Architects* 5, no. 3 (1938): 6.

23. Kapadia, "Presidential Address," 5.

24. Sharada Dwivedi, Rahul Mehrotra, and Umaima Mulla-Feroze, *Bombay: The Cities Within* (Bombay: India Book House, 1995), 69.

25. Kapadia et al., "Ideal Home Exhibition," 319.

26. Editorial, "The Question of Tradition," *Journal of the Indian Institute of Architects* 7, no. 3 (1941): 77–78.

27. Victoria Rosner, *Modernism and the Architecture of Private Life* (New York: Columbia University Press, 2005), 121.

28. Edgar Kaufmann Jr., *What Is Modern Interior Design?* (New York: Museum of Modern Art, 1953), 5.

29. H. J. Billimoria, "Interior Decoration," *Journal of the Indian Institute of Architects*, October 1941: 184–87.

30. Duanfang Lu, ed., *Third World Modernism* (New York: Routledge, 2007).

31. Nancy Kwak, *A World of Homeowners: American Power and the Politics of Housing Aid* (Chicago: University of Chicago Press, 2015).

32. David C. Engerman et al., eds., *Staging Growth: Modernization, Development, and the Global Cold War* (Amherst: University of Massachusetts Press, 2003).

33. See Daniel Lerner, *The Passing of Traditional Society: Modernizing the Middle East* (Glencoe: Free Press, 1958).

34. I borrowed the term *performativity* from Judith Butler's *gender performativity*. See Judith Butler, *Gender Trouble: Feminism and the Subversion of Identity* (New York: Routledge, 1990).

35. For a discussion on the methodological challenge of working on postcolonial South Asian architectural history, see Markus Daechsel, *Islamabad and the Politics of International Development in Pakistan* (New York: Cambridge University Press, 2015), 10.

1. Imagining an Ideal Prototype House for Industrial Workers, 1918–1954

1. Amended Notice Housing of the Working Classes in Bombay, 1918, box 601, folder part 2, Bombay Government Gazette, 469–70, Maharashtra State Archives (hereafter MSA), Mumbai.

2. For a discussion of the formation and evolution of the open plan bungalow as the ideal prototypical house in tropical climate, see Jiat-Hwee Chang, *A Genealogy of Tropical Architecture, Colonial Networks, Nature and Technoscience* (New York: Routledge, 2016). For a discussion of the obsessive fantasy of the colonial entrepreneurs to create a fully automated industrial system, see Tim Barringer, *Men at Work: Art and Labor in Victorian Britain* (New Haven: Yale University Press, 2005).

3. A. E. Mirams, *Plans and Specifications of Houses Suitable for Occupation by the Working Class* (Bombay: Government Central Press, 1919), 8.

4. Rajnarayan Chandavarkar, *The Origins of Industrial Capitalism in India: Business Strategies and the Working Classes in Bombay, 1900–1940* (New York: Cambridge University Press, 2002).

5. Frank F. Conlon, "Industrialization and the Housing Problem in Bombay, 1850–1940," in *Changing South Asia: Economy and Society*, ed. K. Ballhatchet and D. Taylor (Hong Kong: Asian Research Service, 1984).

6. Annual Report of the Municipal Commissioner of Bombay, 1875, 127.

7. Report of the Municipal Commissioner on the Plague in Bombay, 1899, 17–19, 43.

8. B. F. Patel, *History of the Plague in Bombay* (Charleston: Nabu Press, 2010), 22.

9. For a discussion of exploiting contagious disease as a tool for colonial government and urban gentrification, see Gyan Prakash, *Another Reason: Science and the Imagination of Modern India* (Princeton: Princeton University Press, 1999), 123–58.

10. Sandip Hazareesingh, "Colonial Modernism and the Flawed Paradigms of Urban Renewal: Uneven Development in Bombay, 1900–25," *Urban History* 28, no. 2 (2001): 235–55.

11. For a detailed discussion on this matter, see Nikhil Rao, *House, but No Garden: Apartment Living in Bombay's Suburbs, 1898–1964* (Minneapolis: University of Minnesota Press, 2013).

12. Myron Echenberg, *Plague Ports: The Global Urban Impact of Bubonic Plague: 1894–1901* (New York: New York University Press, 2007); Bombay Municipality, Report of the Municipal Commissioners on the Plague in Bombay: With Charts and Diagrams (Bombay: Municipal Commissioner's Office, 1899); P. C. H. Snow, *Report on the Outbreak of Bubonic Plague in Bombay, 1896–97* (Bombay: Printed at the *Times of India* Press, 1897).

13. David Arnold, "Plague: Assault on the Body," in David Arnold, *Colonizing the Body: State Medicine and Epidemic Disease in Nineteenth-Century India* (Berkeley: University of California Press, 1993), 200–239; Prashant Kidambi, "'An Infection of Locality': Plague, Pythogenesis and the Poor in Bombay, c .1896–1905," *Urban History* 31, no. 2 (2004): 249–67; Ira Klein, "Urban Development and Death: Bombay City, 1870–1914," in *Modern Asian Studies* 20, no. 4 (1986): 725–54.

14. James Peter Orr, *Social Reform and Slum Reform* (Bombay: Times Press, 1917), 48. Also see L. W. Michael, *The History of the Municipal Corporation of the City of Bombay* (Bombay: Union Press, 1902).

15. Between 1898 and 1918, two decades after the establishment of the Bombay Improvement Trust, property and house rent were increased by 100–200 percent: *Times of India*, April 18, 1919.

16. Raghunath S. Deshpande, *Modern Ideal Homes for India* (Poona: United Books, 1939), 2.

17. Snow, *Report on the Outbreak of Bubonic Plague*,18–19.

18. James P. Orr, "Social Reform and Slum Reform," printed lectures delivered to the Social Service League, Bombay, September–October 1917. For a brief account of the early history of chawls, see Norma Evenson, *The Indian Metropolis: A View toward the West* (New Haven: Yale University Press, 1989).

19. Arnold, "Plague," 106.

20. James P. Orr, "Light and Air in Dwellings in Bombay," a lecture delivered before the Bombay Sanitary Association, June 27, 1912; James P. Orr, "Density of Population in Bombay," a lecture delivered before the All India Sanitary Conference in Lucknow, Bombay, September 1914; James P. Orr, "How to Check the Growth of Unsanitary Conditions in Bombay," a lecture delivered before the All India Sanitary Conference in Lucknow, Bombay, January 1914.

21. Prashant Kidambi, *The Making of an Indian Metropolis* (Aldershot: Ashgate, 2007), 78.

22. For a contemporary account of Bombay working class housing see: Alexander R. Burnett-Hurst, *Labour and Housing in Bombay: A Study in the Economic Conditions of the Wage-Earning Classes in Bombay* (London: P. S. King, 1925).

23. Government of Bombay, Report of the Special Advisory Committee on the Industrial Housing Scheme (Bombay: Government Central Press, 1927), 10.

24. Rao, *House, but No Garden*, 48.

25. Neera Adarkar, "Salaries and Wages: Girgaon and Girangaon," in *The Chawls of Mumbai: Galleries of Life*, ed. Neera Adarkar (New Delhi: ImprintOne, 2011), 15–25.

26. A. E. Mirams to Government of Bombay (Government Order, General Department File, order no. 3326, Bombay Castle), May 10, 1918, box 262, folder 601, Archives of India, New Delhi.

27. A. E. Mirams to Governtmnet of Bombay, box 262, folder 601; A. E. Mirams to P. R. Cadell, 1918, Poona, General Department, no. 601, Archives of India, New Delhi.

28. A. E. Mirams, *Valuation of Real Property in India with Valuation Tables* (Bombay: Maharashtra State Government Print and Stationery, 1964); A. E. Mirams, Colaba Development, Eastern Section: Preliminary Report, 1919; A. E. Mirams, *Report on the Development of Karachi* (Bombay: Government Central Press, 1923); A. E. Mirams, *An Address to Members of Municipality and Citizens of Poona on the Bombay Town Planning Act of 1915* (Poona: Yeravada Prison Press, 1916); Arthur E. Mirams, *Town Planning in Western Countries and What the Bombay Town Planning Act Means to Karachi: Being a Report of Two Lectures Delivered in Karachi* (Karachi, 1916).

29. Arthur E. Mirams, *Report of the Indian Industrial Commission, 1916–1918* (Calcutta: Superintendent Government Printing, 1918).

30. Oral Evidence by A. E. Mirams, november 23, 1917, in Mirams, *Report of the Indian Industrial Commission*, 369.

31. Oral Evidence by Mirams, 180.

32. "Bombay Working Classes, Exhibition of Housing Design," *Times of India*, June 24, 1918; "Housing Competition Designs, Exhibition Opened in Bombay," *Bombay Chronicle*, June 22, 1918.

33. Amended Notice Housing of the Working Classes in Bombay, 1918, box 601, folder part II: The Bombay Government Gazette, MSA.

34. James Maden and Albert de Bois Shrosbree, *Calcutta Improvement Trust: City and Suburban Main Road Projects* (Calcutta: Calcutta Improvement Trust, 1913).

35. IIC, Evidence, A. E. Mirams, Consulting Surveyor to the GOI, IV, 354, quoted in Chandavarkar, *Origins of Industrial Capitalism*, 178.

36. Caroline E. Arnold, "The Bombay Improvement Trust, Bombay Millowners and the Debate over Housing Bombay's Millworkers, 1896–1918," *Essays in Economic and Business History* 30 (2012): 105–23.

37. Ian Kerr, "On the Move: Circulating Labor in Pre-Colonial, Colonial, and Post-Colonial India," *International Review of Social History* 51 (2006): 85–109.

38. Thomas S. Weir, Census of the City and Island of Bombay taken on the 17th of February (Bombay: *Times of India* Steam Press, 1881), 35.

39. Census of India, 1901, Volume 11: Bombay Town and Island, Part 5, Report (Bombay: *Times of India* Press, 1901), 14, quoted in Sheetal M. Chhabria, "Making the Modern Slum: Housing, Mobility, and Poverty in Bombay and Its Peripheries" (PhD diss., Columbia University, 2012), 208.

40. Bombay State Government, Annual Administrative Report of the BIT (Bombay: Central Government Press, 1919), 3.

41. Bombay State Government, Annual Administrative Report, 8.

42. Government of Bombay, Report of the Special Advisory Committee on the Industrial Housing Scheme (Bombay: Government Central Press, 1927), 1–10.

43. "Municipal Hutments in Sion," *Times of India*, May 21, 1947, 12.

44. Claude Batley, "The Importance of City Planning," in *Bombay Looks Ahead: Eight Lectures*, ed. Clifford Manshardt (Bombay: D. B. Taraporevala Sons, 1934), 36.

45. "The Chawls of Bombay," *Bombay Chronicle*, May 10, 1923. For more of Mistri's comments see: Perin Jamshedji Mistri, "A Letter to the Bombay Chronicle," *Bombay Chronicle*, May 25, 1923.

46. H. Stanley Jevons, "Letter to the Times of India," *Times of India*, May 8, 1923.

47. *Indian Spectator*, January 2, 1898, 11.

48. Annual Report of the Bombay Millowners' Association, 1907, x.

49. Annual Report of the Bombay Millowners' Association, 1907, xi.

50. Speech of Fazulbhoy Currimbhoy, Annual Report of the Bombay Millowners' Association, 1910, v.

51. Written Evidence of Cowasjee Jehangir to the Bombay Development Committee, Annual Report of the Bombay Development Committee (Bombay: Government Central Press, 1914), 94. For more discussion on this topic, see Priyanka Srivastava, "Creating a Healthy and 'Decent' Industrial Force: Health, Sanitation, and Welfare in Colonial Bombay, 1896–1945" (PhD diss., University of Cincinnati, 2012).

52. Annual Report of the Bombay Development Committee, 1914, xi, 76, 94, 130, 257.

53. Statement of C. N. Wadia in Minutes of Evidence, Vol IV, IIC, 1918, 13; written Statement of J. B. Petit, in Annual Report of the Bombay Development Committee, 1914, 130.

54. Proceedings of the Bombay Legislative Council, 1898, 17.

55. Annual Report of the Bombay Development Committee, 1914, 295.

56. Proceedings of the Second All India Sanitary Conference, 1912, MSA, 21.

57. Annual Report of the Bombay Development Committee, 1914, 92–93, 286–87.

58. G. P. Dandekar, "The Revision of Bombay Municipal Building Regulations and By-Laws with a View to Bringing Them up-to-Date,"*Journal of the Indian Institute of Architects* 4, no. 2 (1939): 117–18 (paper read before the Indian Institute of Architects, 1939).

59. Minutes of Evidence Taken before the IIC 1916–1918, Vol IV, 5, quoted in Srivastava, "Creating a Healthy and 'Decent' Industrial Force," 96.

60. IIC, 1916–18 Evidence, Mr. A.E. Mirams, Consulting Surveyor to the Government of India, IV, 371.

61. Mathooradas Tricamjee, *Report of the Rent Enquiry Committee*, Vol. 1, part 1 (Bombay: Government Central Press, 1939), 35.

62. IIC, Evidence, A. E. Mirams, IV, 354.

63. Government of Bombay, Report of the Special Advisory Committee, 12, 14, 20, 22.

64. For a detailed discussion of the connection between Mann and Geddes and their role in establishing the need for a research based sociological study in Bombay, see Henrik C. Aspengren, "Sociological Knowledge and Colonial Power in Bombay around the First World War," *British Journal for the History of Science* 44, no. 4 (2011): 533–48.

65. Sandip Hazareesingh, "The Quest for Urban Citizenship: Civic Rights, Public Opinion and Colonial Resistance in Early Twentieth-Century Bombay," *Modern Asian Studies* 34 (2000): 805.

66. Patrick Geddes, *On Universities in Europe and in India: And a Needed Type of Research Institute, Geographical and Social, Five Letters to an Indian Friend* (Madras: National Press, 1903).

67. Aspengren, "Sociological Knowledge," 544, 542.

68. Noah Hysler-Rubin, *Patrick Geddes and Town Planning: A Critical View* (New York: Routledge, 2011).

69. Chhabria, "Making the Modern Slum."

70. For a detailed discussion of the cause and consequences of these strikes, see Rajni Bakshi, *The Long Haul: The Bombay Textile Workers' Strike* (Bombay: BUILD Documentation Centre, 1986), https://libcom.org/files/TheLongHaul-RajniBakshi.pdf.

71. Neera Adarkar, ed., *The Chawls of Mumbai: Galleries of Life* (Mumbai: ImprintOne, 2011).

72. Sumit Sarkar, *Modern India, 1885–1947* (London: Macmillan, 2005), 176–77.

73. Patrick Geddes, "University of Bolshevism (established in 1920) Worli Bombay," n.d. (1920?), quoted in Aspengren, "Sociological Knowledge," 543.

74. Aspengren, "Sociological Knowledge," 543.

75. Letter, *Times of India*, March 26, 1903.

76. Prashant Kidambi, "Housing the Poor in a Colonial City: The Bombay Improvement Trust, 1898–1918," *Studies in History* 17 no. 1 (2001): 57–59.

77. Kidambi, "Housing the Poor in a Colonial City," 66.

78. For a detailed discussion see Nikhil Rao, *House, but No Garden*, 21–66.

79. Hazareesingh, "Colonial Modernism," 235–55.

80. Government of Bombay, Report of the Bombay Development Committee (Bombay: The Government Central Press, 1914), xviii.

81. J. A. McDonald, "The Bombay Chawls," *Bombay Chronicle*, June 4, 1925.

82. W. C. Hughes, notes on City Improvement Schemes in England, MSA, General Department Files, Vol 40/1901; B. W. Kissan, *Report of Town Planning Enactments in Germany* (Bombay: Government Central Press, 1913).

83. For a detailed discussion see Rao, *House, but No Garden*, 67–96.

84. On the history of improvement trusts, see Robert K. Home, *Of Planting and Planning: The Making of British Colonial Cities* (New York: Routledge, 1997), 98–137; Sundra Rani Singh, *Urban Planning in India: A Case Study of Urban Improvement Trusts* (New Delhi: Ashish, 1979).

85. Stuart Tappin, "The Early Use of Reinforced Concrete in India," paper presented at the the First International Congress on Construction History, Juan de Herrera, Madrid, January 20–24, 2003.

86. P. D. Padukone, "Slum Clearance in Secunderabad," *Indian Concrete Journal* 6, no. 12 (1932): 419–22.

87. J. M. Jardine, "The Modern Coolie House," *Indian Concrete Journal* 5, no. 2 (1931): 43–45.

88. "The Engineering and Industrial Exhibition, Madras: Low Cost, Permanent Concrete House Attracts Considerable Attention," *Indian Concrete Journal* 21, no. 7 (1947): n.p.

89. Ananda G. Mukherjee and Vinod Tagra, *Jawaharlal Nehru: The Architect of Modern India: A Documentary Account of Nehru's Concept of Planning and Development* (New Delhi: Reliance, 1989).

90. Shri P. M. Sundaram, Proceedings, Summary of Nehru at the Inaugural Session, Government of India, Ministry of Labour, 11th Session of the Labour Ministers Conference, New Delhi, november 12–13, 1954, Ministry of Works, Housing, and Supply, file no. HI/1(104)/55 1958, National Archives of India, New Delhi.

91. L. Connor, *Housing Standards and Statistics: The Second Report of the Council for Research on Housing Construction* (London: P. S. King and Son, 1935).

92. "Labour Housing," *Indian Concrete Journal* 21, no. 2 (1947), n.p.

93. *Indian Concrete Journal* 21, no. 2 (1947), n.p. The absence of human subjects suggested, we may assume, that the Indian body was visually incompatible with the notion of modernism and thus Indian subjects were rarely portrayed as owners of colonial-modern space, see James H. Mills and Satadru Sen, ed., "Introduction," in *Confronting the Body: The Politics of Physicality in Colonial and Post-Colonial India*, ed. S. Sen and J. H. Mills, 1–16 (London: Anthem Press, 2004), Conference on "Representing the Body in, Colonial Post-Colonial South, Asia" held at Purdue University, Indiana, February 2001.

94. "The 7th All-India Khadi and Swadeshi Exhibition, Madras, 1939–1940," *Indian Concrete Journal* 14, no. 5 (Supplement to May 15, 1940): 12–18.

95. On the discussion of labour and Gandhi's ashram, see Deepali Dewan, "The Body at Work: Colonial Art Education and the Figure of the 'Native Craftsman,'" in *Confronting the Body: The Politics of Physicality in Colonial and Post-Colonial India*, ed. S. Sen and J. H. Mills, 118–34 (London: Anthem Press, 2004).

96. "Precast Concrete House at the Free India," *Indian Concrete Journal* 22, no. 1 (1948): 12.

97. K. K. Nambiar, "Shenoy Nagar Housing Scheme, Madras," *Indian Concrete Journal* 21, no. 10 (1947): n.p.

98. T. P. Kuttiammu, "A Prefabricated Workman's Hut in Cement Concrete," *Indian Concrete Journal* 22, no. 6 (1948): n.p.

99. Rhodri W. Liscombe, "In-Dependence: Otto Koenigsberger and Modernist Urban Resettlement in India," *Planning Perspectives* 21, no. 2 (2006): 157–78.

100. M. R. Venkataram, "Prefabricated 'Gunite': A Low-Cost Method of Building Concrete Houses." *Indian Concrete Journal* 24, no. 3 (1950): 66–73.

101. "B.B. and C.I.R.L.Y. Build 'Gunite' Houses for Low Wage Earning Staff," *Indian Concrete Journal* 23, no. 8 (1949): 185–87.

102. P. L. Varma, "Use of Soil-Cement in House Construction in the Punjab," *Indian Concrete Journal* 24, no. 4 (1950): 91–96.

103. John H. Whitley, Report of the Royal Commission on Labour in India: Presented to Parliament by Command of His Majesty, June 1931 (London: H. M. Stationery Office, 1931).

104. For LN's role in shaping post-empire Europe and West Asia, see Susan Pederson, *The Guardians: The League of Nations and the Crisis of Empire* (Oxford: Oxford University Press, 2015).

105. Reginald M. Atwater, "Editorial," *American Journal of Public Health and the Nation's Health* 39, no. 4 (1949): 525–27.

106. American Public Health Association, *Basic Principles of Healthful Housing* (New York: American Public Health Association, 1939.

107. American Public Health Association Committee on the Hygiene of Housing, *Housing for Health: Papers Presented under the Auspices of the Committee* (Lancaster: American Public Health Association Science Press, 1941).

108. American Public Health Association, *Basic Principles of Healthful Housing*.

109. Shugan C. Aggarwal, *Industrial Housing in India* (New Delhi: Ministry of Works, Housing, and Supply, 1952), 397.

110. The dispute between industrialists and the state government over rent, loans, subsidies and construction costs had become a long recurring theme. Two examples were recorded in the Ministry File, Ministry of Works, Housing, and Supply, 1955, Material Related to the Dispute between Industrialists and the State Government, file no. HI(104)/54 (dt.19.2.55), National Archives of India, New Delhi.

111. Government of India Subsidised Housing Scheme for Industrial Workers, 1952–53, Grant of Loans and Subsidies Towards Housing Schemes Undertaken by State Governments, Employers and Workers' Co-Operatives (New Delhi: Ministry of Works, Housing, and Supply, 1952).

112. V. R. Caru, "The Making of a Working-Class Area: The Worli BDD Chawls," in *The Chawls of Mumbai: Galleries of Life*, ed. Neera Adarkar (New Delhi: ImprintOne, 2011), 26–36.

113. Government of India, Subsidised Housing Scheme for Industrial Workers, 1952–53.

114. Sundaram, Proceedings, Summary of Nehru at the Inaugural Session, Government of India, Ministry of Labour, no. LC-263 (6) New Delhi, June 12, 1954. Working, Housing and Supply (File no. HI/1(104)/55 1958), Indian National Archives, Delhi.

115. All India Congress Committee, L. N. Nagar, ed., "Housing Schemes," in *The Seventh Year of Freedom, August 1953–August 1954*. (New Delhi: All India Congress Committee, 1954), 181–217.

116. Public Health Engineering Department, *Type Designs for Small Houses* (Calcutta: All India Institute of Hygiene and Public Health, n.d.).

117. Aggarwal, *Industrial Housing in India*.

118. Aggarwal, *Industrial Housing in India*.

119. For a discussion of the working class and the notion of poverty, see Sabyasachi Bhattacharya, *The Labouring Poor and Their Notion of Poverty: Late 19th and Early 20th Century Bengal* (V. V. Giri National Labour Institute, 1998), www.indialabourarchives.org.

120. Aggarwal, *Industrial Housing in India*, 3.

121. Concrete Association of India, *40 Designs for Low Cost Housing* (Bombay: Concrete Association of India, 1952).

122. D. N. Dhar, *Industrial Housing for the Tropics* (Bombay: Concrete Association of India, 1958), 11, 12, 20.

123. For a discussion of the relationship between political institutions and biological entity in the context of postcolonial study, see Dipesh Chakrabarty, "The Climate of History: Four

Theses," *Critical Inquiry* 35, no. 2 (Winter 2009): 197–222; Dipesh Chakrabarty, "Postcolonial Studies and the Challenge of Climate Change," *New Literary History* 43, no. 1 (2012): 1–18.

2. Exhibiting Development

1. Sarvepalli Radhakrishnan, Inaugural address at the United Nations Regional Seminar on Housing and Community Improvement, 1954, n.p., Tyrwhitt Papers, box 29, folder 3, Archive of the Royal Institute of British Architects, London.

2. Jawaharlal Nehru, Inaugural address at the United Nations Regional Seminar on Housing and Community Improvement, 1954, n.p.,Tyrwhitt Papers, box 29, folder 3, Archive of the Royal Institute of British Architects, London.

3. Chatterjee, *Nation and Its Fragments*.

4. Santos Luis Rivera, "An Analysis of Existing Housing Programs in the Commonwealth of Puerto Rico with Special Emphasis on Aided Self-Help Activities," Low Cost Housing in South and South-East Asia, United Nations document ST/SOA/3/Rev. I, July 16, 1951, 13–14.

5. "Spiritual Values Vital to Housing Schemes" (Dr. Radhakrishnan's Call at the United Nations Regional Seminar on Housing and Community Improvement, January 21, 1954), *Times of India*, January 22, 1954.

6. For a quick reference on Weissmann, see Tamara Bjažić Klarin, "Architect Ernest Weissmann: A 'Common' European Immigrant Story," conference paper from Migrants as "Translators": Mediating External Influences on Post World War II Western Europe, 1945–1973, Njemačka, Hamburg, October 24–26, 2013.

7. Richard Harris, "The Silence of the Experts: 'Aided Self-Help Housing,' 1939–1954," *Habitat International* 22, no. 2 (1998): 165–89.

8. Jaqueline Tyrwhitt, Circular Letters to Those to Whom I Have Been Intending to Write for Months, Exhibition Grounds, New Delhi, the February 12, 1954(a), International Federation for Housing and Town Planning South East Asia Regional Conference, New Delhi, February 1–5, 1954, Technical Paper no. R-8, Jaqueline Tyrwhitt Papers, box 32, folder 1, Archive of Royal Institute of British Architects, London (hereafter TyJ/box no./folder no.). For an overview of Tyrwhitt's career, see D. Ladas and C. H. Nagashima, eds., "Mary Jaqueline Tyrwhitt: In Memoriam," *Ekistics* 52 (1985): 314–15; E. Shoshkes, "Jaqueline Tyrwhitt: A Founding Mother of Modern Urban Design," *Planning Perspectives* 21 no. 2 (2006): 179–97.

9. Transcript, London, TyJ/32/1.

10. "Decent Housing at Low Cost: New Delhi's International Exhibition," United Nations Bulletin 16, no. 5 (1954): 186–91.

11. Ministry of Works, Housing, and Supply, International Exhibition on Low-Cost Housing New Delhi, 20th January to 5th March, 1954, Exhibition Souvenir (New Delhi: Government of India, 1954).

12. Joseph Allen Stein, "The Possibility of a Multi-Level Democratic Society," in *Building in the Garden: The Architecture of Joseph Allen Stein in India and California*, ed. Stephen White and Joseph Allen (New York: Oxford University Press, 1993), 313.

13. Stephen White and Joseph Allen Stein, *Building in the Garden: The Architecture of Joseph Allen Stein in India and California* (New York: Oxford University Press, 1993), 317.

14. Garrett I. Eckbo, Robert N. Royston, and Suzanne B. Riess, "Landscape Architecture: The Profession in California, 1935–1940" and "Telesis: Oral History Transcript 1993," unpublished manuscripts, Regional Oral History Office, Bancroft Library, University of California, Berkeley.

15. Peter Bergmann, "The Specter of Amerikanisierung," in *American Culture in Europe: Interdisciplinary Perspectives*, ed. Mike-Frank G. Epitropoulos and Victor Roudometof (Westport, CT: Praeger, 1998), 67–91.

16. Mark Levene, "The Apocalyptic as Contemporary Dialectic: From Thanatos (Violence) to Eros (Transformation)," in *Future Ethics: Climate Change and Apocalyptic Imagination*, ed.

Stefan Skrimshire (London: Continuum, 2010), 107–26; Perry Miller, *Errand into the Wilderness* (Cambridge, MA: Harvard University Press, 1956), 217–44.

17. Advertisement, *Indian Concrete Journal* 20, no. 3 (1946): 201.

18. "Bombay Government's Industrial Housing Scheme," *Indian Concrete Journal* 13, no. 7 (1939): 147.

19. In conversation with Ashok Kumar, principal researcher, CBRI, 2014.

20. J. Leech, "Vacuum Concrete House: An Interesting Exhibit at New Delhi Exhibition," *Indian Concrete Journal*, May 15, 1954. ACC promoted similar structure and its architectural use for some time, see "Ctesiphon Structures in India," *Indian Concrete Journal* 6, no. 6 (October 18, 1932): 20.

21. J. Tyrwhitt, Typescript of Radio Address Broadcast, January 7, 1951, TyJ/32/1.

22. "Aerial View of Bombay," *Indian Concrete Journal* 16, no. 5/6 (1939).

23. *Indian Concrete Journal* 13, no. 9, Special Issue on Air Raid Precaution (1939); *Indian Concrete Journal* 16, no. 5 (1942).

24. Reconstruction Committee of Council (hereafter GIRCC), Record of the Fourth Meeting of the General Policy Committee, held at New Delhi on the 8th and 9th October 1945 (New Delhi: Government of India Press, 1946), 3.

25. Government of Madya Bharat, Request by the Government of Madya Bharat for Additional Financial Assistance for the Tenements Built under the Subsidised Industrial Housing Scheme to Meet the Extra Cost of Foundation in Black Cotton Soil and for Flooring, File No. HI/1(138)/55 Prs No.s HI/1488/55, 883, 1696, Malwa Political Agency, War Branch Indore, 1943 Progs. No.s 25-W, 1943 Technical Training Scheme, Government of India, Ministry of Works, Housing, and Supply, National Archives of India, New Delhi.

26. Proposal to Organise War Services Exhibition throughout India, Progs. Nos. 66-W, 1943, Central Indian Agency, War Branch, National Archives of India, New Delhi.

27. Government of India Information Service (hereafter GIIS), *Planning for India: Sir Ardeshar Dalal's Speech, June 18, 1945*, file no. 3093/mmb/, National Archives of India, New Delhi.

28. GIIS, ed*ucation for All in India Government of India Studies Postwar Proposals*, 3063/cg/ November 3, 1944, 7.

29. GIIS, *India's Post and Telegraph Department in War time*, 3066/mmb/November 25, 1944; GIIS, ed*ucation for All in India Government of India Studies Postwar Proposals*, 3063/cg/November 3, 1944; GIIS, *India's Foreign Trade in Fifth Year of War, Total Foreign Trade Increased More Favourable Trade Balance Trade Trend in 1943–44 Analysed*, 3060/cg/October 23, 1944; GIIS, *Indian Railways Great War Effort*, 3058/cg/October 16, 1944; GIIS, *Government of India's Policy Post War Development of Air Services in India*, no. 3/ 3020/mmh/May 4, 1944; GIIS, *Aid to India's Post-War Development Government Relaxes Capital Issues Restrictions*, no. 33021/mmh/May 13, 1944; GIIS, *India's Post-War Economic Development, Government of India's Plans new Department Created*, 3027/mmh/July 6, 1944.

30. Bureau of Public Information, Government of India, *Post-War Planning: An Outline* (New Delhi: Government of India Press, 1945).

31. GIRCC, Record of the Fourth Meeting of the General Policy Committee.

32. GIRCC, Second Report on Reconstruction Planning (New Delhi: Government of India Press, 1944).

33. "Aerial View of Bombay."

34. "The Indian Town of Tomorrow," *Indian Concrete Journal* 18, no. 6 (1944): 4–5.

35. Ijlal Muzaffar, "The Periphery Within: Modern Architecture and the Making of the Modern World" (PhD diss., Massachusetts Institute of Technology, 2007).

36. Hans Harms, "Historical Perspectives on the Practice and Politics of Self-Help Housing," in *Self-Help Housing: A Critique*, ed. Peter M. Ward (London: Mansell, 1982), 17–53.

37. Inter-American Housing and Planning Center, *Self-Help Housing Guide* (New York: Centro Interamericano de Vivienda, 1961).

38. P. T. Bauer, *Equality: The Third World and Economic Delusion* (Cambridge, MA: Harvard University Press, 1981).

39. Otto Koenigsberger, "Low Cost Housing in South and South-East Asia," *Journal of Environmental Planning and Management* 1–2, no. 3 (1951); United Nations, Tropical Housing Mission, "Low Cost Housing in South and South-East Asia: Report of Mission of Experts, november 22, 1950–January 23, 1951" (New York: United Nations, Department of Social Affairs, 1951).

40. United Nations, Department of Economic Social Affairs, *Self-Help Practices in Housing: Selected Case Studies* (New York: United Nations, 1973).

41. Ian Donald Turner and John F. C. Turner, *Industrialized Housing: The Opportunity and the Problem in Developing Areas* (Washington, DC: US Department of Housing and Urban Affairs, Office of International Affairs, 1971).

42. Inter-American Housing and Planning Center, *Self-Help Housing Guide.*

43. International Federation for Housing and Town Planning, Proceedings of the South East Asia Regional Conference, New Delhi, February 1–7, 1954.

44. Robert L. Tignor, *W. Arthur Lewis and the Birth of Development Economics* (Princeton, NJ: Princeton University Press, 2006).

45. Evsey D. Domar, "Capital Expansion, Rate of Growth, and Employment," *Econometrica: Journal of the Econometric Society* 14, no. 2 (1946): 137–47.

46. Ruth Rempel, "Periodizing African Development History," *African Economic History* 36 (2008): 125–58.

47. Charles Abrams, *Man's Struggle for Shelter in an Urbanizing World* (Cambridge, MA: MIT Press, 1966).

48. United Nations/OS Working Group, Meeting on Cooperation and Coordination of Technical Assistance Activities in the Field of Housing, Building, and Physical Planning in Latin America, november 16, 1954, Minutes, Box 69, folder TAA173/19/011, RAG 2/173, United Nations Archives, New York.

49. Jaqueline Tyrwhitt, Circular Letters to Those to Whom I Have Been Intending to Write for Months, Exhibition Grounds, New Delhi, the February 12, 1954, International Federation for Housing and Town Planning South East Asia Regional Conference, New Delhi, February 1–5, 1954, Technical Paper no. R-8, Tyrwhitt Papers, box 32, folder 1, Archive of the Royal Institute of British Architects, London.

50. G. F. Middleton, *Earth-Wall Construction: Pisé or Rammed Earth, Adobe or Puddled Earth, Stabilized Earth*, rev. ed. (Sydney: Department of Works and Housing, Commonwealth Experimental Building Station, 1956).

51. G. F. Middleton and Lawrence Maxwell Schneider, "Earth-Wall Construction," Department of Housing and Construction Experimental Building Station Bulletin no. 5 (Collingwood, Australia: National Building Technology Centre, 1987).

52. G. F. Middleton, *Build Your House of Earth: A Manual of Pisé and Abode Construction* (Melbourne: Compendium, 1953).

53. Ministry of Works, Housing, and Supply, International Exhibition on Low Cost Housing, Exhibition Souvenir (New Delhi: Government of India, 1954).

54. Sinha, "Lineages of the Developmentalist State," 57–90, 63–64.

55. Patrick Geddes, *Town Planning towards City Development: A Report to the Durbar of Indore* (Indore: Holkore State Printing Press, 1918).

56. Ellen Shoshkes, "Visualizing the Core of an Ideal Domestic Community: Jaqueline Tyrwhitt and Post-war Planning Exhibitions," in *Exhibitions and the Development of Modern Planning Culture*, eds. Robert Freestone and Marco Amati (London: Ashgate, 2014).

57. D. Spencer Hatch, *Up from Poverty in Rural India* (Bombay, Calcutta: Oxford University Press, 1938), 6.

58. S. V. Desai, "Housing in Relation to Redevelopment (with Particular Reference to Bom-

bay City)," in Proceedings of the South East Asia Regional Conference, New Delhi, February 1–7, 1954, 83.

59. Aram Ziai, *Development Discourse and Global History: From colonialism to the sustainable development Goals* (London: Routledge, 2016); also see the classic text Gilbert Rist, *The History of Development: From Western Origin to Global Faith* (London: Zed Books, 1997).

60. Desai, "Housing in Relation to Redevelopment," 85–87.

61. J. D. N. Versluys, "Some Social Aspects of Housing Programmes," in Proceedings of the South East Asia Regional Conference, New Delhi, February 1–7, 1954, 78–82.

62. Deva Raj, "The Redevelopment of Slum Area," in Proceedings of the South East Asia Regional Conference, New Delhi, February 1–7, 1954, 103.

63. United Nations Technical Assistance Mission in India, Social and Economic Aspects of Housing, Basic Substantive Data, TE 3221/India (240–2), UN Archives.

64. Ir. Jac. P. Thijsse, "General Report," in Proceedings of the South East Asia Regional Conference, New Delhi, February 1–7, 1954, 145–55.

65. Charles Abrams (discussant), "Report of the Session, Discussion, Session on Implementation of Planning, February 4, 1954, Chairman: Shri S. K. Joglekar (India)," in Proceedings of the South East Asia Regional Conference, New Delhi, February 1–7, 1954, 403.

66. Mark Wigley, "Network Fever," *Grey Room* 4 (2001): 82–122.

67. Richard Buckminster Fuller, "Eik—Session 7 Part 10," in *Everything I Know* (Los Angeles: Te Buckminster Fuller Institute, 1975, www.bfi.org. The video of the talk is available at https://archive.org/details/buckminsterfuller.

68. J. Tyrwhitt, Typescript of Radio Address Broadcast, January 7, 1951, TyJ/32/1.

69. For an overview of Doxiadis's career, see Alexander Kyrtsis, *Constantinos A. Doxiadis: Texts, Design, Drawings, Settlements* (Athens: Ikaros, 2006).

70. Constantinos Doxiadis, Economic Commission for Europe, Panel on Housing Problem, the Housing Problem of Post-War Europe, Report no. 1, February 1, 1949, Housing Needs and Programmes, United Nations. For a critical discussion, see A. Andreas Kakridis, "Rebuilding the Future: C. A. Doxiadis and the Greek Reconstruction Effort (1945–1950)," *Historical Review/La Revue Historique* 10 (2013): 137.

71. The Harvard Advisory Group (HAG) is a group of economists based at Harvard University to advise on Pakistan government on economic planning. HAG worked closely with World Bank and established the Planning Commission of Pakistan in 1952. HAG was also the driving force to establish the Pakistan Institute of Development Economics in 1957. For a brief history of HAG, see Nadeem Ul Haque and Mahmood Hasan Khan, "The Economics Profession in Pakistan: A Historical Analysis," *Pakistan Development Review* 37, no. 4 (1998): 431–52.

72. Constantinos Doxiadis, *India Notes 1* (October–November 1955), 12, 1, 6, 14, 11, 15, Constantinos A. Doxiadis Archives, Athens.

73. Constantinos Doxiadis, "Discussion on Gandhi's Idea 25.10.55," *Indian Regional Housing Center* 2, January 10, 1956; Doxiadis, *India Notes 1*, 91.

74. Doxiadis, *India Notes 1*, 58, 50.

75. Daechsel, *Islamabad and Politics of International Development.*

76. Doxiadis, *India Notes 1*, 35.

3. The Idea of an Ideal Village

1. Tyrwhitt described the exhibition site as follows: "In this romantic setting, emblematic of the ancient history of India and of its current problems a truly magnificent exhibition," Housing and Community Improvement in Asian Countries, General Report of United Nations Seminar, New Delhi, June 3 1954, TyJ/31/9.

2. Jaqueline Tyrwhitt, Open Letter to Colleagues at the Housing and Community Improvement in Asian Countries, United Nations Seminar, New Delhi, June 3, 1954; TyJ/29/3.

3. Housing and Community Improvement in Asian Countries, General Report of United Nations Seminar, New Delhi, June 3, 1954, Paragraph 56, TyJ/28/7.

4. Housing and Community Improvement in Asian Countries, General Report of United Nations Seminar, New Delhi, June 3, 1954; TyJ/28.

5. The show was sponsored and executed by the Technical Assistance Administration of the United Nations and the Community Project Administration (Planning Commission) with the cooperation of the International Labour Organization, Food and Agriculture Organization of the United Nations, World Health Organization, United Nations Educational, Scientific and Cultural Organization, United nations Children Emergency Fund, Jamia Milia University, Indian Co-Operative Union, 1954.

6. Shoshkes, "Visualizing the Core," 193–208.

7. J. Tyrwhitt, Typescript of Radio Address Broadcast, January 7, 1951, TyJ/32/1.

8. Karin Kirsch and Gerhard Kirsch, *The Weissenhofsiedlung: Experimental Housing Built for the Deutscher Werbund, Stuttgart, 1927* (New York: Rizzoli, 1989), 17.

9. Betts, *Authority of Everyday* Objects, 82–83.

10. Jaqueline Tyrwhitt, Seminar on Housing and Community Improvement, Exhibition Grounds, New Delhi, February 12, 1954, Circular letters, TyJ/31/9.

11. Jaqueline Tyrwhitt, "Technical Paper No. R-8: The Village Centre," in Proceedings of the South East Asia Regional Conference, New Delhi, February 1–7, 1954.

12. The working method was discussed in detail in Tyrwhitt's lecture on rural India, "The Sacred Cow" to York Memorial School, February 18, 1955, Industrial Development Series Housing and Building Materials, May 1954, Economic Commission for Asia and the Far East, TyJ/32/1.

13. Jaqueline Tyrwhitt, Letter to Miss Eleanor M. Hinder, Chief Office for Asia and the Far East Programme Division TAA, December 22, 1953, TyJ/31/9.

14. Jaqueline Tyrwhitt, Typescript of Radio Address Broadcast, January 7, 1951, TyJ/32/1.

15. "Decent Housing at Low Cost."

16. Jaqueline Tyrwhitt, Seminar on Housing and Community Improvement, Exhibition Grounds, New Delhi, February 12, 1954, Circular letters, TYJ/31/9.

17. Joseph S. Alter, "Gandhi's Body, Gandhi's Truth: Nonviolence and the Biomoral Imperative of Public Health," *Journal of Asian Studies* 55, no. 2 (1996): 301–22; Susanne H. Rudolph and Lloyd I. Rudolph, "This-Worldly Asceticism and Political Modernization," in *Postmodern Gandhi and Other Essays: Gandhi in the World and at Home*, ed. Lloyd I. Rudolph and Susanne H. Rudolph (London: University of Chicago Press, 2006), 62–86.

18. J. Tyrwhitt, Letter to Miss Eleanor M. Hinder (Chief Office for Asia and the Far East Programme Division TAA), 1953, TyJ/31/9.

19. Jaqueline Tyrwhitt, Letter to Mr. Gupta, Superintending Engineer, Building and Roads, PWD Jaipur, 1954, Box 31, Folder 9, Jaqueline Tyrwhitt Papers, Royal Institute of British Architecture Archives, London.

20. Housing and Community Improvement in Asian Countries, General Report of United Nations Seminar, New Delhi, June 3, 1954, TyJ/28/7. Also see Mysore Narasimhachar Srinivas, *The Dominant Caste and Other Essays* (Delhi: Oxford University Press, 1994).

21. International Federation for Housing and Town Planning, Proceedings of the South East Asia Regional Conference, New Delhi, February 1–7, 1954, TyJ/32/1.

22. Anand Chakravarti, "The Statutory Panchayat," in *The Village India*, ed. V. Madan (Delhi: Oxford University Press, 2002), 238–51.

23. Sarvepalli Radhakrishnan, Inaugural Address at United Nations Seminar on Housing and Community Improvement, January 21, 1954, Box 29, Folder 3, Jaqueline Tyrwhitt Papers, Royal Institute of British Architecture Archives, London. For a critique of Point Four Program, see Surjuit Mansingh, "India and the United States," in *Indian Foreign Policy: The Nehru Years,*

ed. B. R. Nanda (New Delhi: Radiant Publishers, Nehru Memorial Museum and Library, 1976): 156.

24. Ellen Shoshkes, "Introduction," in Jaqueline Tyrwhitt, *Society and Environment: A Historical Review* (New York: Routledge, 2015).

25. Patrick Geddes, *Patrick Geddes in India*, ed. Jaqueline Tyrwhitt (London: Lund Humphries, 1947). See note 29.

26. For a discussion on Eric Rowse, see Mary O. Ashton, "'Tomorrow Town': Patrick Geddes, Walter Gropius, and Le Corbusier," in *The City after Patrick Geddes*, ed. Volker M. Welter and James Lawson (Bern: Peter Lang, 2000).

27. Paul Hofer, Siegfried Giedion, and Ulrich Stucky, *Hommage à Giedion Profile Seiner Persönlichkeit: Schriften und Dokumente von Siegfried Giedion Sowie Beiträge der Freunde* (Stuttgart: Birkhäuser, 1971), 121–22; Jaqueline Tyrwhitt, personal note on Sigfried Giedion, published in *Hommage à Giedion* (Stuttgart: Birkhäuser, 1954), 121–22, TyJ/60/2.

28. Geddes, *Patrick Geddes in India*, 28.

29. Christine Marsh, "Towards Tagorean Utopia: From Rural Reconstruction to Transition Towns," *Literature Compass* 12, no. 5 (2015): 194–205; Partha Pratim Ray, Bidhan Ch. Biswas, and B.K. Sen, "Knowledge Communication in Tagore's Model For Rural Reconstruction: An Overview," *Annals of Library and Information Studies* 52, no. 3 (2005): 94–102; Christine Marsh, "The Once and Future Village: From Tagore's Rural Reconstruction to Transition Towns," in *Contemporarising Tagore and the World*, ed. Imtiaz Ahmed, Muchkund Dubey, and Veena Sikri (Dhaka: University Press, 2013).

30. "An Architectural Trade Exhibition," *Journal of the Indian Institute of Architects* 3 no. 10 (1938): 305.

31. Eric Paul Mumford, *The CIAM Discourse on Urbanism, 1928–1960* (Cambridge, MA: MIT Press, 2000).

32. Jaqueline Tyrwhitt, José Luis Sert, and Ernesto N. Rogers, eds., *The Heart of the City: Towards the Humanisation of Urban Life* (London: Lund Humphries, 1952), 165.

33. Annie Pedret, *Team 10: An Archival History* (New York: Routledge, 2013); Max Risselada and Dirk van Heuvel, *Team 10: In Search of a Utopia of the Present 1953–1981* (Rotterdam: NAi Publishers, 2005); also see Team 10 online at www.team10online.org.

34. CIAM 8, Open Session, Background of the Core, July 9, 1951, TyJ/45/6.

35. Volker M. Welter, *Biopolis: Patrick Geddes and the City of Life* (Cambridge, MA: MIT Press, 2003): 187–91.

36. Hysler-Rubin, *Patrick Geddes and Town Planning*.

37. Patrick Geddes, "Town Planning Towards City Development: A Report to the Durbar of Indore, 1918 (Part II)," in Geddes, *Patrick Geddes in India*, 28.

38. J. Tyrwhitt, Typescript of Radio Address Broadcast, January 7, 1951, TyJ/32/1.

39. Tyrwhitt assured Hinder on her fear that the CIAM projects might not get a significant place in the India Exhibition. See Tyrwhitt, Letter to Eleanor M. Hinder (Chief Office for Asia and the Far East Programme Division, TAA), november 9, 1953, TyJ/31/9.

40. Tyrwhitt, Sert, and Rogers, *Heart of the City*.

41. Letter from Tyrwhitt to N. P. Dube, Deputy Secretary, Ministry of Works, Housing, and Supply, New Delhi, June 23, 1953, TyJ/31/9.

42. Vandana Madan, "Introduction," in *The Village in India*, ed. V. Madan (New Delhi: Oxford University Press, 2002), 5.

43. George Campbell, *Modern India: A Sketch of the System of Civil Government to Which Is Prefaced Some Account of the Natives and Native Institutions* (London: J. Murray, 1852).

44. Bernard S. Cohn, "Notes on the History of the Study of Indian Society and Culture," in *Structure and Change in Indian Society*, ed. Milton B. Singer and Bernard S. Cohn (Chicago: Aldine, 1968), 3–25.

45. Cohn, "Notes on the History of the Study of Indian Society and Culture," 3–25.

46. Baden Henry Baden-Powell, *The Origin and Growth of Village Communities in India* (London: Swan Sonnenschein, 1899).

47. Bernard Cohn, "Introduction," in *Structure and Change in Indian Society*, ed. Milton Singer and Bernard Cohn (New Brunswick, NJ: Aldine Transaction, 2007).

48. Ronald Inden, *Imagining India* (Indianapolis: Indiana University Press, 2001).

49. Clive Dewey, "Images of the Village Community: A Study in Anglo Indian Ideology," *Modern Asian Studies* 6, no. 3 (1972): 291–328.

50. Bernard S. Cohn, *Colonialism and Its Forms of Knowledge* (Princeton: Princeton University Press, 1996).

51. Patrick Geddes, *Town Planning in Aden, A Report of the Government of Bombay* (Bombay: Government Central Press, 1919), 12, Maharashtra State Archives, General Department 1919, box 26, file 726.

52. Patrick Geddes, "Report on the Towns in the Madras Presidency, 1915: Madura (1915)," in Geddes, *Patrick Geddes in India*, 82.

53. Geddes, "Town Planning towards City Development," 38. See also Patrick Geddes, *Cities in Evolution: An Introduction to the Town Planning Movement and to the Study of Civics* (London: Williams and Norgate, 1915).

54. Geddes, "Town Planning towards City Development," 37.

55. Geddes, "Report on the Towns in the Madras Presidency." See also Patrick Geddes, *Cities in Evolution*, 74.

56. Geddes, *Town Planning in Aden*, 13.

57. Peter H. Hoffenberg, *An Empire on Display: English, Indians, and Australian Exhibitions from the Crystal Palace to the Great War* (Berkeley: University of California Press, 2001).

58. For a critical discussion of Geddesian method of conservative surgery, see Rachel Huworth, "Patrick Geddes Concept of Conservative Surgery," *Architectural Heritage* 11, no. 1 (2000): 37–42.

59. Patrick Brantlinger, "A Postindustrial Prelude to Postcolonialism: John Ruskin, William Morris, and Gandhism," *Critical Inquiry* 22, no. 3 (1996): 466–85.

60. Venugopal Maddipati, "Selfsame Spaces: Gandhi, Architecture and Allusions in Twentieth Century India" (PhD diss., University of Minnesota, 2011), 8.

61. Mark Thomson, *Gandhi and His Ashrams* (Bombay: Popular Prakashan, 1993).

62. Dipesh Chakrabarty, "Adda, Calcutta: Dwelling in Modernity," *Public Culture* 11, no. 1 (1999): 109–45.

63. Susanne H. Rudolph and Lloyd I. Rudolph, "The Coffee House and the Ashram Revisited: How Gandhi Democratized Habermas' Public Sphere," in *Postmodern Gandhi and Other Essays: Gandhi in the World and at Home*, ed. Susanne H. Rudolph and Lloyd I. Rudolph (London: University of Chicago Press, 2006), 140–76.

64. Sris Chandra Chatterjee, *India and New Order: An Essay on Human Planning* (Calcutta: University of Calcutta, 1949); Samita Gupta, "Sris Chandra Chatterjee: The Quest for a National Architecture," *Indian Economic and Social History Review* 28 no. 2 (1991): 187–201.

65. Sris Chandra Chatterjee, *Magadha, Architecture and Culture* (Calcutta: Calcutta University Press, 1942).

66. Pradip Kumar Das, *Henry Irwin and the Indo Saracenic Movement Reconsidered* (Gurgaon, India: Partridge, 2014).

67. Sris Chandra Chatterjee, *Architects and Architecture: Then and Now, An Essay on Human Planning* (Calcutta: University of Calcutta, 1948).

68. Andrzej Piotrowski, "The Spectacle of Architectural Discourses," *Architectural Theory Review* 13, no. 2 (2008).

69. McKim Marriott, ed., *Village India: Studies in the Little Community* (Chicago: University

of Chicago, 1955); Milton B. Singer, *When a Great Tradition Modernizes: An Anthropological Approach to Indian Civilization* (New York: Praeger, 1972).

70. Dipankar Gupta, "The Anti-Utopian Liberal: An Introduction to the Works of André Béteille," in *Anti-Utopia: Essential Writings of André Béteille*, ed. André Béteille (New Delhi: Oxford University Press, 2005), 1–22.

71. André Béteille, *Society and Politics in India: Essays in a Comparative Perspective* (New Delhi: Oxford University Press, 1991), 196.

72. André Béteille, "Civil Society and the Good Society, 12th Zakir Husain Memorial Lecture, February 22, 2000" (New Delhi: Zakir Husain College, University of New Delhi, 2000).

73. *Indian Concrete Journal* 19, no. 2 (1945): 23–25.

74. Associated Cement Companies, *Our Villages of Tomorrow: How Shall We Build Them?* (Bombay: Associated Cement Companies, 1949), n.p.

75. Rod Burgess, "Self-Help Housing: A New Imperialist Strategy? A Critique of the Turner School," *Antipode* 9 no. 2 (1977): 50–59.

76. Peter Ward, ed., *Self-Help Housing: A Critique* (New York: Mansell, 1982).

77. Prem Chowdhry, *Colonial India and the Making of Empire Cinema: Image Ideology and Identity* (Manchester: Manchester University Press, 2000).

78. Bureau of Public Information, *Post-War Planning, An Outline* (Bombay: Government of India, 1945), 28.

79. Jaqueline Tyrwhitt, Seminar on Housing and Community Improvement, Exhibition Grounds, New Delhi, February 12, 1954, Circular letters, TyJ/32/1.

80. Tyrwhitt to Mr. Marcel Schwob, Acting Chief, Office for Asia and the Far East Programme Division, Technical Assistance Administration, Western Court, ND, September 6, 1953, TyJ/31/9.

81. Tyrwhitt to Hinder, Western Court, ND, June 19, 1953, TyJ/31/9.

82. United Nations Housing and Town Planning Bulletin No. 9, The Delhi Seminar on Housing and Planning for South East Asia, 1954, Parts II and III, TyJ/30/1.

83. United Nations Housing and Town Planning Bulletin No. 9.

84. International Federation for Housing and Town Planning, Proceedings of the South East Asia Regional Conference, New Delhi, February 1–7, 1954, 259.

85. Surinder S. Jodhka, "Nation and Village: Images of Rural India in Gandhi, Nehru and Ambedkar," *Economic and Political Weekly* 37, no. 32 (2002): 3343–53.

86. William J. Glover, "The Troubled Passage from 'village communities' to planned new town developments in mid-twentieth-century South Asia," *Urban History* 39, no. 1 (February 2012): 108–27.

87. Andrew Friedman, "The Global Postcolonial Moment and the American New Town: India Reston, Dodoma," *Journal of Urban History* 38, no. 3 (2012): 553–76.

88. Mathew S. Hull, "Communities of Place, not Kind: American Technologies of Neighborhood in postcolonial Delhi," *Comparative Studies in Society and History* 53, no. 4 (2011): 757–90.

89. For a contemporary commentary see Subhash Chandra, "An Evaluation of Urban Community Development in India," *Community Development Journal* 9, no. 3 (1974): 191–202.

90. Charles Horton Cooley, *Social Organization* (New York: Charles Scribner's Sons, 1909). For a critical discussion see Hull, "Communities of Place, not Kind," 757–90.

91. Committee on Rural-Urban Relationship, Ministry of Health and Family Planning, Report of the Rural-Urban Relationship (New Delhi: Government of India Press, 1966), 5 (interim report), United Nations Technical Assistance Mission in India, Urban Community Development, Basic Substantive Data, TE 322/1 India (250–1), UN Archives.

4. Architecture of the New Villages

1. Sinha, "Lineages of the Developmentalist State," 57–90.

2. Nicole Sackley, "Village Models: Etawah, India, and the Making and Remaking of Development in the Early Cold War," *Diplomatic History* 37, no. 4 (2013): 749–77.

3. Albert Mayer, "In Praise of Missionaries," 1947, box 35, folder 4, Albert Mayer Papers on India, Special Collections Research Center, University of Chicago Library, Chicago (hereafter MA/box no./folder no.); Albert Mayer to Govind Ballabh Pant, December 10, 1949, MA/8/13; A. A. Mayer, M. Marriott, and R. L. Park, *Pilot Project, India: The Story of Rural Development at Etawah, Uttar Pradesh* (Berkeley: University of California Press, 1958).

4. Mayer's personal collection of Gandhi's news and photographs: Miscellaneous Collection of News and Photographs of Gandhi, MA/41/27.

5. Albert A. Mayer, 1948, A Letter from Albert Mayer, Appendix II, "What This Pilot Project Is and What It Is Not," Bombay, MA/12/19.

6. Nicole Sackley, "Cosmopolitanism and the Uses of Tradition: Robert Redfield and Alternative Visions of Modernization during the Cold War," *Modern Intellectual History* 9, no. 3 (2012): 565–95.

7. An integrated history of the international history of rural development and community development is yet to be written. In recent times, a major research has been undertaken by Corinna Unger and Marc Frey to study "The International History of Rural Development Since 1950." The research is still in progress and the current status (2017) may be found here: Corinna Unger and Marc Frey, "The International History of Rural Development since 1950," Jacobs University, http://ruraldevelopment.user.jacobs-university.de/index.php. Also see Vermon W. Ruttan, "Integrated Rural Development Programmes: A Historical Perspective," *World Development* 12, no. 4 (1984): 393–401.

8. For a review, see Jessica C. E. Gienow-Hecht, "Shame on US? Academics, Cultural Transfer, and the Cold War: A Critical Review," *Diplomatic History* 24, no. 3 (2000): 465–94. Also see Nils Gilman, *Mandarins of the Future: Modernization Theory in Cold War America* (Washington, DC: Johns Hopkins University Press, 2003).

9. Different countries created their own political fiction regarding rural development. See Kate Merkel-Hess, *The Rural Modern: Reconstructing the Self and State in Republican China* (Chicago: University of Chicago Press, 2016).

10. "Nehru Talks," *Look*, november 2, 1954; "Nehru Warns Nation against Communism, Aims Identical but Paths Different," *Hindu Weekly Review*, October 15, 1956.

11. Praveen K. Chaudhry and Marta Vanduzer-Snow, *The United States and India: A History through Archives, The Formative Years* (Thousand Oaks, CA: Sage, 2008).

12. Chester Bowles to Senator Brian McMahon, January, 3, 1952, Box 81; Memorandum to the Prime Minister of India Nehru, 1952, Box 98, Chester Bowles Papers; Sterling Library, Yale University, New Haven, CT.

13. An account of Mayer's early career: Thomaï Serdari, "Albert Mayer, Architect and Town Planner: The Case for a Total Professional" (PhD diss., Institute of Fine Arts, New York University, 2005).

14. Kermit C. Parsons, "Collaborative Genius," *Journal of the American Planning Association* 60, no. 4 (1994): 462–82.

15. Albert A. Mayer, "Regional Development: The Architect's Role," *American Institute of Architects Journal* 60, no. 10 (1971): 17–19.

16. Richard Pommer, "The Architecture of Urban Housing in the United States during the Early 1930s," *Journal of the Society of Architectural Historians* 37, no. 4 (December 1978): 235–64.

17. Rosemary Wakeman, *Practicing Utopia: An Intellectual History of the New Town Movement* (Chicago: University of Chicago Press, 2016).

18. For Stein's view on town planning and neighborhood design, see Clarence S. Stein, *Toward New Towns for America* (New York: Reinhold, 1957). Also see Clarence S. Stein and Kermit C Parsons, *The Writings of Clarence S. Stein: Architect of the planned community* (Baltimore: Johns Hopkins University Press, 1998).

19. Albert A. Mayer. (1934–1975) Variously Titled, collection of personal papers and correspondence, MA/12/20.

20. Ayala Levin and Neta Feniger, "Introduction: The Modern Village," *Journal of Architecture* 23, no. 3 (2018): 361–66.

21. Alice Thorner, "Nehru, Albert Mayer, and Origins of Community Projects," *Economic and Political Weekly* 16, no. 4 (1981): 117–20.

22. Albert A. Mayer, Research and Action: The Indian Village, Seminar at the University of California Berkeley, 1954, MA/12/20.

23. Albert A. Mayer, Preliminary Outline for Village Planning and Reconstruction, Lucknow, Uttar Pradesh, 1946, MA/11/12. Also see Albert A. Mayer, Specific Programme for the Pilot Intensive Project in Planning, Development Coordination in District Etawah, MA/11/12.

24. Albert Mayer, "This Is the Hunger That We Must Fight," *New York Times*, April 14, 1946, 12; Albert Mayer, "Proposal for Planning," MA/2/17; Albert A. Mayer, Newsletter to Indian Colleagues, August 4, 1952, MA/13/1.

25. Albert Mayer, Newsletter, August 3, 1952, MA/36/7; Albert Mayer, Newsletter, July 8, 1948, MA36/2.

26. Shyama C. Dube, "Cultural Factors in Rural Community Development," *Journal of Asian Studies* 16, no. 1 (1956): 19–30; Albert A. Mayer, "Social Analysis and National Economic Development in India," *Pacific Affairs* 35, no. 2 (1962), 128–40.

27. A. A. Mayer, Variously Titled, 1934–1975, MA/12/20; Albert A. Mayer, Newsletter, 1947, MA/12/20.

28. Albert A. Mayer, A Letter from Albert Mayer, 1947, MA/12/20.

29. A. A. Mayer, "Social Analysis and National Economic Development in India," *Pacific Affairs* 35, no. 2 (1962): 128–40.

30. A list of Trudgett's work as a consultant of the Town and Village Planning Office United Provinces can be found at: List of R. Dudley Trudgett's Work as a Consultant of the Town and Village Planning Office, Uttar Pradesh, 1951–1955, File No. IV (1), R. Dudley Trudgett Collection, Archives of the College of Environment Design, University of California, Berkeley. Albert A. Mayer to Govind Ballabh Patel, Premier of United Province, n.d. MA/12/9.

31. Details Regarding the Town and Village Planning Department and Town Planning in Uttar Pradesh, before and after 1948, Submitted to the Estimates Committee by Town and Village Planning Department, Lucknow, Uttar Pradesh, MA/12/9.

32. Trudgett team's proposal for a prototype model of a circular village, MA/6/7.

33. J. P. Dube, Layout Plan for Bhandra, Hari-Ka-Pura Village, Bhawanipore Village Improvement Scheme; J. P. Dube, Executive Engineer, Town and Village Planning Department, Lucknow, K. N. Misra, Town and village planner, to Uttar Pradesh Government, Lucknow, MA/6/3; J. N. Ghosh, H. K. Mewada, and K. N. Misra, Layout Plan for Bhandra, Jhansi; J. N. Ghosh, engineer Town Planning Department, Lucknow, H. K. Mewada Architect Planner, Town Planning Dept., Lucknow, K. N. Misra, Town and village planner to Uttar Pradesh Government, Lucknow, MA/6/3.

34. Daniel Immerwahr, *Thinking Small: The United States and the Lure of Community Development* (Cambridge: Harvard University Press, 2015), 89.

35. Sinha, "Lineages of the Developmentalist State," 57–90.

36. This statement appears as a note on the drawing of a newly planned village, a development plan for village Bhawanipur, Mahewa, MA/6/7.

37. "All India Technical-cum-Promotion for Planning and Rebuilding of the Villages," mimeograph, January 10, 1957, MA/30/7.

38. For a discussion on Koenigsberger's town planning in India see Liscombe, "In-dependence," 157–78; Sanjeev Vidyarthi, *One Idea Many Plans: An American City Design Concept in Independent India* (New York: Routledge, 2015); Sanjeev Vidyarthi, "Reimagining the American Neighborhood for India," in *Crossing Borders, International Exchange and Planning Practices*, ed. Patsy Healy and Robert Upton (New York: Routledge, 2010). For an overall career of Koenigs-

berger in India, see Rachel Lee, *OK India—Otto Koenigsberger. Architecture and Urban Visions in India* (Berlin: MOD Institute, 2015).

39. Otto H. Koenigsberger, "New Towns in India," *Town Planning Review* 23, no. 2 (1952): 105.

40. Mayer 1950, 174.

41. Harold Robinson, *Aided Self-Help Housing: Its History and Potential* (Washington, DC: US Department of Housing and Urban Development, Office of International Affairs, 1976).

42. A. A. Mayer, Self-Help in Housing and Construction: Some Experiences in India, 1951, MA/35/8.

43. Mayer, Self-Help in Housing and Construction.

44. United Nations, Department of Economic Social Affairs, *Manual on Self-Help Housing* 81 (New York: Department of Economic and Social Affairs, United Nations, 1964).

45. Burgess, "Self Help Housing," 50–59. Also see Reinhard J. Skinner and M. J. Rodell, eds., *People, Poverty and Shelter: Problems of Self-Help Housing in the Third World* (New York: Routledge, 1983).

46. Dhyan P. Singh, Brick Kiln Co-Operatives, *Kurukshetra*, March 1954, Pamphlet Series 1, MA/3/7; Dhyan P. Singh, The Cooperative Brick Kiln Industry in Uttar-Pradesh, *Kurukshetra*, 1954, Pamphlet Series 1, MA/1/7; Dhyan P. Singh, To Co-Workers in Development Projects, Newsletter, 3rd installment, 1954, MA/3/7.

47. Mass Awakening and Mobilization (Shramdan), 1953, Commissioner, Planning and Development, Lucknow, MA/26/1–2.

48. D. P. Singh, The Cooperative Brick Kiln Industry in Uttar Pradesh, 1954, MA/3/7.

49. B. R. Tomlinson, *The Economy of Modern India, 1860–1970* (New York: Cambridge University Press, 1996).

50. Mayer, Self-Help in Housing and Construction.

51. Albert A. Mayer, "Planning in India," *Manchester Guardian*, november 10, 1951.

52. Walt W. Rostow, "The Take-Off into Self-Sustained Growth," *Economic Journal* 66, no. 261 (1956): 31–33.

53. Albert A. Mayer, Newsletter to Indian Colleagues, July 12, 1953, MA/12/19.

54. Albert Mayer, "Research and Action: The Indian Village," speech, January 21, 1954, MA/21/35.

55. Albert A. Mayer, The Pilot Project Etawah Uttar Pradesh: Report for the Period 1940–1950 (October 12, 1948, Appendix II "What This Pilot Project Is and What It Is Not," Bombay), MA/2/18. To get a review of the emotive culture of the New Deal era and its influence on art see Sharon Ann Musher, "Art and the New Deal," in *Interpreting American History: The New Deal and the Great Depression*, ed. Aaron D. Purcell (Kent, OH: Kent State University Press, 2014); Sharon Ann Musher, *Democratic Art: The New Deal's Influence on American Culture.* (Chicago, IL: University of Chicago Press, 2015).

56. Albert A. Mayer, "Homes: Front Line Defence in American Life" (unpublished article, c. 1940), MA/12/6.

57. Mayer, "Homes."

58. Albert A. Mayer, Newsletter to American Friends, July 2, 1950, MA/12/2.

59. Mayer, *Self-Help in Housing and Construction*; Draft of a pamphlet for the United Nations, MA/12/1.

60. Shyama C. Dube, "Some Problems of Communication in Rural Community Development," *Economic Development and Cultural Change* 5, no. 2 (1957): 129–46.

61. Marina R. Pinto, "Rural Development and Bureaucracy in India," *Indian Journal of Political Science* 53, no. 3 (1992): 281.

62. Shyama C. Dube, *India's Changing Villages: Human Factors in Community Development* (Ithaca: Cornell University Press, 1958).

63. Richard L. Park (Asia Foundation and coauthor of Albert Mayer) in interview with

Gerald E. Sussman, in Gerald E. Sussman, "The Road from Etawah: Integrated Rural Development in India" (PhD diss., University of Michigan: Ann Arbor, 1975), 90.

64. Baji N. Singh, Public Opinion in the Mahewa Area, 1952, MA/5/17.

65. Baji N. Singh, Introductory Note on My Report of the Study of Public Opinion, c. 1952–1955, MA/5/17.

66. Sussman, "Road from Etawah," 220.

67. Douglas Ensminger, "Needed: A Bold New Approach to Developing Staff Competence for Community Development," speech, mimeo dated 1962, quoted in Sussman, "Road from Etawah," 110.

68. Immerwahr, *Thinking Small*, 80.

69. Sackley, "Cosmopolitanism and the Uses of Tradition," 565–95.

70. Immerwahr, *Thinking Small*, 72.

71. Mayer, Marriott, and Park, *Pilot Project, India*, 31–32.

72. Mayer, Marriott, and Park, *Pilot Project, India*, 282–83.

73. Albert Mayer, "Research and Action: The Indian: The Indian Village," speech, January 21, 1954, MA/35/21.

74. Albert A. Mayer to M. Park, 1956, MA/11/10.

75. McKim Marriott to Albert Mayer, August 3, 1953, MA/7/6.

76. Jagadish Prasad Gupt, Working of Smokeless Chula at Pilot Project Mahewa, november 27, 1927, Review report on Co-operative Member Education Project, MA/11/20.

77. Barkat Narain, "Housing and Health," *Kurukshetra* (April 1955): 16–17. Barkat Narain was the health adviser to the Community Projects Administration. *Kurukshetra* was a community periodical run by the local development office.

78. Narain, "Housing and Health," 17.

79. Jaqueline Tyrwhitt, United Nations Housing and Town Planning Bulletin no. 9, the Delhi Seminar on Housing and Planning for South East Asia, 1954, Parts II and III, Box 33, folder 29, Jaqueline Tyrwhitt Papers, Royal Institute of British Architecture Archives, London.

80. Tyrwhitt, United Nations Housing and Town Planning Bulletin no. 9.

81. J. N. Ghosh, H. K. Mewada, and K. N. Misra, Layout Plan for Bhandra, Jhansi, MA/6/3.

82. Albert A. Mayer to the Institute of Current World Affairs, Lucknow, May 11, 1949, MA/6/15.

83. George Weller, "Farm Support for India: A New US Bureau," *San Francisco Chronicle*, January 3, 1952, 15.

84. S. N. Agarwal, "Truth About the Etawah Project," *Evening News*, July 19, 1952.

85. George Weller, "India's Farm Experts Fear Huge US Aid," *Daily News*, May 26, 1952.

86. Louis A. Jacob, *American Understanding of India: A Symposium* (Papers read at a conference held at the Library of Congress, October 23–25, 1986) (New Delhi: Manohar, 2001). Also see Arthur G. Rubinoff, "Changing Perceptions of India in the U.S. Congress," *Asian Affairs* 28, no. 1 (Spring 2001): 37–60; Alastair Buchan, "American Perceptions of the Post-War World," *British Journal of International Studies* 3, no. 3 (Oct. 1977): 331–39; Christopher Thomas, "Perceptions of India in the Foreign Press," *India International Centre Quarterly* 20, no. 1/2 (Spring–Summer 1993): 265–73.

87. Harold R. Isaac, *Scratches on Our Minds: American Images of China and India* (New York: John Day, 1958), 243–44, 249, 259, 271.

88. Interview with Hon. John Foster Dulles, in Ramachandra Guha, *India after Gandhi, The History of the World's Largest Democracy* (London: Picador, 2007), 160.

89. Albert Mayer, "The New Capital of the Punjab," Address before Convention symposium I, Urban and Regional Planning, Washington, DC, May 10, 1950. *Journal of the American Institutes of Architects* (October 1950): 166.

90. Description for an Exhibition of Photographs, Excerpt of exhibition catalogue, MA/40/13.

91. Arthur Goodfriend, *The Only War We Seek* (New York: Farrar, Straus and Young, 1951), 97.

92. John P. Lewis, *Quiet Crisis in India: Economic Development and American Policy* (Westport, CT: Greenwood Press, 1962), 252.

93. Chester B. Bowles, *Ambassador's Report* (London: Gollancz, 1954), 199.

94. Bowles, *Ambassador's Report*, 196, 201, 331.

95. Sushil Dey, "The Crisis In Community Development," *Ekistics* 10, no. 58 (August 1960): 114–16.

96. Chester B. Bowles, *Promises to Keep: My Years in Public Life, 1941–1969*, 1st ed. (New York: Harper and Row, 1971), 549.

97. Memorandum to the Prime Minister of India Nehru, 1952, Box 98, Chester Bowles Papers.

98. Chester B. Bowles, Overview of the Chester Bowles Mimeograph, March 5, 1952; The Chester Bowles mimeograph: The Indo-American Development Program: The Problems and Opportunities, Hoover Institution Archives, Stanford University, Stanford, CA.

99. Interview of S. K. Dey, Head of Community Projects Administration and Later Minister for Community Development, in Sussman, "Road from Etawah," 278.

100. Albert A. Mayer, "Americans in India," *Survey Graphic* 35 no. 3 (1947): 202–6.

101. Mayer, Marriott, and Park, *Pilot Project, India*, 313.

102. Albert A. Mayer, Community Projects and National Extension Service Projects in the U.P.: Observations and Recommendations ms. (Mayer to G. B. Pant), 1955, MA/2/13.

103. Albert A. Mayer to Tarlok Singh on the Expansion of the National Extension Service, 1955, MA/14/8.

104. Albert A. Mayer to Selected Old Colleagues, 1955, MA14/6.

105. Douglas Ensminger, Ford Foundation Program Letter, Report no. 114, June 27, 1960, Unpublished India Reports and Memos, Box 2, folder 39, Douglas Ensminger Papers, Ford Foundation Reports, Manuscripts and Archives, Yale University Library, New Haven, CT.

106. Douglas Ensminger, The Research-Cum-Action Program in Environmental Sanitation: Ford Foundation Program Letter, Report no. 110, March 28, 1960, Unpublished India Reports and Memos; Box 1, Douglas Ensminger Papers, Ford Foundation Reports, Manuscripts and Archives, Yale University Library, New Haven, CT.

107. Douglas Ensminger, interview with Gerald Sussman, January 13, 1974, in Sussman, "Road from Etawa," 179.

108. Bowles to Senator Brian McMahon, January 3, 1952, Box 81, Bowles Papers.

109. G. Weller, "Farm Support for India: A New US Bureau," *San Francisco Chronicle*, January 3, 1952, 15.

110. "Community Project Slow Progress, Programme Bodies Frank Report," *Statesman*, november 10, 1954; "American Research in India," *National Herald* (March 21, 1955; "'Leakage' of US Expert's Questionnaire, Indian Research Officer Forced to Resign," *Times of India*, March 26, 1955; "Social Science Research, Need for Making Use of Indian Experts," *National Herald*, March 17, 1955; "University Professor against Social Science Research in India by Foreign Experts," *National Herald*, March 17, 1955; "Will You Vote for Americans!," *National Herald*, March 14, 1955; David Herlihy and Samuel K. Cohn Jr., *The Black Death and the Transformation of the West* (Cambridge, MA: Harvard University Press, 1997).

111. Agricultural Production Team, Ford Foundation Report, *Report on India's Food Crisis and Steps to Meet It* (New Delhi: Government of India, Ministry of Food and Agriculture and Ministry of Community Development and Cooperation, 1959), 46.

112. M. J. Coldwell, René Dumont, and Margaret Read, *Report of a Community Development Evaluation Mission in India, 23 November 1958–3 April 1959* (New York: Ministry of Community Development and Cooperation, United Nations, 1960).

113. Garvin Karunaratne, "Failure of the Community Development Program," *Community Development Journal* 11, no. 2 (1976).

114. Nick Cullather, *The Hungry World: America's Cold War Battle against Poverty in Asia* (Cambridge, MA: Harvard University Press, 2010).

115. S. K. Dey, "Panchayati Raj in Independent India: Some Personal Reflections," in *Panchayati Raj in Karnataka Today: Its National Dimensions*, ed. George Mathew (New Delhi: Institute of Social Science, 1986), 38–39.

116. Partha Chatterjee, *A Possible India: Essays in Political Criticism* (Oxford: Oxford University Press, 1998).

117. Ministry of Community Development and Cooperation, *Main Recommendations and Conclusions* (New Delhi: Government of India, 1961), 57.

118. *Appendix to Pilot Development Projects Etawah and Gorakhpur Interim Report and Appraisal,* Dudley Trudgett Collection, India Documents 1951–55, IV.2, Environmental Design Archives, University of California, Berkeley.

119. Jawaharlal Nehru, quoted in Government of India, Planning Commission, *Report of the Team for the Study of Community Projects and National Extension Service, Vol. 1* (New Delhi: Government of India, 1957), 1.

120. Surrendra Kumar Dey, *Power to the People?: A Chronicle of India, 1947–67* (Bombay: Orient Longmans, 1969), 97.

121. T. K. N. Unnithan and K. B. Singh, *Story of Lalgarh: An Experiment in Self Help and community planning* (New Delhi: Rural Housing Wing, School of Planning and Architecture, 1960), 201, 178.

122. Unnithan, *Story of Lalgarh*, 185.

5. Appropriating Global Norms of Austerity

1. Ministry of Commerce and Industry, *Design for Industry* (New Delhi: Government of India, Ministry of Commerce and Industry, 1960).

2. India Central Small Industries Organisation, *Furniture* (New Delhi: Delhi Manager of Publications, 1962); India Central Small Industries Organisation and India Office of the Development of Commissioner, *Steel Furniture* (New Delhi: Delhi Manager of Publications, 1963); India Central Small Industries Organisation and India Office of the Development of Commissioner, *Wooden Furniture (Northern Region)* (New Delhi: Delhi Manager of Publications, 1963); India Central Small Industries Organisation and India Office of the Development of Commissioner, *Furniture, Doors and Windows* (New Delhi: Delhi Manager of Publications, 1964); India Office of the Development of Commissioner, *Model Carpentry Workshop* (New Delhi: India Central Small Industries Organisation, 1958).

3. India Central Small Industries Organisation, "Small Scale Industry Impact Scheme No. 117" (New Delhi: Ministry of Commerce and Industry, Government of India, 1962).

4. Anand, *Simple Furniture*.

5. S. Bahga and S. Bahga, *Le Corbusier and Pierre Jeanneret: Footprints on the Sands of Indian Architecture* (New Delhi: Galgotia, 2000), 87.

6. Kirsch and Kirsch, *The Weissenhofsiedlung*.

7. Farhan Karim, "Modernity Transfers: The MoMa and Postcolonial India," in *Third World Modernism: Architecture Development and Identity*, ed. Duanfang Lu (New York: Routledge, 2011).

8. The content of the exhibition was published as an edited book, Monroe Wheeler, ed., *Textiles and Ornaments of India: A Selection of Designs* (New York: Museum of Modern Art, 1956). For a discussion of this exhibition, see Karim, "Modernity Transfers," 189–210; Saloni Mathur, "Charles and Ray Eames in India," *Art Journal* 70 no. 1 (2011): 34–53.

9. "Textiles and Ornamental Arts of India on View at Museum of Modern Art," Museum of Modern Art, 1955, www.moma.org.

10. Wheeler, *Textiles and Ornaments of India*, 11.

11. Museum of Modern Art, *Design Today in America and Europe: Publicity*, International

Council and International Program Records, VII.SP-ICE-17–57.2: Press Release, The Museum of Modern Art Archives (hereafter IC/IP, VII.SP-ICE-17–57.2, MoMA Archives, NY.

12. Wheeler, *Textiles and Ornaments of India,* 11.

13. Abigail S. McGowan, "All That Is Rare, Characteristic or Beautiful': Design and the Defense of Tradition in Colonial Idea, 1851–1903," *Journal of Material Culture* 10, no. 3 (2005): 263–87.

14. Kate P. Kent, "The Girard Foundation Collection at the Museum of International Folk Art," *African Arts* 17, no. 1 (1953): 60–64, 88.

15. Museum of Modern Art, *Design Today in America and Europe: Publicity,* IC/IP, VII.SP-ICE-17–57.2, MoMA Archives, NY.

16. IC/IP, VII.SP-ICE-17–57.2, MoMA Archives, NY.

17. IC/IP, VII.SP-ICE-17–57.2, MoMA Archives, NY.

18. "India's Chances in the German Market, Indian Ties with Germany," *Times of India,* September 30, 1959, 30.

19. Monroe Wheeler, *Textile and Ornamental Arts of India* (New York: Arno Press for MoMA, NY, 1956).

20. Several articles that appeared in the *Art in Industry* magazine expressed the view that the Indian sari would soon find its place among global female dress. Subrata Banerjee, "Indian Influence on Western Design," *Art in Industry* 3, no. 1 (1952); Dinesh Dutt, "Traditional Design and Their Modern Implication," *Art in Industry* 2, no. 1 (1950); D. P. Ghosh, "Industrial Application of Ancient Orissan Design," *Art in Industry* 3, no. 1 (1952); Ajit Mokerjee, "Sari Its Role in International Publicity and Contemporary Fashion," *Art in Industry* 2, no. 1 (1950).

21. S. Mansingh, "India and the United States," In *Indian Foreign Policy: The Nehru Years,* ed. B. R. Nanda (New Delhi: Radiant Publishers, Nehru Memorial Museum and Library, 1976), 156.

22. Isaacs, *Scratches on Our Minds;* Arthur Robinoff, "Incompatible Objectives and Short-sighted Politics," in *US-Indian Strategic Cooperation into the 21st Century, More Than Words,* ed. S. Ganguly, B. Shoup, and A. Scobell (New York: Routledge, 2006), 46.

23. US Department of State, *The Subcontinent of South Asia* (Washington, DC: Department of State, 1959), cited in Robinoff, "Incompatible Objectives," 43.

24. R. Guha, *India after Gandhi: The History of the World's Largest Democracy* (Delhi: Harper Perennial, 2008).

25. Charles Eames and Ray Eames, "India Report," *Design Issues* 7, no. 2 (Spring 1991): 63–75.

26. Eames and Eames, "India Report," 63.

27. Charles Eames and Ray Eames, *Mathematica: A World of Numbers . . . and Beyond* Exhibition (Los Angeles: California Museum of Science and Industry, 1961); Charles Eames and Ray Eames, dirs. *Banana Leaf: Something about Transformation and Rediscovery* (unfinished film, Los Angeles: Eames Office, 1972).

28. John Neuhart, Charles Eames, and Ray Eames, *Eames Design: The Work of the Office of Charles and Ray Eames* (London: Thames and Hudson, 1989), xx.

29. Joseph S. Alter, "The *Sannyasi* and the Indian Wrestler: The Anatomy of a Relationship," *American Ethnologist* 19, no. 2 (1992): 317–36.

30. Kenneth Brecher, "The Girard Collection: More Is More," *Los Angeles Times,* December 12, 1982; Kate P. Kent, "The Girard Foundation Collection at the Museum of International Folk Art," *African Arts* 17, no. 1 (1983): 60–64, 88; Michel Monteaux and Henry Glassie, *The Spirit of Folk Art: The Girard Collection at the Museum of International Folk Art* (New York: Harry N. Abrams, 1989); Todd Oldham and Kiera Coffee, *Alexander Girard* (Pasadena, CA: Ammo Books, 2011).

31. Pat Kirkham, "Humanizing Modernism: The Crafts, 'Functioning Decoration' and the Eameses," *Journal of Design History* 11, no. 1 (1998): 15–29.

32. Pat Kirkham, "Humanizing Modernism: The Crafts, 'Functioning Decoration' and the Eameses," *Journal of Design History* 11, no. 1 (1998): 15–29.

33. Dan McMasters, "The Luminous 'Landscape' of Alexander Girard," *Los Angeles Times*, november 3, 1974, 45; Robert Mayer, "The Grand Master of Santa Fe," *Metropolitan Home*, December 1982, 59–68.

34. Pat Kirkham, *Charles and Ray Eames: Designers of the Twentieth Century*. (Cambridge, MA: MIT Press, 1998), 201.

35. Kirkham, *Charles and Ray Eames*, 371.

36. Indian Office of the Development Commissioner (Small Scale Industry), *Steel Furniture* (New Delhi: Indian Office of the Development Commissioner, 1959).

37. "A Commentary upon the 1946 Art in Industry Exhibition Organized by the Indian Institute of Art in Industry," *Art in Industry* 1, no. 2 (1947): 31–49.

38. "Germany Wants to Import More from India," *Times of India*, September 30, 1959.

39. McGowan, "'All That Is Rare,'" 263–87.

40. John Elderfield, ed., *The Museum of Modern Art in Mid-century at Home and Abroad* (New York: Museum of Modern Art, 1994), 138.

41. Arthur Drexler and Greta Daniel, "Introduction," in *Twentieth Century Design: From the Collection of the Museum of Modern Art, New York* (New York: Museum of Modern Art, 1959).

42. Museum of Modern Art, "Design Today in America and Europe: Catalogue," 1959 (Museum of Modern Art Archives, New York, International Program Exhibition Records, VII. SP-ICE-17–57.8, Indian tour).

43. Robinoff, "Incompatible Objectives," 43.

44. Museum of Modern Art, "Design Today in America and Europe: Publicity."

45. "Design Show Opens in India," *Industrial Design*, March 6, 1959, 14.

46. Jack Masey and Conway L. Morgan, *Cold War Confrontations: US Exhibitions and Their Role in the Cultural Cold War* (Baden, Switzerland: Lars Müller, 2008), 58–67. See esp. "A Splendid Pleasure Dome."

47. Museum of Modern Arts, "Textile and Ornamental Arts of India" exhibition, New York, 1955 (Museum of Modern Art Archives, New York, International Program Exhibition Records).

48. Museum of Modern Arts, "Textile and Ornamental Arts of India."

49. Kristin Hoganson, "Cosmopolitan Domesticity: Importing the American Dream, 1865–1920," *American Historical Review* 107, no. 1 (2002): 55–83.

50. Peter D. Bell, "The Ford Foundation as a Transnational Actor," *International Organization* 25, no. 3 (1971): 468.

51. Kathleen D. McCarthy, "From Cold War to Cultural Development: The International Cultural Activities of the Ford Foundation, 1950–1980," "Philanthropy, Patronage, Politics," special issue, *Daedalus* 116, no. 1 (1987): 93–117.

52. Museum of Modern Art, "Design Today in America and Europe."

53. Museum of Modern Art, "Design Today in America and Europe."

54. McCarthy, "From Cold War to Cultural Development," 93–117.

55. Museum of Modern Art, "Design Today in America and Europe."

56. Galen Cranz, *The Chair: Rethinking Culture, Body, and Design* (New York: Norton, 2000), 79–89.

57. Museum of Modern Art, "Design Today in America and Europe," 10.

58. Museum of Modern Art, "Design Today in America and Europe," 9.

59. John E. Crowley, *The Invention of Comfort: Sensibilities and Design in Early Modern Britain and Early America* (Baltimore: Johns Hopkins University Press, 2001), 292.

60. Kaufmann, *What Is Modern Interior Design?*, 5.

61. Kaufmann, *What Is Modern Interior Design?*, 4.

62. Pupul Jayakar, "Textile and Ornamental Arts of India" exhibition catalogue supplement, IC/IP, VI.ICE-D-5–54.2, MoMA Archives, NY.

63. Museum of Modern Art, "Design Today in America and Europe."

64. Museum of Modern Art, "Design Today in America and Europe," 9.

65. Museum of Modern Art, "Design Today in America and Europe."

66. Lisa N. Trivedi, *Clothing Gandhi's Nation: Homespun and Modern India* (Bloomington: Indiana University Press, 2007), 16–17.

67. Peter H. Hoffenberg, *An Empire on Display: English, Indian, and Australian Exhibitions from the Crystal Palace to the Great War* (Berkeley: University of California Press, 2001), 166–71.

68. Barringer, *Men at Work*, 8.

69. Andrzej Piotrowski, "The Spectacle of Architectural Discourses," *Architectural Theory Review* 13, no. 2 (2008): 130–44.

70. Abigail S. McGowan, *Crafting the Nation in Colonial India* (New York: Palgrave Macmillan, 2009), 187–91.

71. Museum of Modern Art, "Design Today in America and Europe."

72. Museum of Modern Art, "Design Today in America and Europe," 6.

73. Museum of Modern Art, "Design Today in America and Europe."

74. Guha, *India after Gandhi*, 682.

75. Deshpande, *Modern Ideal Homes for India*, 34. See also Raghunath S. Deshpande, *Cheap and Healthy Homes for the Middle Classes of India* (Poona: Aryabhushan Press, 1935).

76. *Times of India*, December 13, 1959; Ruth Widmayer, "Equality Is the Basis of U.S. Homes," *Indian Times*, December 13, 1959. This composite bed holding a radio, TV, bedside lamp, and breakfast table was exhibited by Slumberland in London 1959. The *Times of India* published this as "news" as the recent Western progress on the domestic front, "Bed of the Future," *Times of India*, March 3, 1959, as cited in Robert Mayer, "The Grand Master of Santa Fe," *Metropolitan Home* (December 1982): 64.

77. *Times of India*, December 13, 1959.

78. Museum of Modern Art, "Design Today in America and Europe: Catalogue."

79. Wheeler, *Textiles and Ornaments of India*, 11.

80. Pupul Jayakar, "Charles Eames, 1907–1978: A Personal Tribute," *Designfolio (Ahmedabad)*, January 2, 1979; Saloni Mathur, "Charles and Ray Eames in India," *Art Journal* 70, no. 1 (2011): 34–53.

81. Jayakar, "Charles Eames."

82. Ernst Scheidegger and Vilhelm Wohlert, *Proposals for an Institute of Design Training, Service and Research* (New Delhi: Ford Foundation, 1960).

83. Domar, "Capital Expansion, Rate of Growth, and Employment," 137–47.

84. Ashoke Chatterjee, R. K. Bannerjee, and Neera Seth, "40 Years of NID," unpublished report, 1990.

85. Sherry Blankenship, "Flying a Kite: NID Report from and American Visitor," *Design Issues* 21, no. 4 (2005): 25; Sherry Blankenship, "Outside the Center: Defining Who We Are," *Design Issues* 21, no. 1 (2005): 24–31; Katerina Rüedi, *Bauhaus Dream-House: Modernity and Globalization* (New York: Routledge, 2010), 149–52.

86. Saloni Mathur, "Charles and Ray Eames in India," *Art Journal* 70, no. 1 (2011): 49.

87. Stanley Abercrombie, *George Nelson: The Design of the Modern Design* (Cambridge, MA: MIT Press, 2000). For a discussion of the midcentury boom of consumerism see Regina Lee Blaszczyk, *American Consumer Society, 1865–2005: From Hearth to HDTV* (Wheeling, IL: Harlan Davidson, 2009).

88. Samiksha Kothari and Prerak Mehta, "Sudhakar Nadkarni: Interview," *Design in India* (Mumbai, December 2010), www.designinindia.net.

89. Inge Scholl and Dorothee Sölle, *The White Rose: Munich, 1942–1943*, trans. Arthur R. Schultz, 2nd ed. (Hanover, NH: Wesleyan University Press, 1983).

90. Paula Andersen, "Vermittler zwischen Zivilisation und Kultur" (Intermediary between civilization and culture), *Frankfurter Allgemeine Zeitung*, October 4, 1955.

91. Andreas Schüler, *Erfindergeist und Technikkritik: Der Beitrag Amerikas zur Modernisierung und die Technikdebatte seit 1900* (Ingenuity and technology criticism: The American contribution to the debate on modernization and technology since 1900) (Stuttgart: Franz Steiner, 1990); Walter H. Pehle and Peter Sillem, eds., *Wissenschaft im Geteilten Deutschland: Restauration oder Neubeginn nach 1945?* (Science in divided Germany: Restoration or New Beginning after 1945?) (Frankfurt: Fischer, 1992).

92. Quoted in Paul Betts, "Science, Semiotics and Society: The Ulm Hochschule für Gestaltung in Retrospect," *Design Issues* 14, no. 2 (1998): 70.

93. Paul Betts, "The Bauhaus as Cold-War Legend: West German Modernism Revisited," *German Politics and Society* 14, no. 2 (1996): 75–100.

94. Max Bill, "The Bauhaus Idea from Weimar to Ulm," in *Architects Yearbook 5*, ed. Morton Shand (London: Elek, 1953), 29–32.

95. Max Bill was a former Bauhaus disciple and the president of the Swiss Werkbund as first rector of Ulm. Max Bill, "Schönheit Aus Funktion und Als Funktion" (For Beauty and Function as a Function), *Das Werk* 36, no. 8 (1949): 272–74; Martin Krampen and Günther Hörmann, *Die Hochschule für Gestaltung Ulm: Anfänge Eines Projektes der Unnachgiebigen Moderne* (The Ulm School of Design: Beginnings of a Project of Unyielding Modernity) (Berlin: Ernst and Sohn, 2003).

96. Hartmut Seeling, "Geschichte der HfG Ulm, 1953–1968" (The Story of the Design Institute in Ulm) (PhD diss., University of Cologne, Cologne, West Germany, 1985).

97. Heiner Jacob, "HfG Ulm: A Personal View of an Experiment in Democracy and Design Education," *Journal of Design History* 1, no. 3/4 (1988): 221–34.

98. Eva von Seckendorff, *Die Hochschule für Gestaltung in Ulm: Gründung (1949–1953) und* Ära *Max Bill (1953–1957)* (College of Design in Ulm: Foundation Era [1949–1953], and Max Bill [1953–1957]) (Marburg, Germany: Jonas, 1989), 128.

99. Martin Jay, ed., *The Dialectical Imagination: A History of the Frankfurt School and the Institute of Social Research, 1923–1950*, vol. 10, Weimar and Now: German Cultural Criticism (Berkeley: University of California Press, 1996), 282; Thomas Alan Schwartz, *America's Germany: John J. McCloy and the Federal Republic of Germany* (Cambridge, MA: Harvard University Press, 1991), 156–84; Inge Scholl, April 17, 1952, cited in von Seckendorff, *Die Hochschule*, 60. The phrase "spiritual Marshall Plan" was first used by Aicher in his 1948 manuscript "Wer trug der Widerstand?" (Who was the resistance?) cited in Betts, *Authority of Everyday Objects*, 144.

100. Betts, *Authority of Everyday Objects*, 151.

101. Betts, "Science, Semiotics and Society," 73.

102. Jacob, "HfG Ulm," 229.

103. For a view on Ulm's uneasy relations with the profit-driven market, see Abram Moles, "Functionalism in Crisis," *Ulm* 19/20 (August 1967): 24–25.

104. Tomás Maldonado, "Neue Entwicklungen in der Industrie und Die Ausbildung des Produktgestalters" (New Developments in Industry and the Training of Designers)," *Ulm* 2 (October 1958): 33–34.

105. Tomás Maldonado, "Communication and Semiotics in the Trilingual Publication," *Ulm* 5 (July 1959): 69–78.

106. Maldonado, "Communication and Semiotics," 73.

107. Tomás Maldonado, "New Developments in Industry and the Training of Designers," *Architects' Yearbook 9* (London: Elek, 1960): 154.

108. Maldonado, "Neue Entwicklungen," 40.

109. Tomás Maldonado, "Colloquium Con Maldonado e Otl" (Colloquium with Maldonado and Otl), *Design-Italia* 3 (September 1972): 32, as cited in Kenneth Frampton, "Apropos Ulm: Curriculum and Critical Theory," *Oppositions* 3 (May 1974): 17–36.

110. Frampton, "Apropos Ulm," 25.

111. Claude Schnaidt, "Architecture and Political Commitment," *Ulm*, no. 19/20 (August 1967): 34.

112. Martin Krampen and Horst Kächele, *Umwelt, Gestaltung und Persönlichkeit: Reflexionen 30 Jahre nach Gründung der Ulmer Hochschule für Gestaltung* (Environment, design and personality: Reflections 30 years after the founding of the Ulm School of Design) (Hildesheim, Germany: Georg Olms, 1986), 986.

113. Banerjee, "40 Years of NID."

114. Werner Blaser and Hans Gugelot, *Element, System, Möbel: Wege von der Architektur zum Design* (Element, system, furniture: From architecture to design ways) (Stuttgart: Deutsche Verlags-Anstalt, 1984), 57; Hans Gugelot, *System-Design Bahnbrecher* [System-design pioneer]: Hans Gugelot, 1920–1965: The New Collection from the State Museum for Applied Art, Munich, April–June 1984, ed. Otl Aicher and Hans Wichmann (Munich: Die Sammlung [The collection], 1984), 53.

115. Bimal Patel and Ismet Khambatta, "Gajanan Upadhyaya: Furniture Designer," , unpublished monograph (Ahmedabad, India: HCP Design and Project Management and TDW Furniture, 2009); M. P. Ranjan, "Gajanan Upadhyaya: A New Monograph and Exhibition of Furniture Designs," *Design for India*, June 20, 2009.

116. John G. Sommer to Charles and Ray Eames, assistant to the representative, June 18, 1970, Charles Eames and Ray Eames Papers, box 44, folder 2, Library of Congress (hereafter Eames Papers).

117. National Institute of Design, unsigned letter to Harry Wilhelm, Eames Papers, box 44, folder 2.

118. H. Y. Sharada Prasad, prime minister's secretariat, to Charles Eames, August 25, 1972; Eames Papers, box 44, folder 2.

119. Satyavathi Muthu and Chitra Ganapati, "Designing and Evaluating a Washing Machine," *Indian Journal of Home Science* 8, no. 2 (1974): 68–73; Jagjit Kaur Dhesi, R. N. Kaul and Sashi Jain, "Energy Expenditure While Sweeping with different types of brooms held in different posture," *Indian Journal of Home Science* 9, no. 2 (1975): 46–54; Jaggit Kaur Dhesi and Francille Maloch Firebaugh, "The effect of body positions on angels of body bend during chapati making at the ground-level kitchen," *Indian Journal of Home Science* 6, no. 1 (1972): 10–16.

120. J. S. Sandhu, "Design Education in India;" September 1970, Eames Papers, box 44, folder 2.

121. Harry E. Wilhelm, Ford Foundation representative, to Ray Eames, June 1, 1971, Eames Papers, box 44, folder 2.

122. H. Alpay Er, "Development Patterns of Industrial Design in the Third World: A Conceptual Model for Newly Industrialized Countries," *Journal of Design History* 10, no. 3 (1997): 293–307; Sulfikar Amir, "Rethinking Design Policy in the Third World," *Design Issues* 20, no. 4 (2004): 68–75; Karen Fiss, "Design in a Global Context: Envisioning Postcolonial and Transnational Possibilities," *Design Issues* 25, no. 3 (2009): 3–10.

123. Saloni Mathur, "Charles and Ray Eames in India," *Art Journal* 70, no. 1 (2011): 50.

124. Srivastava Balaram, *Thinking Design* (Delhi: Sage, 2011); Ashoke Chatterjee, "The DNA of Design for Development," Indus Valley School of Art and Design, n.d.

125. Lalit Kumar Das, "Culture as the Designer," *Design Issues* 21, no. 4 (2005): 68–77.

126. Michael Erlhoff, "Between Utopia and Reaction," in *Ulm Design: The Morality of Objects: Hochschule für Gestaltung Ulm, 1953–1968*, ed. H. Lindinger (Cambridge, MA: MIT Press, 1991), 38–50.

127. Tomás Maldonado, "Design Education," in *The Education of Vision*, ed. G. Kepes (New York: George Braziller, 1965), 132.

128. Ashoke Chatterjee, "Design in India: The Experience of Transition," *Design Issues* 21, no. 4 (2005): 6.

Conclusion

1. *Housing for the People,* directed and edited by Pratap Parmar (Government of India: A Films Division Production, 1972).

2. Asha Kapur Mehta and Trishna Satpathy, "Escaping Poverty: The Ralegan Siddhi Case," Working Paper no. 119, Indian Institute of Public Administration, 2008.

3. Shahaji Phand and H. P. S. Arya, "Adarsh Gaon Yojana—Way Towards Gandhi's Dream Village: Self Sufficient, Prosperous and Peaceful," *Journal of Rural Development* 26, no. 2 (1998): 207–25.

4. Uday Mehta, "The Impact of Panchayati Raj on Rural India," in *Rural Sociology in India,* ed. Akshayakumar Ramanlal Desia (Bombay: Popular Prakashan, 1969).

5. Gadgil and Ramachandra Guha, *Ecology and Equity: The Use and Abuse of Nature in Contemporary India* (New York: Routledge, 1995), 118–21.

6. A concise history of Hazare's anticorruption movement is available on Hazare's official website, www.annahazare.org.

7. By "post-political" I suggest Slavoj Zizek, Chantal Mouffe, and Jacques Rancière. See Slavoj Zizek, "Carl Schmitt in the Age of Post Politics," in *The Challenge of Carl Schmitt,* ed. Chantal Mouffe (London: Verso, 1999); Slavoj Zizek, *The Ticklish Subject: The Absent Centre of Political Ontology* (London: Verso, 2009).

8. See Arif Dirlik, *The Postcolonial Aura: Third World Criticism in the Age of Global Capitalism* (Boulder, CO: Westview Press, 1997).

9. Felix Driver, "Global Times and Spaces: On Historicizing the Global," *History Workshop Journal* 64, no. 1 (2007): 321–22; Felix Driver and Raphael Samuel, "Rethinking the Idea of Place," Editorial, *History Workshop Journal* 39, no. 1 (1995): v–vii; Alan Lester, "Imperial Circuits and Networks: Geographies of the British Empire," *History Compass* 4, no. 1 (2006): 124–41; Doreen B. Massey, *For Space* (London: Sage, 2005); Peter Stearns, "Part I: Social History and Spatial Scope," *Journal of Social History* 39, no. 3 (2006): 613–14.

10. Andrew E. G. Jonas, "Pro Scale: Further Reflections on the 'Scale Debate' in Human Geography," *Transactions of the Institute of British Geographers* 31, no. 3 (2006): 399–406.

11. Robert N. Bellah, a prominent disciple of Parson, argued that in Japan the modernization process took a very different course than the anticipated Western model. Robert N. Bellah, *Tokugawa Religion: The Cultural Roots of Modern Japan* (New York: Free Press, 1985).

12. Bonnie H. Erickson, "The Context Challenge: Generalizing Social Capital Processes across Two Different Settings," in *Contexts of Social Capital: Social Networks in Markets, Communities, and Families,* ed. Ray-May Hsung, Nan Lin, and Ronald Breiger (New York: Routledge, 2009), 93–114.

13. Nan Lin, *Social Capital: A Theory of Social Structure and Action* (Cambridge, UK: Cambridge University Press, 2001), 12.

BIBLIOGRAPHY

Archival Sources

Archives of the College of Environment Design, University of California, Berkeley
Dudley Trudgett Collection
Joseph Allen Stein Collection

Archives of the United Nation, New York

Constantinos A. Doxiadis Archives, Benaki Museum, Athens

Library of Congress, Washington, DC
Eames Collection

Library of the National Archives of India, Delhi

Library of the National Institute of Design, Ahmedabad

Maharashtra State Archives, Mumbai
General Department files

Museum of Modern Art Library and Archives, New York
International Council and International Program Records

National Archives of India, Delhi

Rare Collection Library of the Associated Cement Companies Limited, Mumbai

Rare Collection National Library of India, Kolkata

Royal Institute of British Architects Library Drawings and Archives Collection, London
Jaqueline Tyrwhitt Papers

University of Chicago Library, Special Collection, Chicago
Albert Mayer Collection

Yale University Library Manuscripts and Archives, New Haven
Chester Bowles Papers
Douglas Ensminger Papers

Reports, Catalogues, Unpublished Manuscripts, and Films

All India Congress Committee. *The Seventh Year of Freedom, August 1953–August 1954*. New Delhi: All India Congress Committee, 1954.

Anand, D. N. *Simple Furniture and Interior Decoration*. New Delhi: Directorate of Extension and Training, Ministry of Food and Agriculture, 1959.

Associated Cement Companies. *Our Villages of Tomorrow: How Shall We Build Them?* Bombay: Associated Cement Companies, 1949.

Bhattacharya, Sabyasachi. "The Labouring Poor and Their Notion of Poverty: Late 19th and Early 20th Century Bengal." Revised version of a lecture delivered at V. V. Giri National Labour Institute at the inauguration of the Integrated Labour History Research Programme on July 24, 1998. Uttar Pradesh: V. V. Giri National Labour Institute, 1998. www.indialabourarchives.org/.

Bombay Labour Office. Moral Corruption and Congested Chawl Housing: Report on Working Class Budgets in Bombay City. Bombay: Bombay Central Press, 1924.

Bombay Labour Office. Report on an Enquiry on Middle Class Unemployment in the Bombay Presidency. Bombay: Government Central Press, 1927.

Bueneman, Ervan. *Special Report on Techniques of Aided Self-Help Housing: Some Examples of US and Overseas Experience*. Washington, DC: Department of Housing and Urban Development, Office of International Affairs, 1973.

Burnett-Hurst, Alexander R. *Labour and Housing in Bombay: A Study in the Economic Conditions of the Wage-Earning Classes in Bombay*. London: P. S. King, 1925.

Burroughs, Wynn St. John. *Thoughts on House and Land Improvement and Homesteads for the Native Poor*. Calcutta: Stanhope Press, 1885.

Burroughs, Wynn St. John. *A Difficult Problem Solved: Shewing What Sanitation Is, the Evils Arising from a Want of It, and the Means Necessary to Remove Them, with Remarks on Urban Improvements—Moral, Social and Physical*. Calcutta: Stanhope Press, 1886.

Campbell, George. *Modern India: A Sketch of the System of Civil Government to which Is Prefaced Some Account of the Natives and Native Institutions*. London: J. Murray, 1852.

Chatterjee, Ashoke. "The DNA of Design for Development." Convocation address, Indus Valley School of Art and Design, Karachi, 2005.

Concrete Association of India. *40 Designs for Low Cost Housing*. Bombay: Concrete Association of India, 1952.

Council for Research on Housing Construction. Housing Standards and Statistics: The Second Report of the Council for Research on Housing Construction. London: P. S. King and Son, 1935.

Crane, Jacob L. "Improvement of Shelter and Home Environment." Paper presented at the West Indian Housing Conference, 1966.

Eames, Charles, and Ray Eames. "The Eames Report April 1958." *Design Issues* 7, no. 2 (1991): 63–75.

Eames, Charles, and Ray Eames. *Mathematica: A World of Numbers . . . and Beyond*. Exhibition. Los Angeles: California Museum of Science and Industry, 1961.

Eames, Charles, and Ray Eames, dirs. *Banana Leaf: Something about Transformation and Rediscovery*. Film (unfinished). Los Angeles: Eames Office, 1972.

Eckbo, Garrett I., Robert N. Royston, and Suzanne B. Riess. "Landscape Architecture: The Profession in California, 1935–1940," and "Telesis: Oral History Transcript 1993." Unpublished manuscript, Berkeley: Regional Oral History Office, Bancroft Library.

Government of Bombay. Report of the Special Advisory Committee on the Industrial Housing Scheme. Bombay: Government Central Press, 1927.

India Central Small Industries Organisation. "Small Scale Industry Impact Scheme No. 117." New Delhi: Ministry of Commerce and Industry, Government of India, 1962.

International Federation for Housing and Town Planning. Proceedings of the South East Asia Regional Conference, New Delhi, February 1–7, 1954. New Delhi: United Nations, 1957.

Jain, Nidhi. "Connection between Spirituality and Sustainable Development." Master's thesis, University of Calgary, Alberta, Canada, 2001.

Kaji, H. L. "Housing Conditions among the Lower Middle Class in Bombay (South)." *Local Self-Government Gazette* 11, no. 2 (1925): 105–10.

Kissan, B. W. *Report of Town Planning Enactments in Germany*. Bombay: Government Central Press, 1913.

Kothari, Samiksha, and Mehta Prerak. "Sudhakar Nadkarni: Interview." *Design in India* (December 2010). www.designinindia.net.

Lewin, A Chris. *Housing Co-operatives in Developing Countries: A Manual for Self-Help in Low Cost Housing Schemes*. New York: Intermediate Technology Publications, 1981.

Maddipati, Venugopal. "Selfsame Spaces: Gandhi, Architecture and Allusions in Twentieth Century India." PhD diss., University of Minnesota, Minneapolis, 2011.

Maden, James, and Albert de Bois Shrosbree. *Calcutta Improvement Trust: City and Suburban Main Road Projects*. Calcutta: Calcutta Improvement Trust, 1913.

Malik, M. L. *Guide to Chandigarh*. Chandigarh: Navjivan News Agency, 1968.

Mass Observation. Home Propaganda: A Report Prepared by Mass Observation for the Advertising Service Guild. London: John Murray for the ASG, 1941.

Mass Observation. An Enquiry into People's Homes: A Report Prepared by Mass Observation for the Advertising Service Guild. London: John Murray for the ASG, 1943.

Mehta, Asha Kapur, and Trishna Satpathy. *Escaping Poverty: The Ralegan Siddhi Case*. Manchester: Chronic Poverty Research Centre, 2008.

Merrill, Dennis. "Bread and the Ballot: The United States and India's Economic Development, 1947–1961." PhD diss., University of Connecticut, Storrs, 1986.

Michael, L. W. *The History of the Municipal Corporation of the City of Bombay*. Bombay: Union Press, 1902.

Middleton, George Frederick. *Earth-Wall Construction: Pisé or Rammed Earth, Adobe or Puddled Earth, Stabilized Earth*. Revised ed. Sydney: Department of Works and Housing, Commonwealth Experimental Building Station, 1956.

Middleton, George Frederick and Lawrence Maxwell Schneider. *Earth-Wall Construction*. Department of Housing and Construction Experimental Building Station Bulletin No. 5. Canberra: Australian Government Publishing, 1976.

Middleton, George Frederick and Lawrence Maxwell Schneider. *Earth-Wall Construction*. Commonwealth Scientific and Industrial Research Organisation Bulletin No. 5. Collingwood, Australia: National Building Technology Centre, 1987.

Ministry of Commerce and Industry. *Design for Industry*. New Delhi: Ministry of Commerce and Industry, Government of India, 1960.

Mirams, Arthur E. *An Address to Members of Municipality and Citizens of Poona on the Bombay Town Planning Act of 1915*. Poona: Printed at Yeravada Prison Press, 1916.

Mirams, Arthur E. *Town Planning in Western Countries and What the Bombay Town Planning Act Means to Karachi: Being a Report of Two Lectures Delivered in Karachi*. Karachi, 1916.

Mirams, Arthur E. *Report of the Indian Industrial Commission, 1916–1918*. Calcutta: Superintendent Government Printing, 1918.

Mirams, Arthur E. *Valuation of Real Property in India with Valuation Tables*. Bombay: Maharashtra State Government Print and Stationery, 1964.

Municipal Corporation of Greater Bombay. City of Bombay Municipal Act No. III of 1888. Bombay: Printed at the *Times of India* Steam Press, 1888.

Murdoch, John. *The History of the Plague and How to Stop Its Ravages*. Madras: Christian Literature Society for India, 1898.

Muzaffar, Muhammad Ijlal. "The Periphery Within: Modern Architecture and the Making of the Modern World." PhD diss., Massachusetts Institute of Technology, Cambridge, 2007.

National Institute of Design. *40 Years of NID*. Unpublished manuscript. Ahmedabad: National Institute of Design, 1999.

Office of the Chief Adviser of Factories. *Low-Cost Housing for Industrial Workers*. New Delhi: Government of India, Ministry of Labour, 1954.

Orr, James Peter. "Light and Air in Dwellings in Bombay." A lecture delivered before the Bombay Sanitary Association, June 27, 1912. Bombay: British India Press, 1912.

Orr, James Peter. "Density of Population in Bombay." A lecture delivered before the All India Sanitary Conference in Lucknow, Bombay, September 1914. Bombay: British India Press, 1914.

Orr, James Peter. "How to Check the Growth of Unsanitary Conditions in Bombay." A lecture delivered before the All India Sanitary Conference in Lucknow, Bombay, January 1914. Bombay: British India Press, 1914.

Orr, James Peter. *Social Reform and Slum Reform*. Bombay: Times Press, 1917.

Ranjan, M. P. *Katlamara Chalo: A Design for Development Strategy, Design as a Driver for the Indian Rural Economy*. Ahmedabad: Centre for Bamboo Initiative at the National Institute of Design, 2001.

Renner, Andrea. "Housing Diplomacy: US Housing Aid to Latin America, 1949–1973." PhD diss., Columbia University, 2011.

Robinson, Harold. *Aided Self-Help Housing: Its History and Potential.* Washington, DC: US Department of Housing and Urban Development, Office of International Affairs, 1976.

Rotary Club of Bombay and Bureau of Research Publications. *Dharavi: An Economic and Social Survey of a Village in the Suburbs of Bombay.* Bombay: Tata Institute of Social Science, 1944.

Royal Commission on Labour in India. Report of the Royal Commission on Labour in India: Presented to Parliament by Command of His Majesty, June 1931. London: H. M. Stationery Office, 1931.

Scheidegger, Ernst, and Vilhelm Wohlert. *Proposals for an Institute of Design Training, Service and Research.* New Delhi: Ford Foundation, 1960.

Seeling, H. "Geschichte der HfG Ulm, 1953–1968" (The story of the Design Institute in Ulm). PhD diss., University of Cologne, 1985.

Serdari, Thomaï. "Albert Mayer, Architect and Town Planner: The Case for a Total Professional." PhD diss., Institute of Fine Arts, New York University, 2005.

Srivastava, Priyanka. "Creating a Healthy and 'Decent' Industrial Force: Health, Sanitation, and Welfare in Colonial Bombay, 1896–1945." Phd diss., University of Cincinnati, 2012.

Sundaram, Shri P. M. Proceedings, Summary of Nehru at the Inaugural Session, Government of India, Ministry of Labour, no. LC-263 no. 6. New Delhi, June 12, 1954. 11th Session of the Labour Ministers Conference, New Delhi, november 12 and 13, 1954. Ministry of Works, Housing, and Supply, File no. HI/1(104)/55 1958. National Archives of India: New Delhi, 1955.

Sussman, Gerald. "The Road from Etawah: Integrated Rural Development in India." PhD diss., University of Michigan, Ann Arbor, 1975.

Terner, I. D., and J. F. C. Turner. "Industrialized Housing: The Opportunity and the Problem in Developing Areas." US Department of Housing and Urban Affairs. Washington, DC: Office of International Affairs, 1971.

Tricamjee, Mathooradas. *Report of the Rent Enquiry Committee,* Vol. 1, part 1. Bombay: Government Central Press, 1939.

US Department of State. *The Subcontinent of South Asia.* Near and Middle Eastern Series No. 41. Washington, DC: Department of State, 1959.

Published Sources

Abercrombie, Stanley. *George Nelson: The Design of the Modern Design.* Cambridge, MA: MIT Press, 2000.

Abrams, Charles. *Man's Struggle for Shelter in an Urbanizing World.* Cambridge, MA: MIT Press, 1966.

Adarkar, Neera, ed. *The Chawls of Mumbai: Galleries of Life.* New Delhi: ImprintOne, 2011.

Adarkar, Neera. "Salaries and Wages: Girgaon and Girangaon." In *The Chawls of Mumbai: Galleries of Life,* edited by Neera Adarkar, 15–25. New Delhi: ImprintOne, 2011.

Aggarwal, Shugan Chand. *Industrial Housing in India.* 1st ed. New Delhi: Ministry of Works, Housing, and Supply, 1952.

Aguiar, Marian. *Tracking Modernity: India's Railway and the Culture of Mobility.* Minneapolis: University of Minnesota Press, 2011.

Alpay Er, H. "Development Patterns of Industrial Design in the Third World: A Conceptual Model for Newly Industrialized Countries." *Journal of Design History* 10, no. 3 (1997): 293–307.

Alter, Joseph S. "The *Sannyasi* and the Indian Wrestler: The Anatomy of a Relationship." *American Ethnologist* 19, no. 2 (1992): 317–36.

Alter, Joseph S. "Gandhi's Body, Gandhi's Truth: Nonviolence and the Biomoral Imperative of Public Health." *Journal of Asian Studies* 55, no. 2 (1996): 301–22.

Alter, Joseph S. *Gandhi's Body: Sex, Diet, and the Politics of Nationalism.* Philadelphia: University of Pennsylvania Press, 2000.

American Public Health Association. *Basic Principles of Healthful Housing*. New York: American Public Health Association, 1939.

Amir, Sulfikar."Rethinking Design Policy in the Third World." *Design Issues* 20, no. 4 (2004): 68–75.

Appadurai, Arjun, ed. *The Social Life of Things: Commodities in Cultural Perspective*. Cambridge, UK: Cambridge University Press, 1988.

Appadurai, Arjun. *Modernity at Large: Cultural Dimensions of Globalization*. Minneapolis: University of Minnesota Press, 1996.

Arnold, Caroline E. "The Bombay Improvement Trust, Bombay Millowners and the Debate Over Housing Bombay's Millworkers, 1896–1918." *Essays in Economic and Business History* 30 (2012): 105–23.

Arnold, David. *Colonizing the Body: State Medicine and Epidemic Disease in Nineteenth-Century India*. Berkeley: University of California Press, 1993.

Ashton, Mary O. "'Tomorrow Town': Patrick Geddes, Walter Gropius, and Le Corbusier." In *The City after Patrick Geddes*, edited by Volker M. Welter and James Lawson. Bern: Peter Lang, 2000.

Aspengren, Henrik C. "Sociological Knowledge and Colonial Power in Bombay around the First World War." *British Journal for the History of Science* 44, no. 4 (2011): 533–48.

Atwater, Reginald M. Editorial. *American Journal of Public Health and the Nation's Health* 39, no. 4 (1949): 525–27.

Baden-Powell, Baden Henry. *The Origin and Growth of Village Communities in India*. London: Swan Sonnenschein, 1899.

Bahga, Sarbjit, and Surinder Bahga. *Le Corbusier and Pierre Jeanneret: Footprints on the Sands of Indian Architecture*. New Delhi: Galgotia, 2000.

Bakshi, Rajni. *The Long Haul: The Bombay Textile Workers' Strike*. Bombay: BUILD Documentation Centre, 1986.

Balaram, Singanapalli. "Design Pedagogy in India: A Perspective." *Design Issues* 21, no. 4 (2005): 11–22.

Balaram, Singanapalli. *Thinking Design*. Delhi: Sage, 2011.

Banerjee, Subrata. "Indian Influence on Western Design." *Art in Industry* 3, no. 1 (1952): 16–20.

Barringer, Tim. *Men at Work: Art and Labour in Victorian Britain*. New Haven: Published for the Paul Mellon Centre for Studies in British Art by Yale University Press, 2005.

Barringer, Tim, and Tom Flynn. Introduction. In *Colonialism and the Object: Empire, Material Culture, and the Museum*, edited by T. J. Barringer and T. Flynn, 1–8. New York: Routledge, 1998.

Basu, Aparna. *Mridula Sarabhai: Rebel with a Cause*. Delhi: Oxford University Press, 2003.

Batley, Claude. "The Importance of City Planning." In *Bombay Looks Ahead: Eight Lectures*, edited by Clifford Manshardt. Bombay: D. B. Taraporevala Sons, 1934.

Batley, Claude. *Bombay's Houses and Homes*. Bombay: National Information and Publications, 1949.

Bauer, Péter Tamás. *Equality, the Third World and Economic Delusion*. Cambridge, MA: Harvard University Press, 1981.

Bay, Joo-Hwa, and Boon Lay Ong, ed. *Tropical Sustainable Architecture: Social and Environmental Dimensions*. Oxford, UK: Elsevier, 2006.

Bayly, Christopher Alan. "The Origins of Swadeshi (Home Industry): Cloth and Indian Society, 1700–1930." In *The Social Life of Things: Commodities in Cultural Perspective*, edited by Arjun Appadurai, 285–322. Cambridge, UK: Cambridge University Press, 1988.

Bell, Peter D. "The Ford Foundation as a Transnational Actor." *International Organization* 25 no. 3 (1971): 465–78. doi: 10.1017/S0020818300026266.

Bergmann, Peter. "The Specter of Amerikanisierung." In *American Culture in Europe: Interdisciplinary Perspectives*, edited by Mike-Frank G. Epitropoulos and Victor Roudometof, 67–91. Westport: Praeger, 1998.

Béteille, André. *Society and Politics in India: Essays in a Comparative Perspective*. New Delhi: Oxford University Press, 1991.

Béteille, André. "Civil Society and the Good Society, 12th Zakir Husain Memorial Lecture, February 22, 2000." New Delhi: Zakir Husain College, University of New Delhi, 2000.

Béteille, André, ed. *Anti-Utopia: Essential Writings of André Béteille*. New Delhi: Oxford University Press, 2005.

Betts, Paul. "The Bauhaus as Cold-War Legend: West German Modernism Revisited." *German Politics and Society* 14, no. 2 (1996): 75–100.

Betts, Paul. "Science, Semiotics and Society: The Ulm Hochschule für Gestaltung in Retrospect." *Design Issues* 14, no. 2 (1998): 67–82.

Betts, Paul. *The Authority of Everyday Objects: A Cultural History of West German Industrial Design*. Berkeley: University of California Press, 2004.

Bhatt, Vikram, and Peter Scriver. *After the Masters: Contemporary Indian Architecture*. Seattle: University of Washington Press, 1990.

Bill, Max. "Schönheit aus funktion und als funktion" (For beauty and function as a function). *Das Werk* 36, no. 8 (1949): 272–74.

Bill, Max. "The Bauhaus Idea from Weimar to Ulm." In *Architects Yearbook 5*, edited by M. Shand, 29–32. London: Elek, 1953.

Billimoria, H. J. "Interior Decoration." *Journal of the Indian Institute of Architects*, October 1941: 184–87.

Billimoria, H. J. "The Origin and Growth of the Indian Institute of Architects: A Brief History." *Journal of the Indian Institute of Architects* 8, no. 3 (1942): 203–10.

Bittner, Regina and Kathrin Rhomberg. "The Bauhaus in Calcutta, World Art Since 1922: On the Topicality of an Exhibition." In *The Bauhaus in Calcutta: An Encounter of the Cosmopolitan Avant-Garde*, edited by Sria Chatterjee and Boris Friedewald. Ostfildern: Hatje Cantz, 2013.

Blanchard, Jean-Marc F., edward D. Mansfield, and Norrin M. Ripsman. "Power and the Purse: Economic Statecraft, Interdependence, and National Security." In *Power and the Purse: Economic Statecraft, Interdependence and National Security*, edited by Jean-Marc F. Blanchard, edward D. Mansfield, and Norrin M. Ripsman, 1–14. London: Frank Cass, 2000.

Blankenship, Sherry. "Flying a Kite: NID Report from and American Visitor." *Design Issues* 21 no. 4 (2005): 23–31.

Blankenship, Sherry. "Outside the Center: Defining Who We Are." *Design Issues* 21, no. 1 (2005): 24–31. doi: 10.1162/0747936053103084.

Blaser, Werner, and Hans Gugelot. *Element, system möbel: Wege von der architektur zum design* (Element, system furniture: From architecture to design ways). Stuttgart: Deutsche Verlags-Anstalt, 1984.

Blunt, Alison. "Imperial Geographies of Home: British Domesticity in India, 1886–1925." *Transactions of the Institute of British Geographers* 24, no. 4 (1999): 421–40.

Bowles, Chester B. *Ambassador's Report*. London: Gollancz, 1954.

Bowles, Chester B. *Promises to Keep: My Years in Public Life, 1941–1969*. 1st ed. New York: Harper and Row, 1971.

Bramall, Rebecca. *The Cultural Politics of Austerity: Past and Present in Austere Times*. New York: Palgrave Macmillan, 2013.

Brantlinger, Patrick. "A Postindustrial Prelude to Postcolonialism: John Ruskin, William Morris, and Gandhism." *Critical Inquiry* 22, no. 3 (1996): 466–85.

Burgess, Rod. "Self Help Housing: A New Imperialist Strategy? A Critique of the Turner School." *Antipode* 9, no. 2 (1977): 50–59. doi: 10.1111/j.1467-8330.1977.tb00710.x.

Burgess, Rod. "The Limits of State Self-Help Housing Programmes." *Development and Change* 16, no. 2 (1985): 271–312. doi: 10.1111/j.1467-7660.1985.tb00211.x.

Caldwell, John. "Malthus and the Less Developed World: The Pivotal Role of India." *Population and Development Review* 24, no. 4 (1998): 675–96.

Callinicos, Alex. *Making History: Agency, Structure, and Change in Social Theory*. Leiden, The Netherlands: Brill Academic, 2009.

Caru, V. R. "The Making of a Working-Class Area: The Worli BDD Chawls." In *The Chawls of Mumbai: Galleries of Life*, edited by Neera Adarkar, 26–36. New Delhi: ImprintOne, 2011.

Chadha, Rajni. *The Emerging Consumer: A Changing Profile of the Urban Indian House-Wife and Its Implications*. New Delhi: New Age International, 1995.

Chakrabarti, Mohit. *The Gandhian Philosophy of the Spinning Wheel*. New Delhi: Concept Publishing, 2000.

Chakrabarty, Dipesh. "Adda, Calcutta: Dwelling in Modernity." *Public Culture* 11, no. 1 (1999): 109–45. doi: 10.1215/08992363.

Chakrabarty, Dipesh. *Postcolonial Thought and Historical Difference*. Princeton: Princeton University Press, 2000.

Chakrabarty, Dipesh. *Habitations of Modernity: Essays in the Wake of Subaltern Studies*. Chicago: University of Chicago Press, 2002.

Chakravarti, Anand. "The Statutory Panchayat." In *The Village India*, edited by Vandana Madan, 238–51. Delhi: Oxford University Press, 2002.

Chandavarkar, Rajnarayan. *The Origins of Industrial Capitalism in India: Business Strategies and the Working Classes in Bombay, 1900–1940*. New York: Cambridge University Press, 2002.

Chandavarkar, Rajnarayan. *History, Culture and the Indian City: Essays on Indian History*. New York: Cambridge University Press, 2009.

Chandra, Subhash. "An Evaluation of Urban Community Development in India." *Community Development Journal* 9, no. 3 (1974): 191–202. doi: 10.1093/cdj/9.3191.

Chang, Jiat-Hwee. "Building a Colonial Technoscientific Network: Tropical Architecture, Building Science and the Politics of Decolonization." In *Third World Modernism: Architecture, Development and Identity*, edited by Duanfang Lu, 211–35. New York: Routledge, 2010.

Chang, Jiat-Hwee. *A Genealogy of Tropical Architecture, Colonial Networks, Nature and Technoscience*. New York: Routledge, 2016.

Chatterjee, Ashoke. "Design in India: The Experience of Transition." *Design Issues* 21, no. 4 (2005): 4–10. doi: 10.1162/074793605774597514.

Chatterjee, Partha. *The Nation and Its Fragments: Colonial and Postcolonial Histories*. Princeton: Princeton University Press, 1993.

Chatterjee, Sris Chandra. *Modern Indian Architecture*. Calcutta: Calcutta University Press, 1930.

Chatterjee, Sris Chandra. *Magadha, Architecture and Culture*. Calcutta: Calcutta University Press, 1942.

Chatterjee, Sris Chandra. *Architects and Architecture, Then and Now: An Essay on Human Planning*. Calcutta: Calcutta University Press, 1948.

Chatterjee, Sris Chandra. *India and New Order: An Essay on Human Planning*. Calcutta: Calcutta University Press, 1949.

Chattopadhyaya, Kamaladevi. *America: The Land of Superlatives*. New York: Phoenix, 1946.

Chaudhuri, Supriya. "Modernisms in India." In *The Oxford Handbook of Modernisms*, edited by Peter Brooker, A. Gasiorek, D. Longworth, and A. Thacker, 942–60. Oxford: Oxford University Press, 2010.

Chhabria, Sheetal M. "Making the Modern Slum: Housing, Mobility, and Poverty in Bombay and Its Peripheries." PhD diss., Columbia University, 2012.

Chopra, Preeti. *Joint Enterprise: Indian Elites and the Making of the British Bombay*. Minneapolis: University of Minnesota Press, 2011.

Chouliaraki, Lilie, and Norman Fairclough. *Discourse in Late Modernity: Rethinking Critical Discourse Analysis*. Edinburgh: Polygon, 1999.

Chowdhry, Prem. *Colonial India and the Making of Empire Cinema: Image Ideology and Identity*. Manchester: Manchester University Press, 2000.

Cohn, Bernard. *Colonialism and Its Forms of knowledge*. Princeton: Princeton University Press, 1996.

Cohn, Bernard S. "Notes on the History of the Study of Indian Society and Culture." In *Structure and Change in Indian Society*, edited by Milton Singer and Bernard S. Cohn, 3–25. New Brunswick, NJ: Aldine Transaction, 2007.

Collingham, E. M. *Imperial Bodies: The Physical Experience of the Raj, c. 1800–1947*. Cambridge: Polity, 2001.

Conlon, F. F. "Industrialization and the Housing Problem in Bombay, 1850–1940." In *Changing*

South Asia: Economy and Society, edited by Kenneth Ballhatchet and David Taylor, 153–68. Hong Kong: Asian Research Service, 1984.

Coomaraswamy, Ananda K. *The Indian Craftsman*. London: Probsthain and Co. 1909.

Coser, Rose Laub. "The Complexity of Roles as a Seedbed of Individual Autonomy." In *The Idea of Social Structure: Papers in Honor of Robert K. Merton*, edited by Lewis A. Coser, 237–63. New York: Harcourt Brace Jovanovich, 1975.

Craig, Gary, Marjorie Mayo, Keith Popple, Mae Shaw, and Marilyn Taylor, eds. *The Community Development Reader: History, Themes and Issues*. Portland: Policy Press, 2011.

Cranz, Galen. *The Chair: Rethinking Culture, Body, and Design*. New York: W. W. Norton, 2000.

Crowley, John E. *The Invention of Comfort: Sensibilities and Design in Early Modern Britain and Early America*. Baltimore: Johns Hopkins University Press, 2001.

Cullather, Nick. *The Hungry World: America's Cold War Battle against Poverty in Asia*. Cambridge: Harvard University Press, 2010.

Daechsel, Markus. *Islamabad and the Politics of International Development in Pakistan*. New York: Cambridge University Press, 2015.

Dalvi, Mustansir. "'Domestic Deco' Architecture in Bombay: G. B.'s Milieu." In *Buildings That Shaped Bombay: Works of G. B. Mhatre, FRIBA, 1902–1973*, edited by K. Iyer, 14–21. Mumbai: Kamla Raheja Vidyanidhi Institute of Architecture and Environmental Studies, 2000.

Dandekar, G. P. "The Revision of Bombay Municipal Building Regulations and By-Laws with a View to Bringing Them up-to-Date." Lecture delivered to the Indian Institute of Architects. *Journal of the Indian Institute of Architects* 5, no. 4 (1939): 117–18.

Das, Lalit Kumar. "Culture as the Designer." *Design Issues* 21, no. 4 (2005): 41–53. doi: 10.1162/074793605774597523.

Das, Pradip Kumar. *Henry Irwin and the Indo Saracenic Movement Reconsidered*. India: Partridge, 2014.

Datta, Partho. "How Modern Planning Came to Calcutta." *Planning Perspectives* 28, no. 1, 139–47. doi: http://dx.doi.org/10.1080/02665433.2012.737247.

Dauer, Richard P. *A North-South Mind in an East-West World: Chester Bowles and the Making of United States Cold War Foreign Policy, 1951–1969*. Westport, CT: Praeger, 2005.

d'Auria, Viviana. "From Tropical Transitions to Ekistic Experimentation: Doxiadis Associates in Tema, Ghana." *Positions: On Modern Architecture and Urbanism/Histories and Theories*, no. 1 (2010): 40–63.

d'Auria, Viviana, Bruno De Meulder, and Kelly Shannon, eds. *Human Settlements: Formulations and (Re)Calibrations*. Amsterdam: SUN Academia, 2010.

Desai, S. V. "Housing in Relation to Redevelopment (with Particular Reference to Bombay City)." In Proceedings of the South East Asia Regional Conference New Delhi, February 1–7, 1954. New Delhi: Conference proceedings, 1954.

Deshpande, Raghunath S. *Cheap and Healthy Homes for the Middle Classes of India*. Poona: Aryabhushan Press, 1935.

Deshpande, Raghunath S. *Modern Ideal Homes for India*. Poona: United Books, 1939.

Dewey, Clive. "Images of the Village Community: A Study in Anglo-Indian Ideology." *Modern Asian Studies* 6, no. 3 (1972): 291–328.

Dhar, D. N. *Industrial Housing for the Tropics*. Bombay: Concrete Association of India, 1958.

Dinshaw, F. N. "The Cement Merger." *Indian Concrete Journal* 10, no. 1 (1936).

Domar, Evsey D. "Capital Expansion, Rate of Growth, and Employment." *Econometrica: Journal of the Econometric Society* 14, no. 2 (1946): 137–47.

Drexler, Arthur, and Greta Daniel. *Introduction to Twentieth Century Design: From the Collection of the Museum of Modern Art, New York*. New York: Museum of Modern Art, 1959.

Dube, Shyama Charan. "Cultural Factors in Rural Community Development." *Journal of Asian Studies* 16, no. 1 (1956): 19–30.

Dube, Shyama Charan. "Some Problems of Communication in Rural Community Development." *Economic Development and Cultural Change* 5, no. 2 (1957): 129–46.

Dube, Shyama Charan. *India's Changing Villages: Human Factors in Community Development*. Ithaca: Cornell University Press, 1958.

Dumont, Louis. "The 'Village Community' from Munro to Maine." In *The Village in India*, edited by V. Madan, 31–50. New Delhi: Oxford University Press, 2002.

Dutt, Dinesh. "Traditional Design and Their Modern Implication." *Art in Industry* 2, no. 1 (1950): 25–32.

Dutta, Arindam. *The Bureaucracy of Beauty: Design in the Age of Its Global Reproducibility*. New York: Routledge, 2007.

Dwivedi, Sharada, Rahul Mehrotra, and Umaima Mulla-Feroze. *Bombay: The Cities Within*. Bombay: India Book House, 1995.

Easterly, W. R. *The Elusive Quest for Growth: Economists' Adventures and Misadventures in the Tropics*. Cambridge: MIT Press, 2001.

Echenberg, Myron J. *Plague Ports: The Global Urban Impact of Bubonic Plague, 1894–1901*. New York: New York University Press, 2007.

Eisenstadt, Shmuel Noah. *Revolution and the Transformation of Societies: A Comparative Study of Civilizations*. New York: Free Press, 1978.

Eisenstadt, Shmuel Noah. *The Political Systems of Empire*. New Brunswick, NJ: Transaction Publishers, 1993.

Elderfield, J., ed. *The Museum of Modern Art in Mid-Century at Home and Abroad*. New York: Museum of Modern Art, 1994.

Engerman, David C., N. Gilman, M. H. Haefele, and M. E. Latham, eds. *Staging Growth: Modernization, Development, and the Global Cold War*. Amherst: University of Massachusetts Press, 2003.

Erlhoff, Michael. "Between Utopia and Reaction." In *Ulm Design: The Morality of Objects, Hochschule für Gestaltung Ulm, 1953–1968*, edited by H. Lindinger, 38–50. Translated by D. Britt. Cambridge, MA: MIT Press, 1991.

Evenson, norma. *The Indian Metropolis: A View toward the West*. New Haven: Yale University Press, 1989.

Fiss, Karen. "Design in a Global Context: Envisioning Postcolonial and Transnational Possibilities." *Design Issues* 25, no. 3 (2009): 3–10.

Forty, Adrian. *Objects of Desire: Design and Society since 1750*. 1st ed. London: Thames and Hudson, 1986.

Frampton, Kenneth. "Apropos Ulm: Curriculum and Critical Theory." *Oppositions*, May 3, 1974: 17–36.

Frampton, Kenneth. *Le Corbusier*. New York: Thames and Hudson, 2001.

Frankel, F. R., R. Bhargava, B. Arora, and Z. Hasan. *Transforming India: Social and Political Dynamics of Democracy*. Oxford: Oxford University Press, 2000.

Friedewald, Boris. "The Bauhaus and India: A Look Back to the Future: Building! Design! Gothic!—India!" In *The Bauhaus in Calcutta: An Encounter of Cosmopolitan Avant-Gardes*, edited by Sria Chatterjee and Boris Friedewald. Ostfildern: Hatje Cantz, 2013.

Friedman, Andrew. "The Global Postcolonial Moment and the American New Town: India Reston, Dodoma." *Journal of Urban History* 38, no. 3 (2012): 553–76.

Gadgil, Madhav, and Guha, Ramachandra. *Ecology and Equity: The Use and Abuse of Nature in Contemporary India*. New York: Routledge, 1995.

Galston, William A., and Peter H. Hoffenberg, ed. *Poverty and Morality: Religious and Secular Perspectives*. New York: Cambridge University Press, 2010.

Gandhi, Mahatma K. *India of My Dreams*. Ahmedabad, India: Navjivan, 2000.

Geddes, Patrick. *Cities in Evolution: An Introduction to the Town Planning Movement and to the Study of Civics*. London: Williams and Norgate, 1915.

Geddes, Patrick. *Patrick Geddes in India*. Edited by Jaqueline Tyrwhitt. London: Lund Humphries, 1947.

Geddes, Patrick. "Town Planning towards City Development. A Report to the Durbar of Indore, 1918 (Part II)." In Patrick Geddes, *Patrick Geddes in India*, edited by Jaqueline Tyrwhitt. London: Lund Humphries, 1947.

Gerrard, C. R. "Tradition and the Modern Architect." *Journal of the Indian Institute of Architects* 8, no. 3 (1942): 252–54.

Ghose, Rajeshwari. "Design, Development, Culture, and Cultural Legacies in Asia." *Design Issues* 6, no. 1 (1989): 31–48.

Ghosh, D. P. "Industrial Application of Ancient Orissan Design." *Art in Industry* 3, no. 1 (1952): 20–23.

Gienow-Hecht, J. C. E. "Shame on US? Academics, Cultural Transfer, and the Cold War: A Critical Review." *Diplomatic History* 24, no. 3 (2000): 465–94. doi: 10.1111/0145-2096.00227.

Gilman, Nils. *Mandarins of the Future: Modernization Theory in Cold War America.* Baltimore: Johns Hopkins University Press, 2003.

Gloag, John. *Victorian Comfort: A Social History of Design from 1830–1900.* London: Adam and Charles Black, 1961.

Glover, William J. "Objects, Models and Exemplary Works: Educating Sentiment in Colonial India." *Journal of Asian Studies* 64, no. 3 (2005): 539–66.

Glover, William J. "The Troubled Passage from 'Village Communities' to Planned New Town Developments in Mid-Twentieth-Century South Asia." *Urban History* 39, no. 1 (2012): 108–27. doi: 10.1017/S0963926811000800.

Gordon, Leonard A. "Wealth Equals Wisdom?: The Rockefeller and Ford Foundations in India." *Annals of the American Academy of Political and Social Science* 554, Special Issue: The Role of NGOs: Charity and Empowerment (November 1997): 104–16.

Goswami, M. *Producing India: From Colonial Economy to National Space.* Chicago: University of Chicago Press, 2004.

Grier, Katherine C. *Culture and Comfort: People, Parlors, and Upholstery, 1850–1930.* Amherst: University of Massachusetts Press, 1989.

Guha, Ramachandra. *India after Gandhi: The History of the World's Largest Democracy.* New York: HarperCollins, 2007.

Gupta, Dipankar. "The Anti-Utopian Liberal: An Introduction to the Works of André Béteille." In *Anti-Utopia: Essential Writings of André Béteille*, edited by A. Béteille, 1–22. New Delhi: Oxford University Press, 2005.

Gupta, Pankaj V., A. Dilwali, and R. Ganguli. *Golconde: The Introduction of Modernism in India.* New Delhi: Urban Crayon Press, 1910.

Gupta, Samita. "Sris Chandra Chatterjee: The Quest for a National Architecture." *Indian Economic and Social History Review* 28, no. 2 (1991): 187–201. doi: 10.1177/001946469102800204.

Hancock, Mary. "Home Science and the Nationalization of Domesticity in Colonial India." *Modern Asian Studies* 35, no. 4 (2001): 871–903. doi: 10.1017/S0026749X01004048.

Haque, Nadeem Ul, and Mahmood Hasan Khan. "The Economics Profession in Pakistan: A Historical Analysis." *Pakistan Development Review* 37, no. 4 (1998): 431–52.

Harris, Richard. "Slipping through the Cracks: The Origins of Aided Self-Help Housing, 1918–53." *Housing Studies* 14, no. 3 (1999): 281–309.

Harms, Hans. "Historical Perspectives on the Practice and Politics of Self-Help Housing." In *Self-Help Housing: A Critique*, edited by P. M. Ward, 17–53. London: H. W. Wilson, 1982.

Havell, E. B. *Essays on Indian Art, Industry and Education.* Madras: G. A. Natesan, 1915.

Hazareesingh, Sandip. "The Quest for Urban Citizenship: Civic Rights, Public Opinion and Colonial Resistance in Early Twentieth-Century Bombay." *Modern Asian Studies* 34 (2000): 797–829.

Hazareesingh, Sandip. "Colonial Modernism and the Flawed Paradigms of Urban Renewal: Uneven Development in Bombay, 1900–25." *Urban History* 28 no. 2 (2001): 235–55. doi: 10.1017/S096392680100205X.

Hepworth, Mike. "Privacy, Security and Respectability: The Ideal Victorian Home." In *Ideal Homes?: Social Change and Domestic Life*, edited by T. Chapman and J. L. Hockey, 17–29. London: Routledge, 1999.

Herlihy, David. *The Black Death and the Transformation of the West.* Cambridge, MA: Harvard University Press, 1997.

Herman, Arthur. *Gandhi and Churchill: The Epic Rivalry that Destroyed an Empire and Forged Our Age.* London: Hutchinson, 2008.

Hettne, Björn. *Development Theory and the Three Worlds*. New York: Wiley, 1990.

Hobsbawm, Eric J. "Introduction: Inventing Traditions." In *The Invention of Tradition*, edited by E. J. Hobsbawm and T. Ranger, 1–14. Cambridge, UK: Cambridge University Press, 1992.

Hofer, P., S. Giedion, and U. Stucky. *Hommage à Giedion: Profile seiner persönlichkeit: Schriften und dokumente von Sigfried Giedion sowie beiträge der freunde* (Profile of his personality: Writings and documents from Sigfried Giedion and contributions of friends). Stuttgart: Birkhäuser, 1971.

Hofstadter, Richard. *Social Darwinism in American Thought*. Boston: Beacon Press, 1992.

Hogan, Michael. *The Marshall Plan: America, Britain, and the Reconstruction of Western Europe, 1947–1952*. Cambridge, UK: Cambridge University Press, 1989.

Hoganson, Kristin. "Cosmopolitan Domesticity: Importing the American Dream, 1865–1920." *American Historical Review* 107, no. 1 (2002): 55–83.

Home, Robert K. *Of Planting and Planning: The Making of British Colonial Cities*. New York: Routledge, 1997.

Huber, V. A. *Die Selbsthülfe der Arbeitenden Classen Durch Wirtschaftsvereine und Innere Ansiedlung* (The Self-Help Classes of Workers by Industry Associations and Internal Settlement). Berlin: Besserache, 1848.

Hull, Mathew S. "Communities of Place, not Kind: American Technologies of Neighborhood in postcolonial Delhi." *Comparative Studies in Society and History* 53, no. 4 (2011): 757–90.

Huworth, Rachel. "Patrick Geddes Concept of Conservative Surgery." *Architectural Heritage* 11, no. 1 (2000): 37–42.

Huxley, J. *UNESCO: Its Purpose and Its Philosophy*. London: Euston Grove Press, 2010.

Hysler-Rubin, noah. *Patrick Geddes and Town Planning: A Critical View*. New York: Routledge, 2011.

Immerwahr, Daniel. *Thinking Small: The United States and the Lure of Community Development*. Cambridge, MA: Harvard University Press, 2015.

Inchbald, Michael. "Furnishing Ferozepur." *Art in Industry* 1, no. 1 (1947): 69–73.

Inden, Ronald. *Imagining India*. Indianapolis: Indiana University Press, 2001.

Isaacs, H. R. *Scratches on Our Minds: American Views of China and India*. New York: John Day, 1958.

Iyer, Kamu, ed. *Buildings That Shaped Bombay: Works of G. B. Mhatre, FRIBA, 1902–1973*. Mumbai: Kamla Raheja Vidyanidhi Institute of Architecture and Environmental Studies, 2000.

Iyer, Kamu. "G. B. Mhatre: The Man and His Work." In *Buildings That Shaped Bombay: Works of G. B. Mhatre, FRIBA, 1902–1973*, edited by Kamu Iyer, 22–43. Mumbai: Kamla Raheja Vidyanidhi Institute of Architecture and Environmental Studies, 2000.

Jacob, Heiner. "HfG Ulm: A Personal View of an Experiment in Democracy and Design Education." *Journal of Design History* 1 no. 3/4 (1988): 221–34.

Jayewardene-Pillai, S. *Imperial Conversations: Indo-Britons and the Architecture of South India*. New Delhi: Yoda Press, 2007.

Joas, Hans, and Wolfgang Knöbl. *Social Theory: Twenty Introductory Lectures*. Cambridge: Cambridge University Press, 2009.

Jodhka, Surinder S. "Nation and Village: Images of Rural India in Gandhi, Nehru and Ambedkar." *Economic and Political Weekly* 37, no. 32 (2002): 3343–53.

Johnson-Marshall, P. "Special Issue Dedicated to Mary Jaqueline Tyrwhitt: Tribute." *Ekistics* 52, no. 314/315 (1985): 16–18.

Joshi, Chitra. *Lost Worlds: Indian Labour and Its Forgotten Histories*. London: Anthem Press, 2005.

Kakridis, Andreas. "Rebuilding the Future: C. A. Doxiadis and the Greek Reconstruction Effort (1945–1950)." *Historical Review/La Revue Historique* 10 (2013): 137.

Karim, Farhan S. "Modernity Transfers: The MoMA and Post Colonial India." In *Third World Modernism: Architecture, Development and Identity*, edited by D. Lu, 189–210. New York: Routledge, 2010.

Kasturi, Poonam Bir. "Designing Freedom." *Design Issues* 21, no. 4 (2005): 68–77.

Kaufmann, edgar Jr. *What Is Modern Interior Design?* New York: Museum of Modern Art, 1953.

Kaul, Chandrika. "England and India: The Ilbert Bill, 1883, A Case Study of the Metropolitan Press." *Indian Economic and Social History Review* 30, no. 4 (1993): 413–36. doi: 10.1177/001946469303000402.

Kent, Kate P. "The Girard Foundation Collection at the Museum of International Folk Art." *African Arts* 17, no. 1 (1983): 60–64, 88.

Kepes, György. *The New Landscape in Art and Science*. Chicago: Paul Theobald, 1956.

Kerr, Ian J. "On the Move: Circulating Labour in Pre-Colonial, Colonial, and Post-Colonial India." *International Review of Social History* 51, supplement (2006): 85–109. doi: 10.1017/S0020859006002628.

Kidambi, Prashant. "Housing the Poor in a Colonial City: The Bombay Improvement Trust, 1898–1918." *Studies in History* 17, no. 1 (2001): 57–79. doi: 10.1177/025764300101700103.

Kidambi, Prashant. "'An Infection of Locality': Plague, Pythogenesis and the Poor in Bombay, c. 1896–1905." *Urban History* 31, no. 2 (2004): 249–67. doi: 10.1017/S0963926804002135.

Kidambi, Prashant. *The Making of an Indian Metropolis: Colonial Governance and Public Culture in Bombay, 1890–1920*. Aldershot, UK: Ashgate, 2007.

Kidambi, Prashant. "Consumption, Domestic Economy and the Idea of the 'Middle Class' in Late Colonial Bombay." In *Towards a History of Consumption in South Asia*, edited by D. Haynes, A. McGowan, T. Roy, and H. Yanigasawa, 108–35. Delhi: Oxford University Press, 2010.

Kinross, Robin. "Hochschule für Gestaltung Ulm: Recent Literature." *Journal of Design History* 1, no. 3/4 (1988): 249–56.

Kirkham, Pat. *Charles and Ray Eames: Designers of the Twentieth Century*. Cambridge, MA: MIT Press, 1998.

Kirkham, Pat. "Humanizing Modernism: The Crafts, 'Functioning Decoration' and the Eameses." *Journal of Design History* 11, no. 1 (1998): 15–29.

Kirsch, Karin, and Gerhard Kirsch. *The Weissenhofsiedlung: Experimental Housing Built for the Deutscher Werkbund, Stuttgart, 1927*. New York: Rizzoli, 1989.

Klarin, Tamara Bjažić. "Architect Ernest Weissmann: A 'Common' European Immigrant Story." Conference paper from Migrants as "Translators": Mediating External Influences on Post World War II Western Europe, 1945–1973, Njemačka, Hamburg, October 24–26, 2013.

Klein, Ira. "Urban Development and Death: Bombay City, 1870–1914." *Modern Asian Studies* 20, no. 4 (1986): 725–54. doi: 10.1017/S0026749X00013706.

Knight, W. Andy, ed. *Adapting the United Nations to a Postmodern Era: Lessons Learned*. New York: Palgrave Macmillan, 2001.

Koenigsberger, Otto. "Low Cost Housing in South and South-East Asia." *Journal of Environmental Planning and Management (Series 1)* 2, no. 3 (1951): 17–23.

Krampen, Martin. *Umwelt, gestaltung und persönlichkeit: Reflexionen 30 jahre nach gründung der Ulmer Hochschule für Gestaltung* (Environment, design and personality: Reflections 30 years after the founding of Ulm School of Design). Hildesheim, Germany: Georg Olms, 1986.

Krampen, Martin. *Die Hochschule für Gestaltung Ulm: Anfänge eines projektes der unnachgiebigen moderne* (The Ulm School of Design: Beginnings of a project of unyielding modernity). Berlin: Ernst and Sohn, 2003.

Murthy, Krishna. *Ancient Indian Furniture*. Delhi: Sundeep Prakashan, 1982.

Kumar, Shanti. *Gandhi Meets Primetime: Globalization and Nationalism in Indian Television*. Urbana: University of Illinois Press, 2005.

Kusno, Abidin. *Behind the Postcolonial: Architecture, Urban Space, and Political Cultures in Indonesia*. New York: Routledge, 2000.

Kusno, Abidin. "Tropics of Discourse: Notes on the Re-Invention of Architectural Regionalism in Southeast Asia in the 1980s." *Fabrications* 19, no. 2 (2010): 58–81.

Kuttiammu, T. P. "A Prefabricated Workman's Hut in Cement Concrete." *Indian Concrete Journal* 22, no. 6 (1948): n.p.

Kwak, Nancy. *A World of Homeowners: American Power and the Politics of Housing Aid*. Chicago: University of Chicago Press, 2015.

Kyrtsis, Alexander. *Constantinos A. Doxiadis: Texts, Design, Drawings, Settlements*. Athens: Ikaros, 2006.

Lang, John, Madhavi Desai, and Miki Desai. *Architecture and Independence: The Search for Identity—India 1880 to 1980*. Delhi: Oxford University Press, 1997.

Le Corbusier. *The Athens Charter*. Translated by A. Eardley. New York: Studio, 1973.
Legg, Stephen. *Spaces of Colonialism: Delhi's Urban Governmentalities*. Wiley-Blackwell, 2007.
Legg, Stephen. "Of Scales, Networks and Assemblages: The League of Nations Apparatus and the Scalar Sovereignty of the Government of India." *Transactions of the Institute of British Geographers* 34, no. 2 (2009): 234–53. doi: 10.1111/j.1475-5661.2009.00338.x.
Lerner, Daniel. *The Passing of Traditional Society: Modernizing the Middle East*. New York: Free Press, 1958.
Levene, M. "The Apocalyptic as Contemporary Dialectic: From Thanatos (Violence) to Eros (Transformation)." In *Future Ethics: Climate Change and Apocalyptic Imagination*, edited by S. Skrimshire, 107–26. London: Continuum, 2010.
Lewis, John P. *Quiet Crisis in India: Economic Development and American Policy*. Westport, CT: Greenwood Press, 1962.
Lindinger, Herbert., ed. *Ulm Design: The Morality of Objects: Hochschule für Gestaltung Ulm, 1953–1968*. Translated by D. Britt. Cambridge, MA: MIT Press, 1991.
Lindley, Mark. *J. C. Kumarappa: Mahatma Gandhi's Economist*. Mumbai: Popular Prakashan, 2007.
Lu, Duanfang. *Remaking Chinese Urban Form: Modernity, Scarcity and Space, 1949–2005*. London: Taylor and Francis, 2006.
Madan, Vandana, ed. *The Village India*. Delhi: Oxford University Press, 2002.
Majumdar, Bimanbehari. *Gandhian Concept of State*. Calcutta: M. C. Sarkar, 1957.
Maldonado, Tomás. "Neue Entwicklungen in der Industrie und Die Ausbildung des Produktgestalters [New Developments in Industry and the Training of Designers]." *Ulm* 2 (October 1958): 25–40.
Maldonado, Tomás. "Communication and Semiotics in the Trilingual Publication." *Ulm* 5 (July 1959): 69–78.
Maldonado, Tomás. "New Developments in Industry and the Training of Designers." In *Architects' Yearbook* 9, 174–80. London: Elek, 1960.
Maldonado, Tomás. "Design Education." In *The Education of Vision*, edited by G. Kepes, 122–35. New York: George Braziller, 1965.
Maldonado, Tomás. "Colloquium con Maldonado e Otl" (Colloquium with Maldonado and Otl). *Design-Italia* 3 (September 1972): 32.
Maniaque-Benton, Caroline. *French Encounters with the American Counterculture, 1960–1980*. London: Ashgate, 2011.
Mansingh, S. "India and the United States." In *Indian Foreign Policy: The Nehru Years*, edited by Bal Ram Nanda. 150–69. New Delhi: Radiant Publishers, Nehru Memorial Museum and Library, 1976.
Marriott, McKim, ed. *Village India: Studies in the Little Community*. Chicago: University of Chicago, 1955.
Marsh, Christine. "The Once and Future Village: From Tagore's Rural Reconstruction to Transition Towns." In *Contemporarising Tagore and the World*, edited by Imtiaz Ahmed, Muchkund Dubey, and Veena Sikri, 194-205. Dhaka: University Press, 2013.
Marsh, Christine. "Towards Tagorean Utopia: From Rural Reconstruction to Transition Towns." *Literature Compass* 12, no. 5 (2015): 194–205.
Masey, Jack, and Conway L. Morgan. *Cold War Confrontations: US Exhibitions and Their Role in the Cultural Cold War*. Baden, Switzerland: Lars Müller, 2008.
Mathur, Saloni. "Living Ethnological Exhibits: The Case of 1886." *Cultural Anthropology* 15, no. 4 (2000): 492–524. doi: 10.1525/can.2000.15.4.492.
Mathur, Saloni. *India by Design: Colonial History and Cultural Display*. Berkeley: University of California Press, 2007.
Mathur, Saloni. "Charles and Ray Eames in India." *Art Journal* 70, no. 1 (2011): 34–53.
Mazzarella, William. "Branding the Mahatma: The Untimely Provocation of Gandhian Publicity." *Cultural Anthropology* 25, no. 1 (2010): 1–39. doi: 10.1111/j.1548-1360.2009.01050.x.
McCarthy, Kathleen D. "From Cold War to Cultural Development: The International Cultural Activities of the Ford Foundation, 1950–1980." *Daedalus* 116, no. 1, Special Issue: Philanthropy, Patronage, Politics (1987): 93–117.

McDonald, G. "Selling the American Dream: MoMA, Industrial Design and Post-War France." *Journal of Design History* 17, no. 4 (2004): 397–412.

McGowan, Abigail S. "All That Is Rare, Characteristic or Beautiful: Design and the Defense of Tradition in Colonial Idea, 1851–1903." *Journal of Material Culture* 10, no. 3 (2005): 263–87. doi: 10.1177/1359183505057145.

McGowan, Abigail S. *Crafting the Nation in Colonial India*. New York: Palgrave Macmillan, 2009.

McGowan, Abigail S. "Ahmedabad's Home Remedies: Housing in the Re-Making of an Industrial City, 1920–1960." *Journal of South Asian* Studies 36, no. 3 (2013): 397–414. doi 10.1080/00856401.2013.8147492013.

McKeon, M. *The Secret History of Domesticity: Public, Private, and the Division of Knowledge*. Baltimore, MD: Johns Hopkins University Press, 2005.

Meherally, Yusuf. *At the Cross-Roads*. Edited by Kamaladevi Chattopadhyaya. Bombay: National Information and Publications, 1947.

Mehta, Rustam J. *The Handicrafts and Industrial Art of India*. Bombay: Taraporevala, 1960.

Mehta, U. "The Impact of Panchayati Raj on Rural India." In *Rural Sociology in India*, edited by A. R. Desai, 560–98. Bombay: Popular Prakashan, 1969.

Mendelsohn, Oliver, and Marika Vicziany. *The Untouchables: Subordination, Poverty and the State in Modern India*. Cambridge, UK: Cambridge University Press, 1998.

Menoret, Pascal. *Joyriding in Riyadh: Oil, Urbanism and Road Revolt*. Cambridge, UK: Cambridge University Press, 2014.

Metcalf, Thomas R. "Architecture and the Representation of Empire: India, 1860–1910." *Representations*, no. 6 (1984): 37–65.

Metcalf, Thomas R. *An Imperial Vision: Indian Architecture and Britain's Raj*. Berkeley: University of California Press, 2002.

Middleton, George Frederick. *Build Your House of Earth: A Manual of Pisé and Abode Construction*. Melbourne, Australia: Compendium, 1953.

Mills, James H., and Satadru Sen. Introduction. In *Confronting the Body: The Politics of Physicality in Colonial and Post-Colonial India*, edited by S. Sen and J. H. Mills, 1–16. London: Anthem Press, 2004.

Minor, Robert N. *The Religious, the Spiritual, and the Secular: Auroville and Secular India*. Albany: State University of New York Press, 1999.

Misra, Bankey Bihari. *The Indian Middle Classes: Their Growth in Modern Times*. Oxford, UK: Oxford University Press, 1961.

Moles, A. "Functionalism in Crisis." *Ulm*, August 19–20, 1967: 24–25.

Monteaux, Michel, and Henry Glassie, H. *The Spirit of Folk Art: The Girard Collection at the Museum of International Folk Art*. New York: Harry N. Abrams, 1989.

Monteyne, David. *Fallout Shelter: Designing for Civil Defense in the Cold War*. Minneapolis: University of Minnesota Press, 2011.

Mukerjee, Madhusree. *Churchill's Secret War: The British Empire and the Ravaging of India during World War II*. New York: Basic Books, 2011.

Mukherjee, Ananda G., and Vinod Tagra. *Jawaharlal Nehru: The Architect of Modern India, A Documentary Account of Nehru's Concept of Planning and Development*. New Delhi: Reliance, 1989.

Mumford, Eric Paul. *The CIAM Discourse on Urbanism, 1928–1960*. Cambridge, MA: MIT Press, 2000.

Murthy, K. Krishna. *Ancient Indian Furniture*. Delhi: Sundeep Prakashan, 1982.

Nadkami, S. K. "The Saraswat Cooperative Housing Buildings in Tardeo." *Indian Concrete Journal* 14, no. 10 (1940): 370–71.

Nambiar, K. K. "Shenoy Nagar Housing Scheme, Madras." *Indian Concrete Journal* 21, no. 10 (1947): n.p.

Nandy, Ashish. *The Intimate Enemy: Loss and Recovery of Self under Colonialism*. Delhi: Oxford University Press, 1983.

Nandy, Ashish. *At the Edge of Psychology: Essays in Politics and Culture*. Delhi: Oxford University Press, 1990.

Nandy, Ashish. *An Ambiguous Journey to the City: The Village and Other Odd Ruins of the Self in the Indian Imagination*. New Delhi: Oxford University Press, 2001.

Nehru, Jawaharlal. "12 March 1950, 23rd Annual Session of the Federation of Indian Chambers of Commerce (Ficci), New Delhi." In *Selected Works of Jawaharlal Nehru, Second Series*, edited by Sarvepalli Gopal, 624–30. Vol. 14, Part 1: November 15, 1949—April 8, 1950. New York: Oxford University Press, 1993.

Nehru, Jawaharlal. *The Discovery of India*. Calcutta: Signet Press, 1946. Reprint, New Delhi: Oxford University Press, 2004.

Neuhart, John, Charles Eames, and Ray Eames. *Eames Design: The Work of the Office of Charles and Ray Eames*. London: Thames and Hudson, 1989.

Note, Osamu. "Designing after the Modern: The Making of Designers and Their Imagining of the Future in Postcolonial Southern India." *South Asia: Journal of South Asian Studies* 29, no. 2 (2006): 255–77. doi: 10.1080/00856400600809948.

Nye, Joseph. *Soft Power: The Means to Success in World Politics*. New York: Public Affairs, 2004.

Oldham, Todd, and Kiera Coffee. *Alexander Girard*. Pasadena, CA: Ammo Books, 2011.

Overy, Paul. *Light, Air and Openness: Modern Architecture between the Wars*. London: Thames and Hudson, 2008.

Panton, Jane Ellen. *Suburban Residences and How to Circumvent Them*. London: Ward and Downey, 1896.

Parel, Anthony. "Symbolism in Gandhian Politics." Paper presented at the American Association of Asian Studies Annual Sessions, Boston, 1962. *Canadian Journal of Political Science* 2, no. 4 (1969): 513–27.

Parsons, Kerit C. "Collaborative Genius." *Journal of the American Planning Association* 60, no. 4 (1994): 462–82. doi: 10.1080/01944369408975605.

Patel, B. F. *History of the Plague in Bombay*. Charleston, NJ: Nabu Press, 2010.

Patel, Indraprasad Gurdanbhai. *Glimpses of Indian Economic Policy: An Insider's View*. New Delhi: Oxford University Press, 2002.

Pederson, Susan. *The Guardians: The League of Nations and the Crisis of Empire*. Oxford: Oxford University Press, 2015.

Pedret, Annie. *Team 10: An Archival History*. New York: Routledge, 2013.

Pehle, Walter H., and Peter Sillem, eds. *Wissenschaft im geteilten Deutschland: Restauration oder neubeginn nach 1945?* (Science in divided Germany: Restoration or new beginning after 1945). Frankfurt: Fischer, 1992.

Phand, Shahaji, and H. P. S. Arya. "Adarsh Gaon Yojana-Way towards Gandhi's Dream Village: Self-Sufficient, Prosperous and Peaceful." *Journal of Rural Development* 26, no. 2 (2007): 207–25.

Pieris, Anoma. "Is Sustainability Sustainable?: Interrogating the Tropical Paradigm in Asian Architecture." In *Tropical Sustainable Architecture: Social and Environmental Dimensions*, edited by Joo-Hwa Bay and Boon Lay Ong, 267–86. Oxford: Elsevier, 2006.

Piotrowski, Andrzej. "The Spectacle of Architectural Discourses." *Architectural Theory Review* 13, no. 2 (2008): 130–44. doi: 10.1080/13264820802216528.

Plamper, Jan. "Introduction." *Slavic Review* 68, no. 2, Special Issue: Emotional Turn?: Feelings in Russian History and Culture (2009): 229–37.

Preston, Peter Wallace. *Development Theory: An Introduction*. Cambridge, MA: Blackwell, 1996.

Pyla, Panayiota. "Hassan Fathy Revisited: Postwar Discourses on Science, Development, and Vernacular Architecture." *Journal of Architectural Education* 60, no. 3 (2007): 28–39. doi: 10.1111/j.1531-314X.2007.00093.x.

Radkau, Joachim. "'Wirtschaftswunder' Ohne Technologische Innovation? Technische Modernität Den 50er Jahren" ("Economic miracle" without technological innovation? Technical modernity in the 50s"]. In *Modernisierung Im Wiederaufbau: Die Westdeutsche Gesellschaft der 50er Jahren* (Modernization in the reconstruction: The West German society of the 50s), edited by Axel Schildt and Arnold Sywottek, 129–53. 2nd ed. Bonn: J. H. W. Dietz, 1993.

Raedt, Kim De. "Between 'True Believers' and Operational Experts: UNESCO Architects and School Building in Post-colonial Africa." *Journal of Architecture* 19, no. 1 (2014): 19–42.

Rao, Nikhil. *House, but No Garden: Apartment Living in Bombay, 1898–1948*. Minneapolis: University of Minnesota Press, 2013.

Rauchway, Eric. *The Money Makers: How Roosevelt and Keynes Ended the Depression, Defeated Fascism, and Secured a Prosperous Peace*. New York: Basic Books, 2015.

Ray, Partha Pratim, Bidhan Ch. Biswas, and B. K. Sen. "Knowledge Communication in Tagore's Model For Rural Reconstruction: An Overview." *Annals of Library and Information Studies* 52, no. 3 (2005): 94–102.

Ray, Raka, and Seemin Qayum. "Masculinity, Femininity, and Servitude: Domestic Workers in Calcutta in the Late Twentieth Century." *Feminist Studies* 26, no. 3, Special Issue: Points of Departure: India and the South Asian Diaspora (2000): 691–718.

Ray, Raka and Seemin Qayum. *Cultures of Servitude: Modernity, Domesticity, and Class in India*. Stanford: Stanford University Press, 2009.

Rempel, Ruth. "Periodizing African Development History." *African Economic History* 36 (2008): 125–58.

Risselada, Max, and Dirk van Heuvel. *Team 10: In Search of a Utopia of the Present, 1953–1981*. Rotterdam: NAi Publishers, 2005.

Rist, Gilbert. *The History of Development: From Western Origin to Global Faith*. London: Zed Books, 1997.

Robertson, R. M. "The Young Architect and His Job." *Journal of the Indian Institute of Architects* 3, no. 2 (1936): 134.

Robinoff, Arthur. "Incompatible Objectives and Shortsighted Politics." In *US-Indian Strategic Cooperation into the 21st Century, More Than Words*, edited by Sumit Ganguly, Brian Shoup, and Andrew Scobell, 38–60. New York: Routledge, 2006.

Rosner, Victoria. *Modernism and the Architecture of Private Life*. New York: Columbia University Press, 2005.

Rostow, Walt Whitman. "The Take-Off into Self-Sustained Growth." *Economic Journal* 66, no. 261 (1956): 25–48.

Rothermund, Dietmar. *An Economic History of India: From Pre-colonial Times to 1991*. New York: Routledge, 1993.

Rudolph, Lloyd I., and Susanne Hoeber Rudolph. "The Coffee House and the Ashram Revisited: How Gandhi Democratized Habermas' Public Sphere." In *Postmodern Gandhi and Other Essays: Gandhi in the World and at Home*, edited by Lloyd I. Rudolph and Susanne Hoeber Rudolph, 140–76. London: University of Chicago Press, 2006.

Rüedi, Katerina. *Bauhaus Dream-House: Modernity and Globalization*. New York: Routledge, 2010.

Rurup, Rurup. "Problems of the German Revolution, 1918–19." *Journal of Contemporary History* 3, no. 4 (1968): 109–35.

Sarkar, Sumit. *Modern India, 1885–1947*. London: Macmillan, 2005.

Sassatelli, Roberta. *Consumer Culture: History, Theory and Politics*. 1st ed. London: Sage, 2007.

Schnaidt, Claude. "Architecture and Political Commitment." *Ulm*, no. 19–20 (August 1967): 27–34. Lecture given at the Academy of Fine Arts, Hamburg, March 2, 1967.

Scholl, Inge, and Dorothee Sölle. *The White Rose: Munich, 1942–1943*. Translated by A. R. Schultz. 2nd ed. Hanover, NH: Wesleyan University Press, 1983.

Schüler, Andreas. *Erfindergeist und technikkritik: Der beitrag Amerikas zur modernisierung und die technikdebatte seit 1900* (Ingenuity and technology criticism: The American contribution to the debate of modernization and technology since 1900). Stuttgart: Franz Steiner, 1990.

Schwartz, Thomas Alan. *America's Germany: John J. McCloy and the Federal Republic of Germany*. Cambridge, MA: Harvard University Press, 1991.

Scott, Felicity D. *Outlaw Territories: Environments of Insecurity/Architectures of Counterinsurgency*. New York: Zone Books, 2016.

Scriver, Peter, and Vikramaditya Prakash, eds. *Colonial Modernities: Building, Dwelling and Architecture in British India and Ceylon*. Abingdon, UK: Routledge, 2007.

Scriver, Peter, and Amit Srivastava. *India: Modern Architecture in History*. London: Reaktion Books, 2016.

Sharma, Ursula. *Women's Work, Class, and the Urban Household: A Study of Shimla, north India*. London: Tavistock Publications, 1986.

Shoshkes, Ellen. "Jaqueline Tyrwhitt: A Founding Mother of Modern Urban Design." *Planning Perspectives* 21, no. 2 (2006): 179–97. doi: 10.1080/02665430600555339.

Shoshkes, Ellen. "Jaqueline Tyrwhitt and Transnational Discourse on Modern Urban Planning and Design, 1941–1951." *Urban History* 36, no. 2 (2009): 262–83. doi: 10.1017/S0963926809006282.

Shoshkes, Ellen. "Visualizing the Core of an Ideal Domestic Community: Jaqueline Tyrwhitt and Post-war Planning Exhibitions." In *Exhibitions and the Development of Modern Planning Culture*, edited by Robert Freestone and Marco Amati, 193–208. London: Ashgate, 2014.

Shoshkes, Ellen. "Introduction." In Jaqueline Tyrwhitt, *Society and Environment: A Historical Review*, 1–5. New York: Routledge, 2015.

Simon, David. ed. *Fifty Key Thinkers on Development*. London: Routledge, 2006.

Singer, Milton B. *When a Great Tradition Modernizes: An Anthropological Approach to Indian Civilization*. New York: Praeger, 1972.

Singer, Milton B., and Bernard S. Cohn, eds. *Structure and Change in Indian Society*. Chicago: Aldine, 1968.

Singh, Sundra R. *Urban Planning in India: A Case Study of Urban Improvement Trusts*. New Delhi: Ashish, 1979.

Sinha, Subir. "Lineages of the Developmentalist State: Transnationality and Village India." *Comparative Studies in Society and History* 50, no. 1 (2008): 57–90.

Skinner, R. J., and M. J. Rodell, eds. *People, Poverty and Shelter: Problems of Self-Help Housing in the Third World*. New York: Routledge, 1983.

Sparke, Penny. *Furniture*. London: Bell and Hyman, 1986.

Srinivas, Mysore Narasimhachar. *The Dominant Caste and Other Essays*. Delhi: Oxford University Press, 1994.

Steger, Manfred B. *Gandhi's Dilemma: Nonviolent Principles and Nationalist Power*. New York: St. Martin's Press, 2000.

Stein, Joseph A. "The Possibility of a Multi-Level Democratic Society." In *Building in the Garden: The Architecture of Joseph Allen Stein in India and California*, edited by Stephen White and Joseph Allen Stein, 313. New York: Oxford University Press, 1993.

Tapan, Neeta. *Micro Credit, Self-Help Groups (SHGs) and Women Empowerment*. New Delhi: New Century Publications, 2010.

Tappin, Stuart. "The Early Use of Reinforced Concrete in India." *Construction History* 18 (2002): 79–98.

Tarlo, Emma. *Clothing Matters: Dress and Identity in India*. Chicago: University of Chicago Press, 1996.

Tendulkar, Dinanath Gopal. *Mahatma: Life of Mohandas Karamchand Gandhi*. Vol. 2. Delhi: Publications Division, Ministry of Information and Broadcasting, Government of India, 1969.

Thakurdas, Pursotamdas. *Memorandum Outlining a Plan of Economic Development for India*. Harmondsworth, UK: Penguin, 1954.

Thomson, John Arthur, and Patrick Geddes. *Life: Outlines of General Biology*. Vols. 1 and 2. London: Harper and Brothers, 1931.

Thomson, Mark. *Gandhi and His Ashrams*. Bombay: Popular Prakashan, 1993.

Thorner, Alice. "Nehru, Albert Mayer, and Origins of Community Projects." *Economic and Political Weekly* 16, no. 4 (1981): 117–20.

Tignor, Robert L. *W. Arthur Lewis and the Birth of Development Economics*. Princeton, NJ: Princeton University Press, 2006.

Tilly, Charles. *Big Structures, Large Processes, Huge Comparisons*. New York: Russell Sage Foundation, 1984.

Tipps, Dean C. "Modernization Theory and the Comparative Study of Societies: A Critical Perspective." *Comparative Studies in Society and History* 15, no. 2 (1973): 199–226.

Tomlinson, Brian Roger. *The Economy of Modern India, 1860–1970*. New York: Cambridge University Press, 1996.

Trivedi, Lisa N. "Visually Mapping the 'Nation': Swadeshi Politics in Nationalist India, 1920–1930." *Journal of Asian Studies* 62, no. 1 (2003): 11–41.

Trivedi, Lisa N. *Clothing Gandhi's Nation: Homespun and Modern India*. Bloomington: Indiana University Press, 2007.

Unnithan, Thottamon Kantan Kesavan Narayan, and K. B. Singh. *Story of Lalgarh: An Experiment in Self Help and Community Planning*. New Delhi: Rural Housing Wing, School of Planning and Architecture, 1960.

Volwahsen, Andreas. *Living Architecture: Indian*. Translated by A. E. Keep. London: Macdonald, 1969.

von Seckendorff, E. *Die Hochschule für Gestaltung in Ulm: Gründung (1949–1953) und Ära Max Bill (1953–1957)* (The College of Design in Ulm: Foundation Era [1949–1953], and Max Bill [1953–1957]). Marburg, Germany: Jonas, 1989.

Vyas, Kumar H. "Design History: An Alternative Approach." *Design Issues* 22, no. 4 (2000): 27–34.

Vyas, Kumar H. *Design, the Indian Context: Learning the Historical Rationale of the Indian Design Idiom*. Ahmedabad: National Institute of Design, 2000.

Walters, Francis Paul. *A History of the League of Nations*. Oxford: Oxford University Press, 1963.

Ward, Peter, ed. *Self-Help Housing: A Critique*. New York: Mansell, 1982.

Ward, Peter and Sylvia Chant. *Community Leadership and Self-Help Housing*. New York: Pergamon, 1987.

Welter, Volker M. "Post-War CIAM, Team X, and the Influence of Patrick Geddes: Five Annotations." In *CIAM-Team 10: The English Context*, edited by D. L. Camp, D. van den Heuvel, and G. de Waal, 87–110. Delft, The Netherlands: Delft Technische Universiteit, 2001.

Welter, Volker M. *Biopolis: Patrick Geddes and the City of Life*. Cambridge, MA: MIT Press, 2003.

Wheeler, Monroe, ed. *Textiles and Ornaments of India: A Selection of Designs*. Based on an exhibition held at the Museum of Modern Art in 1955. New York: Museum of Modern Art, 1956.

White, Stephen. *Building in the Garden: The Architecture of Joseph Allen Stein in India and California*. New York: Oxford University Press, 1993.

Wigley, Mark. "Network Fever." *Grey Room* 4 (2001): 82–122.

Windsor Liscombe, Rhodri. "In-Dependence: Otto Koenigsberger and Modernist Urban Resettlement in India." *Planning Perspective* 21, no. 2 (2006): 157–78. doi: 10.1080/02665430600555305.

Ziai, Aram. *Development Discourse and Global History: From Colonialism to the Sustainable Development Goals*. London: Routledge, 2016.

INDEX

Note: Page numbers in *italics* refer to figures.